The Gospel
on Campus

The Gospel on Campus

A Handbook of Campus Ministry Programs and Resources
Department of Education • United States Catholic Conference

Dr. Michael
Galligan-Stierle
General Editor

Second Edition

United States Catholic Conference • Washington, D.C.

In its 1990 planning document, as approved by the general membership of the United States Catholic Conference in November 1989, the Department of Education was authorized to publish the resource manual for campus ministers that had been initiated by Bro. Peter Clifford, then representative for higher education and campus ministry. *The Gospel on Campus: A Handbook of Campus Ministry Programs and Resources* is the fruition of that project, which involved the work of hundreds of campus ministers throughout the United States. Under the general editorship of Dr. Michael Galligan-Stierle, and under the direction of Rev. Charles H. Hagan, USCC representative for higher education and campus ministry, the text for the second edition of *The Gospel on Campus: A Handbook of Campus Ministry Programs and Resources* was submitted for review and approved by Bishop Robert J. Banks, chair of the Committee on Education, and is authorized for publication by the undersigned.

Monsignor Dennis M. Schnurr
General Secretary
NCCB/USCC

Photos by CNS/The Crosiers, Michael Hoyt/Catholic Standard, and Rick Reinhard used with permission.

Standards for Campus Ministers is published by the Catholic Campus Ministry Association, 300 College Park Avenue, Dayton, Ohio 45469-0001. Copyright © 1990 by CCMA. Used with permission. All rights reserved. No part of this work may be reproduced or by any means, electronic or mechanical, including photocopy, recording, or any information storage and retrieval system without permission in writing from the publisher.

Introduction to The Context of Campus Ministry and *The Commuter Student*, copyright © June Meredith Costin. Used with permission. All rights reserved.

Excerpts from the revised Code of Canon Law, Latin-English Edition, copyright © 1983 by the Canon Law Society of America, Washington, D.C. Used with permission. All rights reserved.

ISBN 1-57455-031-4

Contents

The Newman Prayer

May God support us all the day long
till the shadows lengthen
and the evening comes
and the busy world is hushed
and the fever of life is over
and our work is done—
then in this mercy—
may God give us a safe lodging
and a holy rest
and peace at the last.

Cardinal John Henry Newman

Preface to the Second Edition of the Gospel on Campus

Rev. Charles H. Hagan, S.T.D.

I am delighted to present the second edition of *The Gospel on Campus: A Handbook of Campus Ministry Programs and Resources*. The first edition of the handbook appeared in 1991 and was an immediate success, selling well over 6,000 copies. Campus ministers of all denominations were lavish in their praise of this very practical resource for ministry. The idea of a second edition was conceived at a board meeting of the Catholic Campus Ministry Association (CCMA). Suggestions had been sent to CCMA through a program reply sheet in the first edition, which is reprinted in this second edition of *The Gospel on Campus*.

In this edition all program and resource sections have been updated. Several articles from the first edition have been revised and expanded significantly. New articles on Catholic faculty, certification, diversity, the challenge of the generations, and vocation ministry on campus have been included.

I am most grateful to Dr. Michael Galligan-Stierle, the general editor, to Mr. Donald McCrabb, and to Ms. Amina Noah for their invaluable assistance in completing this important project. I am also most grateful to the writers and program contributors, from those who authored or revised articles to those who suggested articles or sent us information for publication. This second edition of *The Gospel on Campus* is one more example of the unique spirit of cooperation that makes campus ministry such an exciting venture.

Preface

*Dr. Michael
Galligan-Stierle
General Editor*

In November 1987, Bro. Peter Clifford, the USCC representative for campus ministry and higher education, invited twelve campus ministers to dinner in an effort to solicit suggestions on furthering campus ministry nationwide and on implementing the bishops' pastoral letter, *Empowered by the Spirit: Campus Ministry Faces the Future.*

The group endorsed his idea to create a campus ministry handbook of resources. That is, eleven out of the twelve endorsed the idea. I strongly opposed it, proclaiming: "The last thing the Church needs is more printed matter about what we ought to be doing!" I was overruled, and today I can see why. The handbook is full of excellent resources that can be utilized by any campus minister to concretize the vision of the bishops' pastoral letter.

Six months after that dinner, I agreed to be the handbook editor. Nine months after the dinner, a steering committee of twelve formulated an outline and began gathering materials. Two years after the dinner, the committee had gathered so many resources that Bro. Peter and I approached the USCC Office for Publishing and Promotions Services and asked them to consider a series of volumes on campus ministry. Unable to gauge the demand for such a project, we agreed to begin with a one-volume work that would address the key areas of campus ministry, categorize the best programs available, and provide a framework for future writings.

What you hold in your hands is the finest thinking and the best programming ideas for Catholic campus ministry ever assembled in one volume. The vast number of programs submitted for publication testifies to the vitality and creativity of those who minister. Contained within, you will find more than forty articles, two hundred programs, and one hundred annotated bibliographic entries—all related to campus ministry.

You will notice that *The Gospel on Campus: A Handbook of Campus Ministry Programs and Resources* can stand as a book, or it can be disassembled and placed in a three-ring binder. Once in the binder, new articles or programs related to campus ministry can be added to the appropriate chapters. New programming ideas can be exchanged by filling out the Program Reply Sheet at the end of the book and mailing it to the Catholic Campus Ministry Association, 300 College Park Avenue, Dayton, Ohio 45469-2515.

A project of this size can only be completed with the support of family, friends, and colleagues. Special thanks to my family, both immediate and extended, who surrounded me with a loving environment and tolerated my out-of-town trips and long hours of writing and editing manuscripts. Thanks to my many friends who listened when I needed an ear and talked when I needed companionship.

My warm and heartfelt thanks to Dr. Carol Fowler, Mr. Donald R. McCrabb, and Rev. George M. Schroeder, the three associate editors, who worked long and hard during the final two years, steering the content and massaging the text. Thanks to all the writers and program contributors, from those who authored articles to those who suggested unique programs and sent us information for publication. Special thanks to those who helped at USCC, especially Norma Williams for her proficient typing of manuscripts, the USCC Office for Publishing and Promotion Services, and Bro. Peter Clifford and Fr. Charles Hagan.

Finally, a word of thanks to all those campus ministers who find themselves at the intersection of higher education and the Church. May you be a guiding light to all those searching for direction at that intersection.

Campus Ministry:
An Invitation to Mission

Campus ministry is an expression of the Church's special desire to be present to all who are involved in higher education (cf. *Empowered by the Spirit: Campus Ministry Faces the Future* [ES], 13) and to further the dialogue between the Church and the academic community. The Church brings to this dialogue its mission to preach the Gospel of Christ and to help the human family achieve its full destiny (cf. ES, 17). From the beginnings of campus ministry with the Melvin Club in 1883 at the University of Wisconsin, the Newman Apostolate (Movement) in 1893 at the University of Pennsylvania, and the pastoral works of the religious communities and Catholic educators at Catholic colleges and universities throughout the years, Catholic church members have sought to support and to be present to those in higher education in our country.

Today, as we approach the twenty-first century, many people in our society experience alienation, impersonalism, and other forms of brokenness. Members of the academic community struggle with similar questions. At the same time, there is a growing interest and a great reservoir of energy and talent that can be utilized in the service of the Church and the world (cf. ES, 11).

Campus ministry seeks to proclaim the Good News to the academic community and to a pluralistic society in a prophetic yet reconciling voice. Lay, religious, and ordained campus ministers constitute this professional, pastoral ministry in the Church today. These campus ministers gather all the members of the Church on campus to form the faith community (cf. ES, 34-44); to appropriate the faith (cf. ES, 45-58); to form a Christian conscience (cf. ES, 59-60); to educate for justice (cf. ES, 70-82); to facilitate personal development (cf. ES, 83-92); and to develop future leaders for Church and society (cf. ES, 93-101).

The eye of faith discerns campus ministry, where commitment to Christ and care for the academic world meet in purposeful activity to serve and realize the kingdom of God (cf. ES, 21). With this intention in mind, campus ministry embraces the hope that all individuals will be "empowered by the Spirit" to recognize their own dignity and worth and to reach out to others on the campus to collaborate in building God's kingdom of love and justice.

1

The History of Campus Ministry

Mr. P. Gerard Shaw

For over a century, Catholic campus ministry in our country, empowered by the Spirit, has been forming communities of faith which witness to the presence of the risen Christ. Now we are at the beginning of a new era filled with opportunities to build up the faith community on campuses and to promote the well-being of higher education and society as a whole. (ES, 1)

The first U.S. colleges and universities were founded by religious groups and modeled after English and German universities. These institutions, whether private or public, took responsibility for the religious and moral development of their students. Eventually, as the university became increasingly secular, students themselves formed religious clubs to nurture their own religious convictions and to give expression to the missionary zeal of their day. The Young Men's Christian Association (YMCA) was one such student organization.

Catholics, on the other hand, enrolled in Catholic institutions of higher learning. The bishops of the United States insisted on Catholic schooling at all levels, due to the perceived threat of Protestantism. By the mid- to late-1800s, Catholics began to attend public and private non-Catholic colleges and universities, attempting to balance their intellectual lives with their faith lives. Often, students found the university hostile to Catholicism. Some came to church leaders looking for help. The need of Catholic students to grow in their college careers at public universities ignited what became known as the Newman Movement.

On Thanksgiving Day, 1883, at the home of Mr. and Mrs. John C. Melvin, just across the street from the University of Wisconsin, in Madison, John J. McAnaw, a prelaw student from Ohio, complained that a Medieval Studies professor had slandered the Catholic Church. Before the night ended, young McAnaw found himself president of "The Melvin Club," which for the next fifteen years held discussions on various Catholic topics (see Evans, p. 19).

One student in the group, Timothy L. Harrington, carried the Melvin Club memory with him to medical school at the University of Pennsylvania in 1892. He was deeply impressed by the writings of the recently deceased Cardinal John Henry Newman of England. Following Christmas vacation, Harrington suggested to his returning classmates that they form a club similar to what he had experienced in Madison. Eighteen of them agreed, and in 1893 "The Newman Club" was established. It was an organization of young Catholics seeking to improve themselves socially, intellectually, and religiously in a university setting. The students were ministering one to another with very little "official" support other than permission and tolerance.

By 1905, Catholics had organized similar clubs on fifteen campuses as scattered as Cornell (1888), Michigan (1889), Minnesota (1890), Brown (1892), Harvard (1893), Berkeley (1898), and, after 1900, Chicago, Columbia, and several other public universities in the Midwest. . . . Typically, the clubs arose either from an

Michael Hoyt/Catholic Standard

experience of supposed anti-Catholicism or from sudden enthusiasm for some aspect of Catholic culture; they were mainly Irish in membership; they flourished for a few years as literary societies, but usually lapsed into dancing clubs upon graduation of their founders; clubs helped by professors or other adults more often remained true to their original aims than did those lacking such attention, and clubs aided by priests usually did the best of all. . . . Nearly identical purposes emerged for all these groups: to learn, defend, and spread the Catholic faith; to pursue cultural ideals generally; to offer mutual help to members. (Evans, p. 21)

On September 17, 1906, Fr. Henry C. Hengell, curate at Madison's Holy Redeemer Parish, was assigned to the University of Wisconsin, making him the first full-time Catholic chaplain at a state university. Following the example of Milwaukee Archbishop Sebastian Messmer, and inspired by Pope Pius X's encyclical on education, *Acerbo Nimis,* three other bishops took similar steps in Rochester (New York), Austin (Texas), and San Francisco (California). The educational role of these student groups was always seen as essential. In 1915, the Paulist Fathers, serving the Newman Club at the University of Texas in Austin, arranged to

offer bible classes for academic credit. In 1919, Fr. John A. O'Brien, Catholic chaplain at the University of Illinois, made a similar arrangement with that school's Protestant chaplain. By 1920, 40,000 Catholics were attending non-Catholic universities (see Evans, p. 47).

In 1921, the Catholic bishops of the United States, speaking through the newly formed National Catholic Welfare Conference (NCWC), stated that Newman Clubs were "one of the most powerful aids" for developing Catholic leaders in higher education. In 1942, NCWC created its Youth Department by joining the Newman Club Federation, begun as the Federation of Catholic College Clubs in New York on October 28, 1915, with the National Association of Catholic College Students, begun at Purdue University in 1908. The Federation of Catholic College Clubs had taken on the Newman identity in 1938.

It is interesting to note that, while positive things were being said about this work, ominous clouds darkened the horizon. Negative voices, emerging largely from religious orders running Catholic colleges and universities, feared that official church support for Catholics attending state schools threatened the survival of Catholic higher education. The post-World War II wave of thousands of returning veterans to both Catholic and non-Catholic campuses, supported by the GI Bill, swept away these clouds as Newman Centers and Clubs sprang up everywhere across the country.

In 1962, the National Catholic Educational Association (NCEA) recognized the educative role of Newman Clubs by amending its bylaws to provide associate membership for Newman educational centers. The NCWC, with then-Archbishop John Krol of Philadelphia as moderator of the Youth Department, established the National Newman Apostolate "to promote the intellectual and moral development . . . the religious education . . . the apostolic formation" of Catholics in non-Catholic colleges and "to promote their responsible participation in the academic and civic communities" (Evans, p. 129).

Finally, the constituent sections of this movement (i.e., the National Newman Club

Federation, the National Newman Club Chaplains Association, the National Newman Alumni Association, the John Henry Cardinal Newman Honorary Society, the National Newman Association of Faculty and Staff, and the National Newman Foundation) became the National Newman Apostolate, with Archbishop Paul J. Hallinan of Atlanta as its episcopal moderator. The NCWC Youth Department established a separate office to coordinate this apostolate and named Fr. Charles Albright, CSP, as its first coordinating secretary. Further restructuring took place between 1966 and 1969, when national discussion determined that the apostolate might better be served if some components were organized locally rather than nationally. Diocesan directors took on more responsibility, while many lay and religious women and men were hired as campus ministers.

Against the worldwide events of the Second Vatican Council, the assassinations of John F. Kennedy and Martin Luther King, Jr., and the Vietnam War, the Church, the country, and the campuses were forced to examine their very roots. Even as these events impacted secular and private, non-Catholic campuses, Catholic colleges and universities were undergoing major governance shifts. As sponsoring religious orders divested themselves of administrative responsibilities, they turned their institutions over to boards of trustees, composed mainly of lay people. While Catholic colleges restructured, the chaplain's office redefined itself as ministering to the whole campus—students, faculty, and staff—and consequently, on many campuses, chaplains began to refer to themselves as campus ministers, similar to their non-Catholic campus colleagues. Some began to be accountable directly to the president of the institution.

Most Catholic campuses today have campus ministry staffs who work in a variety of ways: living in residence halls; fostering a liturgical life on campus; counseling and ministering in ways that meet the needs of their communities; and challenging students, faculty, and staff to an authentic sense and life of gospel justice and peace. Campus ministers at Catholic colleges and universities continue to share with their colleagues on other campuses and grow together with them.

In 1969, as a direct outgrowth of the National Newman Chaplains' Association, the Catholic Campus Ministry Association (CCMA) was established. Fr. Charles Forsyth, OSB, University of Colorado at Boulder, last president of the chaplains group, was named CCMA's first president. While the Newman group had limited its membership to ordained chaplains at non-Catholic colleges, CCMA opened its doors to Catholic campus ministers at all campuses. As the work of CCMA's president increased, the board agreed to hire a full-time administrator. Sr. Margaret M. Ivers, IBVM, was hired in 1977, and the first executive office was established at Wayne State University (Detroit, Michigan). In 1989, CCMA had a twentieth-anniversary membership of well over 1,000. It continues to serve as the professional organization for Catholic campus ministers throughout the United States.

In November 1983, at Madison, Wisconsin, the birthplace of the Newman Movement, diocesan directors of campus ministry established their own group, the National Association of Diocesan Directors of Campus Ministry (NADDCM), to serve their specific needs.

In January 1985, at St. Thomas University (Miami Shores, Florida), the National Catholic Student Coalition (NCSC) established itself in service to local and regional groups of Catholic students at colleges and universities across the country.

In November 1985, the Catholic bishops of the United States overwhelmingly approved *Empowered by the Spirit: Campus Ministry Faces the Future,* a pastoral letter describing, endorsing, and supporting the presence of the Church to the total world of higher education. This comprehensive document has become the benchmark for all campus ministry plans and programs. It complements and expands the bishops' 1981 document, *Catholic Higher Education and the Pastoral Mission of the Church.*

Catholic campus ministry has a long and lively history, demonstrating its ability to respond to and grow with the signs of the times. From a small club of concerned Catholics, to an officially recognized ministry by the National Conference of Catholic Bishops (NCCB), this growth has involved thousands of lay people, men and women religious, and clergy—students, faculty, and staff members—who have given generously of themselves. As Catholic campus ministry moves into its second century and faces the third millennium, it continues to invite and challenge Catholics in higher education—and higher education itself—to think critically, to believe intelligently, to love unselfishly, and to live realistically the Gospel of Jesus Christ.

Resources for the History of Campus Ministry

Books

DeMan, Thomas, OP. *Dominican Campus Ministry: 1908-1988.* Marysville, Wash.: Tulai Bay Press, 1988.

Evans, John Whitney. *The Newman Movement: Roman Catholics in American Higher Education, 1883-1971.* Notre Dame, Ind.: University of Notre Dame Press, 1980.

Newman, John Henry Cardinal. *The Idea of a University.* Westminster, Md.: Christian Classics, Inc., 1973. In 1852, Newman delivered a series of lectures on the nature of a university and his philosophy of education. Six years later, these lectures were amplified and published in book form. This book continues to be studied by people in higher education as an excellent apology for liberal education, which directs the role of higher education toward the humanistic rather than the utilitarian. Newman considered theology to be of critical importance in the educational process.

Shedd, Clarence P. *The Church Follows Its Students.* New Haven, Conn.: Yale University Press, 1938. This is an extensively researched history of the development of the university pastorate as a special field of ministry in the churches. The major emphasis is on the period from about 1900 to the 1930s. Each of the major Protestant denominations, along with the Catholic and Jewish ministries, is treated separately. For those interested in the early evolution of campus ministry.

———. *Two Centuries of Student Christian Movements.* New York: Associated Press, 1934. A detailed history of the inception and the development of student-founded Christian associations, many of which grew to attain international scope and character. A work of interest to those who seek to understand the role of student initiatives in the genesis of ministry on campus.

Shockley, Donald G. *Campus Ministry: The Church Beyond Itself.* Louisville: Ky.: Westminister John Knox Press, 1989.

The Quest for Wisdom

Reflections on Campus Ministry and the Relationship Between the Church and Higher Education

Rev. George M. Schroeder *(Compiled from the Writings of Rev. James J. Bacik, Sr. Maureen Schaukowitch, OSF, and Dr. Joachim Viens)*

We believe that the faith community and the institutions of higher learning are involved in a common pursuit of the life of wisdom. (ES, 19)

The passionate search for the "life of wisdom," as Pope John Paul II has indicated, is at the center of the "deep bond that exists between the Church and the university" (1982, p. 250). In the ideal life of wisdom, human beings achieve a richer personal synthesis which is the fulfillment of the pursuit of truth; discover the highest principles which integrate all knowledge; and learn to combine the theoretical with the practical, self-fulfillment with a concern for the common good, and knowledge with the light of love. The Church and higher education are natural partners in the quest for this kind of wisdom. Both sides should work together for the welfare of individuals and society. As Pope John Paul II stated: "If then there is not established ever more profoundly a bond between the Church and the university, it is the human person who will be harmed as a result; . . . nor will the culture be fully humanized (1982, p. 251). (Bacik, *The Quest for Wisdom*)

These "Human Persons"

More than 12 million students are enrolled in over 3,300 institutions of higher learning

in the United States. Almost 10 million attend public colleges and universities. The rest attend private institutions. Of all college and university students, some 4.5 million— between 36 and 39 percent—identify themselves as Roman Catholic.

The National Opinion Research Center tells us that in 1960, 25 percent of U.S. college graduates were Catholic; now 45 percent are Catholic. Half of the Catholics in the United States have attended college. The proportion of well-educated Catholics will increase more in the next fifteen years than it did in the last fifteen.

A 1989 Gallup poll on the religious beliefs and sexual attitudes and behaviors of college students, commissioned by the Christian Broadcasting Network, indicates that 80 percent of college students say religion is important in their lives, but their faith has relatively little impact on their sexual behavior:

Many of the Catholic students, representing 29 percent of the students in the survey, appeared to reject outright some of the major teachings of the Church: They approve of premarital sex (75 percent), trial marriages (59 percent), divorce on

grounds of incompatibility (76 percent), and abortion (53 percent). (*Summary Report,* p. 2)

These are the "human persons" who will be shaping the world, nation, culture, and the Church—perhaps, the universe. These are the people who will search out cures for AIDS and cancer, strive for peace among nations, and wrestle with environmental issues and new technologies.

The rugged individualism and personalism bemoaned by Robert Bellah, et al. in *Habits of the Heart: Individualism and Commitment in American Life,* and the breakdown of American family life have produced young people who are extremely ego-centered, who see themselves under tremendous pressure and stress, and who give as the primary reasons for going to college earning more money and getting a good job.

Ernest Boyer, in *College: The Undergraduate Experience in America,* argues that "through an effective college education, students should become personally empowered and also committed to the common good" (1987, p. 69).

Table 1 shows the results of three separate samplings, in which undergraduates were asked to indicate the "essential" outcomes of a college education. Between the first and third surveys, the goals of "training and skills for an occupation" and a "detailed grasp of a specialized field" have jumped from near the bottom to the top. Conversely, "learning to get along with people" and "formulating values and goals for life" have become much less important to those surveyed.

It is also disturbing that almost two out of every five undergraduates polled indicate they feel no sense of community at their college. But despite this diminishing sense of community, respondents showed signs of hope and inspirations that reach beyond personal gain. In their searching, students are torn between a moral idealism and a "realism" to pursue challenging careers, leaving them politically and socially isolated. They struggle for meaning and identity like other college students before them.

A growing number of students are coming to believe they can make a difference. They are willing to reach out a helping hand to others. Table 2 indicates students' participation in various voluntary services during their college years.

This trend toward volunteer service and attention to basic human needs is a mark of success for the university. According to Boyer, "the goal of the undergraduate experience is not *only* to prepare the undergraduates for careers, but to enable them to live lives of dignity and purpose; not *only* to give knowledge to the student, but to channel knowledge to humane ends" (1987, p. 219).

The University Culture

As we move into the last decade of the twentieth century, American higher education is reexamining itself. From different corners of academe come insightful critiques and reflections: *College: The Undergraduate Experience in America* (Boyer), quoted above; *Cultural Literacy: What Every American Should Know* (Hirsch); *The Closing of the American Mind* (Bloom); *A Free and Ordered Space: The Real World of the University* (Giamatti); and *Reforming Education: The Opening of the American Mind* (Adler).

Contrary to an ever-increasing demand for technical training, these authors—albeit,

Table 1

What Undergraduates Believe the "Essential" Outcomes from a College Education Should Be

(Carnegie, 1969, 1976, 1984)

College Outcome	1969	1976	1984	1969-1984
Learning to get along with people	76%	69%	65%	-11%
Formulating values and goals for my life	71%	63%	63%	-8%
Detailed grasp of a particular field	62%	68%	70%	+8%
Training and skills for an occupation	59%	64%	73%	+14%
Well-rounded general education	57%	58%	60%	+3%

with varying intensities, viewpoints, and solutions—urge the importance of a liberal education; the study of the humanities; the skills of critical thinking, careful analysis, and creative responses.

Boyer, particularly, argues that a sense of community on campus must be vigorously affirmed. He defines community as "an undergraduate experience that helps students go beyond their own private interest, learn about the world around them, develop a sense of civic and social responsibility, and discover how they, as individuals, can contribute to the larger society of which they are a part" (1987, pp. 67-68). To accomplish this, colleges need to recognize that, although we live alone, we also are deeply dependent upon one another. "Through an effective college education, students should become personally empowered and also committed to the common good" (1987, p. 69).

Boyer describes an effective college as one with a clear and vital mission, where goals are determined by the needs of society, as well as by the needs of those individuals searching for education. This double set of needs—those of society and those of individuals—says Boyer, can never be separated or seen in isolation.

Meanwhile, amidst this dialogue over the ideal, various professions and disciplines (e.g., law, medicine, business) are caught up in debates over ethics. But who is asking the prior questions: What is the essence of right and wrong? the nature of civic virtue? the basic meaning and purpose of moral behavior?

On our college campuses, racism, recreational sex, drug and alcohol abuse, surrogate test-takers, and computer hackers exist cheek-by-jowl with the latest technologies, the newest psychological theories, and the best libraries in the world. Selling one's academic soul for research money, unprincipled investment policies, and college athletic scandals continue to cloud our country's campuses with mixed messages about altruism, higher education, true sportsmanship, and special interests.

While more substantial scholarship, grant, and loan money is available to college students, college costs are still rising faster than the cost of living, and defaults on student loans are at an all-time high.

Building the Wisdom Community

So, what is the connection between the Church and higher education? Is campus or university ministry just an opportunity to increase church membership? University ministry that is worthy of the name *ministry* must be seriously and sincerely interested in the goals and purposes of the university. And so, it follows, where a project or a situation is integral to the goals of the university, and when it also calls forth a faith stance, there exists a classic opportunity for campus ministry.

Think of the richness and variety in the university: from military, political, and natural sciences and the behavioral and social sciences, to communications, literature, the arts, and philosophy. The university is a freeze-frame, a microcosm of the culture. If

Table 2
Participation of College Students in Volunteer Activities
(Carnegie, 1984)

Activity	Percent Participation
Fund Raising	47%
Service Activity	45%
Church Service Project	41%
Charity Organization	31%
Election Campaign	20%
Elderly and Retirees	19%
Environmental Project	17%
Hospital Service	12%

the Church enters into a true dialogue with the university, it will be a dialogue between faith and culture. The result would be a wisdom in the people who fill the positions of importance in the world. This wisdom would appear when the university is consulted on rice production in Asia or on acid rain in New England or on city planning or on foreign policy. If the world is to survive, it needs more than knowledge or skill; it cries out for wisdom.

The university as an institution can guarantee the acquisition of knowledge, skills, and perhaps arts. It requires objective credentials of instructors; it grants degrees and diplomas after appropriate testing. But none of that guarantees wisdom. It takes community to cultivate wisdom. Wisdom is learned in conversation, in friendships, in small communities, from and with wisdom figures. Wisdom is an interpersonal endeavor. Wisdom is more than knowledge and skill, it includes value and a grasp of one's own ultimate meaning. This is where religious tradition becomes relevant to the university's search for wisdom.

As institutions, the Church and the university have some common problems, as well as some common strengths and conflicts. For example, some of the religious tradition's most cherished language is not easily assimilated in a university milieu (e.g., words such as *preaching, message, mission, evangelization, authority, magisterium*). But these two wisdom communities have much in common and can easily and fruitfully complement each other.

The Church is expected to be a wisdom community. For the early Christians, Jesus was a wisdom figure. The entire Sermon on the Mount portrays Jesus as a wisdom figure, bringing good judgment to law. The priest is expected to be a wisdom figure. The campus minister is expected to be a wisdom figure, and students are in search of faculty who will be wisdom figures for them. But wisdom in both Church and university needs a community context, and campus ministers need to create that context. Wisdom also needs solitude and reflection, and authentic campus ministry must work to create that atmosphere as well.

Where Will the Dialogue Take Place?

The dialogue between the university and the religious tradition takes place first of all in the heart of the person to whom both faith and learning are dear. It takes place in friendships. It also takes place in articles and lectures. It takes place in interdisciplinary studies, especially when they have a theological component. Both religious inquiry and academic inquiry could profit greatly from this dialogue between faith and culture.

The times call for action; the future of society demands a renewed effort by both higher education and the Church. In this effort, higher education is accountable to the citizens of the country who support it and require its services. Students, faculty members, administrators, and trustees have a

responsibility to work diligently so that their particular institution lives up to its best ideals. The Church on campus is accountable to Jesus Christ the risen Lord, as well as to the diocesan Church and all who need campus ministry. All the members of the Church on campus must be responsive to the Spirit by contributing their best efforts to making their community of faith a genuine sign and instrument of the kingdom.

Ultimately, the world will be a better place because of this dialogue. Without it, faith makes no contribution to culture, and culture tends to overlook the depth dimensions of human life and the realm of ultimate meanings. Without such a dialogue, culture makes no contribution to religion, and such a religion becomes alien and alienating to the new generations who are growing up in a new culture, different from the one in which the religious tradition was shaped and given expression.

As the officially mandated presence of the Church in university culture, campus ministry occupies the crossroads between religious wisdom and university wisdom. Empowered by comprehensive and challenging programming, competent and committed staff, this dialogue becomes a major intersection for modern culture built on the triad foundations of Gospel, university, and Church.

Resources for the Church and Higher Education

Books/Articles

Adler, Mortimer J. *Reforming Education: The Opening of the American Mind.* New York: Collier Books, 1989. In direct rebuttal to Allan Bloom's *The Closing of the American Mind,* Dr. Adler draws from a lifetime devoted to education to address the controversy of what should be taught in our schools, how it should be made available, and what end it should serve. Adler "argues for the restoration of form and substance to the dishwater mixture we currently call education in America."

Bacik, James J. "The Making of a Pastoral Letter: The Quest for Wisdom Revisited" in *The Journal of the CCMA.* The NCCB document *Empowered by the Spirit: Campus Ministry Faces the Future,* published in 1986, is a "completely revised version of an earlier draft entitled *The Quest for Wisdom: The*

Church in Dialogue with Higher Education," writes Bacik. He then traces the history of the campus ministry pastoral and the premise on which it was written. He critiques the present document, while describing some of the main differences between the original draft and the final product. The article presents some of the thinking of the original authors and the bishops.

Bellah, Robert, Richard Madsen, William Sullivan, Ann Swidler and Steven Tipton. *Habits of the Heart: Individualism and Commitment in American Life.* New York: Perennial Library/Harper and Row, 1985. This five-year study of various American communities has much to say to campus ministers concerning the isolation and loneliness that college students experience. It traces some of the history of the conflict experienced today between individualism and the need for community and commitment to others.

Bloom, Allan. *The Closing of the American Mind.* New York: Simon and Schuster, Inc., 1987. This best seller raises serious questions about the nature and quality of higher education in America today. Despite the fact that he provides very few footnotes, Bloom, a professor of social thought at the University of Chicago, stirred a national discussion, an understanding of which is essential to anyone working professionally in campus ministry. He argues that the social and political crisis of twentieth-century America is really an intellectual crisis and offers his own solutions.

Boyer, Ernest. *College: The Undergraduate Experience in America.* New York: Harper and Row, 1987. This three-year study of American campus experience follows closely the findings of Bellah, et al. It finds that students today tend to look more for job security in the future than the excitement of learning. It finds that there is a definite confusion over goals, which leaves students fragmented and unfocused.

Braxton, Edward. "The Church and the University: Ministry on Campus" in *Origins* 14:47 (May 9, 1985): 763-770.

Campus Ministry Pastoral Letter Editorial Committee. Most Rev. William B. Friend, chairman. *The Quest for Wisdom: The*

Church in Dialogue with Higher Education (Draft). Washington, D.C.: United States Catholic Conference, 1984. The first draft of what eventually was published as *Empowered by the Spirit: Campus Ministry Faces the Future,* this document examines the relationship between the Church and the university in the pursuit of truth.

Carnegie Foundation for the Advancement of Teaching. *The Campus Life: In Search of Community.* Lawrenceville, N.J.: Princeton University Press, 1990. A thoughtful look at the challenges campus leaders face in contemporary student life, based on a yearlong study in conjunction with the American Council on Education. Includes survey results from college and university presidents and student affairs offices and highlights examples of programs that help build community on campus.

Giamatti, A. Bartlett. *A Free and Ordered Space: The Real World of the University.* New York: Norton Publishers, 1988. Written by the former president of Yale University and short-lived commissioner of baseball, this book is a rich and rewarding analysis of the moral and academic issues that animate our society's continuing efforts to define the role of colleges and universities and the purpose of a liberal education.

Hirsch, Jr., E.D., ed. *Cultural Literacy: What Every American Needs to Know.* Boston: Houghton Mifflin Company, 1987. The best-seller examines the lack of knowledge that even the most-educated Americans have about their culture, the reasons for it, and some suggestions for reversing this lack.

John Paul II. "The Church of the University" in *The Pope Speaks* 27:3 (Fall 1982): 249-251. This pastoral speech of John Paul II was given to the clergy of Rome during their annual Lenten meeting, March 8, 1982. It addresses the Church's need for the university, as well as the university's need for the Church. It then reflects on various pastoral questions such as liturgy and hospitality.

McBrien, Richard. "Gospel, University, and Church" in *The Journal of the CCMA* 1:3 (Winter 1988): 9-12. McBrien first considers each of the three themes: Gospel, university, and Church. After reflecting on each of them separately, they are considered in relationship to one another. He finally concludes with a fourth topic—ministry—which in his view binds together the other three. The directive offered in each of these sections, which McBrien views as essential, is that of evangelization: the proclamation of the Good News, the Gospel.

Vatican Congregation for Catholic Education and the Council for the Laity. "Pastoral Ministry on the University Campus" in *Origins* 6:13 (September 16, 1976): 197, 199-204.

Vatican Congregation for Catholic Education, Pontifical Council for the Laity, and Pontifical Council for Culture. "The Church in the University and in University Culture" in *Origins* 24:5 (June 16, 1994): 74-80.

Other

Gallup Organization. *Religious Beliefs and Sexual Attitudes and Behaviors of College Students.* Princeton, N.J.: The Gallup Organization, 1989. Prepared for The Christian Broadcasting Network, Inc., this is the first poll to cover both topics simultaneously. It is an attempt to find out where this nation's future leaders stand on family and moral issues and to discover what role religion plays in the lives of American college students today.

Viens, Joachim. *Wisdom and Higher Education* (Homily). Fort Collins, Colo.: John XXIII University Center, September 1, 1988. This unpublished work addresses, for the campus ministry parish, the challenge of the Gospel in university life and suggests practical paths of cooperation.

The Context of Campus Ministry

Introduction

Dr. June
Meredith Costin

Higher education benefits the human family through its research, which expands our common pool of knowledge. By teaching people to think critically and to search for the truth, colleges and universities help to humanize our world. The collegiate experience provides individuals with attitudes and skills that can be used in productive work, harmonious living, and responsible citizenship. (ES,14)

The context of higher education can be examined in two directions: the campuses where ministry professionals serve, and the students who meet these ministers in formal and informal ways.

The Campuses

Colleges of the last half of the 1990s face issues on a number of fronts as this century draws to a close. A number of national commissions (particularly since 1983) have addressed areas for reform in higher education. Today's changes, even as reflected from the last decade, run the gamut from those of technology to government, from judicial to administrative. The rate of change challenges the academic community to catch its breath (*Chronicle of Higher Education,* September 1, 1995, p. 5). Catching one's breath is a luxury! Areas of concern, both short-term and long-term, that were identified in 1989 (*Chronicle of Higher Education,* September 1, 1989, p. 5) not only remain with us, but have intensified vis-à-vis the social arena. Short-term concerns include tight budgets, increasing

the enrollment as projections for full-time enrollments show decreasing numbers, and the retention of minority students. Longer term critical areas include the projection of fewer faculty for the close of the decade, increasing tensions and violence on campus, the type of curriculum offered, and funding. As serious concerns (alcohol/drug abuse, racial/ethnic tensions, violence and crime) about quality of life permeate our society, these questions also permeate and confront campuses. The outlook is "both lively and sobering" (*Chronicle,* 1989, p. 5).

In 1994, there were 3,632 colleges and universities in the United States, 1,625 are public institutions and 2,007 are private ones, as well as 6,737 vocational institutions. More than half (1,021) of the public institutions are two-year colleges, while the majority (1,586) of the private institutions are four-year (*Chronicle,* 1995, p. 5). Some of the private four-year institutions are Catholic with a pervasive church presence. While two-year colleges and vocational institutions are less likely than traditional four-year campuses to have full-time ministerial support, the

presence of students in any learning environment challenges the Church to be attuned to their special needs.

Geographical location is another way to divide today's campuses: metropolitan, 22.6 percent; city, 27 percent; small town, 37.6 percent; and rural, 12.8 percent. (*Peterson's Higher Education Directory,* p. 10) While these campus statistics are from 1989—the most recent available to the author in this format—the percentages are close to today's since the total campus statistics have been relatively stable in the seven-year time span. Synthesizing these with the divisions of public, private, and vocational, one can imagine great differences, for example, between the four-year, private rural campus and the two-year, public city campus. An added consideration is campus size. The small campus setting does not match that of the larger. Campus ministry exists in a wide variety of campus settings, with diverse supporting structures.

This chapter presents yet another division for consideration: Catholic institutions, community colleges, commuter students, and residential campuses. These types of campuses and students cut across the categories above (public, private, and vocational; metropolitan, city, small town, and rural).

For effective ministry, the campus minister must consider the campus type, location, size, and the particulars of the campus setting. Campuses do not operate in a vacuum. Some circumstances affecting one campus affect others. Challenges facing the campus are challenges facing the ministry. Campus ministry can be instrumental in the educational quest of the college or university. Campus ministry must be supportive when hardships and struggles befall the campus, encouraging equitable resolutions.

This chapter will sketch a variety of campus contexts. The following selections attempt to encourage and assist campus ministers in their critical tasks.

The Students

An article in a 1966 UNESCO report on higher education states that "for the first time in human history, though many have not really accepted the fact, it is possible to think of higher education as a goal for all," (UNESCO, 77). If this were a true goal for all, then to ask who students are would be similar to asking a country's demographics or characteristics. (The reader is asked to note the date of thirty years ago. Has our society accepted this fact yet?)

The total student enrollment at the four-year institutions (1993-1994) was 8,739,791 (*Chronicle*, 1995, p. 5). These numbers are important when one reflects that there is an opportunity for the Church to support, nourish, and interact with more than eight million persons through campus ministries at these four-year institutions. If one includes two-year institutions, as well as graduate and professional schools, there were 14,305,658 students (*Chronicle,* 1995, p. 5) Using the latter number, students are more then 5 percent of the total population of 260,341,000, but the potential influence of this minority is great. These students will be (and some already are) decision-makers in society and around the world.

What motivates today's students and what are their goals? The *Chronicle of Higher Education* (January 12, 1996, A35), citing the annual survey of freshmen across the nation published by the American Council on Education and University of California at Los Angeles, lists reasons important to students in their decisions to go to college. Responses listed by a majority of incoming respondents were the following:

▲ to be able to get a better job: 77.3 percent (M: 76.4 percent, F: 78.1 percent)

▲ to learn more about things: 74 percent (M: 69.8 percent, F: 77.5 percent)

▲ to be able to make more money: 72.3 percent (M: 75.3 percent, F: 69.7 percent)

▲ to gain general education: 62.5 percent (M: 55.8 percent, F: 68.1 percent)

It should be noted that the survey eliminated the category of "to prepare for graduate school" (from the 1990 norms) in 1995. The different priorities given to money and knowledge and general education by men and women should be noted. Regardless of the differences, however, all agreed that their highest priority was a better job.

These answers correlate with the responses to questions regarding students' objectives. Essential or very important objectives were

▲ being very well off financially: 74.1 percent (M: 76 percent, F: 72.5 percent)

▲ becoming an authority in one's field: 64.5 percent (M: 65.9 percent, F: 63.4 percent)

Academic and professional knowledge as well as financial security concern students as well as campus administrators, who seek to develop institutions of fiscal solvency and academic excellence (*Chronicle,* 1996, p. 17).

Of these students, 28.6 percent had no concern about financing their college education, 52.3 percent had some concern, and 10.1 percent had major concerns (*Chronicle,* 1996, p. 35). If college costs continue to escalate as in the past, these percentages may change. When students have to work to subsidize their education as they study, stress levels often increase as time for extracurricular activities, including ministry programs, decreases. Ministers planning programs need to be cognizant of their students' employment responsibilities.

The majority (54.3 percent) of the students surveyed described themselves as middle of the road, politically. The far right included only 1.6 percent and the far left, 2.7 percent (*Chronicle,* 1996, p. A35). These numbers may or may not describe political apathy on the part of some. Ministers may wish to poll their own student populations in this regard, particularly in light of social justice and social outreach programming. As is seen below, the environment is a popular issue with students of this study.

A survey of attitudes yielded strongest agreement with the statement that just because a man thinks that a woman has "led him on" he is not entitled to have sex with her; the agreement was 88.7 percent, with 82.9 percent of male respondents in agreement, and 93.4 percent of female respondents. The next strongest agreement came regarding the statement that better education and more job opportunities would substantially reduce crime: 85.6 percent agreement (84.5 percent male; 86.5 percent female). Of the twenty-one viewpoints presented, ranging from political to racial and sexual issues, three other points that yielded over 80 percent agreement were that the government isn't controlling pollution (83.5 percent agreement: 80 percent

male; 86.4 percent female), that the federal government should do more to control the sale of handguns (agreement of 80.8 percent: 70.2 percent male; 89.7 percent female), and better education and more job opportunities would substantially reduce crime (85.6 percent agreement: 84.5 percent male; 86.5 percent female). At the other end of the scale, the statement least agreed to was that marijuana should be legalized. Only 19.3 percent of those surveyed concurred: 22.8 percent, male; 16.4 percent female (*Chronicle,* 1996, p. A35)

Campus ministry has traditionally been the Church's response to students under 25 years of age. The generation of today's traditional-age college students was born in the late 1970s, after the Second Vatican Council. Their experience of Church is indeed post-conciliar, but may also be an experience of Church in transition. It is important for campus ministries to offer theological education as well as programs related to spiritual and theological development in order to strengthen students' understanding of the significance of this council in the life of Catholicism and in the life of the Catholic Church in the United States. Traditionally the ages of eighteen to twenty-five represent times of questioning, searching and oftentimes significant faith development. Today's students may still fall into this category, but life experiences for young people are incredibly complex in today's society compared with that of even twenty years ago. Students may have faced serious crises of life and faith long before college or age eighteen. The task for ministers is increased.

Student values respond to events and pressures in the society at large. Campus ministers are familiar with religious responses (and changes) to events and pressures in the personal lives of students. The reaction to society at large becomes more evident as society becomes more global and interconnected at the same time. A study by Dean R. Hoge, Raymond H. Potvin, and Hart M. Nelson, *Religion and American Youth: With Emphasis on Catholic Adolescents and Young Adults,* using fifty years of data on student values, showed both consistent trends (values of freedom, autonomy, changes in moral orientation) and shifts in response to social pressures. The Potvin, Hoge, Nelsen study states that there are factors beyond the Church and its personnel that influence religious commitments. Family, community, employment and national commitments have a strong influence on religious commitment. Religious commitment cannot be seen in isolation.

A word needs to be added about the over-twenty-five student population, a group that continues to increase as education permeates our lives. Even though developmental needs of the young adult differ from those of the older student, campus ministers have gifts to share with all students. It is important to understand the relationship of spiritual needs to psychological and emotional development and to remember that students of the same age may be diverse developmentally. Similarly, faith development does not necessarily coincide with age or other facets of one's maturity.

Campus ministers know from experience, however, that no study or survey can fully describe the students in their ministries. The ministry's context must be all-inclusive. The world, from its poverty to its riches, from its peace and justice to its violence and brutal inequities, is the larger context of campus ministry and of higher education. The more one knows about this context—campus, student, and society—the better one can bring God's light and life into focus and into reality.

Bibliography

Jacoby, Barbara. *The Student as Commuter: Developing a Comprehensive Institutional Response.* ASHE-ERIC Higher Education Report 7, 1989. Series Editor, Jonathan D. Fife. Washington, D.C.: George Washington University, School of Education and Human Development.

Kaye, Kim R., Robert E. Henne, and Richard E. Bohlander, eds. *Peterson's Higher Education Directory 1989.* Princeton: Peterson's Guides, 1989.

Potvin, Raymond H., Dean R. Hoge, and Hart M. Nelsen. *Religion and American Youth: With Emphasis on Catholic Adolescents and Young Adults.* Washington, D.C.: United States Catholic Conference, 1976.

Chronicle of Higher Education. September 6, 1989, 5-24.

Chronicle of Higher Education. September 1, 1995, 5-26.

Chronicle of Higher Education. January 5, 1996, A33-35.

UNESCO. *World Survey of Education.* Paris: UNESCO, 1966.

Multiculturalism and Campus Ministry in a Changing University Culture

Rev. Edward B. Branch, D.Min.

We belong to a Church spanning a world where every corner is in someone's parish, so the question of multiculturalism ought not be such a problem or so great a challenge. Yet we in the United States find ourselves as confused as any politician. So confused in fact that we tend to abandon our theological prerogatives to approach the phenomenon from solely sociological or psychological points of view. A tendency to frame the discussion in terms of majority-minority issues would inevitably construct an "us and them" dichotomy perhaps producing much heat but little light. I would propose, rather, to begin this construction of a Catholic perspective on multiculturalism from the perspective of a people of faith theologically reflecting, first, on our ministerial context and, second, on our various cultures as constitutive vehicles of revelation. It is important to situate this discussion in the context of where we are (the university), who we are (Catholic), and consequently what we are supposed to be doing (pastoral mission).

The Vatican Congregation for Catholic Education[1] and the pontifical councils for laity and culture have done us a great service in isolating some pertinent issues in university culture which touch on the question of multiculturalism and its meaning for Christians in the university setting. The congregation describes culture as all that through which the human person cultivates identity as such. As a creator of culture the university is confronted by several contemporary challenges. First, the professionalization of the university creates in these institutions career training centers to provide for the needs of technological and industrial society. This is not always compatible with the formation of a sense of values in professional ethics. Rather such needs place emphasis on the other disciplines as a complement to necessary specialization. Secondly, the congregation cites the prevailing secularism, which can give rise to skepticism or an ill-defined religious searching inviting the proliferation of cults and fundamentalist sect activity. In the first instance as a developer of culture, the university is exposed to the risk of passively submitting to dominant cultural influences or becoming marginal in relation to them. In the second instance there is a tendency toward nationalism or conformity.

This crisis of culture in the university is of concern to ministry, because we as Christians have a stake in the search for value and truth. More importantly, the option for a culture of technological efficiency affects the progress of peoples and solidarity with the marginalized and oppressed, both very Catholic concerns. These are the hallmark of now three papacies and a constitutive element in the preaching of the Gospel. Our concern as Christian ministers must be our ability to effect an ethos that will safeguard the university's cultural imperative. We cannot allow ourselves to be subrupted by a dominant culture which may already have students and faculty consider their university presence a parenthesis in their life of faith. It is for this reason and others that the question of multiculturalism is for us who believe a question of the relationship between faith and culture. As Pope John Paul II[2] has often said, it is a question of creating a culture of solidarity or a culture of efficiency. Will we see people as human and in relationship with us, or will we see them as a problem to be solved, a bother to be managed?

Msgr. Albacete[3] advances our discussion with his reflection on faith and culture given at San Antonio to the Hispanic Convocation

'95. His reflection speaks not only to the Hispanic experience or for that matter to a difference of language alone. He offers us a way of seeing culture and faith transmission as integrally related. He offers a way of viewing our Catholic experience and evangelization within it as interdependent. We cannot be catholic or Catholic unless we cultivate a faith that is multicultural. A faith that is multicultural manifests the Gospel and its values in a way that is integral to the life pattern, traditions, and values of peoples outside our normal experience. If we are not able to hear the word in our time, it may be because we are not in tune with those for whom God has a preferential option—especially the poor of those cultures in which Christianity is firmly incarnated. He says strongly with John Paul II that a faith that does not become a culture is no faith at all. In our time to be able to understand these cultures is to be open to revelation. As campus ministers, then, it is our goal to cultivate a multicultural literacy in our programs but more importantly in our way of functioning and relating on a daily basis.

As a tradition, ours is a house of many cultures, dependent on many cultures to reveal the face of the risen Christ in our time. Cultivating a multicultural literacy is not a matter of doing justice for helpless, dependent people, or having a few non-majority people around as an emblem of credibility. It is rather a matter of openness to revelation. It is a matter of whether we will become a world Church in fact. Karl Rahner[4] said it well:

> But if the Church really is or must become an actual world Church not only in theory but in concrete life and practices as well, then clearly there will also have to be theologies in all the world that differ from a specifically European theology.

We continue to give the impression that only Europe has anything worthwhile to say about human and transcendent experience. Now that there are interactive discs and video recorders, it is our business to use them as a voice among our own people to carry the Pentecost message that the good news is broadcast in many tongues and may be discovered in the ethos of many peoples.

Sometimes I think Coca-Cola may have preached its good news around the world better than we have the Gospel.

Developing such a literacy is to confront perhaps the prevailing culture in the university and even among our own people. It is a character of evangelization or re-evangelization for which we as ministers are present in the community. We are creating a culture of faith that supports the university in being itself—a culture seeking truth—rather than a feeder for the needs of industry and technology and professional athletics. Ours is a tradition that speaks in many voices. Albacete's admonition to see in the Hispanic religio-cultural experience a paradigm of the dynamic between faith and culture will motivate us to engage in theological reflection through the filter cultural languages not our own. If Hispanic theologians see their faith as generating culture and, therefore, a culture of evangelization, it is important for all the faithful to understand and encounter it. Preparation for such reflection begins with consideration of our environments for ministry.

Multicultural literacy begins as language proficiency begins: with personal interaction. Pictures on the walls, magazines on the rack, and random musical offerings can speak to our ministerial clientele of the diversity that is our Church. For me to advertise an event with French signs decorated with symbols from francophone Africa tells the whole campus that Africans are Catholic and tells African students that this is a place where somebody wants to talk to them. To have a Caribbean night—or four or five—tells students from that part of the world that not just African Americans are welcome here. It is helpful as well to invite Hispanic and African and Asian and Oceanic Pacific professors and graduates who are on campus (there almost always is one or two of the above) to speak on some non-ethnic topic. This creates the occasion for a new perspective on a perhaps familiar issue. African and African American representations of Christ are not out of place in majority white institutions. Nor is it inappropriate to display Christian art from Central and South America and Asia. Pictures of responsible adult African, Hispanic, and Asian (as well as African

American) adults teaching small white children send the message that others in the Church are not always dependent. These initiatives inform the subconscious that the Church is larger that those of Euro-American extraction. Our campus centers must be reservoirs for and about everybody in our global family.

A second phase is in the attempt to facilitate circumstances in which those not of our majorities are able to tell their stories. I will never forget the two black students at Catholic University (one American, the other Jamaican), themselves marginal in the university's social culture, who took a Belgian student who knew no English under their wing for three months (they knew little or no French). They shared greetings and reflections on life now eight years later. Christianity had become a mentality in the ethos of their lives. Americans especially must learn to evoke and listen to the stories of others.

These attempts to "change the wallpaper" are a beginning, a sort of pre-evangelization. There are yet mindsets that are barriers to an openness to personal interactions and the voice of the Spirit carried in cultures not our own. The ever-stronger notion of an American Church, the good and the bad of it, often conflicts with the reality of a Church universal. We give the impression that what is not American is not welcome. More and more, American Church and American culture are becoming synonymous. The deep roots of racism, materialism, secularism, and impersonality do not provide nurture for the tired, poor, huddled masses from Mexico, the Caribbean, Africa, Asia, or the Middle East. Nor do these roots evidence the inculturation of a Christian faith in solidarity with the suffering, struggling outsider. California Catholics voting for Proposition 187 do not place our Mexican coreligionists at ease.

The stride toward community is sometimes a stride toward uniformity, a second barrier. The effort to be a community sometimes can discourage those uncomfortable interactions that create the one heart and one mind we seek. Structures that do not encourage freedom of expression do not invite non-native presence or participation.

They do not encourage voices from cultures of faith, contemporary sources of revelation.

There are barriers among non-natives which from an evangelization point of view form the agenda for ministry-internalized oppression, the attitude that what is American is best, the notion that the safest place is by myself or among my own. Our outreach must speak to these attitudes if we are to be able to free these other voices to speak. It is to be remembered that at all times our ministry agenda is a new evangelization—to be able to hear the voice of contemporary revelation as it comes through cultures of faith.

In reflecting on Hispanic experience, Albacete reminds us that creating a culture of faith on campus is, if not dangerous, an uncomfortable business, because there are forces that do not like Catholics—not because of doctrine and religiosity but because of counterculture rooted in faith that would institutionalize a preferential option for the marginalized. Our American culture is actively seized by a culture of individual morality and structures of sin that deny solidarity with the poor. We are confronted, Albacete reminds us, by the questions of freedom of choice and religious conviction as private matters and purely legalistic issues. There are powerful forces—economic, cultural, and political currents—which encourage and support this notion and encourage a society exclusively concerned with efficiency, a war of the powerful against the weak.

There are, on the other hand, equally powerful forces from below, cultures born of the efforts to follow Christ which have become a mentality in the ethos of peoples. These are those where faith and culture have met and become tools for evangelization and liberation. Hispanic cultures are an example, but the African American voice was heard early as documented by Joseph R. Washington[5] in his *Politics of God*, Gayraud Wilmore[6] in his *Black Religion and Black Radicalism* and Albert Raboteau in *Slave Religion: The Invisible Institution in the Antebellum South*[7]. Joseph Donders[8] points us to the prophetic voice from African cultures in *Non-Bourgeois Theology*. There are also Native American sources of prophecy for our time. All of these cultures come together and are present to us on campus to evangelize us anew and become a source for a culture of faith that will become an ethos in the mentality of our people. Is this not our mission, to fashion of ourselves a people in solidarity with those whom God loves?

The imperatives of the search for truth and value, for which the university exists and which campus ministry serves, requires that we look like the global Church we are and learn the language of our global family members. Solidarity with God's favored people demands it. This new evangelization of our own people begins with our efforts to somehow present these voices even when their faces are not physically present.

Notes

1. **The Vatican Congregation for Catholic Education and the Pontifical Councils for the Laity and for Culture.** "The Presence of the Church in the University and the University Culture." *Origins* 24:5: 74.

2. **John Paul II.** *Redemptor Hominis,* no. 1.

3. **Albacete, Lorenzo,** "The Hispanic Presence in the Church in the United States." *Origins* 25:10: 157.

4. **Rahner, Karl,** *Theological Studies* 401979 716-727.

5. **Washington, Joseph R.,** *The Politics of God.* Garden City: Doubleday, 1967.

6. **Wilmore, Gayraud,** *Black Religion and Black Radicalism.* Maryknoll, N.Y.: Orbis Books, 1984.

7. **Raboteau, Albert,** *Slave Religion: The Invisible Institution in the Antebellum South.* N.Y.: Oxford University Press, 1980.

8. **Donders, Joseph,** *Non-Bourgeois Theology: An African Experience of Jesus.* Maryknoll, N.Y: Orbis Books, 1985.

Ministering on a Catholic Campus

This pastoral document envisions a Catholic university or college as an enterprise wholly committed to evangelical ministry. To relegate this ministry to the institution's periphery in an isolated department or office of "campus ministry," is to fault the university's or college's essential Catholic identity. (Catholic Higher Education and the Pastoral Mission of the Church, 44)

Rev. Charles H. Hagan, S.T.D.

The Context

The setting of a Catholic college or university provides a unique situation where academic theology and practical pastoral experience can interact for the enrichment of the whole community. In the apostolic constitution *On Catholic Universities*, Pope John Paul II describes a Catholic college or university as a privileged place where students and faculty "work toward a higher synthesis of knowledge in which alone lies the possibility of satisfying that thirst for truth which is profoundly inscribed on the heart of the human person" (16). The Catholic college or university is a privileged setting for the encounter between faith and culture, based on the institutional commitment to the task of mediating faith and culture.

The outward appearance of Catholic campuses is characterized by the presence of a chapel, religious names and symbols, and often a religious community. The particular Catholic institution often has a very specific character, reflecting the charism or mission of the religious community that founded it. The catalog of course offerings includes courses in theology, pastoral ministry, and religious education, which further set the institution apart from its secular counterparts.

The role of theology in the life of the Catholic college or university is essential since theology is the integrating discipline that sets the Catholic institution apart and brings the various disciplines together in a dialogue characteristic of true Christian humanism. The Catholic bishops of the United States, in their pastoral letter *Catholic Higher Education and the Pastoral Mission of the Church,* describe theology's role in the life of the institution in these words:

The early American Catholic colleges were founded, in part, to protect the faith of students. The mission of Catholic institutions has broadened considerably since that time. They are full partners in the higher education community of the nation, offering wide diversity of academic programs and degrees. With all this diversity, however, theological education has maintained a role that is central to their mission. (21)

The Structure

Campus ministry at a Catholic college or university can provide many occasions to help students discover the profound unity of truth and diverse traditions that weave the rich fabric of the Church's life. To ensure the overall success of the campus ministry program, the director of campus ministry at a Catholic college or university should be a vice president or have a title that clearly defines campus ministry's place in the administrative structure. It is equally important that the director of campus ministry have direct access to the school's president. This not only identifies the person responsible for the spiritual life of the campus but also clearly indicates the importance given to campus ministry in the life of the institution. For this reason, the director of campus ministry ought to be a full-time position.

Many campus ministry programs are served by more than one full-time salaried person. In these particular settings, it is crucial for the success of the campus ministry program that the individual campus ministers work as a team. In the team model, each person is hired for a particular specialization or assumes a number of very specific responsibilities to serve the whole community and also contributes to the spiritual and personal growth of other team members.

In addition to the full-time salaried campus ministry staff, other people participate in campus ministry's service to the college community. Staff from student activities, counseling services, and residential life can serve as resource persons for campus ministry programs. In addition, there usually is a special relationship between theology or religious studies programs and the campus ministry program. Sometimes, Catholic campus ministers teach one or more theology courses. In many campus ministry settings, students, faculty members, and administrators perform services on campus, such as a coordinator of volunteers, and are considered to be part of the larger campus ministry program.

The Programs

Isolation is one of the most commonly described experiences on a college or university campus today. Students are often separated from one another by competition for grades and for acceptance by peers and campus organizations. Graduate and undergraduate students on the same campus are frequently separated from each other by differences in age and interests. Faculty and administrators sometimes see themselves in opposition by reason of different perspectives and responsibilities. Faculty members, especially in larger institutions, are frequently separated from one another by departmental loyalties. The call to form community based on faith flows from the nature of the Gospel itself and offers the very real possibility of overcoming differences based on age, roles, or social position.

The eucharist is the primary focus for the creation of community on a Catholic campus. Within the eucharist, the homily can be a powerful instrument for applying the Gospel to the situation of a particular campus. There is no adequate substitute for a well-planned and well-attended liturgical celebration as an experience of community building. Campus ministers need to recognize the priestly vocation of all the faithful by involving students, faculty, and administrators in appropriate liturgical roles and by encouraging them to invite others in the college community to the celebration of

eucharist. The Sunday liturgy, in particular, is often the best place to educate the community about Catholic social teaching and to inform students, faculty, and staff about retreat programs, education programs, and programs of community outreach, which are powerful ways of building community throughout the week. The community building aspects of the Sunday eucharist can be enhanced by the opportunity to share food together immediately after the liturgical celebration. Campus ministers, in particular, have the responsibility of helping the campus community feel part of the universal Church, the local Church, and the neighboring community that surrounds the campus. The eucharist can also provide occasions throughout the academic year for special liturgical celebrations for the Catholic community to appreciate the charism or mission of the religious community that founded the institution.

A Catholic college or university reflects the great mosaic of American society with its divergent views and different lifestyles. The challenge for students, administrators, or staff members on a Catholic campus today is well expressed in the words of Pope John Paul II, in his apostolic constitution *On Catholic Universities*:

> Catholic universities will seek to discern and evaluate both the aspirations and the contradictions of modern culture, in order to make it more suited to the total development of individuals and people. (45)

The critical ministry moment when one faces the intellectual challenge to faith posed by the writings of an atheistic humanist or agnostic scientist on campus or the disillusionment of a fallen away Catholic is also a springboard to grow in the direction of a more mature and personal faith. The theology department, library, and personal faith stories of administrators, faculty, and students are powerful resources for those who face a challenge to faith. These resources can be found in Catholic colleges and universities in a more comprehensive form than elsewhere in higher education. However, the widespread availability of these resources does not guarantee their use for personal faith development. The campus ministry program is charged in a special way to utilize the institutional resources for the sake of personal faith development. In particular, a campus minister can be the instrument for helping an individual to see the relationship between one's faith commitment and the need to make the culture more human and more Christian. In an increasingly secularized society, campus ministers can alert the culture to its religious roots and help individuals achieve personal integration.

Many students who come to Catholic colleges or universities today have not had the benefit of a consistent and positive religious education program. Often, specific programs on the foundations of the Catholic faith or on learning how to form a Christian conscience can attract these students. All students, both Catholic and non-Catholic, are influenced by the society at large, which equates moral decisions with personal feelings and touts the virtue of tolerance as the height of civility. Catholic colleges can be attractive, at least in part, because of opportunities to be of service to others before graduation. This service may, in fact, be expressed in the particular charism of the founder of the religious community who established the school. Campus ministry can respond to student and faculty desires to serve others by offering well-planned and adequately supervised programs of community outreach that encourage appropriate personal theological reflection as an integral part of the program.

The setting of a Catholic college or university provides a unique situation where academic theology and practical pastoral experience can interact for the enrichment of the whole community. Through its various programs, campus ministry can be a lead agent in combating the fragmentation of knowledge present on so many campuses today. Campus ministry on a Catholic college or university can be a clear voice calling upon the various disciplines, such as economics and theology, arts and sciences, to dialogue with one another. It also needs to be a persistent advocate for ethics in research, administration, athletics, and in the professions. Furthermore, justice and peace issues can often find fuller reflection and discussion under the impetus of campus ministry than elsewhere on campus.

Collaboration

The context of a Catholic college or university brings significant opportunities, advantages, and problems to campus ministry. Ongoing communication with administrators and faculty members, as well as the development of a truly collaborative ministry on campus, will help ensure that the pastoral letter *Empowered by the Spirit* can be fully and uniquely implemented on Catholic campuses throughout the United States.

Resources for Ministering on a Catholic Campus

Books/Documents

The Catholic Bishops of the United States. *A Letter to College Students.* Washington, D.C.: United States Catholic Conference, 1996.

Hunt, Michael J. *College Catholics: A New Counter-Culture.* New York and Mahwah, N.J.: Paulist Press, 1993.

John Paul II. *On Catholic Universities.* Apostolic Constitution. Washington, D.C.: United States Catholic Conference, 1990. This is the most comprehensive statement available for understanding the role of a Catholic college or university in the world today.

National Conference of Catholic Bishops. *Empowered by the Spirit: Campus Ministry Faces the Future.* Washington, D.C.: United States Catholic Conference, 1985.

United States Catholic Conference. *Catholic Higher Education and the Pastoral Mission of the Church.* Washington, D.C.: United States Catholic Conference, 1980.

Other

Hagan, Charles H. "College Education/ Values Education," *Origins* 22:35 (February 11, 1993): 602-604.

Campus Ministry at a Community College

Mr. John Rivera and Dr. Michael Galligan-Stierle

At these two-year colleges, the ministry of presence is especially important, as is securing the support and active involvement of interested faculty members. These institutions are often open to the addition of religious courses into the curriculum. Skills in marriage and career counseling are especially valuable. It is important for these campus ministers to maintain close relationships with neighboring parishes because that is where many students will find their primary faith community. (ES, 30)

Learning the Community College Demographics

In the fall of 1987, 5 million students attended 1,500 public and private two-year institutions within the United States.[1] These community college students accounted for 37 percent of the 13 million college students nationwide.

A visit to most two-year institutions reveals a growing population of older students, second-career people, and divorced students. Many students are employed, preferring to pay for their courses as they attend school, rather than their four-year counterparts who are more likely to defer their payment through grants and loan programs.[2] Students with limited financial means are attracted to the 50 percent lower tuition and fee expenses of the community college compared with four-year institutions.[3] Some students attend a particular community college for a specific vocational program. Others enter the local college to live at home, while they become accustomed to the academic and social life of higher education. Some students transfer to a four-year institution upon completion of their associate degree.

Faculty, staff, and administrators at a two-year institution have a different profile from their four-year school counterparts as well. Those at two-year institutions earn significantly less than those at four-year institutions. For example, professors at two-year public schools earn $7,000 less, while those at two-year private schools earn $14,000 less.[4] Consequently, professors at a two-year institution are likely to move to a four-year institution or into the business world when an opportunity of greater value presents itself. On the other hand, faculty at two-year institutions often have a greater emphasis on teaching rather than research.

These national impressions of the two-year institution need to be modified with specific statistical demographics obtained from the dean of students' office of the school where one is ministering, as well as with personal observations and interviews with faculty, college officials, and students. In short, the campus minister must be attuned to the unique characteristics of people who attend and work at the community college.

Ministry Plan and Focus

A campus minister can use three different ministry strategies in a community college setting: (1) a higher education focus emphasizes the chaplain working to enhance the goals and mission of the college and usually includes some teaching or guest lecturing; (2) faculty, staff, and administration focus concentrates on serving and empowering the college officials to develop their faith life and to share their faith with students; and (3) student-group focus concentrates on the establishment of a Catholic student group/club that serves as the programming base for pastoral and social student activities. Each of these avenues can become the focus of the entire ministry, although a blending of these three areas is usually the more successful approach at a community college.

Higher Education Focus

Campus ministry can enrich the mission and goals of the community college. The campus community welcomes people who are knowledgeable about its history, mission, and goals. Details of the college's mission and goals can be obtained from the college's publications and personnel. Support for these goals can be garnered from the campus community, nearby parishes, and diocesan staff. College administrators can elaborate on the current challenges and opportunities facing the institution.

The campus minister could join college committees or assist in the retention of students, an area college officials are always interested in improving. In addition, campus ministers can assist in classroom lecturing. This provides opportunities to speak on issues of faith, ethics, morality, history, peace, and justice. For those with the proper credentials, teaching at the college provides visibility and excellent student/faculty contacts. Frequently, a speaking or teaching invitation will follow the distribution of a resume and personal contact with faculty and administrators throughout the college.

Faculty, Staff, and Administrator Focus

Ministry to faculty is ministry to students. This is especially true at the community college. Faculty, administrators, and staff have pastoral needs. Many are interested in discussing topics of religion and spirituality. Spending time with these members of the community can provide mutually beneficial dividends since these people are the college's stable population.

Invaluable knowledge about college employees may be obtained by visiting all college departments. Names of Catholic faculty, staff members, and administrators will emerge along with those persons interested in ministry, whether Catholic or not. An excellent place to meet faculty is at faculty senate meetings or in the faculty dining room (if they are open).

Student-Group Focus

Club status gives official recognition to campus ministry. By law, any privilege or benefit given to a college club at a public institution must also be offered to campus ministry. If there is lack of institutional support, the club approach may be the only way to get on campus. By submitting a club constitution with a list of officers, club members, and a faculty advisor, Catholic students can

The first time I stepped onto a community college campus, I was overwhelmed and scared. As I sat down in a state of shock, I observed students of various ethnic backgrounds, ages, and clothing styles. On this particular campus, there were 12,000 students, 900 faculty, plus staff members and administrators. The only similarity is their diversity. I felt like Jonah being spit out of a large fish onto the shore of a strange land. After an hour, I walked away a discouraged and lonely person.

Like Jonah, I, too, could not see the concerns and opportunities for ministry. My only focus was the undesirable aspects of this particular assignment. Yet, today, my focus is the challenges and possibilities for ministry at a community college. With the support of many people, my perspective has changed and ministry has grown.

Mr. John Rivera
Incarnate Word College

establish such an official campus organization. At some colleges, student government is allowed to provide funds to campus ministry for certain activities if club status has been conferred by the college.

The small number of students interested in joining a club or attending student meetings may be frustrating. Many students work and have family commitments. The campus minister must be aware of this reality. Focusing energy on one-to-one contacts, such as marriage or career counseling, can help the campus minister reach out to students.

In most community colleges, campus ministry is seen as part of the student activities department. The student activities director is usually open to programming oriented toward developing the leadership skills of students. For example, campus ministry involvement can prove fruitful in the area of student government. Consideration of other departments, especially business and community affairs, could complement involvement with student activities.

Gathering Support for Community College Campus Ministry

No community college campus minister should ever try to "go it alone." Reaching out is necessary for the growth of the minister and the ministry.

Diocesan Resources

Diocesan directors of campus ministry can provide programming resources and be a liaison between the individual campus minister and the bishop. Cluster meetings and networking with other campus ministers can provide colleague support and an exchange of ideas. In addition, the diocesan offices of worship, catechetics, peace and justice, family life, and youth and young adult ministry are available for the campus minister's use.

Local Parish

The cooperation and involvement of local parishes are essential, and the parish may be a good place for students to meet, plan meaningful events, and be of service to the community. The parish is also an excellent resource. Help may be obtained from the parish priests, deacons, religious education directors, or parishioners. The parish may even hire part-time or full-time campus ministry staff, especially if the numbers of students and faculty actively involved in the parish are significant. A parishioner may serve as a volunteer, a lay minister, an advisory board member, or as a financial contributor. Locating, inviting, and motivating these individuals are essential. Although working with volunteers may sometimes be difficult, in an era of tight budgets and lay ministry development, it is essential for community college campus ministry. Sometimes it is necessary to locate lay volunteers and clergy from parishes other than those immediately surrounding the college. This is particularly necessary when a local parish or pastor may not sense the urgent need, does not have a gift for working with young adults, or is currently overburdened with parish concerns.

The Campus Itself

Locating and training a few key students and a few faculty, staff, and/or administrators for campus ministry programming are the most important tasks a new community college campus minister can undertake.

Spending time developing the potential gifts within a student can forever alter the vocational choices made by that student. As a stable force, faculty can support the goals of campus ministry by living their vocations as teachers. In their daily contact with students, they can be an example of Christian adulthood. Faculty members may be interested in assisting with programming or being mentors for young adult students.

Involvement of the Larger Community Using Communication Vehicles

Getting out the good news to the larger community is no easy task. There are, however, a number of communication vehicles that can be used to spread the word. Students may take responsibility for some or all of these activities:

▲ *Community Newspapers.* Can be used to list volunteer needs and announce programs, especially in the local section.

▲ *Diocesan Newspaper.* Can be utilized to solicit volunteer help, as well as to announce retreats, faith-sharing opportunities, and social events.

▲ *School Newspaper.* Can be an important ministry tool. If the minister is new on campus, a feature article may be possible.

▲ *Regular Campus Ministry Newsletter.* Can be an effective means of gathering support from the campus community and for communicating coming events, workshops, and retreats.

▲ *Parish Bulletins.* Can be utilized to solicit volunteer help, as well as to announce retreats, faith sharing opportunities, and social events.

▲ *Posters.* Can best be used for a single message or event, such as a retreat.

▲ *Introductory Letter.* Can be an effective means of introducing campus ministry to the campus community. The student activities director may allow an introductory letter to be sent to staff, describing the areas served by the ministry. A similar letter may be circulated to the faculty through the office of the academic dean. Mail can be sent through campus facilities

Rick Reinhard

when campus ministry has club status. If there is no club status, postage for mailings needs to be built into the budget.

▲ *Comprehensive Mailing Lists.* Can be developed to announce regular and special events. These lists can serve as an indicator of the numbers of people contacted and those involved.

Pastoral Ministry Programs

Programming on a community college campus is never an easy task. Nevertheless, the following endeavors can truly enrich students' lives, even if the number of commuter-student participants is small:

▲ *Worship.* Worship can be held at a nearby parish or in a reserved space on campus (at most institutions). These services can celebrate significant religious, national, or campus events. The celebration of eucharist at the opening and closing of the academic year, on holy days, and on Ash Wednesday usually draws Catholic faculty, staff, and administrators.

▲ *Bible Study.* An open discussion of Scripture—its meaning and application to personal experience—is frequently a viable program. Joining with other Christian groups to discuss a biblical topic is beneficial for ecumenical relationships.

▲ *Faith Sharing.* Select faculty may be enthusiastic about volunteering to facilitate a faith-sharing group. Making the connection between faith and everyday life builds community and helps people appropriate their faith.

▲ *Social Events.* Picnics, sports events, movies, and going out for pizza are some possibilities. Remember, the social event itself is not as important as the students who come. If their friends plan to come, they will come. Keeping it simple is easier on budgets and usually makes people feel more comfortable when talking and eating.

▲ *Special Events.* Find out when key college events are celebrated and see how they might be enriched by campus ministry. A core of enthusiastic students can be helpful in designing the program and carrying out the details.

Conclusion

Students at a community college are all commuters, with diverse histories and cultures. Campus ministry enriches learning by understanding student needs, by understanding the mission and goals of the community college, and by responding to each area in a pastoral way. Parish and faculty/staff support can help discern what it means to minister at the college, as well as assist in the ministry process. Whatever ways campus ministry is present, it is most important that the ministry activities assist the college in the fulfillment of its mission. Finally, the creative use of gifts and talents of the minister and the volunteers within the college can address the unique concerns of this ministerial setting.

Notes

1. According to the fall 1987 U.S. Department of Education Statistics, there were 12,768,307 college students, of which 7,992,085 were at 2,135 four-year institutions and 4,776,222 were at 1,452 two-year institutions.

2. According to the fall 1986 U.S. Department of Education Statistics, 47.3 percent of students at public four-year institutions receive financial assistance compared with 28.5 percent of students at public two-year institutions. Only 7.8 percent of community college students take out loans compared with 24.7 percent of students attending four-year institutions.

3. According to the 1986-87 U.S. Department of Education Statistics, the average tuition costs are $1,414 at public four-year institutions, and $660 at two-year institutions. For private institutions, costs are $6,658 at four-year institutions and $3,684 at two-year institutions.

4. According to the 1987-88 U.S. Department of Education Statistics, for nine-month contracts, the average pay for professors at public four-year institutions was $37,903 compared with $30,960 at public two-year institutions. Those at private four-year institutions received $35,747, while those at private two-year institutions received $21,692.

The Commuter Student

Dr. June Meredith Costin

Campus ministers find that the unique stations of their particular campuses create their own concerns and opportunities. For example, campus ministers at community colleges must respond to the needs of students who live at home and have jobs. They often need assistance in defining their roles and responsibilities in the home. Many students are married and are present on campus only for their classes. Some ministers have been able, in these situations, to form small faith communities around shared prayer or social action projects. (ES, 30)

The above paragraph from *Empowered by the Spirit* is directed to two-year community colleges while, at the same time, it addresses ministry with commuter students. Since commuter colleges are, by their very nature, nonresidential, it is these campuses that quickly come to mind when one thinks of commuter students. The words of the bishops on ministry with commuters extend, however, to another group of students: those who commute to colleges or universities that include a residential population.

In terms of programming, many similarities exist between those students who commute to an all-commuter campus, such as a community college, and those who commute to a campus with residential students. This article refers to all commuters, on both types of campuses. It should be noted, however, that if there are residential students, the campus minister is encouraged to involve them in programs with commuters, for they offer friendship and campus stability. The programming should not focus on residential students only. The commuters should not be treated as second-class citizens. If there are only commuters, the campus minister is encouraged to seek a neighboring parish or gathering of faculty to offer a community base. The support of these significant local persons is often most needed and welcomed by both the commuter and the campus minister.

According to the U.S. Department of Education, Center for Education Statistics, in the fall of 1986, 81 percent of all college and university students commuted. When one looks at that percentage in terms of undergraduates only, the population traditionally served by campus ministry, the percentage of commuters is 80. Of these, 50.4 percent live off campus, not with their parents, and 29.8 percent live at home (see U.S. Department of Education, p. 10). These percentages may be surprising. The college "experience" is often equated with four years of residence, halls of ivy, and the social whirl of sororities and fraternities. The college experience for many, for more than three out of every four students, is vastly different, though the buildings may indeed be ivy covered.

The freshman student who resides in an off-campus apartment is in a different environment than a resident freshman. The independence required to deal with leases, landlords, prompt payment of bills, neighbors, lawns, noise, housemates, and furniture may demand a maturity not required of the freshman who has a resident advisor, parents directly paying all major bills, and peers close at hand (see Gribbon, pp. 33-36). In these two circumstances, the opportunities for decision making differ greatly. The student's environment is a significant factor in determining that student's needs. Campus ministers must be aware of the variety of environments in order to minister effectively to all students.

Assumptions, Stereotypes, and Myths

Students affairs professionals who have studied commuters and their campus experiences have discovered that often assumptions are made that have unjust consequences for the commuter student. In a study of commuter experience, L. Lee Kenefelkamp and Sylvia S. Stewart list four common assumptions:

1. The definition of being a college student traditionally has been equated with living in residence halls.

2. The residence experience is considered the normative experience of students.

3. The characteristics associated with residence students are positive and reflective of all student development.

4. The characteristics associated with resident living facilitate development and are attributed exclusively to resident living (Kenefelkamp and Stewart, p. 62).

Another study of commuters goes further to assign commuters some negative characteristics. Because all of us—campus ministers included—are subject to the milieu in which we live, these are listed here as a reminder, lest we find ourselves unconsciously adopting them as fact. William R. Baggett of Georgia State University lists some stereotypes that connote a negative image:

1. As "townies," not residents, they merely infiltrate the campus from time to time— they don't really belong there.

2. Lacking sufficient maturity to go away to school, they are no doubt "tied to mother's apronstrings."

3. They are likely to be "troublemakers," those who refuse to follow conventional rules.

4. They don't really care for the campus; if they did, they would want to live there (Baggett, pp. 5-6).

An article by James J. Rhatigan lists other popular myths:

1. Commuting students are less committed to their education.

2. Commuting students are less able academically.

3. Commuting students have no interest in campus life beyond their classes.

4. Since many commuting students attend part time, it costs less to provide them with instruction and the spectrum of campus services (Rhatigan, pp. 4-5).

Some Realities

If these are assumptions and myths, what are the realities about commuter students? Who are commuters? This is not always an easy question to answer. For example, one university in the Northeast provided a listing of commuters that had students "commuting" to the campus from as far away as Florida and Montana. It is a student's responsibility to give the administration accurate information regarding address, but when this does not occur, the university cannot (or does not) always pursue the student.

Though definitions of *commuter* may vary, the one used by the National Clearinghouse for Commuter Programs, the Council for the Advancement of Standards for Student Services/Development Programs, and the National Association of Student Personnel Administrators (NASPA) may be considered normative. They define a commuter as any student who does not live in campus-owned housing. As will be shown, commuters are in residence in many locations, near and far from campus. The term does not give any indication of how great the commute may be, though seldom is it realistic to think it is across many states!

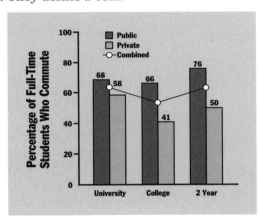

Figure 1

Figure 1 shows the percentage of full-time students who commute, by institutional type. Although these statistics date from 1982, they are the latest available in this format. These statistics are illustrative for the decade of the 1990s as well. The percentage of full-time students who commute at public two-year colleges is only 76 percent, meaning that 24 percent are residential students. Not all two-year colleges are community colleges. Another misconception held by some is that there are many commuter students at campuses other than community colleges, but these are the part-time students. If one considers the full-time enrollment of all institutions combined, the chart shows that over half of that student population commutes (see Stewart and Rue, p. 7).

A study by Sylvia S. Stewart and Penny Rue considers three variable combinations, which yield eight possible types of commuters (see Figure 2). The three variables in the study of commuters are dependent or independent (not living with a parent or relative); traditional (eighteen to twenty-four) or nontraditional (twenty-five and above) age; and part-time or full-time (see Stewart and Rue, p. 5). Combinations of these variables, from the dependent, traditional-age, full-time student to the nondependent, nontraditional-age, part-timer yield subgroups for ministry evaluation. An office of campus ministry should determine which subgroups reflect their commuters and use this data for planning.

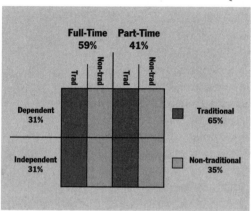

Figure 2

To further compound the number of subgroups possible, commuters can also be considered in terms of whether they have a long commute or a short one; whether they are in-state or out-of-state students (cost factors are involved here); whether they are members of a cultural/social minority groups; and whether they are graduate or undergraduate students, first-time students or those in second-degree programs, career-change, or continuing education. As is evident, the word most descriptive of commuters is diverse. Commuter students can best be characterized by their heterogeneity (see Jacoby, March 7, 1986, Keynote).

Nonetheless, the "literature on these students prior to the 1960s tended to view this population as generally homogeneous" (Andreas, p. 12). While there may have been fewer commuters then than now, surely those were members of the above-mentioned subgroups. In their 1980 study, Rosalind R. Andreas and Jan Kubic find commuters nearly as heterogeneous in quality as they are in quantity. They believe one could almost place each individual commuter in a different subgroup (see Ibid.).

Characteristics of Commuters

William R. Baggett lists nine characteristics of commuter students that cut across these subgroups. In comparing commuters with resident students, he finds the following commuter characteristics:

1. More conflict with parents.

2. More conformity to parental expectations.

3. More dependent emotionally on their parents.

4. Less affectionate with their parents and less likely to communicate well with them.

5. Lower rate of participation in extracurricular activities.

6. Less likely to complete a degree in four years.

7. For adult commuters, the return to school is often triggered by a life transition, such as a career change, divorce, or death of spouse.

8. More prone to stress because of tightly scheduled lives.

9. Seek vocational preparation as the main purpose of college (Baggett, p. 8).

As with the myths, one should not assume that any individual commuter is described by any or all of these characteristics. The sensitive campus minister should, however, be aware of all of them. In addition, this list gives the campus minister a number of areas to consider as sermon or workshop topics, areas that reflect genuine concerns for some commuters.

Needs of Commuters

An individual's needs are directly related to that person's identity. Barbara Jacoby, of the National Clearinghouse for Commuter Programs, names the common core of needs for students who commute. She identifies mobility, multiple life roles and time demands, integrated support systems, and a sense of belonging. The primary need is mobility.

Mobility

While it is primary, mobility can also be the most stressful circumstance that a student encounters each day. The time it takes a student to travel each day, the ease or difficulty of that travel, and the variability of weather all influence how the day is spent. Commuters often need to be conscious of the fact that the car is needed by other family members, sometimes at a precise time. If the student commutes by public transportation, that too presents a variable over which there is often no control. Because of the need to travel, commuters do not have the same amount of time available to them on campus as do residents. Commuters may also find that their time is precisely defined. The need to meet carpoolers or to return the car at a given time is demanding. The meeting with a campus minister or a program that runs overtime presents difficulties not experienced or even considered by a student returning to the dorm.

Campus ministry programming must be accessible. If the location of the program involves parking difficulties or a long walk from a parking lot, participation is severely jeopardized. The willingness to move a program to a location accessible for students may be impeded by the fact that there is no such location. A common problem on many campuses is parking. Campus officials often maintain that, although adequate parking is available, students want parking spaces next to their classroom buildings. The ten- or twenty-minute walk across campus generates the belief that parking is a problem. One reality to consider is that the parking search itself may have taken another ten, twenty, or more minutes. While students must allow time to travel to and from the parking lot, the variable in the amount of time causes added frustration. Often the parking problem must simply be acknowledged and events scheduled accordingly.

Multiple Life Roles and Time Demands

While mobility affects all commuters in some way, the second need, the area of multiple life roles and time demands, causes the greatest diversity among them. This need touches the core of a student's identity. The multitude of roles in which students find themselves include child, parent, grandparent, spouse, babysitter, employer, employee. Each role requires the commuter to consider its own special demands that often conflict with demands of other roles. Students may

be unable to develop another relationship. Relationships require an investment of self, and if the individual already feels caught in a multiplicity of roles, an additional person or group may be unwelcome. Campus ministry should support commuters in their existing roles, rather than initially assigning those students new roles as club officers or committee members.

Integrated Support Systems

Surrounding the many roles of the commuter are complex support systems. A resident student will develop a circle of friends in classes, dorms, and extracurricular activities. These support groups are many and cut across different campus lines, but at least they share proximity on campus. For the commuter, however, support systems include home or job contacts in addition to those of campus. Their off-campus family, friends, and colleagues do not always have a clear perception of the campus environment. For example, parental support becomes a hindrance when parents do not understand the exigencies of campus life. If an individual's support system, particularly a major one such as that of the home, breaks down, that student is more than ever in need of the services of a concerned campus minister.

Support systems involve a student's relationship with family, work, and campus. The term campus ecology has been used to describe the student, his or her environment, and the relationship between the two. One aspect of campus ecology is highlighted in an article entitled "Parents of Dependent Commuters, A Neglected Resource," by Barbara Jacoby of the National Clearinghouse for Commuter Programs (see Jacoby, pp. 49-60). The author has used a positive, rather than a negative, title and an encouraging perspective. Jacoby, however, within the context of that study, cites both negative and positive influences, including, on the one hand, the lack of independence, parental pressure for grades, and domestic duties, and, on the other hand, financial and emotional security. The role of the parent in the life of his or her dependent commuter student may be a new one for the parent, as well as for the student. This area is a worthy topic for programming.

The need for a support system can be translated into pastoral terms. If our relationship with Christ and Church has meaning, it mandates that we are to be Christ for each other, in loving and caring support. A universal goal for campus ministry is the building of community. This community, this support system, does not need to replace other support systems, but rather, the Christian community reinforces and influences other groups. If one has no friends or contacts within the ministering community and never crosses paths with those individuals outside of the church setting, membership becomes a formality and may not survive the test of time. The building of friendships among students is important. The commuter may find it harder to make friends on campus than the resident and may be especially appreciative of gatherings that include both residents and commuters.

A *Sense of Belonging*

Last on Jacoby's list is the need to develop a sense of belonging. This is related to the need for a support system. If one "belongs," then the group to which one belongs often serves as a support system. Conversely, if one has a support system, the sense of belonging follows naturally. Many persons may participate in Sunday worship communities without a sense of belonging, but particularly on campus, the expectations are high that one "belongs" to groups. Students are encouraged to join activities, and some counseling centers assist students in those choices. Students expect to belong to something. That expectation is also shared by the college administration, which promotes student programming and rewards extracurricular involvement. The administration becomes concerned if students do not belong to campus organizations.

Campus ministry wears two hats in this regard. As a recognized student organization on many campuses, it is a club to which students belong. At the same time, the services of a campus minister extend far beyond that of club moderator to the pastoral and sacramental life of the Church. The two hats that campus ministry wears are both important, but the commuter student needs to be aware that both facets of the ministry are available.

For the busy commuter who has too much to do, too many people to relate with, and too little time, the pastoral guidance of a campus minister must be made visible and not hidden behind a club motif. A counseling opportunity may be a welcome gift for the student, while that student is not attracted to another club.

If the need to belong is not met, the loss is more greatly felt in a setting where expectations are high. The opposite of the sense of belonging is the sense of alienation. Campus ministry, by its very nature, strives to serve those who feel alienated. The commuter who is in a minority on a residential campus may well be such a person.

With the assumption that time on campus is limited, Andreas states that "efforts must be made to ensure that the commuter feels welcome and that he or she belongs on campus." She offers questions for self-assessment. These questions attempt to determine whether a sense of belonging is facilitated by academic affairs, student services, and administrative offices (see Andreas, pp. 19-20). Campus ministry should also consider its contribution toward facilitating a sense of community for the commuter. In some cases, failures of the overall campus community can have tragic consequences. Feelings of belonging and of being welcomed can offer buffers against loneliness, depression, and suicide.

While it is hard to discard one's view of the campus population as the traditional-age, four-year, residential-college students of earlier years, this author hopes that campus ministry increasingly recognizes the significance of the commuter population. Commuters do not represent "maturational deficiencies" from a norm but rather "logical and predictable individual and group differences." Statistics of today and predictions for the future tell us clearly that on many campuses the commuter student replaces the residential student as the norm (see Kenefelkamp and Stewart, p. 62).

Ministry and the Commuter

The author hopes that this discussion of the diversity of commuters does not discourage campus ministers from offering programming, fearing that they may not meet such diversity of needs. Anyone who ministers with commuters faces immense difficulties in scheduling programs and discouragement with small attendance at these programs. At the same time, since at least 81 percent of all college and university students commute, ministry with this population cannot be ignored. In fact, in light of these statistics, that ministry takes on an oft-forgotten urgency.

Following is a list of some practical suggestions. It is hoped that the reader will be inspired to think of other strategies and will be willing to experiment. Many offices of student affairs have developed special outreach to their commuter populations. Campus ministry may find opportunities to join their efforts, as well as to develop cosponsorship of services. The one ministry service that is always welcomed is that of counseling. If no other outreach to commuters takes place, a listening, counseling campus minister provides an immensely valuable service. The students who are met one on one may be the nucleus to guide the ministry into new and challenging directions.

Practical Programming

The following areas are important to any ministry. These topics are addressed here specifically in their relationship with commuter ministry. This list does not claim to be complete, but it does hope to encourage one's efforts. The value of a program for one or two persons is not always diminished because they were the only ones present.

Ways to meet students:
▲ Find the most popular place(s) on campus.

▲ Use the cafeteria as an "office" in the midst of much activity; it is an excellent place for scheduled presence.

▲ Attend athletic events that draw a crowd.

▲ Join other clubs for their events.

▲ Set up a table in a high-traffic area, with coffee and donuts (or flowers on Valentine's Day), for example, and ministry identification.

Ways to develop visibility on campus:
▲ Offer one's services for blessings at major events such as convocations,

graduations, commissioning ceremonies. (Related to the above, but visibility includes visibility with faculty/staff on a professional basis.)

▲ Attend major campus events such as those cited above. In addition, student orientation programs; faculty/staff meetings, where possible; lectures; and sports events are all areas for visibility.

Importance of faculty, staff, administration contacts:
▲ These contacts are especially important where the student population is large and/or only on campus for two years. The campus minister is minister for these persons themselves, and they may join in ministerial outreach.

Linkage with residential programs:
▲ Provides a good support base to assist in making the commuter feel welcomed on campus. It is important, however, to be sure that these residential programs do not treat the commuter as a "second-class" citizen (see the myths and assumptions cited above).

Publicizing programs:
▲ While this is always important, it is crucial where commuters are involved. They often do not have campus mailboxes— there is a cause for one's efforts—and the campus minister is challenged to use every possible means, including posters, bulletins, flyers, campus media, and, where possible, announcements through faculty members.

Other campus groups that may be an avenue for meeting students:
▲ The campus minister's attendance at events sponsored by other groups (e.g., departmental clubs, the athletic department) may offer an introduction to students.

The scheduling of events:
▲ Select mealtimes, which are good occasions—especially if food is freely given. Early in the day may also be good, even breakfast.

▲ Cooperate with faculty in scheduling a classroom presentation (campus minister or outside speaker obtained through the ministry), with follow-up discussion outside of class.

▲ Ask students whom you know to give you their schedules and track the patterns.

▲ Avoid Mondays and Fridays, which are generally not good, and on Monday through Thursday campuses, avoid Thursday, which is also bad.

▲ Utilize seasonal and special events. Thanksgiving, Advent, Christmas, Lent, Black History Month, World Food Day, Holocaust Memorial are some good examples.

The ecumenical dimension:

▲ Since most ministries share common goals of meeting students and involving them in programming, there may be value in a united effort.

▲ Some campuses are willing to provide lists of students by religious denominations and are encouraged to do so if more than one denomination makes the request. Collaboration is encouraged here, with the realization that this may not always be possible.

Types of programs:

▲ An invitation to eat—even a meal with no program—where the food is good, cheap, or free is always popular at almost any time of the day or night. Exam times are most welcomed, but there is less opportunity for conversation during these periods. Also, it need not be a complete meal; it can be something as simple as serving lemonade to students during registration and/or orientation.

▲ A sponsored guest speaker, with a meal, either at lunch, dinner, or on a weekend (when students return to the library on weekends to study).

▲ Exhibits in central areas on campus can heighten awareness of ministry and/or areas of local or global concern. These may or may not link with other programming.

▲ International awareness—including opportunities to fast, to donate money saved by not eating, to break-the-fast meal with a Third-World menu—is a popular area for programming on many campuses. This also gives an opportunity to join with another campus international or multicultural organization or division.

▲ Book displays on timely topics (with cooperation/permission of local campus bookstore and/or campus library) provide an opportunity for education in particular areas. These can be used in conjunction with the above or alone.

▲ Displays mentioned above, if they are displays of religious writing, can be done in conjunction with other campus religious groups. For example, persons often look for spiritual reading during Advent and Lent and may welcome access to current publications. An opportunity to browse and to buy is particularly appropriate if there is no religious bookstore nearby (and the campus bookstore approves, of course).

▲ Topics for speakers or workshops could call attention to the unique needs of commuters as mentioned in the text.

▲ Bible discussions offer programs where the presence of only a few persons does not detract from the quality of the event. This is also an area where faculty, staff, administration, and students may gather together.

Social outreach projects:

▲ Projects such as a one-day-a-month visit to a nursing home; recycling bottles, cans, paper, plastics, and so forth; clothing drives; helping in a soup kitchen for one meal a month are all possibilities. If the commuter student can bring a donation to someone who will route it for them or if he or she can give an hour or two to a project, outreach programs can be most successful.

Resources for Ministering to the Commuter Student

Books/Articles

Andreas, Rosalind R. "Institutional Self-Study: Serving Commuter Students" in *Commuter Students: Enhancing Their Educational Experiences,* Series No. 24, pp. 9-24. Sylvia S. Stewart, ed. *New Directions for Student Services.* Ursula Delworth and Gary R. Hanson, editors-in-chief. Washington, D.C.: Jossey-Bass Publishers, Inc., 1983. One of a series of articles in a work specifically directed to commuters. Reflections for ministry, as well as institutions.

Baggett, William R. *"Who are Commuter Students?"* Unpublished manuscript. Atlanta, Ga.: Georgia State University, 1989. Talk given at Baptist Campus Ministers Conference gives examples of differences in student circumstances. The author knows well the commuter population.

Chickering, Arthur W. and Associates. *The Modern American College.* San Francisco: Jossey-Bass Publishers, Inc., 1981. A detailed scholarly study by a well-known authority in higher education.

Delworth, Ursula and Gary R. Hanson, editors-in-chief. *New Directions for Student Services.* Washington, D.C.: Jossey-Bass Publishers, Inc., 1983. Recommended reading for all those ministering with commuter students. An excellent collection.

Gribbon, R. T. *Students, Churches, and Higher Education: Congregational Ministry in a Learning Society.* Valley Forge, Pa.: Judson Press, 1981. One chapter is specifically devoted to the community college and the local church. Another, directed to the characteristics and needs of older students, is also directly related to commuter student ministry.

Hallman, W. E. *So There's a Community College in Your Town: A Guide for Local Church Ministry with the Nearby Community College.* New York: UMHE Communication Office, 1976. Includes a practical guide for initiating ministering relationships between parish and community college. Also includes a chapter of case studies.

Jacoby, Barbara. "Parents of Dependent Commuters: A Neglected Resource" in *Commuter Students: Enhancing Their Educational Experiences,* Series No. 24, pp. 49-60. Sylvia S. Stewart, ed. *New Directions for Student Services.* Ursula Delworth and Gary R. Hanson, editors-in-chief. Washington, D.C.: Jossey-Bass Publishers, Inc., 1983. Insights into the relationships of parents and commuting students that could be helpful for programming as well as counseling.

Kenefelkamp, L. Lee and Sylvia S. Stewart. "Toward a New Conceptualization of Commuter Students: The Developmental Perspective" in *Commuter Students: Enhancing Their Educational Experiences,* Series No. 24, pp. 61-70. Sylvia S. Stewart, ed. *New Directions for Student Services.* Ursula Delworth and Gary R. Hanson, editors-in-chief. Washington, D.C.: Jossey-Bass Publishers, Inc., 1983. Helpful in terms of understanding the commuter perspective.

Rue, Penny and Ludt. "Organizing for Commuter Student Services" in *Commuter Students: Enhancing Their Educational Experiences,* Series No. 24, pp. 25-48. Sylvia S. Stewart, ed. *New Directions for Student Services.* Ursula Delworth and Gary R. Hanson, editors-in-chief. Washington, D.C.: Jossey-Bass Publishers, Inc., 1983. While campus ministry does not directly offer "commuter student services," this article may give the campus minister some ideas for ministry.

Stewart, Sylvia S. and Penny Rue. "Commuter Students: Definition and Distribution" in *Commuter Students: Enhancing Their Educational Experiences,* Series No. 24, pp. 25-48. Sylvia S. Stewart, ed. *New Directions for Student Services.* Ursula Delworth and Gary R. Hanson, editors-in-chief. Washington, D.C.: Jossey-Bass Publishers, Inc., 1983. May assist one in defining commuters on their campus.

Other

Consortium of Student Affairs Professional Organizations. *CAS Standards and Guidelines for Student Services/Development Programs.* Council for the Advancement of Standards for Student Services/Development Programs. 1986. Standards for student affairs professionals and recommended reading for campus ministers, particularly those who find themselves in advocacy positions.

Jacoby, Barbara. Keynote Address. Delaware Undergraduate Student Congress Symposium. Newark, Del.: University of Delaware, March 7, 1986. Dr. Jacoby and other members of the National Clearinghouse, cited below, are available for workshops and consultation.

National Clearinghouse for Commuter Programs, 1195 Adele Stamp Student Union, The University of Maryland, College Park, MD

20742. A most valuable resource for anyone ministering with commuters. They publish a quarterly, *The Commuter,* and also a directory of types of programs offered by student services on various campuses. Annual membership is an excellent investment.

Researching and Ministering to Commuter Students. May 22-25, 1989. Baptist Student School Board, Charles B. Johnson, director, Student Ministries Department, 127 Ninth Avenue North, Nashville, TN 37234. The proceedings of this conference, directed to commuter student services, fills a large loose leaf binder. Copies of presentations are included. A wealth of resource material is contained therein.

UME (United Ministries in Education) Communication Office, c/o Educational Ministries—ABC, Valley Forge, PA 19481. The denomination has a number of publications on campus ministry, specifically under a Community College Program.

U.S. Department of Education, Center for Education Statistics. *The 1987 National Postsecondary Student Aid Study.* Washington, D.C.: 1989. One's own campus personnel can give important information from a number of perspectives. Everyone from the part-time employee to the full-time administrator can help the campus minister better know his or her campus environment and its population.

The Residential Campus

The experience of Christian community on campus is important to the life of the whole Church. Students who have such a positive experience and are taught their responsibilities to the larger Church will continue to be a very valuable resource for family, parish, and diocesan life when they leave school. (ES, 43)

Dr. Carol
Fowler

Introduction

It is a warm September day, early and electric in College Town, USA. The residence halls open today, and by evening, thousands of new and returning students will have this normally peaceful burg hopping. No more easy access to restaurants, shopping, or parking. No more quiet weekends in the residential areas close to campus. Parties, loud music, congestion, problems at local bars, pre- and post-game football activities are about to replace the summer tranquility. Yet no one is really upset. The city or town that is home to the residential college or university gratefully depends upon this institution for the local economy and often for its culture. Among those most focused by the students' return are the campus ministers at the Newman Center or university parish near campus.

This article will examine four points: (1) the residential college or university; (2) the special concerns of residential students; (3) the nature of campus ministry at these schools; and (4) some practical programs for residential campus ministry.

The Residential College or University Setting

Numerous residential campuses exist throughout the United States. While the majority of full- and part-time college and university students tends to gravitate to urban and suburban commuter schools, a very large number of students, especially full-time, traditional-aged undergraduates with good high school academic records, attend residential campuses. Such schools also have large graduate and international student enrollments. This article focuses on the residential campus characterized by a high percentage of students living on or near campus for the purpose of attending school, rather than on the primarily commuter school, which may have a small residential population. Student living arrangements in such residential campuses include residence halls, fraternity and sorority houses, rental apartments and houses, cooperatives, and rooms in local homes.

Special Concerns of Residential Students

Among the many issues facing undergraduate and graduate students, some are particular to those students who reside on or near campus rather than with their family of origin or in their hometown.

Freshmen and other new residential students must make multiple adjustments to a new lifestyle. Roommate problems often arise. Overcrowding in residence halls is common, especially early in the academic year. Space sharing and privacy needs, when and how to have personal guests, and noise problems are among the many possible tensions in a new living situation. Younger undergraduates and international students often experience serious homesickness. Those who live close enough may go home frequently and not give themselves a chance to enter fully into the learning possibilities of the residential experience. It is important to note that weekends offer many programming opportunities for campus ministers.

For many students, going away to school is their first experience with significant financial responsibilities. They are offered credit cards and quickly accumulate debts they cannot pay. Many juggle school, a new living situation, and part-time jobs. The pressures of independence multiply.

The residential campus is many students' first experience living in socioeconomic, cultural, racial, and sexual diversity. They also discover their newfound freedoms sometimes more akin to license in regard to alcohol and drug use. Some residential campuses, even more than commuter schools, exhibit a subculture that consistently encourages alcohol abuse and other irresponsible behavior. On some campuses, for example, Thursday night is known as "bar night" or "party night." Campus ministers face the question of whether or not to do any programming on such nights or perhaps program other activities as viable alternatives.

Other activities and interests on the residential campus also grab the attention of students. Fraternities and sororities (the Greek system) have needs that could well be addressed by campus ministry. These organizations, many of which are also housing units, have the reputation—sometimes well-deserved—that parties and alcohol consumption are their primary reason for existence.

Intercollegiate athletics often play a predominant role in residential college life. Some teams have chaplains. Catholic campus ministers are often asked to serve in these roles. Young Christian Athletes are active on many campuses. Their influence on Catholics is sometimes negative if their local leadership leans toward fundamentalism. The ethics of intercollegiate athletics and the predominance of athletics in institutional decision making certainly demand attention as the campus minister works to influence the environment of the college or university where he or she ministers.

Graduate students, many of whom are international students, have particular needs. Many large universities have graduate and married student housing that is small and crowded. The academic, time, and financial pressures on these students often cause personal and marital problems. Divorce rates are high among this group.

Campus ministry can foster relationships among many varied groups of people on the residential campus. Student government, union boards, and student services are all concerned with the quality of life of the residential student—sometimes with little concern for the commuter student. These university groups often have financial resources that campus ministers can use for nonsectarian programming for students.

The residence hall staffs are particularly important. Campus ministers can have a significant role in residence hall (never call them "dorms") programming and services. It is important to know the housing director and the resident advisors (RAs). Counseling and student health services are two other significant areas of contact. Fostering relationships with parents, who are often among the greatest supporters of campus ministry, is invaluable. By knowing the permanent residents of the neighborhood, town, or city where the campus is located, "town and gown" tensions can sometimes be reduced. Campus ministry can be a significant mediating presence in these situations.

The Nature of Campus Ministry at Residential Colleges and Universities

What does campus ministry look like at residential schools? With all the diversity of formats and styles, the most common form of ministry at public and non-Catholic institutions is the Newman Center located on campus or, more frequently, on the campus perimeter with easy access. These Newman Centers may be canonically established university parishes, which are usually nonterritorial, or quasi-parishes that function in most ways like a parish. Liturgy and sacraments are major parts of Newman Center ministry, as they are at residential Catholic institutions. Marriage preparation and weddings may be common. The RCIA has proven to be very successful in these settings. Excellence in liturgy, preaching, and music has been a hallmark of campus ministry throughout the United States. Newman Center staffs usually use a team model with a pastor or director named by the diocese or religious order responsible for the Newman Center. The campus minister serving at a Newman Center or a Catholic residential school often faces long hours of work, including nights and weekends. The pace slows down when students are on holiday, quarter, semester, or summer breaks. Rarely does the work stop, even when students are gone. Sunday liturgy often continues, usually with a reduced schedule. Christmas and Easter may be difficult because the main body of worshipers and the liturgical ministers are away from campus.

Tensions can arise in the Newman Center setting. Finances are often difficult. Most dioceses expect those doing the ministry to raise significant funds for ministry support. Some Newman Centers are completely self-supporting and even pay diocesan assessments. Permanent parishioners are very important to the financial well-being of these Newman Centers, providing stability and ongoing ministerial resources to the community. However, sometimes the services they expect in return (e.g., catechesis for their children) may conflict with the primary mission of the center, which is to serve students, faculty, and staff of the university. It is important that these permanent parishioners, who use the Newman Center as an alternative parish, accept the mission of the center or university parish before becoming members. It is sometimes too easy for campus ministers to be so caught up in all of the work of center maintenance and ministry that they do not focus enough on campus. "On-campus presence" is a constant challenge to campus ministers who serve at Newman Centers.

Newman Centers are the dominant Catholic campus ministry image in this country. It is important to accept this format as only one of various styles of ministry operative today at our colleges and universities. Serving as a campus minister in this particular setting is often challenging and exhausting, but always satisfying and, at times, even exhilarating.

Programs for the Residential Campus

1. Outreach to Residence Halls

This outreach tries to provide students with programs that respond to their needs. The meetings are practical and informational and presented in a dialogic style. Target groups are students in residence halls and those in the Greek system. RAs or others who are responsible for programming in the living unit do the actual scheduling. Some program ideas include (1) *An Evening with Leo* (tapes of Leo Buscaglia); (2) *The College Dating Game—Who Wins?*; (3) *What Are We Really Fighting About?* (communication and

listening in the midst of conflict); (4) *Alcohol: Fact and Fiction*; (5) *Comfort not Come-on* (intimacy and friendship); (6) *Could This Be Magic?* (the occult, Satanism, and the New Age Movement); (7) *The Joy of the 36-Hour Day* (time management); (8) *I Think I'm Cracking Up!* (stress management); and (9) *It's Over. Now What?* (surviving broken relationships).

Contact:
Newman Catholic Student Center
512 Normal Road
DeKalb, Illinois 60115
Tel. 815-758-6667

Place:
Northern Illinois University

2. Care Packages

About a month prior to final exams, a letter is sent to parents of students who are registered at the Newman Center. Enclosed with each letter are two order forms. Parents complete the order form and return it with their check; then, baskets and ingredients are purchased wholesale. The baskets are assembled and students are contacted to come and pick up their "care package." For some, it is the first time they have been to the Catholic Center. Baskets include fruit, popcorn, cheese and crackers, an inspirational leaflet along with a note of encouragement from their parents.

Contact:
Pat Lynch, OSU
St. Lawrence Catholic Campus Center
1631 Crescent Drive
Lawrence, Kansas 66044
Tel. 913-843-0357

Place:
University of Kansas

3. Residence Hall Representatives

One or two students from each residence hall who have been active in campus ministry serve as contact persons for that hall. They are responsible for publicity; residence hall programs by campus ministers; contact with Catholic students, especially new students; and giving feedback to the campus ministers about urgent student concerns that need to be addressed.

4. *Sunday Night Supper*

Many residence halls do not serve food on Sunday nights. Students often prefer Sunday liturgy in the late afternoon or early evening. This can be combined with supper and some kind of short program.

Contact:
Ms. Jan Slattery
700 S. Morgan Street
Chicago, Illinois 60607
Tel. 312-829-0670

Place:
Archdiocese of Chicago

Resident Assistant Training

Campus ministers endeavor to become part of the training for staff resident assistants at the beginning of each semester or quarter. These RAs are essential to the residence hall's effectiveness and vitality. Campus ministers can be excellent resources to RAs for counseling, religious questions, and programming.

Persons Who Serve on Campus

Introduction

*Sr. Judith A.
Rinek, SNJM*

*Thus, all the baptized members of the academic community have the opportunity and
the obligation, according to their unique talents and situations, to join with others to help
higher education reach its full potential. (ES, 22)*

Though once the exclusive domain of
the ordained, campus ministry has
broadened to include men and
women, both laity and clergy. What
has brought about this shift? Vatican II's
Dogmatic Constitution on the Church roots
the Christian vocation to ministry in baptism and confirmation. Elaborating on this
with contemporary theology, Richard P.
McBrien, in *Ministry*, describes "designated
Christian ministry" as "any general service
rendered to others in Christ and because of
Christ in the name of the Church and for
the sake of helping the Church fulfill its mission" (McBrien, p. 12). Furthermore, ministry is grounded in the "empowering,
charism bestowing" Holy Spirit and is oriented to God's kingdom (Ibid., p. 13).

Applying this perspective to campus ministry, the Catholic bishops of the United
States, in their pastoral *Empowered by the
Spirit: Campus Ministry Faces the Future*,
state: "The faithful are called not only to
bring Christian witness to the academic
world, but also to exercise their baptismal
prerogatives by helping to build up the
Church on campus" (ES, 23). One implica-
tion is that a professional campus minister
empowers Catholics on campus to do

ministry: "Their task is to identify, call forth,
and coordinate the diverse gifts of the Spirit
possessed by all members of the faith community" (ES, 24). The name of this empowering style of leadership is *collaboration* or
teamwork. Affirming this way of doing ministry, the bishops write: "We encourage the
formation of such team ministries, which
serve as models of ministry and community
for the rest of the Church" (ES, 26).

Teamwork may take place in a formal
group of full-time ministers or in an ad hoc
group called together to complete a task. In
Collaborative Ministry, Carroll Juliano and
Loughlan Sofield define collaborative ministry as "the identification, release and
union of the gifts of all baptized persons" (p.
11); thus, it is related to the sacrament that
joins each person to the Body of Christ.

Evelyn and James Whitehead note, in *The
Emerging Laity*, that the dynamics of collaboration are similar to those of the Body of
Christ. Members of the Body of Christ are
equal and interdependent. Integral to the
development of this interdependence among
team members are processes that expand
dialogue, articulate the vision, include all in
the decision making, manage tension and
conflict, and foster mutual accountability

and forgiveness. Being an organic reality, teams grow and mature. In studies of groups, social scientists have identified a vital role for the designated leader in each stage of development: orientation, inclusion, control, conflict, cohesion, faith sharing, intimacy, and termination. Each member has a unique role in building up the body as well; and all the gifts are needed (see 1 Cor 12:4-37). The closer the parts became united to Christ, the more fully this body experiences growth (see Eph 4:13,16). Eventually, collaboration matures into an energetic, creative, inclusive, and effective ministry.

Behaviors, processes, and structures that foster mutuality are quite an accomplishment for persons raised in the patriarchal structures of Church and society. Usually, differences in needs, in assumptions, and in cultural and gender experiences breed misunderstanding. Furthermore, research has shown that a high percentage of men and women in ministry are adult children of alcoholic families; thus, they have a tendency to addictive behavior and low self-esteem. Individuals with low self-esteem manifest some behaviors identified as obstacles to collaboration: competitiveness, parochialism, arrogance, burnout, hostility, unwillingness to deal with conflict or loss, learned helplessness, inability to share faith, and lack of sexual integration. Consequently, it is possible that those committed to teamwork are not yet capable of doing it.

Ironically, these very obstacles reveal the potential of a collaborative style of ministry. By coming to terms with their levels of personal and professional growth, ministers will seek the healing, knowledge, support, and skills necessary for healthy functioning in a team. Moreover, as they discern the effect of systemic injustice on their dynamics as a group, ministers will develop a sensitivity to sexism, racism, clericalism, and such. Finally, as they search for a spirituality that integrates all aspects of the person, campus ministers will engage the power of the Spirit in renewing society and the Church. Such a spirituality notices God in every experience, enables risk, learns from suffering and failure, and moves to compassionate action. In short, teamwork calls men and women, both laity and clergy, to conversion. And who can

predict the long-term effect of pooling Spirit-ignited visions, feelings, and enthusiasms to "function as one Body, with one life and one mission, namely Christ's" (Sofield and Juliano, p. 10)?

Resources for Persons Who Serve on Campus

Books/Articles

Cowan, Michael A., ed. *Alternative Futures for Worship.* vol 6: *Leadership Ministry in Community.* Collegeville, Minn.: The Liturgical Press, 1987. This book explores leadership, power, and ministry in the Christian community in the context of tradition, socio-psychological theory and research, and liturgical and pastoral theology. It emphasizes empowerment and includes rituals for celebrating different forms of leadership.

Ferder, Fran and John Heagle. *Partnership: Women and Men in Ministry.* Notre Dame, Ind.: Ave Maria Press, 1989. This book gives a scriptural rationale for the mutuality of women and men in ministry. Containing a critique of patriarchal attitudes toward women and of the theology of sexuality, it suggests a new vision of the human person and new images for ministry and the Church.

McBrien, Richard P. *Ministry: A Theological, Pastoral Handbook.* San Francisco: Harper and Row, 1988. This handbook gives a clear theological grounding to a wide variety of ministries in the Church. It defines ministry in a modern ecclesial perspective and identifies the qualities of a minister and the spirituality that enables ministry. The analysis of historical development of the concept of "ministry" is very insightful.

Sofield, Loughlan and Carrol Juliano. *Collaborative Ministry: Skills and Guidelines.* Notre Dame, Ind.: Ave Maria Press, 1987. This practical handbook helps to assess readiness for collaboration. It looks at the skills needed, discusses the obstacles, and provides guidelines for effective management of meetings and conflict. Emphasis is on baptismal giftedness. Elements for a spirituality that enables collaboration are presented.

Whitehead, Evelyn Eaton and James D. *The Emerging Laity: Returning Leadership to* *the Community of Faith.* Garden City, N.J.: Doubleday and Company, Inc., 1986. Emphasizing biblical images of leadership, this book critiques the present exercise of church leadership. From the perspective of sociology, it explores contemporary theories of leadership, discusses power and empowerment, and gives practical suggestions for effective leadership in all aspects of Church.

The Professional Campus Minister

Sr. Joann Plumpe, OP, and Mr. Donald R. McCrabb

Some members of the Church on campus are called to lead the faith community. Ideally, these men and women are professionally trained and exercise the kind of leadership that serves and empowers others. As officially appointed campus ministers, they are sent to form the faith community so that it can be a genuine sign and instrument of the kingdom. (ES, 24)

Identity

Each campus minister brings to his or her ministry a rich background of personal, educational, and professional experiences that gives the ministry color, texture, and depth. Campus ministers come from a variety of vocations: diocesan priests, religious order priests, women religious, men religious, lay men and women, and deacons. For the most part, campus ministers are highly educated. Most hold a master's degree in theology—or its equivalent. Some have doctorates of ministry or of philosophy. Virtually all campus ministers are college graduates. Few campus ministers begin their ministry on campus without previous ministerial or professional experience. Some campus ministers have been associate pastors, pastors, teachers, principals, vocation ministers, professors, college presidents, counselors, musicians, and theologians. There are also different routes to becoming a campus minister. Some people have pursued, and expect, a career in campus ministry; others see their involvement in campus ministry as temporary. Most campus ministers have had to go through some application process to secure their position, while there are some who have been appointed to campus ministry. Some campus ministers are full time; others are part time, with other duties on or off campus.

Given the different backgrounds campus ministers bring to their ministry, is there a common identity that all campus ministers share? Of course, each campus setting is unique. The possibilities range from a four-year, residential, Catholic, doctorate, research university to a two-year, commuter, public, associate degree, technical school. Some universities are very open and accepting of campus ministry; others are more tentative.

Servant Leader

The Church calls the campus minister to be a servant leader of the faith community on the university campus, a truly unique setting for such a community. The university provides an intellectually stimulating environment but often fails to address adequately the religious and spiritual needs of its members. People need a place to be open and honest with their feelings and ideas—especially regarding faith. A healthy faith community is a place that breeds trust and openness, where individuals recognize and affirm their worth before God and others. In such a place, persons are valued for who they are and for who they can become, not measured merely by the body of knowledge they possess.

Faith community leaders in this setting must provide direction and vision. Campus ministers need "to identify, call forth, and coordinate the diverse gifts of the Spirit possessed by all the members of the faith community" (ES, 24). Specifically, campus ministers discover people who have been nurtured and can now nurture others, individuals willing to take responsibility for the development of the faith community. This is networking at its best.

Calling forth the gifts of the community is particularly challenging when a large percentage of the members change yearly. Student leaders often last only one or two years. Campus ministers must prepare for rapid turnover with adequate formation/training programs and cultivation of new student leaders. The great gift campus ministry gives to the broader Church is graduates willing and able to serve in leadership roles within both the Church and society.

The vision campus ministers are called to embrace is no less than forming their community of faith as a "sign and instrument" of the reign of God. The six aspects of campus ministry begin to embody how the faith community is a "sign and instrument" for the good of its own members, the university, the Church, and the world.

Areas of Competency

The campus minister must possess certain talents and skills in order to fulfill this awesome responsibility. The Catholic Campus Ministry Association has identified three areas of competency for the campus minister: (1) personal, (2) theological, and (3) professional.

Every professional must have that sense of self, that personal maturity that enables them to use their knowledge and skills for the good of others. What is unique to campus ministers is their faith, their commitment to community, and their love of learning.

If campus ministers are responsible for forming the faith community on campus, then they need to be people of prayer and people who like other people. How can campus ministers challenge the members of their community to share openly their prayer lives with one another if they are incapable of doing it themselves? This ministry needs people who have experienced their own sinfulness and are in the process of redemption. The ministry needs emotionally healthy persons of prayer who desire community and possess the necessary social skills for its development.

Campus ministers need a solid foundation in theology and the ability to interpret that perspective for others. Many college students are eager for answers that are theologically correct and still in harmony with their life experiences. So many students today have had little formal or adequate religious education. Effective campus ministers know how to accept the questions students struggle with and can point to the revelation of God's love in the midst of those

very struggles. Professional competencies include basic ministerial skills expected of most people doing an official ministry of the Church and skills unique to the university environment.

Love for Learning

Love for learning is an exciting and life-giving dimension of the university. The life of the campus minister needs to exemplify this. In academic circles, a great deal of value is placed on "higher degrees" and the ability to express and to share realms of knowledge. For credibility among faculty and administrators, for a greater chance to take an active role in the institution, and for their own self-development, it is important that campus ministers actively pursue knowledge and truth.

"Campus ministers with solid training and good credentials will have more opportunities to enter into the mainstream of academic life on campus" (ES, 28). It is much easier for ministers to point out that "higher degrees" are but one aspect of life if they lived through the rigors of intellectual life. Academic experience also gives campus ministers greater empathy for those struggling toward a degree.

Finally, part of the integrity of the professional campus minister is his or her fidelity to the vision of campus ministry outlined in *Empowered by the Spirit: Campus Ministry Faces the Future*. If certain aspects of the vision are ignored, then the faith community is not given the opportunity to flourish as the "sign and instrument" it is called to be.

Professional Worth

Certainly, all campus ministers do not possess the above-mentioned skills and abilities to the same degree. Each will tend to be stronger in one area or another. The crucial factor for all campus ministers—as for every minister—is the ability to recognize one's own strengths and limitations. No one can do it all. Each campus minister will have to develop the skill of self-limiting. With all the opportunities and possibilities on campus, realistic self-appraisal is the personal skill most needed by the campus minister.

The Catholic Campus Ministry Association is committed to helping campus

Standards and Certification
A Brief Explanation

by Rev. William Lum

The notion of standards and certification may be a new idea to some people. The point of certification is to document that a person has reached a level of competence, a level of ability, a level of training, a level of preparation. Standards establish the norm in which one must become proficient in order to be certified. No one imagines that the establishment of standards or the certification process is the absolute guarantee of a perfect campus minister. It is only one more indicator—with all the usual limitations of paper credentials. But it can be a very helpful tool if properly employed.

Standards. What are the standards by which one decides who is certified? One determines the appropriateness of certifying a campus minister by the use of standards. One can document the level of competence of a campus minister by using standards of competence and achievement. The term *standard* or *standards* measures competency. The term describes a level of competence.

Certification. Is this campus minister seeking certification? Has CCMA certified John Jones or Mary Smith? This campus minister has been granted certification by meeting the appropriate standards. The term *certification* or *certify* describes the process whereby one seeks to have a level of competence formally documented and endorsed by an appropriate organization. For campus ministers, certification is the process whereby a campus minister seeks to have a level of competence documented and endorsed by the Catholic Campus Ministers Association (CCMA), a professional association empowered by the United States Catholic Conference (USCC) to provide this service to campus ministers.

We can contrast the term *certification* with other terms that, at first, seem similar but really are different:

Licensing is a process that controls who may practice a praticular profession. Doctors are licensed to practice medicine in one state or another. Pharmacists are licesned to dispense drugs and medicines. Certification does not control who may practice campus ministry. Rather, it attests to a level of competence and achievement. Not all campus ministers may wish to be certified. Some campus ministers may wish to limit themselves to one particular area of campus ministry and see no need to be certified for a wider competence and a wider place of accomplishment. Some campus ministers may simply choose not to demonstrate in a documentable way their level of competence. Certification is a voluntary process.

Accredidation is frequently confused with certification. Institutions or programs of education are accredited; persons are certified.

Standards and certification begin to give campus ministers a professional identity and to raise their self-esteem. Standards and certification outline elements that are important for the training of campus ministers. In addition, they can be useful in other ways by:

- getting a church agency to become more serious about paying a just wage;
- getting a church agency to become more serious about continuing education of campus ministers;
- obtaining education and professional development;
- making candidates for campus ministry more aware of the appropriate requirements for the job.

Grandparenting is another term frequently used when certification is discussed. Grandparenting is the modification of the ordinary process of certification for those who have been active in campus ministry for many years and can show that they have met the standards in other ways. This gives the experienced campus ministers an opportunity to demonstrate their competencies and their levels of accomplishment.

When an organization establishes a certification program it must do two things: (1) write standards: competency statements that describe the profession; and (2) design the certification process and procedures: the method the organization uses to assure an equitable and objective assessment of an individual's competency. The next step is to develop an equitable and objective certification process that respects the competency of the person and the substance of the standards.

ministers assess their own strengths and limitations through professional standards and certification. The Standards for Campus Ministries were approved in May 1990 and revised in December 1995. The process for certification involves writing a theology of campus ministry, assessing competency in light of the standards, and peer review.

Certification is a voluntary process that enables a person to document one's competence to carry out the duties and responsibilities of a particular role. Certification does not control who "does" campus ministry. It is simply a supportive process that helps a person name and own his or her abilities to lead the faith community on campus.

Each campus minister needs to take responsibility for his or her professional development. CCMA exists on the national level to facilitate the professional and theological growth of campus ministers. There are also regional and local opportunities for professional growth. Key to any significant professional growth is the development of peer support. Campus ministers cannot carry out their responsibility to lead the faith community on campus without the honest and critical feedback of others in the ministry. Those who have been in campus ministry the longest continue to attest to the need for professional growth. The very nature of campus ministry—in a setting that is constantly expanding the horizons of human knowledge—demands professional growth. Just as professors spend hours weekly to stay abreast of their discipline, campus ministers need to have regular opportunities for study, theological reflection, and prayer.

Campus ministry is clearly a profession. Campus ministers are called by the Church to lead the faith community on campus. It is their job to help the community grow as a "sign and instrument" of the reign of God. This responsibility calls for personal, theological, and professional competencies unique to campus ministry. Interweaving the talents and dreams of the faith community within the intellectually alive and demanding environment of the university is certainly a challenge. And yet, for many campus ministers, it is this very challenge that signifies the emergence of the reign of God.

Certification for Catholic Campus Ministers

Sr. Beth Hassel, PBVM, D.Min.

Campus ministers have a unique responsibility and an extraordinary opportunity to breathe vibrant life into the Gospel as it is lived and understood on college campuses at this change of the millennium. The magnitude of this opportunity some thirty years after the Second Vatican Council cannot be minimized; it is the opportunity to influence the future of the Church and American society with the message of the Gospel. Continually, the Church must call forth talented and gifted ministers to serve in this ministry. It is not a task that the Church can afford to take lightly, for her very future is at stake. In a world where professional competency is valued and demanded at all levels, the training and certification of those who minister on our college campuses is of great concern to the whole Church, for campus ministry is "where commitment to Christ and care for the academic world meet in purposeful activity to serve and realize the kingdom of God."[1]

This article will trace the efforts of the Catholic Campus Ministry Association (CCMA) to respond to this need for professional certification in a complex world, and to answer the call of the bishops in their pastoral letter on the future of campus ministry. We shall have to ask if certification is really necessary and then look briefly at the history and rationale of the process of setting standards for certifying those who would minister on the campuses of our colleges and universities. We shall trace the process of certification and place the certification documents and standards in appendices.

Is There a Need for Certification?

The questions are familiar: "Why should I be certified? I have a secure ministry position at a private Catholic university. I don't need to be certified. Isn't my ordination certification enough?" "I have a master's degree in theology (or counseling, etc.) so why do I need something more?" "I've been doing ministry for twenty years; this can't help me." "I don't have the time!" "Do I receive more benefits if I am certified?"

The certification of professional competency can be a difficult thing at first. But who would argue today with the certification required of physicians for medical specialities? Who could disagree with the need to certify counselors in their general skills and then in the specialities in which they practice? Do we not even check to see if the mechanic who works on our car is certified to tamper with our expensive investment? Few hospitals today will employ chaplains, ordained or not, who have not also been certified because of the special demands of ministry in a hospital setting. The same is true for those who would minister on a college campus; it is a unique setting with specific problems and opportunities that demand competencies not needed for other forms of ministry. Gone are the days when the "chaplain" could expect consistent Mass attendance or lines for confession, or anticipate that the young adult students would be knowledgeable in the basics of their faith. Gone is the time when sacramental ministry was a primary focus. A proactive leadership on the part of campus ministers is essential on Catholic, non-denominational, or secular campuses. This leadership demands a significant level of ongoing personal and professional development.

In their pastoral letter, *Empowered by the Spirit: Campus Ministry Faces the Future,* the bishops made it clear that there are struggles and challenges that the campus minister faces unique to the college setting and thus they challenged all serving in this ministry, with the need for professionalization.[2] Such "professionalization" is increasingly important at American colleges and universities where professional qualifications receive significant emphasis. The real reason for professionalization is, however, the need and the obligation of ministers to be fully qualified and to engage in ongoing education in ministry and in theology. Those who would minister on a campus must therefore take seriously the call to professionalism.

Response to the Bishops' Challenge

The Catholic Campus Ministry Association (CCMA) was established in 1969 to foster the professional and theological development of Catholic campus ministers and to promote the mission of the Church in higher education.[3] The CCMA is a national voluntary organization of individuals and groups of campus ministers who associate to foster their theological and professional growth and to promote the ministry of the Catholic Church in higher education. The CCMA, in dialogue with the American bishops, its own membership, and other professional societies, seeks continuously to articulate a vision for this ministry and to develop its human and financial resources to further this mission. The association promoted active leadership and participation of its constituents at national, regional, and local levels in planning and evaluation.

The CCMA began to investigate certification in 1986 when it became an associate member of the United States Catholic Conference Commission on Certification and Accreditation. Early consultations among the CCMA membership indicated a strong desire for certification among the lay members of the association and some reluctance among the ordained members.

From the outset, the certification program was conceived first and foremost as a means for ongoing personal and professional development and for the endorsement and confirmation of one's competencies by professional peers knowledgeable about ministry in one's specific locale. Thus, the process is oriented specifically to the individual minister as an aid for growth, for facilitating the individual's review and assessment of his or her own competencies in this ministry, and for encouraging the development of a concrete plan for professionalism. Continued growth as a person and as a professional is

thus the underlying goal of the process, and this goal led the association to base certification on the recommendations of peer ministers in the general locale of the candidates.

The development of the certification program took place in two phases. First, a national certification task force gathered to research and develop standards for certification (Appendix A) and a code of ethics (Appendix B) for campus ministers nationwide. The general membership of the association had the opportunity to critique three drafts of the working documents. The CCMA executive board approved "Standards for Certification" in May 1990. The code of ethics was completed and approved in May 1992. In the second phase of development, a process for certification of the current and future membership of the association was discussed and approved. The USCC's Commission on Certification and Accreditation approved the CCMA "Standards," "Code of Ethics," and the certification process (Appendix C) on October 16, 1992. Thus, campus ministers are certified by the United States Catholic Conference upon the recommendation of the Catholic Campus Ministry Association.

The CCMA executive board appointed the first national certification committee at its May 1993 meeting.[4] The first meeting of the committee was in September 1993. In the spring of 1993 the CCMA began its certification with an open "grandparenting" process for those active in the association. The grandparenting process saw over 300 campus ministers certified. The certification is valid for those under the grandparenting process and for those certified through the normal process for seven years. Recertification will depend upon an evaluation of continuing education and ministerial experience since initial certification.

Purpose of Certification

The certification program of the association is designed to assist the individual in assessing his or her own competency recognized at the national level. It is clear from the experience of certifying boards in many professions and from the experience of the CCMA that effective ministry depends on a comprehensive, reflective self-assessment which is then reviewed, supported and confirmed by one's peers in the profession.

▲ **Self-Assessment.** Candidates for certification gather valuable information about their strengths and weaknesses as campus ministers by assessing their own competencies in light of the standards developed by the CCMA. This self-review aids campus ministers in discerning weaknesses, in capitalizing on strengths and in charting an appropriate course of continuing education so as to enhance their ability to minister on campus.

▲ **Confirmation by Peers.** Confirmation of one's competencies by experienced professionals provides support for the individual's ministry and strengthens one's confidence in the face of the sometimes overwhelming difficulties and complexities of the young adult and faculty/staff ministry on a campus. This is particularly helpful in a university environment, where objective verification of a person's qualifications, ability, and professional competence is so highly valued. Although based on the person's own review, the peer review helps the campus minister objectively assess his or her own personal, theological, and professional competencies in the light of the concrete needs of ministry. Peer review thus functions as an aid in the process of critically assessing one's abilities and a means of professional recognition.

Overview of the Certification Process

In order to make the certification process as comprehensive as possible, local interview teams assess the candidate and make recommendations for certification. The candidate first applies to the national office for the packet of application materials and then submits his or her application and the processing fee according to the calendar published by the CCMA. The executive director determines the eligibility of the candidate and forwards the certification materials to the national certification committee (NCC).

The NCC then appoints a local interview team whose members are knowledgeable about the general needs and challenges of campus ministry in the local area. It is this team of certified campus ministers who evaluate, make suggestions, and finally

recommend the candidate to the NCC for certification. The actual certification is made by the NCC of the CCMA in the name of the United States Catholic Conference.

Appendix A

Standards for Campus Ministers

A college or university is a primary forum in our society where public debate takes place, where opinions are shaped, and where values are formed. Campus ministry is "where commitment to Christ and care for the academic world meet in purposeful activity to serve and realize the kingdom of God."[5] Campus ministers have the unique responsibility to enhance the presence and the ministry of the Church within higher education and to influence the future of the Church and society with the message of the Gospel. The official Church calls forth and commissions talented and gifted people to serve in this challenging ministry. Therefore, the Catholic Campus Ministry Association offers these standards to promote a level of competency for campus ministry. They provide a means to gauge performance in the ministry and to foster a high degree of professional excellence. The living out of these standards bears witness to discipleship with Jesus and his pastoral prophetic call.

I. Personal Competencies

A Catholic campus minister is a practicing, believing, fully initiated member of the Catholic Church who

a. is able to articulate knowledge of and faith in the teaching of Christ and the Church and shares this knowledge and faith through one's own unique gifts and talents

b. nourishes this faith and knowledge through membership in a worshiping Catholic community, personal spiritual direction, annual retreats and days of prayer, reconciliation, prayer and liturgy

c. publicly adheres to church teaching and the CCMA Code of Ethics

d. demonstrates a healthy integration of one's own sexuality

e. demonstrates a balanced lifestyle, showing concern for physical and spiritual components of one's life

f. manages stress, arbitrates conflict, accepts failure and ambiguity in morally and socially acceptable ways

II. Theological Competencies

A campus minister is expected to

a. have a basic understanding[6] of Roman Catholic dogma and doctrine in the following areas:
- God, Christ, Church
- Ethics and Moral Theology
- Theology of Campus Ministry
- Spirituality and Prayer
- Scripture and Scripture Interpretation
- Church History: World and American
- Pastoral Theology
- Liturgy and Sacrament
- Justice and Peace
- Canon Law

b. pursue theological reflection and education

c. have a familiarity with other religious traditions and practices

III. Professional Competencies

A. Pastoral Skills

A campus minister demonstrates

1. basic communication and motivation skills
2. effective assessment, intervention, and referral skills
3. the ability to initiate, deepen, and terminate ministerial relationships
4. the ability to organize, facilitate, administer, and share responsibility and decision-making
5. the ability to articulate the faith through preaching, teaching, writing, and spiritual direction
6. the ability to discern the needs of the campus community and to call forth and coordinate the diverse gifts of the community for worship and service

B. Conceptualization Skills

A campus minister is able to articulate an understanding of

1. the nature and purpose of higher education
2. the experience and perspective of the student in higher education
3. human growth and development (faith, moral, spiritual, ritual) and how psychosocial, developmental, cultural, and ethnic dynamics affect ministerial practices
4. the interrelationship between the campus ministry, the campus minister, the Church and higher education

5. the six aspects of campus ministry as delineated in *Empowered by the Spirit*, the pastoral letter on campus ministry

C. Ministerial Skills

A campus minister demonstrates the ability to

1. develop and sustain effective professional relationships by maintaining membership in local, regional, and national organizations of campus ministry
2. minister in an interfaith and multicultural environment
3. minister collaboratively
4. initiate and sustain relationships with other college or university professionals

Appendix B

Code of Ethics

We, the members of the Catholic Campus Ministry Association, profess the dignity and sanctity of all individuals. In light of our specialized ministry in and to higher education, we commit ourselves:

To the People We Serve

We serve students, faculty, staff, and administrators who gather at institutions of higher education to search and learn. Although called to serve the Catholic community, we will not restrict our ministry to persons of a particular age, gender, race, creed, physical ability, or sexual orientation.

Our first concern is for the well-being of those we serve as they join with us in the mission of the Church in higher education. As leaders within the faith community, we seek no unfair advantage that our position may give to us. We adhere to appropriate interpersonal boundaries in relating with those we serve.

To Gospel and Pastoral Values

We look to Scripture, the rich heritage of the Roman Catholic Church, and the movement of the Spirit of God throughout the entire human story to promote the value and dignity of the person and the unfolding of the reign of God in human history.

We commit ourselves to providing a safe and healthy environment in which to conduct our ministry. This environment would be free of any form of harassment.

To Discipleship and Service Within Our Church

We promise our community of faith an active discipleship in the spirit and mission of Jesus. We will relate with others in ways that respect their dignity as persons and their freedom of conscience without compromising our own beliefs.

We recognize the privileged relationship we have with the people we serve and promise them acceptance and confidentiality. We will give our community of faith dedicated service. We will work hard, given a reasonable job description and work schedule.

To Personal Faithfulness, Integrity, and Well-Being

We will actively pursue our own faith development and enrichment.

We will seek not only personal integrity but also an integration of our faith, our ministry and our lifestyle.

We will care for our own health and personal well-being, lest our own needs interrupt or undermine our ministry.

To Higher Education

We embrace the goals and purposes of higher education and seek to enrich the local community of faith, and the universal Church, with its fruits.

To Broader Social Concerns, Justice, and Peace in the World

We recognize the university as a privileged place for public debate on the many social concerns facing our society today.

We promise our community of faith that we will speak the gospel values within this forum and collaborate with others in the pursuit of peace and justice in the world.

To the Standards of Our Profession

We strive for holiness, wholeness, and excellence in our ministry.

Our standards give us a starting point from which we can grow as professionals in service to the Church and higher education.

Accountability

We pray that our Church, our community of faith, and our colleagues will support us and challenge us to live out these ethical principles.

We believe that any violation of these principles needs to be handled on the local level through the due process available to the person or persons in question.

The CCMA executive board has the right to withhold membership and revoke certification from a person who has violated this code of ethics. Endorsement definition from USCC:

> The formal recognition of a person for ministry by the bishop of the diocese of the minister seeking endorsement, recognition by a person delegated by the bishop to endorse ministers, or recognition by a major religious superior, if the minister is a member of a religious order.

Decertification Procedure

High standards of professional competence and compliance with our code of ethics are expected of CCMA members. Violating the association's code of ethics is grounds for losing certification. The formal process for removing certification is termed Decertification Procedure.

1. Any member or group of members of CCMA may file a complaint against a certified campus minister who has violated the CCMA code of ethics.
2. A complaint is filed by writing the chair of the CCMA executive board by registered mail within sixty (60) days following an awareness or knowledge of an alleged incident(s) or court decision.
3. Minimum information to be included in the complaint:
   a. Name, address, and phone number of the person filing the complaint (hereafter "petitioner")
   b. Date the grievance is filed
   c. Date the alleged incident(s) occurred
   d. Name and address of the campus minister involved in the alleged incident(s) (hereafter "respondent")
   e. A complete account of the alleged incident(s)
4. The chair of the CCMA executive board will mail a copy of the complaint to the respondent via registered mail within five days of receipt from the petitioner.
5. The chair will appoint a three-person ethics panel from the executive board to review the grievance.

6. The decertification panel will gather information from the petitioner and respond to appropriate sources pertinent to proper review of the grievance. It is understood that options for local resolution of this matter will have already been explored.

7. The decertification panel will convene a formal review either by conference call or in person within sixty (60) days of receiving a grievance. The panel will render a binding decision with either of the following options:
   a. The complaint is without merit in the context of CCMA's standards or code of ethics.
   b. A serious violation of CCMA's standards or code of ethics has occurred with the specified area named. The panel must then choose either to reprimand the respondent or to suspend certification for a certain time period or indefinitely.

8. The decertification panel will give written notification of its decision within five (5) days to the respondent, the petitioner, the chair of CCMA executive board and to the CCMA executive director for proper documentation. The decision will be final and binding for the association and kept on file in the national office.

Appendix C

CCMA Certification Process

I. Purpose

The Catholic Campus Ministry Association (CCMA) certifies campus ministers in the name of the United States Catholic Conference Commission on Certification and Accreditation.

The certification process is designed to call the campus minister to accountability in ministry and to assess his or her personal, theological, professional competencies as outlined by the standards of CCMA (approved by the CCMA executive board, May 5, 1992).

II. Process

A. Minimum Requirements

1. Ecclesiastical endorsement: A commission to function as a campus minister by the local ordinary, his delegate, or the major of a religious congregation

2. An advanced degree (beyond bachelor degree)

3. At least 18 graduate credits in theology from an accredited college or university

4. Satisfactory completion of 400 hours of supervised ministry, with detailed reporting and evaluation of that practice, and an individual contract for learning, e.g., one unit of accredited Clinical Pastoral Education (CPE)[7]

5. Two years full-time professional experience in campus ministry (five years part-time)

6. Current membership in the Catholic Campus Ministry Association

B. Documentation
1. Letter of Ecclesiastical Endorsement
2. Transcripts
3. Reflection Paper[8]
4. Self-Review[9]
5. Review by others[10]

C. Application

A completed application form and application fee must be submitted to CCMA's national office by the due date published in *Crossroads*. The national office will forward the names of those eligible for certification to the chair of the national certification committee.

D. Interview

The chair of the national certification committee will appoint a local interview team. The candidate will contact the chair of the local team. Results of the interview will be sent to the chair of the national certification committee.

E. Certification

The national certification committee will review all documentation and grant or deny certification or grant provisional certification pending completion of specified requirements by a set date. Certification is granted for seven years. If denied, the candidate will be informed what he or she needs for certification.

III. Procedures

A. The national certification committee will be appointed for a three-year term by the CCMA executive board. It will consist of a representative from each of the four regions and one at-large. The certification committee will annually elect its own chairperson. Initial appointments will be structured as follows to provide continuity:

1. Two regional representatives for six-year term
2. Two regional representatives for three-year term
3. One at-large representative for four-year-term
4. All subsequent appointments for three-year terms

B. Interview teams will be appointed by the national certification committee in consultation with the local diocesan director of campus ministry. Each team will consist of three certified campus ministers who have been trained in the certification process. Each region will have a number of teams to minimize travel experiences for the candidates.

The interview teams will follow a standardized process for the sake of uniformity and fairness. The team will send their recommendations to the national certification committee. The decision to render or deny certification rests with the national certification committee.

Interview teams will be trained by the national certification committee. This training will review the certification process, the standards, the composition and function of the team, and the process that will be used for the interview as well as the procedures for decision-making and notifying candidates.

The interview is a key element in the certification process. The interview will be conducted according to a standardized process which is both challenging to the candidate and consistent with the standards of CCMA. The process will be one of dialogue between the candidate and the interview team. It will be conducted in an atmosphere of affirmation and honesty and should attempt to surface both the strengths and limitations of the candidate.

C. The interview process will have a distinct role for each member of the interview team:

1. **Chair:** The chair of the interview team will serve as facilitator of the interview
   a. Coordinating place, date, and time of interview
   b. Disseminating written documentation

c. Chairing the pre-interview meeting where the presenter's summary will be discussed and areas of special focus identified. Following the discussion of presented materials, areas for questioning will be assigned to each member of the interview team
d. Introducing the candidate to the interview team
e. Explaining the procedure and process to the candidate
f. Keeping time and maintaining an appropriate balance in length and breadth for each area of questioning
g. Ensuring that the interview team covers all questions raised in the presenter's summary
h. Conducting the decision-making process using the following model:
   I. Soliciting from each team member an opinion concerning the candidates competencies
   II. Facilitating a discussion on any areas of the candidate's noncompliance with standards
   III. Facilitating efforts to reach unanimous decision about certification
i. Communicating the interview team's recommendation to the candidate
j. Returning two copies of the documentation to the candidate

2. **Presenter:** The presenter's responsibilities consist of preparing a written summary of the documentation supplied by the candidate. The summary will raise areas to be discussed in the interview. The presenter may consult the other members of the interview team in preparing the report. The presenter sends a copy of his or her report to the members of the interview team. The presenter's report needs to

   a. List name, address, and phone number of candidate
   b. State time and place of interview
   c. List names, addresses, and roles of interviewers
   d. Summarize candidate's background, education, work history, and supervised ministry experience
   e. Delineate specific issues that the presenter feels should be discussed during the interview addressing both the strengths and areas for growth for the candidate

3. **Recorder:** The recorder is the third member of the interview team. The recorder's duties consist of
   a. Taking minutes of the interview
   b. Writing a report after the interview
   c. Typing and signing the recorder's report
   d. Sending the presenter's and recorder's reports to the CCMA national office, which distributed these reports to the national certification committee. The candidate is given copies of these reports once the national certification committee has rendered its decision.

D. Code of Ethics: Commitment to the Catholic Campus Ministry Association code of ethics is required as part of the certification process. Violation of the code could result in the loss of certification.

E. Family Education Rights and Privacy Act of 1974: This act allows the candidate a choice of waiving or claiming his or her option to view recommendations followed with his or her signature. CCMA's policy is that all certification documents are available for review by the candidate.

F. Grievance and Appeals: A candidate denied certification has the right to appeal the decision of the national certification committee.
1. Upon receiving the decision the candidate has thirty (30) days to write to the chair of the CCMA executive board requesting an appeal. The candidate must state the specific grounds for the appeal.
2. The chair of the executive board will
   a. Appoint a three-member certification appeal review team from the executive board and designate one of them as chair
   b. Notify the candidate of the three-member review team
3. The members of the review team shall have no personal or professional conflict of interest with the candidate and shall not have participated in the original interview team.
4. The candidate sends each member of the review team the grounds for the appeal as well as the original documentation and the interview team's report.

5. The review team studies all the materials and renders a decision to uphold or deny the appeal.
6. The chair of the review team will communicate the decision to the national certification committee, the chair of the original interview team, and the candidate. The decision of the review team is final and binding for the association.

G. Grandparenting is a one-time recognition by CCMA that grants certification to those eligible based on experience. All CCMA members with ecclesiastical endorsement and five years of full-time professional campus ministry experience (eight years part-time) who request certification by the published deadline are eligible for grandparenting.

H. Recertification is a process that validates a campus minister's professional growth every seven years. Campus ministers use a standard form sent to them by the national office to record their continuing education, retreats, and ministry experience. They review the form with a peer campus minister prior to submitting it to the national certification committee.
1. At the end of the calendar year prior to the year in which the candidate is to be recertified, the CCMA national office sends the candidate
   a. Letter of notification
   b. Application
   c. Report form
   d. Name and address of the chair of the national certification committee
2. The CCMA national office sends the chair of the national certification committee the names of those to be recertified that year.
3. The candidate sends completed documentation to the chair of the national certification committee.
4. The chair arranges to have the national certification committee review the materials.
5. The committee reviews the materials and renders a decision.
6. The chair of the national certification committee notifies the candidate and the CCMA national office of the decision.
7. The CCMA national office updates the file and sends the campus minister a new certificate.

Notes

1. National Conference of Catholic Bishops. *Empowered by the Spirit: Campus Ministry Faces the Future*, no. 21.

2. National Conference of Catholic Bishops. *Empowered by the Spirit: Campus Ministry Faces the Future,* nos. 21-32.

3. United States Catholic Conference Commission on Certification and Accreditation. CCMA Organizational Report, p.4.

4. Chair: Patrick Corcoran; CCMA Executive Director Ex-Officio: Donald McCrabb; Regional Representatives: Kysha Cox (West), Brother Cosmas Rubencamp (South), Rev. Daniel Zak (Midwest), Sr. Beth Hassel (Northeast). Presently, Maureen Pryor is Regional Representative of the West due to the resignation of K. Cox in 1994.

5. National Conference of Catholic Bishops. *Empowered by the Spirit: Campus Ministry Faces the Future,* no. 21.

6. "Basic understanding" refers to familiarity with the major concepts and language of these areas and an ability to access additional resources.

7. The CCMA executive board has approved the campus minister mentoring program as fulfilling half of this requirement.

8. Candidates will be asked to reflect on their theological and pastoral framework for ministry and their perspective on the Church's ministry in higher education. (Maximum length: ten double-spaced pages).

9. A standardized form is used for the self-review.

10. A standardized form is used for these reviews.

Formation of the Campus Minister

Campus ministers with solid training and good credentials will have more opportunities to enter into the mainstream of academic life on campus. (ES, 28)

Sr. Joan Hartlaub, CSJ

People enter campus ministry from a wide variety of training and experience. Different campuses and different campus ministry positions demand different competencies and skills. Most employers require at least a master's degree in some closely aligned field (e.g., religious education, theology, religious studies, pastoral care, counseling). Individual job descriptions usually specify the needed qualifications.

The Catholic Campus Ministry Association (CCMA) offers a set of professional standards to all in this ministry, as well as to those who employ them, be they directors of centers, Catholic college and university administrators, or diocesan directors of campus ministry. Anyone who is interested in entering campus ministry should examine these CCMA standards, perhaps with a friend or a qualified mentor, and determine for oneself just how many of the standards are already met. The seasoned campus minister can also use these standards as a guide to continuing education.

As with other ministries, it is vital that the campus minister take a proactive stance regarding her or his further education and training, determine long- and short-range goals, and choose those that most benefit both the ministry and the minister. In this pursuit of further education and training, several important specific campus ministry programs are worth considering.

1. Campus Ministry Internships

Internships are available, some with opportunities for graduate classes or degrees. Internships generally target the person who has a bachelor's degree and little ministry experience, usually a single young adult. Since these opportunities often change, ask for a list of current internship programs.

Contact:
300 College Park Avenue
Dayton, Ohio 45469-2515
Tel. 513-229-4648

2. Graduate Degrees with Campus Ministry Emphasis

Many institutions of higher education offer graduate degrees in ministry. Some offer a concentration in campus ministry. Ask for a list of colleges with approved concentrations in campus ministry.

Contact:
300 College Park Avenue
Dayton, Ohio 45469-2515
Tel. 513-229-4648

3. Frank J. Lewis Institute for Campus Ministry Orientation

For those employed as campus ministers, with one year or less experience, the United States Catholic Conference (USCC) offers this summer program. For more than thirty years, these institutes have provided high-quality professional preparation for campus ministers. Two institutes are presented each summer, one in the East and one in the West. They provide nine-day programs with a core curriculum based on *Empowered by the Spirit*. Each institute, limited to forty participants, focuses on the needs of those entering the field of campus ministry or those just completing their first year. About half of the institute cost is covered by a grant from the Frank J. Lewis Foundation, which is administered through the USCC. The remaining portion is usually paid by the hiring agent (i.e., diocese or institution). The institutes are supported and staffed by members of CCMA and NADDCM, in cooperation with the USCC Department of Education. Applications for the institute can be obtained from your diocesan director for campus ministry or from the USCC representative for higher education and campus ministry.

Contact:
Department of Education
United States Catholic Conference
3211 Fourth Street, N.E.
Washington, D.C. 20017-1194
Tel. 202-541-3165

4. *Campus Ministry Mentoring Program*
Those who complete the Frank J. Lewis Institute program are eligible for acceptance into the yearlong Campus Ministry Mentoring Program. This in-depth ministry program joins the relatively new campus minister with a more experienced mentor. An application can be obtained from:

Contact:
Department of Education
United States Catholic Conference
3211 Fourth Street, N.E.
Washington, D.C. 20017-1194
Tel. 202-541-3165

Contact:
CCMA
300 College Park Avenue
Dayton, Ohio 45469-2515
Tel. 513-229-4648

5. *CCMA- and NADDCM-Sponsored Programs*
Both organizations sponsor various study weeks, conventions, institutes, retreats, and so forth, geared to the development of campus ministry and the needs of campus ministers. CCMA membership accesses one to all this information.

Contact:
CCMA
300 College Park
Dayton, Ohio 45469-2515
Tel. 513-229-4648

In addition to the specific campus ministry training programs mentioned above, individual study and reading are essential for professional development. Individual study can occur on one's own campus by taking a class each semester. Such classes are excellent opportunities to further one's education, meet people, and experience higher education directly. Many times, various local, regional, or national conferences offer valuable workshops and experiences applicable to some aspect of campus ministry. Semester breaks and summers often afford such opportunities.

Reading can keep one current on church and higher education issues, as well as on local, national, and global issues that impact society in general and the campus in particular. Publications such as *America, Commonweal, Origins,* and the London *Tablet* can be helpful for this. *The Chronicle of Higher Education,* published weekly, is a must for anyone who wants to be informed on issues affecting higher education. Contact: 1255 Twenty-Third Street, N.W., Washington, D.C. 20037. In the campus ministry field itself, CCMA's monthly *Crossroads* and Lutheran Campus Ministry's national *Entree* are two practical publications for information and programming ideas.

Finally, selecting a spiritual director or mentor can be a significant way to personalize one's growth. This individual can help one to develop a spiritual life and/or to sharpen one's skill as a minister.

The professional campus minister is someone engaged in lifelong learning. Ministry in the academic world calls the minister to continue to work to obtain and improve the "solid training and good credentials [necessary to] have more opportunities to enter into the mainstream of academic life on campus" (ES, 28).

Campus Ministry Personnel: People, Policies, and Processes

To prepare for meeting all these challenges, we encourage campus ministers to take responsibility for their own personal and professional development. Clear contractual arrangements that include carefully defined expectations and procedures for accountability and evaluation help to set a proper framework for their personal enrichment. (ES, 29)

Ms. Mary Anne Kasavich

Campus ministers are the most valuable resource for the Church's ministry in higher education today. It is important, therefore, that campus ministry develop and implement personnel systems that ensure that qualified and competent professionals continue to find their campus ministry work affirming, challenging, and rewarding. This section examines some of the elements of such a campus ministry personnel system.

The Supervisors

1. The Diocesan Director

The diocesan director has many responsibilities: stewarding the vision of campus ministry within the diocese on behalf of the bishop; gathering the resources to implement that vision; hiring personnel; evaluating both the ministry and the ministers. These responsibilities demand careful attention. Diocesan directors must balance their concerns for personnel with the gathering of resources, planning with evaluation, and so forth. An excessive focus on any of these responsibilities, such as the accountability of campus ministers, with little attention to resource development or planning, will severely damage the credibility of the diocesan director and retard the growth of the ministry. Nevertheless, the effectiveness of any vision of campus ministry and the primary resources to achieve that vision are dependent on the people in the ministry. Consequently, diocesan directors spend a considerable amount of time with their campus ministers—planning, evaluating, learning, praying, listening, and teaching.

Most dioceses do not enjoy the services of a full-time diocesan director for campus ministry. In some cases, the director of one of the campus ministries takes on these responsibilities on a part-time basis. Other possibilities are a "diocesan contact," either elected by fellow campus ministers or appointed by the bishop, or a "diocesan administrator," who has the responsibilities of being the diocesan director for other ministries in addition to campus. In these situations, the persons involved need to be clear as to how the basic responsibilities of the diocesan director will be fulfilled and/or delegated. Such an arrangement should be approved by the bishop and the campus ministers.

2. The Campus Ministry Director

A director of campus ministry is the person responsible for stewarding campus ministry at a particular university or college. This person could be the pastor at a university parish; the director of a campus ministry department at a Catholic college; a university vice president for ministry at a large Catholic university; a director of a Newman Center; or the chaplain of a small interfaith campus ministry office. Obviously, the depth and complexity of a campus ministry depends on the size of the college or university, the size of the campus ministry program, and the human and financial resources available. Nevertheless, the administrative responsibilities—stewarding the vision, gathering the responses, hiring, and evaluating—are the same.

Unlike the diocesan director, however, the campus ministry director will be involved in

the plans, policies, and activities of the university. At a secular school, the director will be concerned about building bridges of cooperation with the administration of the school and with campus ministers of other faiths. The director at a Catholic college or university will be heavily involved in the overall direction and development of the school itself as a Catholic institution.

The campus ministry director must rely on people for the development and implementation of the vision for campus ministry. In addition to paid staff, the campus ministry director also has colleagues and volunteers who are willing and able to help the ministry develop.

Personnel Policies for Campus Ministers

The most critical responsibility that either a campus ministry director or a diocesan director faces on a day-to-day basis is the supervision of campus ministers. This section outlines the specific tasks involved with this responsibility.

1. Job Descriptions

A job description is a list of duties and responsibilities that are well-defined,

measurable, and easily evaluated. A proper description includes the position title, context, basic qualifications, required activities, and expected results. It should be based on the vision statement of the campus ministry department or organization, reflect the perceived needs of the particular context, and implement the mission of campus ministry as articulated in *Empowered by the Spirit*.

2. Contracts or Letters of Agreement

A written contract or letter of agreement offers protection to both parties in the agreement and enhances job security and better communication. Such a document should specify salary, employment status, benefits, and length of employment. A contract that does not specify an expiration date can only be terminated when agreed upon procedures for dismissal or resignation are followed. The campus minister's job description should accompany the contract.

3. Performance Appraisal

A performance appraisal process provides the campus ministry staff, as well as the director, with structures of mutual accountability, responsible stewardship, dialogue, and professional growth. The National Association of Church Personnel Administrators (NACPA) highlights some other benefits: enhanced job satisfaction, greater sense of ownership and responsibility, greater job security, perspective on the inner workings of the larger organization, and a context within which to address each employee as unique and valuable (see Drexler, pp. 14-15).

Finally, performance appraisal furthers the work of the Church:

> Whenever persons who work for the Church grow and have a sense of fulfillment, and whenever the institution grows, the work of the Church is being furthered. The reign of God is made manifest in the world. This is the goal, the result which all who work for the Church ultimately seek. (Drexler, p. 19)

The Appraisal Process and Instrument

A well-designed process respects the principle of subsidiarity: the administrator of the performance appraisal should be the person closest to the campus minister and the job performance. Campus ministers who are being appraised should have input into the process and adequate information concerning their appraisal. The process should be flexible and adaptable to individual ministers and campus ministry contexts. Finally, the process should be clear and direct in its implementation and not require an unreasonable expenditure of time and energy.

Successful implementation of the appraisal process will depend on careful preparation. Performance appraisal should take place in a positive and supportive climate. A written procedure for the appraisal process should be available to campus ministers so that they have sufficient information and can be comfortable with their participation in the process. Campus ministry directors should be trained in the implementation of the particular performance appraisal process. Further, an in-service opportunity should be provided for campus ministry personnel to present the appraisal process, answer questions, clarify procedures, and help create an atmosphere of openness and trust.

The appraisal instrument must be fair, accurate, regularly reviewed as a tool, and revised when necessary. When based on a well-defined job description, it will provide feedback on verifiable behavior and accomplishments. Ideally, the director and campus minister will have defined together the objectives to be attained and quantitative and qualitative criteria for those objectives. NACPA recommends a collaborative, goal-oriented appraisal system in all jobs where tasks vary, flexibility is required, and decision making is necessary (see Drexler, p. 32). Campus ministry fulfills these requirements.

The Performance Appraisal Interview

A full performance appraisal should be done once a year and supplemented with informal sessions three times a year (see Drexler, p. 35). In the case of newly hired campus ministers, a progress report should occur within the first three months of employment. The time-line for performance appraisal should be published, and individual interviews should be scheduled with some advance notice for preparation.

Both the administrator and the employee have homework to do before the actual interview. The campus minister is given the appraisal form for reflection and completion of the self-appraisal phase. The administrator gathers previous appraisals, identifies accomplishments and failures of the employee, and reviews other communications between the administrator and campus minister regarding job performance.

NACPA suggests nine steps in the actual appraisal interview session:

There is as much variety in the job descriptions and in the actual influence of diocesan directors of campus ministry as there are variations in the populations, needs, and locations of dioceses in the United States. For a sample packet of diocesan director job descriptions, contact: Rev. Michael J. Newman, SDS; 5900 Newman Court, Sacramento, California 95819; Tel. 916-454-4188.

▲ Self-Review. The campus minister gives his or her self-assessment of performance.

▲ Past Accomplishments. The director affirms past accomplishments.

▲ Additional Accomplishments. The director lists any additional accomplishments that the campus minister may have forgotten.

▲ Improvements and Updated Expectations. Based on the data gathered, the director discusses improvements that could be made, additional assignments, and changing priorities as the campus minister gains more experience and knowledge of the ministry.

▲ Problem Solving. The campus minister and director discuss mutual goals around any particular problem areas.

▲ Appraiser Review. The director reviews the total assessment.

▲ Action Plan. The campus minister and director put in writing goals for continued and improved performance.

▲ Follow-Up Date. The next informal appraisal session is scheduled.

▲ Response. The campus minister has an opportunity to indicate in writing areas of agreement and disagreement with the appraisal report.

4. Record Keeping

The campus ministry department should have written policies governing the keeping of personnel records, including performance appraisal reports. Campus ministry personnel should also have some input into the disposition of their personnel records.

Federal privacy of information acts, which currently apply to employment practices within government agencies, provide useful guidelines for the private sector as well. Some states also have enacted laws relating to privacy of employment records. The rights of an employee include the right to know what information is collected; to participate in decisions concerning the content, use, and disclosure of that information; access to the information; and the opportunity to challenge and correct that information. The employer has the responsibility to record only necessary and relevant data; to gather and use information for specific purposes; to store employee records in a secure way; to provide information only to persons who need it; to check records for accuracy and relevance; and to delete obsolete or inaccurate information (see Drexler, pp. 52-53).

5. Personnel Termination

A campus minister can be separated from a ministry position through retirement, resignation, or the elimination of the position itself (reduction). There are also two ways that personnel termination may result from performance appraisal: *nonrenewal* and *dismissal/termination*.

Nonrenewal occurs when the administrator chooses not to offer another contract to the campus minister or chooses not to continue employment for the subsequent employment period. Ordinarily, this results when the campus minister fails to meet the performance standards set up between the administrator and the campus minister. In such instances, the administrator notifies the campus minister in writing of the intent not to renew thirty days prior to the

Job descriptions vary from diocese to diocese, from campus to campus, and from position to position. The Catholic Campus Ministry Association has a sample packet of campus minister job descriptions for the asking. Contact: CCMA, 300 College Park Avenue, Dayton, Ohio 45469-2515; Tel. 513-229-4648.

contract's end. The administrator is not required by law to state the reason for nonrenewal. The campus minister who is given a notice of intent not to renew may discuss the matter with the administrator informally to determine whether there are alternatives to nonrenewal. If no alternative is found, the nonrenewal would become effective automatically at the expiration of the thirty days.

If it is necessary to terminate employment during the course of the contract/ employment period, the administrator should notify the employee in writing. The administrator must show cause for the decision to terminate employment and detail what corrective efforts were taken. The campus minister should have an opportunity for a hearing at which he or she is fully informed of the reasons for dismissal and is able to respond to the charges. If circumstances require that action be taken before such a hearing can take place, NACPA recommends that the employee be suspended with pay until the conclusion of the hearing. Only after such a due-process procedure is followed and the dismissal decision upheld in the hearing, should formal dismissal occur and written notice be given to the employee.

Once again, the importance of a comprehensive personnel policy should be stressed. If careful attention is given to the candidate selection process; if campus ministry job descriptions include standards of effectiveness; if there is a clear listing of the knowledge, skills, tasks, and behavior critical to the job; the likelihood of employment termination will be lessened.

Resources for Campus Ministry Personnel

Books/Articles

Daly, William P. and Joseph T. Graffis. *Parish Personnel Administration.* Cincinnati, Ohio: NACPA, 1988. This manual is a practical and comprehensive aid for pastors and persons in the parish who have responsibility for personnel administration. The topics cover the various aspects of the relationships of the parish with its employees: Parish Staff Analysis; Position Descriptions; Recruitment Process; Application Materials;

Selection and Hiring Procedures and Records; Salary and Benefit Plans; Performance Appraisal; Workplace Problems; and Separations.

Drexler, Charles H., Donald C. Lozier and Ann Margaret O'Harra. *Performance Appraisal: A Manual for Church Administrators.* Cincinnati, Ohio: NACPA, 1988. This manual presents the principles of performance appraisal and guidelines for the development of a performance appraisal process for all employees within the church system. It describes the different types of performance appraisal instruments for a variety of positions and includes samples of these instruments.

NACPA. *Just Treatment for Those Who Work for the Church.* Cincinnati, Ohio: NACPA, 1986. This twenty-one page booklet, which comes with an eleven-page study guide, is the finest historical, ethical, and comprehensive approach to just treatment of church workers to be published. This little document is a must for every church employer.

Setting Up a Peer Ministry Program

Sr. Shirley Osterhaus, OSF

A good way for campus ministers to multiply their effectiveness is by facilitating peer ministry programs. . . . In all such peer ministry approaches, it is important that those serving others are well prepared through proper grounding in gospel ideals and church teachings. . . ." (ES, 66)

Peer ministry might be described as "the multiplication of the bread." Peer ministers act as yeast among the multitudes, activating and nourishing life. As yeast, they invite other students to rise to the call of growth and service; they gather the ingredients of students' lives to celebrate in community; they challenge students to stretch beyond comfortable boundaries. In turn, peer ministers themselves grow through the act of giving and in a warm and supportive environment.

On a college or university campus, peer ministry is ministry by young adults for young adults. The uniqueness of peer ministry lies in the peer minister's ability to relate to young adults as social equals, sharing faith and friendship. This special peer witness provides a model to other young adults of individuals striving to integrate Christian values in their lives, while offering service to another.

There are numerous reasons to develop a student peer ministry program on college campuses. Peer ministry offers students the opportunity to be bread for other students, while developing and reevaluating their place in the Church. It offers the campus community role models of students in service leadership positions. Peer ministers are a supplement to the professional staff's outreach on campus. These student leaders are not the primary ministers for other students. Rather, student peer ministers are called to enable other students in accepting leadership positions and in fulfilling outreach opportunities.

A peer ministry program includes the following important elements:

▲ recruitment
▲ job description
▲ wages
▲ personal support
▲ leadership and ministry development
▲ supervision
▲ evaluation

Both personal invitation and open job applications to the Catholic student community are avenues for recruitment. In recruitment, clear job descriptions are essential—be it for peer minister of retreats, of liturgy, of parish community outreach, or other specified areas. Included in the job description are expectations, the number of work hours, and payment per hour. Many peer ministers receive a stipend or a salary for their ministry, although some do not. Whenever possible, this monetary commitment serves as a model of justice in the Church for those choosing careers in lay ministry. Along with personal support and community building among the peer ministers and the professional staff, there is need for consistent supportive supervision of the student ministers (i.e., weekly individual and/or group meetings). Whereas the peer ministers supplement the professional staff with outreach, the professional staff is generous with their time commitment to the student peer ministers.

One important ingredient in the making of the one bread among the peer ministers and the professional staff is community building. Without the trust and security a sense of community offers, problems in communication arise, as well as feelings of isolation and aloneness. An experience of bondedness enables the student peer ministers to express their needs and any concerns that arise. At times, a campus minister can expect too much of the peer ministers in light of their age, maturity, and other demands. Or the campus minister may expect too little and limit the peer ministers' creativity and energy. It is important that the relationship between the campus minister and the peer ministers be clear in order to avoid problems such as inadvertently relating as colleague or gofer.

There are many ways of kneading, shaping, and financing a peer ministry program. Catholic universities offer possibilities of personally selecting work-study students; of giving course credit over a semester on a graduate level; of setting up intern programs, where older undergraduate students can receive room/board and stipend; or of being a part of a graduate religious studies intern program. In state universities where internships are required (e.g., in the human service field), students may find peer ministry an avenue for a community outreach internship. The financing of a peer ministry program calls for creative outreach. The students themselves, as well as the students' parents and the alumni, are a resource for ideas and finances. Local area churches might make a commitment to fund a position with an "adopt-an-intern" program. Grant monies from the (arch)diocesan "career ministry" office offers another possibility.

There are many campuses that have peer ministers. If you have the opportunity to develop such a program on your campus, seize it. Young adults ministering to other young adults is the clearest way to multiply and to enrich the lives of students. Campuses with peer ministry programs can wait for the bread to rise—within the students' ministering and within the campus community life.

Campuses with Peer Ministry Programs

Contact:
Sr. Frances Nosbisch, OSF
3303 Rebecca Street
Sioux City, Iowa 51104
Tel. 712-279-5485

Place: Briar Cliff College

Contact:
John Donaghy
St. Thomas Aquinas Center
2210 Lincoln Way
Ames, Iowa 50010
Tel. 515-292-3810

Place:
Iowa State University

Contact:
Pat Lynch, OSU
1631 Crescent Road
Lawrence, Kansas 66044
Tel. 913-843-0357

Place:
St. Lawrence University Center

Contact:
Seton Cunneen, SND
Campus Ministry
Washington, D.C. 20017-1094
Tel. 202-939-5263

Place:
Trinity College

Resources for Peer Ministry

Books/Articles

Bacik, James J. "Peer Ministry: Leadership and Services on Campus" in *Community and Social Support for College Students.* Norman S. Giddan, ed. Toledo, Ohio: University of Toledo, 1988. Bacik explores the key aspects of peer ministry: community building, liturgical participation, formation, working for justice, and service to the academic world.

Hanrahan, Peg and Joanne Seiser. "Peer Ministry: A Model for Campus Ministry" in *Process.* Dayton, Ohio: CCMA, Spring 1978. An excellent article describing the peer ministry program in the Archdiocese of Chicago. It identifies the positive and negative aspects of peer ministry, the recruiting and supervision processes, and the necessary support system for this ministry.

Lutheran Campus Ministry and Educational Services. *Student to Student Ministry.* Chicago, Ill.: Lutheran Campus Ministry and Educational Services, November 1978. A packet of eight articles and a resource section on peer ministry. The packet contains articles on "Live-in Communities"; "Salaried Peer Ministers"; and "Unique Models for Peer

Ministry." For further information, contact Lutheran Campus Ministry and Educational Services, 35 East Wacker Drive, Chicago, Illinois 60601.

Reynolds, Brian. *A Chance to Serve: A Leader's Manual for Peer Ministry.* Winona, Minn.: St. Mary's Press, September 1984. This resource workbook is a helpful guide for those who are beginning a peer ministry program. It offers theoretical foundations and eighteen sessions that are components of a formations program for students involved with peer ministry.

Varenhorst, Barbara, Ph.D. *Curriculum Guide for Student Peer Counseling Training.* Palo Alto, Calif.: December 1980. An excellent resource for training students who will be involved in peer ministry. This workbook offers fifteen sessions on a variety of skills needed by peer ministers. For further information, contact 25 Churchill Avenue, Palo Alto, California 94306.

Working with Volunteers

All the faithful on campus, by virtue of their baptism, share in the task of bringing the humanizing light of the Gospel to bear on the life of the academic community . . . (ES, 22). Officially appointed campus ministers . . . identify, call forth, and coordinate the diverse gifts of the Spirit . . . to multiply the centers of activity and to unleash the creative power of the Spirit. . . . (ES, 24)

Rev. Thomas Welbers

All professional (i.e., paid) ministers will find themselves devoting a great part of their time and energy ministering with and to volunteer (i.e., unpaid) ministers. If we take seriously the call to ministry of all baptized and confirmed Christians, then an important aspect of those with an "official" ministerial role is to promote and support the ministry of everyone else.

This means that most ministry will actually be accomplished by volunteers, and the professionals work largely to serve them. This should not be too surprising, considering the meaning of the word *ministry* and the example of Jesus, who is normative for us.

Volunteers offer to do something because they want to do it. Often, however, professionals who supervise volunteers see them as unreliable or uncontrollable. Problems arise because supervisors assume a level of motivation, commitment, skill, or time that is above or below what the volunteer actually possesses. Also, supervisors do not have the same sort of power over volunteers that they have over employees.

The following observations and guidelines may help campus ministers to work with volunteers:

1. Successful recruitment requires a boldness that does not advertise a task, but rather promotes a process or movement in which people like to participate. If people are sold on the cause, they will be motivated to do the tasks needed to further the cause. There is a core of self-interest deep inside all altruism. Such self-interest is good, not bad. But it requires the recruiter to ask seriously at the outset: "What is it worth to potential volunteers?"

2. Causes, in themselves, do not recruit people. People recruit people. Successful recruitment of good volunteers does not come from generic advertising, but from one-to-one contact. In other words, if you want to get people, you have to ask them, personally and directly, to join your cause.

3. When you ask for volunteers, have something ready for them to do, even though you may not always get the people with the precise capabilities for the job as you see it. This means that you have to plan and organize the work before you start recruiting.

4. Never minimize the work ("Anyone can do it . . ."). People want to feel part of something important. Nobody is going to get a sense of accomplishment doing something anybody can do. Rather, affirm the capabilities you see in them to be part of the mission.

5. Clearly define the task(s) and the expectations. Be flexible in your expectations, allowing a variety of competence levels among the volunteers.

6. Assess your volunteers' capabilities and assign them the tasks that they find interesting and can complete. There are several types of people:

   a) Organizational Detail People. They prefer to be behind the scenes and are extraordinarily faithful when they find their work satisfying and they are appreciated. They do not want to be in charge and often will not perform well if they are.

   b) "People" People. These are the loving, touching, reaching out types. They could care less about ideas or the organization, but they want to know who will be there, who they will help, and how they should do it.

c) Performers. These are the busy ones, and you should talk organization and ideas with them. They need to see the big picture and know where they can fit in and how they can find work satisfaction without overextending themselves.

7. Once you have the volunteers working, remember their ongoing need to feel involved in the whole mission. Look for ways of nurturing their sense of involvement. Job satisfaction is all you have got to hold them.

8. Recognize and accept the limitations of your volunteers—both in time and in talent—and help them to do the same. Generosity and belief in a cause can sometimes blind people to their limitations. Help them bite off only what they can chew—a difficult task when there is more work than volunteers.

9. Remember that "Thank you!" needs to be said frequently and in many ways. Appreciate and reward your volunteers. Formal recognition, awards banquets, parties, and gifts are all immensely important. However, they are no substitute for careful and loving attention to the good work that your volunteers are doing. Seize every opportunity to offer a word of appreciation, to give feedback on their work, and to underscore what their efforts mean to the organization.

Resources for Working with Volunteers

Tape Series

Noonan, Bill. *Volunteerism in Campus Ministry.* Tape Series. Dayton, Ohio: CCMA, 1986. Given as a lecture at the 1986 CCMA Western Study Week, Noonan describes the essentials for volunteerism on a college campus: purpose, recruitment, relationship, support, training, and evaluation. Using his experience at the University of California, Los Angeles, Noonan gives concrete examples for campus ministry volunteerism.

Thero, Cyndi. *Many Hands: Making Volunteer Ministry Work.* Tape Series. Kansas City, Mo.: NCR Credence Cassettes, 1984. In a three-set tape series, nationally known Thero elaborates in detail on the various dimensions of volunteerism. While not specifically given for campus ministers, Thero's insights on church volunteerism are essential in building a sound volunteer program.

Catholic Faculty and Campus Ministry

Rev.
Vincent
Krische

The Catholic faculty members of our respective universities form a valuable resource for the enhancement and strengthening of our campus ministry. *Empowered by the Spirit: Campus Ministry Faces the Future*, a pastoral letter, speaks eloquently of the ministry and the important, almost indispensable role of the Catholic faculty. The letter states,

> All the faithful on campus, by virtue of their baptism, share in the task of bringing the humanizing light of the Gospel to bear on the life of the academic community. They are called to live out Christian values while engaging in the teaching, learning, research, public service, and campus life that constitute the academic world. . . . The faithful are called not only to bring Christian witness to the academic world, but also to exercise their baptismal prerogatives by helping to build up the Church on campus." (*Empowered by the Spirit*, nos. 22-23)

The Vatican document, *The Church's Presence in the University and in University Culture* affirms the role of the Catholic faculty within the university itself. The document states,

> "The Christian vocation is, of its nature, a vocation to the apostolate." This statement of the Second Vatican Council, when applied to university pastoral action, is a resounding challenge to responsibility for Catholic teachers, intellectuals and students. The apostolic commitment of the faithful is a sign of the vitality and spiritual progress for the whole Church. (*The Church's Presence in the University and in University Culture*, section III, paragraph 2)

Accepting the indispensable role of the Catholic faculty in developing a strong campus ministry, one may raise the question, "How do you accomplish this on a practical level?" Let me offer a few suggestions.

We must consider ministry to the Catholic faculty and ministry with the Catholic faculty. Regarding the first opportunity, I suggest the formation of a Catholic faculty discussion group. To accomplish this, one must first "find" the Catholic faculty within the university. This can usually be done through effective networking (i.e., asking those you know to be Catholic to let you know of others whom they know to be Catholic). Although you may not discover every Catholic, you will find the majority. You could begin by gathering a small group of the faculty and asking them to take responsibility for the formation of the group, the development of the program, the discernment of issues that need to be addressed, and the timetable for meetings.

It is possible that two or more groups could be established. There may be some who would enjoy theological reflection opportunities through discussing various issues relative to the Church today. Using the bishops' pastoral letter and the recent Vatican document can be an excellent place to start. Other books, periodicals, and articles could be used as the group continues. These groups should also allow some time for shared prayer.

Other faculty may be interested in a "support" group. As we all know, faculty experience many needs within academia. They are concerned with issues such as the lack of respect among students, rampant dishonesty and cheating, unethical practices of colleagues, insensitivity of administration, and other professional concerns. Today, some faculty experience higher education as a very different environment than they previously knew or had anticipated. This kind of support group can be tremendously helpful.

Some faculty enjoy socializing with each other along with informal conversion during social events. Friday afternoons with "TGIF" opportunities can be refreshing. Many faculty do this within their departments or specialized groups already, gathering at a local place for refreshments and relaxation. The Catholic center could provide such a place and encourage the Catholic faculty to attend.

Catholic faculty families could look for "family events," such as pot-luck suppers, summer picnics, Christmas, and other holiday gatherings. People socializing can build a strong sense of community.

Christmas holidays can always be very busy for people, so it might be helpful to sponsor a Valentine Party for faculty, provided Lent starts after Valentine's Day.

Trying to find new Catholic faculty who may move into the community at the beginning of the academic year can be very difficult. The university will have a list of all new faculty. One could get that list and send a welcome letter to all whose names are there, informing them of your particular campus ministry and inviting them to be a part of your community. Those who are Catholic may respond and become part of your ministry. Those who are not Catholic will appreciate the letter of welcome and invitation, even though they may not respond.

Ministry with Catholic faculty has many possibilities. It is, first of all, important to invite the Catholic faculty to share your responsibilities in campus ministry. In exercising their baptismal commitment, they become "campus ministers" themselves, seeking to build the faith within the academic environment.

The "ministry of presence" is very effective. For Catholic faculty to be invited to join in all of the activities and to be present with the students is very helpful. For the students to see the faculty involved in the Church speaks a very strong message. If faculty exercise ministries within the liturgies, it affirms for the students that academicians too find meaning in life through developing a strong and dynamic faith. It is also a witness to the fact that there is no conflict or contradiction between "faith and reason." Students are strengthened in their faith as they observe their teachers and university administration and staff personnel actively pursuing a faith life.

Faculty can also assist in sacramental preparation classes for students. Most campus ministries serve a large number of students who are planning to marry. The married faculty can serve an invaluable role by being "lead couples" in marriage preparation programs. Inviting engaged couples to their home for discussion of the various aspects of marriage brings mutual benefit to the married couple and the engaged couples. This is a very important ministry today, especially as we hear the call from every unit of society to build and restore the strength of the family. The moral crises in the society of our day are directly related to the breakdown of family life. In campus ministry, we are in a unique position to form "a new type of family" for the next generation as we prepare our young couples for marriage.

In her presentation to campus ministers at the 1996 Eastern Study Week in Orlando, Florida, Dr. Sharon Parks of Harvard encouraged us to establish "mentoring groups" for students. The faculty could easily provide this ministry in various ways.

First, they could offer to give assistance to any Catholic student who is studying within their discipline (e.g., a student may be experiencing terrible difficulty in calculus). A Catholic faculty member may be willing to lend a hand. This could be set up either personally/privately or in a more public manner. In a personal way, a campus minister could serve as a "broker." Catholic faculty may be asked individually or personally if they would be willing to offer this service, and if the campus minister knows a student to have this particular need, he/she could match them up. Some faculty may be willing to have their names published in the bulletin, newsletter, or on a bulletin board within the center with information on what they are willing to offer and how the students could contact them. Permission should first be obtained from the faculty member for this public notice.

Campus ministers, along with faculty, could establish "faith reflection" groups within particular disciplines. The purpose of the group would be to bring the light of faith, the moral practices, and the spiritual insight of the tradition into that particular profession. An example would be the formation of a Catholic law students' group. This group would meet regularly to discuss issues relating to "Law and Faith," both as regards particular principles as well as theological reflection on current issues. In this way, students would be empowered to integrate their faith and professional lives. In this way, they would understand how to bring the Gospel into the marketplace of law, legislation, and the judicial system. A student would then be able to distinguish between a lawyer who happens to be Catholic and a Catholic lawyer. This could be repeated in all fields, such as business, education, journalism, architecture, and social welfare. The faculty who are committed to both their faith and their discipline are a tremendous resource.

Faculty who are in special areas of study could be ideal teachers for religious/theology classes at the Catholic center or campus ministry. This would be particularly true for someone in humanities studies. One who is learned in American history, for example, could have knowledge of the Catholic Church in the United States and could teach such a course to the Catholic students. This could be set up in the form of what was once called the "Free University."

Catholic faculty teaching in disciplines where the Church has a very concentrated interest could help Catholic students reflect on Church teachings as they relate to these disciplines. A fine example of this would be the social teachings of the Church as they affect studies in sociology, social welfare, and political science. Many papal encyclicals, bishops' pastoral letters, and historical teachings of the Church can shed a very different light upon these disciplines by careful study. This is particularly true for students and faculty in secular higher education.

These are just a few ways by which one may invite the faculties into particular areas of the education ministry.

Catholic faculty should also be asked to share in the administrative responsibilities of the campus ministry. They are very capable of serving on councils, budget and finance committees, strategic planning committees, and review committees. Sharing with them the vision of campus ministry as expressed in Church documents can help us actualize the potential of our ministry. Our faculty know many people, can be great ambassadors for the ministry, lend credibility to the ministry, and facilitate a more effective ministry. The more faculty involved in your ministry, the stronger and better your ministry will be.

Campus ministry is called not only to serve the students, but to be a partner in the education and formation of students. We share with the university the mission of enabling students to reach their highest potential. Keep in mind that the faculty are the "key" to the university itself. They can open many doors for you within the institution itself; they can bring your concerns to the pertinent people in administration; they can introduce you to important people within the university, and they can lend tremendous credibility to the Church.

The above suggestions and ideas are only the beginning of the role the faculty can exercise within the Church. As the pastoral letter *Empowered by the Spirit* challenges us to give Catholic faculty an essential and integral part in our campus ministry program, the promise of a bright future will be realized. As the challenge of the pastoral letter to give Catholic faculty an integral part in our campus ministry is actualized, we can look forward to an enhanced program of ministry on campus.

Organizing Campus Ministry

Beginning Campus Ministry

Some members of the Church on campus are called to lead the faith community. . . . One of the most important functions of campus ministers is to provide a vision and a sense of overall direction that will encourage and guide the other members to contribute to the well-being of the academic community and the Church on campus. (ES, 24)

Rev. F. Stephen Macher, CM, and Rev. Lawrence Gibbs

Beginning a new position or a new ministry is never easy, especially if you are called to lead the faith community. Unlike parish-based ministry, where parishioners come to you or to a program at the parish for nourishment, university ministry calls you to serve those in higher education who are seeking the transcendent within their lives. Within this academic environment, you will become the sacramental and liturgical presence of the Church. There, at the intersection where higher education seeks religious meaning, the campus minister finds the location for service.

Becoming Acquainted with the World of Academic Endeavor

Whether the minister is plowing a new arena or is watering where a former campus minister has planted, introduction to this new "arena" is primary. Personal introductions to key persons on campus are necessary: the administration, the dean of students, the coordinator of student activities, and the residence hall directors. Individually meet each member of the Religious Studies faculty. The campus

minister should inform all key persons how and where he or she can be reached. Regularly share campus ministry news.

Most often, the minister's first colleagues will be found in the student life and development sectors. Their task is nonacademic. They organize student activities and the more comprehensive concerns of the quality of campus life. Making one's time and energy available to these professionals will allow them to see the campus minister as a kindred spirit and foster the minister's entry into campus life.

While students, and sometimes even faculty and administrators, tend to be in transition, the staff is usually deeply rooted and knows the campus well. The staff remains constant, and the campus minister can rely upon them with a high degree of dependability. Taking time to meet them will draw out a wealth of collaboration. These people have a feel for what is happening on the campus just below the surface. They know the rumors, the gossip, and the troubles.

The minister should also have firsthand knowledge of the leadership in student government, fraternities and sororities, newspaper and yearbook staffs, intramural and

recreation departments, and the counseling staff. It would also help if the campus minister is able to become a resource person for class lectures or campus committees.

Making the cafeteria or student union center a second "office" will provide an opportunity for the different people on campus to see the campus minister in a relaxed setting. Some call this "loitering with intent" or "ministry of presence." An occasional coffee break in the faculty lounge and lunch in the faculty dining room can help the campus minister with new contacts and referrals.

Become familiar with the library, and, if possible, acquire a faculty ID card and a parking sticker. The campus minister's name should be on the campus mailing list to receive faculty newsletters, university newspapers, public relations materials, and student publications. Post a school calendar in your office (see *Texas Campus Ministry Handbook*, 1984).

The Role of the Minister

The Catholic campus minister is an active member of the Catholic Church. The community looks to the minister to lead the campus faith community. Meet with the bishop and the diocesan director; in the case of a Catholic-sponsored institution, meet with your immediate supervisor and the president of the school. The campus minister in a public university or college should have a letter of introduction from the bishop and the diocesan director to the proper campus authorities.

At this beginning stage, the minister should meet with other campus ministers at the institution and with other Catholic campus ministers in the diocese. The minister needs to begin to build bridges with the local Catholic parishes and the diocese. Since the campus minister will find students from many faiths, it will be very helpful to visit local Protestant pastors and rabbis. Such visits will enrich the ministry and also expose these religious leaders to the realities of higher education (see McCrabb, 1988).

Begin with some tried and true programs such as service projects for the hungry and the homeless, talks on human sexuality and intimacy, prayer services centered on the liturgical seasons, and bible study. Identify other established programs the ministry could cosponsor: a hunger drive, a Christmas toy collection, or a symposium on such topics as ecology or international politics. Each campus presents different situations that will call forth the minister's initiative and creativity in designing and implementing programs suited for those circumstances. If the community is diffuse or grieving the departure of a popular campus minister, the task may be complicated. Remember, patience and perseverance are essential.

Survival Needs of the New Campus Minister

A first-year minister needs to stay in touch with the initial expectations that led to the acceptance of the particular ministry. A job description will serve as a guide. Daily tracking of activities, with brief notations will help with time efficiency and accountability (see Conlee, 1987). Learning to adjust to the various roles of minister (e.g., spiritual guide, adult faith companion, religious expert, and academic colleague) will alleviate stress.

From the beginning, the minister should schedule a balance between time spent at job-related activities and time for solitude, recreation, and socializing outside the work sphere. The help of a spiritual director or mentor will prove very beneficial for the minister's life and for the ministry (see Conlee, 1987).

Awareness of personal limitations and needs may cause the minister to feel the need for a support group. The minister cannot depend on the students for peer support. Participation in a local and/or regional campus ministers' group can prove mutually supportive and challenging. A minister who

Key People to Meet

VIPs

President/Chancellor/Provost

Vice President of Academic Affairs

Dean of Student Activities

Dean of Religious Studies

Director of Resident Life

Professional Counseling Staff

Mainstays

Secretaries

Security Staff

Medical/Infirmary Staff

Janitorial Staff

Food Services Staff

Director of Recreational Facilities

Director of Residence Halls

Student Leaders

Newman Club Officers

Student Government Officers

Presidents of Fraternities/Sororities

Editor of School Newspaper

Editor of Yearbook

Graduate/Resident Assistants in Residence Halls

works alone will also need to call forth the gifts within the community (see McCrabb, 1988). It is unrealistic to think that one person alone has all the gifts necessary for ministering to a whole campus.

The minister should join the Catholic Campus Ministry Association (CCMA). This national organization offers programs, newsletters, and educational materials that can greatly assist the ministry. The minister should also consider attending the nine-day Frank J. Lewis Institute for Campus Ministry Orientation the summer immediately following the first year. The Institute, ordinarily held in the Northeast in June and in the West in July/August, is sponsored by the United States Catholic Conference (USCC), with the expressed goal of educating and orienting clergy, religious, and laity in their unique role as campus minister. In addition, the new campus minister should consider enrolling in the national Campus Ministry Mentoring Program through the USCC or, at a minimum, find a local mentor. A mentoring program is not only professionally correct but also provides the atmosphere in which a minister consciously grows. Support systems and mentors chosen for the minister's own enrichment can be one of the most nourishing pieces of the minister's overall life.

A Cooperative Quest for Wisdom

Just as there is a hunger for meaning throughout society, so too will students seek deeper insights that help to integrate the knowledge unfolding in their classes. It is here that the campus minister finds the heart of the mission: joining the intellectual, artistic, and athletic achievements of the university with the beliefs and teachings of the Church.

Most students are concerned primarily with their self-concepts, relationships, intimacy, and careers. The minister will find that "students today do believe in God but are not always articulate about their beliefs since many students are religiously illiterate" (McCrabb, 1988). The minister serves these students by helping them to "'make sense' of the Church's teaching in light of the intellectual rigors of the modern university" (Ibid.).

Current literature aids the minister in understanding a young student's need for mentoring. Be aware of this mentor role since some collegians may unconsciously expect the minister to act as such. Be discerning in deciding to whom you will be a mentor. The minister may eventually find it necessary to recruit volunteer professionals on campus or from neighboring parishes who can help fill this need.

God calls us into service and partnership with himself. God shares with us the joy of young faith developing into maturity. We share with our students privileged and holy time as we see them take their place side by side with other members of the Church, ready to serve others' needs.

Resources for Beginning Campus Ministry

Books/Articles

Texas Catholic Ministers Association (TCMA). *Texas Campus Ministry Handbook: Checklist for New Campus Ministers.* Texas Catholic Ministers Association, 1984. This handbook gives guidelines and a checklist for the new campus minister. It has several articles regarding campus ministry, the constitution and by-laws of the TCMA, a revealing chart on the development of the Newman Movement, and an interesting article on Cardinal John Henry Newman.

Other

Conlee, Mary Beth. Surviving Lay Ministry: The Beginning Lay Minister in the Church Today. Master's thesis. Houston, Texas: St. Thomas University, 1987. This text is oriented to the new campus minister. It has survival guidelines for those about to enter their first year in this ministry. It also explores two issues facing the Church today: theology of vocations and mentoring.

Job-Related Fundamentals

Job Description

Accountability Process

Daily Appointment Book

Scheduled Days Off and Vacation Time

Annual Retreat

Daily Scheduled Prayer Time

Campus Essentials

Campus Map

Faculty ID Card

Parking Sticker

Library Card

Faculty Mailbox

Student Handbook

School Calendar

School Catalog

McCrabb, Donald. An Orientation to Campus Ministry. Lecture given at Frank J. Lewis Chaplains School. Washington, D.C.: Georgetown University, Summer 1988. This document gives an overview of campus ministry. It speaks of today's students who do believe in God but who are not always articulate about their beliefs. It also speaks of building bridges to the local parishes to inform others about the reality of higher education.

Church and State Legal Issues Relating to Campus Ministry

The time has come . . . to forge a new relationship between the Church and higher educa-
tion that respects the unique character of each. We remain convinced the "cooperation
between these two great institutions, Church and university, is indispensable to the
health of society." (ES, 13)

Rev.
George M.
Schroeder

P art of today's demanding reality in achieving effective campus ministry on any campus is a working knowledge of the various church and civil laws that directly or indirectly impact the Church's presence and programs. This article will first look at those ecclesiastical regulations that can impact upon campus ministry and then at civil law and procedure that can directly and indirectly affect the Church's presence on campus. Finally, the article briefly addresses liability issues.

Church Law

Listed below in numerical order are canons or sections of canons from the Church's 1983 revised *Code of Canon Law* that relate to campus ministry. These can be especially helpful in discussions with various parish and church officials in developing and supporting campus ministry.

Book II/Part II/Title III/Chapter VI
Parishes, Pastors and Parochial Vicars

Can. 518—As a general rule a parish is to be territorial, that is, it embraces all the Christian faithful within a certain territory; whenever it is judged useful, however, personal parishes are to be established based upon rite, language, the nationality of the Christian faithful within some territory or even upon some other determining factor.

Book II/Part II/ Title III/Chapter VIII
Rectors of Churches and Chaplains

Can. 564—A chaplain is a priest to whom is entrusted in a stable manner the pastoral care, at least in part, of some community or particular group of the Christian faithful, to be exercised in accord with universal and particular law.

Can. 566—§1. A chaplain ought to be given all the faculties which proper pastoral care requires. . . .

Can. 568—To the extent it is possible, chaplains are to be appointed for those who cannot avail themselves of the ordinary care of a pastor because of the condition of life, such as migrants, exiles, refugees, nomads, sailors.

Book III/Title III
Catholic Education

Can. 794—§1. The duty and right of educating belongs in a unique way to the Church which has been divinely entrusted with the mission to assist men and women so that they can arrive at the fullness of the Christian life.

Can. 795—Since a true education must strive for the integral formation of the human person, a formation which looks toward the person's final end, and at the same time toward the common good of societies, children and young people are to be so reared that they can develop harmoniously their physical, moral and intellectual talents, that they acquire a more perfect sense of responsibility and a correct use of freedom, and that they be educated for active participation in social life.

Book III/Title III/Chapter II
Catholic Universities and Other Institutes of Higher Studies

Can. 812—It is necessary that those who teach theological disciplines in any institute of higher studies have a mandate from the competent ecclesiastical authority.

Can. 813—The diocesan bishop is to have serious pastoral concern for students by erecting a parish for them or by assigning priests for this purpose on a stable basis; he is also to provide for Catholic university centers at universities, even non-Catholic ones, to give assistance, especially spiritual, to young people.

In addition to the above official church canons, also be alert to any local diocesan, institutional, or parish documents, structures, mission statements, policies, guidelines, and so forth, that relate to campus ministry and its programs, either directly or indirectly.

Civil Law

Federal law places very clear restrictions on the authority of university personnel at public institutions to limit the program or speech of campus ministry.

Widmar v. Vincent, 454 U.S. 263 (1981). In this case, decided by the U.S. Supreme Court in 1981, Missouri State University was ordered to permit Mr. Vincent, a student of the college, to meet with his religious group on campus for bible study and other related religious activities. This decision allows a religious group the same access to university facilities as non-religious groups.

Keegan v. University of Delaware, 349 A.sd (Delaware Supreme Court, 1975). In this case, the Supreme Court of the State of Delaware ordered the college to permit Fr. Keegan to say Mass in the college student center.

In both cases the college was required to permit either students, or their campus ministry, staff support to use the college facility for legitimate campus ministry. Ministry was defined as both worship and conversations and related activities that use religious language.

The college has the responsibility to see that meetings and events on its campus do not interfere with the legitimate ongoing functions of the college. Thus, programs cannot block halls, interrupt classes (except at the invitation of the faculty person in charge), disrupt food service, or jeopardize the safety of persons in the building.

Two other major pieces of law also govern the situation. The college cannot discriminate against people on the basis of their language. Unless it is censoring the content of speech of every group which uses the campus, it may not do so to campus ministry. Further, to censor in this way would be to violate freedom of speech. Thus, the college may not censor the speech of campus ministry or place prior restraints on the content of that language in any way.

The second piece of law covers the right of association. Any organization or association must be treated with equal rules and procedures. The clergy associations of the communities of the college district have equal rights with every other club or organization that meets at the campus and holds its events open to the public (Creel, 1982).

Rosenberger v. Rector and Visitors of University of Virginia (1995). In this case the United States Supreme Court upheld the right of a Christian group to receive funding for a religious publication as long as the group was a recognized student group that followed the procedures outlined by the university for receiving funding. This ruling is a logical extension of Widmar.

Experience has demonstrated that some college or university officials are not aware of these decisions. From time to time, the U.S. Supreme Court and lower courts decide on further cases that may impact campus ministry activity directly or indirectly. The campus minister should be clear about his or her right to be on campus based upon these civil laws and court decisions.

Experienced campus ministers, especially those at state colleges and universities, report that the most effective approach to a cooperative effort is taking time to meet and getting to know various university officials and staff who make the decisions about religious groups and activities on campus. Oftentimes, a religious affairs council or committee exists on campus. Engage with them in an explanation of the institutional, state, federal, and other regulations by which these activities are regulated. Request a firsthand examination of the pertinent documents. Do not be afraid to ask questions, especially in light of the above cases.

Once you understand the possibilities and the limits, use them in the best interests of the ministry and the campus. If necessary, consult with your diocesan director, experienced campus ministers in your area, or the Catholic Campus Ministry Association.

Liability Issues

As with other employers, campus ministers must exercise due care to make sure that their conduct does not cause harm to others. Their actions in the performance of their ministry could subject the diocese or the university to civil lawsuits. They could also be sued personally for intentional or negligent conduct injurious to others. Such lawsuits could result from automobile accidents, at one extreme, to assault and battery at the other. Therefore, take time to understand pertinent university and church policies and regulations concerning discrimination, confidentiality, sexual harassment and abuse, malpractice, and similar concerns.

Be clear about what you are hired for, the scope of your duties and responsibilities, what your credentials and competencies are—and are not. Clarify any concerns or confusion with your employers. Every state, every diocese, and every school has laws, policies, and regulations that may affect you in your job. Try to have as thorough an understanding of these as possible before something happens, and know who to contact if something does occur that could threaten a lawsuit.

Resources for Legal Issues and Campus Ministry

Books/Articles

Canon Law Society of America. *Code of Canon Law.* Latin-English Edition. Washington, D.C.: Canon Law Society of America, 1983.

Creel, Marilyn, K. "Federal Law and Public Higher Education." Brief Paper. Illinois: United Community College Ministry Organizing Board for Illinois, 1982.

Hagan, Charles H. "The Logic of *Rosenberger v. Rector and Visitors of University of Virginia* and its Implications for Campus Ministry." *Crossroads* XXVII (September 1995); 1 and 4.

White, Lawrence. "The Profound Consequences of the 'Rosenberger' Ruling," *Chronicle of Higher Education* XLI, 44 (July 14, 1995); B1-3.

Other

Center for Constitutional Studies, Notre Dame Law School, Notre Dame, IN 40556; Tel. 219-239-5864.

United States Catholic Conference, Office of the General Counsel, 3211 Fourth Street, N.E., Washington, D.C. 20017-1194; Tel. 202-541-3300.

Developing a Mission Statement and Goals

Mr. Donald R. McCrabb

Campus ministry can be defined as the public presence and service through which properly prepared baptized persons are empowered by the Spirit to use their talents and gifts on behalf of the Church in order to be sign and instrument of the Kingdom in the academic world. (ES, 21)

Introduction

A mission statement is the heart of any organization. It clearly states an organization's purpose and intent:

A mission statement tells the world why the organization exists and what general categories of activities are within its purview. (Wolf, p. 76)

For Catholic organizations such as campus ministry centers, departments, or offices, a mission statement describes the purpose of the Church at a particular time and in a specific place.

Establishing a Mission Statement

A helpful framework for a mission statement is a set of questions that describes the persons involved, the purpose of the organization, and the manner in which the purpose will be carried out:

1. Who are we? Who are we called to be?
2. Whom do we serve? Whom are we called to serve?
3. What do we promise those we serve? What are we called to promise those we serve?
4. In what style or manner do we carry out our promise? In what manner or style are we called to carry our promise?

The first set of questions on identity describes those responsible for the purpose of the organization. This description must reflect the history of the group, its current demographics, and any potential changes in the population.

The second set identifies the organization's constituencies. This set of questions focuses the purpose of the organization, since no ministry can serve everyone. Clearly understanding one's constituency significantly impacts the development of

goals and objectives for a campus ministry program.

The third set describes the promise of the organization to the constituency. The promise details those general activities that the organization is committed to on behalf of the people it serves. In many ways, the promise describes both the needs of the constituency and the competency of the organization.

Finally, the fourth set of questions gives the organization an opportunity to state how it intends to implement its purpose. Will campus ministry carry out its activities with warmth and hospitality or be cold and sterile?

How to Develop a Mission Statement

Campus ministers who formulate a mission statement have consistently reported that the process proved to be as valuable as the statement itself. Developing a mission statement is a very simple process, but it is time consuming if all the members of the organization work together. If they are involved, common ownership for the mission takes place within the entire community.

There are many ways of developing a mission statement. Perhaps the most common is the four-step process outlined below:

1. The community leadership drafts a statement that responds to the four sets of questions listed above.
2. The draft document is circulated to the members of the organization for comments, suggestions, and deletions.
3. The leadership redrafts the statement, incorporating the suggestions.
4. Steps 1, 2, and 3 are repeated as often as necessary until the community decision makers officially adopt the statement.

Goals, Objectives, and Strategies

The mission statement tells the public why an organization exists. Goals set the direction of the organization. They give a framework for setting objectives. The six aspects of campus ministry listed in *Empowered by the Spirit* are goals. They do not indicate programs for a specific campus ministry but, rather, set direction for all campus ministries.

With goals, an organization can set specific and measurable objectives. If the goal is "to provide life-giving worship experiences for the campus community" then one objective could be "to establish a student choir for the 8:00 p.m. Sunday liturgy within two years." The objective is the specific destination within a broader direction and carries with it a measurable target or benchmark.

Strategies are action plans directed to an objective. They outline how the organization will reach its destination and how much it will cost. A simple action plan for the objective "to establish a student choir . . ." would involve (1) recruitment efforts, (2) training, (3) practices, (4) instruments, and (5) music. Each of these actions can be budgeted.

Just Do It

Once objectives have been written into action plans and those plans are funded, then it is time to work the plan. This is best done by scheduling the different steps to the action plan on a calendar and monitoring the progress of each step. Adjustments may be necessary in the middle of the plan—as long as they remain focused on the objective.

Evaluation

Objectives are very specific. Evaluation asks the questions: Did we achieve our targets? Why or why not? How can we do better next time? Evaluation is an essential step that needs to be scheduled once the objective is completed. Frequently, people begin to evaluate an objective before all the strategies have been taken. Or, worse, people fail to evaluate at all. Evaluation provides very helpful information for developing future strategies, objectives, and goals.

Conclusion

The mission statement clearly states to the public the purpose of campus ministry, and it serves as a foundation document for the development of goals and objectives. With this defined purpose, it is easy to establish goals, objectives, and strategies. All actions will be precise and mission centered. The basis for evaluation will reflect the uniqueness of the ministry but still provide some measure of growth.

Sample Mission Statements

The sample mission statements that follow come from (1) a Newman Center at a public university, (2) a diocese, (3) a Catholic university, and (4) an interfaith campus ministry. These statements are unique, and yet they all address, in some way, the four questions listed above.

1. Newman Center

The Newman Center is a Catholic presence at the University of Minnesota, Twin Cities Campus, and exists to serve university students, faculty, and staff, as well as persons from the Twin City area who share and assist in its mission:

▲ to create among members a more enlightened mind in matters of Catholic faith;

▲ to instruct and to aid them in the study of contemporary religious and justice issues; and

▲ to create among the students, faculty, staff, and alumni of Newman an environment of social interaction and a spirit of friendship.

All members of the Newman community are called to exercise their own ministries in creating a truly humane and nourishing environment for growth and faith. Newman seeks to build a strong, active, and welcoming community united in worship, study, service, and work for justice. The Newman community strives to cooperate with other religious centers on campus and within the archdiocese in order to carry out their mutual ministries.

Contact:
The Catholic Center
University of Minnesota
Twin Cities Campus
1701 University Avenue, S.E.
Minneapolis, Minnesota 55414-2076
Tel. 612-331-3437

2. A Diocese

Campus ministry is the official presence of the Church on the college and university campuses within the Archdiocese of Boston.

As campus ministers, we join with the men and women of our faith community to make present and real the person of Jesus Christ.

We gather as the Catholic community to celebrate the sacraments, to listen to Scripture, to educate, to counsel, and to serve one another.

We affirm, complement, and challenge our communities of higher education in light of our Catholic tradition.

We collaborate ecumenically, especially in the pursuit of justice and peace.

Thus, we are present on campus as a sign of faith and as a companion on the faith journey.

Contact:
Archdiocese of Boston
20 Arrow Street
Cambridge, Massachusetts 02138
Tel. 617-868-6586

3. A Catholic College and University

The mission of Campus Ministry at the University of Dayton is to lead the university in fostering a faith community among its members. This faith is manifested

▲ in personal and communal devotion to God, specifically as revealed in Jesus Christ and handed down in Roman Catholic tradition;

▲ in common worship;

▲ in efforts at sharing the gospel with one another in the university community and with persons beyond the university;

▲ in a sense of ministry to one another in the university community and to persons beyond the university;

▲ in the quality of relationships extant among the members of the community and in its relationships with persons beyond the university community; and

▲ in efforts at enriching humanity and the world through the articulation of moral and religious values and their implementation.

Contact:
University of Dayton
300 College Park Avenue
Dayton, Ohio 45469
Tel. 513-229-3339

4. An Interfaith Campus Ministry

The Auraria Interfaith Ministry is a cooperative endeavor of several mainline religious denominations in Denver to provide services to the Auraria campus community, as well as to other metro-Denver constituencies. These denominations allocate responsibility to a staff person (and in some cases a ministerial support board) for working cooperatively on the Auraria Interfaith Ministry Team.

Contact:
Auraria Interfaith Ministry
1030 St. Francis Way
Denver, Colorado 80204
Tel. 303-556-3864

Resource for Developing a Mission Statement

Wolf, Thomas. *The Non-Profit Organization: An Operating Manual.* Englewood Cliffs, N.J.: Prentice-Hall, Inc., 1984. An excellent overview of eight major areas needed to manage any nonprofit organization. Campus ministers will find the sections on the "Board," "Planning," "Staff," and "Fund Raising," particularly helpful.

Evaluating Campus Ministry

To prepare for meeting all these challenges, we encourage campus ministers to take responsibility for their own personal and professional development. Clear contractual arrangements that include carefully defined expectations and procedures for accountability and evaluation help to set a proper framework for their personal enrichment. (ES, 29)

Dr. Carol Fowler

Short- and long-range planning necessitates good evaluation of the needs and effectiveness of campus ministry at local and diocesan levels. Ministry evaluation involves an examination of the personnel involved and the personnel needed to accomplish the ministry's goals. However, this article is not about performance appraisals of ministers but, rather, a critical review of the ministry.

A good evaluation tool can be built around the six aspects of campus ministry as listed in *Empowered by the Spirit: Campus Ministry Faces the Future*. In addition, the dimensions of campus ministry found in the pastoral letter, and elucidated by Rev. James J. Bacik in the Introduction to Chapter VII of this book, can serve as a foundation for evaluation. These dimensions are spirituality, evangelization, and ecumenism. The evaluation tools included within this article reflect these foundational principles. They are offered here as guidelines only; people should custom-design an instrument specifically for their particular situation.

The first instrument model is from the Diocese of Richmond, Virginia. This extensive evaluation is done every three years. A team of two people go to the site and interview campus ministers, students, faculty, staff, and other interested persons. An annual-report format from Richmond is also available and is listed in the resource section.

The second, briefer instrument, is used annually in the Archdiocese of Chicago. Campus ministers complete a written report, answering the evaluation instrument questions. If there is more than one campus minister at a ministry site, they work on the

written report together. Campus ministers are interviewed by the diocesan director both as a team and individually to supplement the written materials.

A third effective evaluation process is Colleague Consultation from CCMA, especially when an outside and more objective view of the ministry is needed. In all three cases, the intent is to provide a solid basis for future planning and more effective campus ministry.

Process for the Visitation of the Catholic Campus Ministries of the Diocese of Richmond

1. A visitation team visits each full-time campus ministry every three years.
2. In the early spring of the visitation year, the campus minister sends to the diocesan director a 1,500-word retrospective evaluation of the ministry, including the strengths and weaknesses he or she perceives.
3. This is circulated to the visitation team, chaired by the diocesan director and including one or two members of the diocesan campus ministry committee (one member selected by a campus minister at the site being evaluated), a member chosen by the local board (if applicable), and a member of the diocesan staff and/or a knowledgeable parish staff member from another part of the diocese.
4. The diocesan director also makes available to the visitation team copies of the annual reports from the previous two years, as well as pertinent position descriptions, and so forth.
5. The visitation team meets at the campus ministry site for a two-day visit, according to the following schedule:

First Day

11:00 a.m.
Team meeting

12:00 p.m.
Meeting with the campus minister
(on the self-evaluation)

2:00 - 5:00 p.m.
Each member interviews three to five
persons (half-hour or hour interviews,
as appropriate)

7:00 - 8:00 p.m.
Meeting with local board/committee
(on their functions, as they perceive
them) [This could be followed by an
open "town meeting" session.]

Second Day

9:00 a.m.
Each member interviews two to four
persons

11:00 a.m.
A "reality check" with the campus
minister

12:00 p.m.
Lunch meeting of the team (to formulate some recommendations for the
local board/committee and campus
minister)

4:00 p.m.
Diocesan director shares
recommendations with the campus
minister

6. The persons to be interviewed are
selected by the local campus minister
and include faculty, an administrator
or two whose responsibilities include
relating to campus ministries, students,
area pastors, and ecumenical campus
ministry colleagues.

7. The visitation team uses as a basis for the
interviews the standard worksheet for the
visitation team.

8. The final written report is done by the
diocesan director after circulating a draft
among the members of the visitation
team for their approval.

Campus Ministry Triennial Visitation of the Diocese of Richmond

Worksheet for Visitation Team

1. Forming Faith Community (including worship and social activities)
Strengths: _____
Weaknesses: _____

2. Passing on the Faith
Strengths: _____
Weaknesses: _____

3. Forming Christian Conscience
Strengths: _____
Weaknesses: _____

4. Educating for Justice (including outreach)
Strengths: _____
Weaknesses: _____

5. Facilitating Personal Development
Strengths: _____
Weaknesses: _____

6. Developing Leaders for the Future
Strengths: _____
Weaknesses: _____

7. Ecumenical Dimension of the Ministry
Strengths: _____
Weaknesses: _____

9. The campus minister(s) of the campus visited should write a brief response to the report, which is appended to it before the final report is circulated.
10. Those responsible for the local campus ministry use the report as the basis for their own goal setting for the next year.

Campus Ministry Annual Review of the Archdiocese of Chicago

Focus Question: In light of the goals for your campus ministry setting this year and your job description, please list strengths, weaknesses, and ideas or plans for change or improvement for each of the following areas:

I.   Faith Development (educational programs, RCIA, evangelization, sacramental preparation, teaching opportunities, other);

II. Spiritual Development (liturgy, prayer, sacramental life, retreats, other);

III. Personal Development (counseling, spiritual direction, conscience formation, ministry opportunities, other);

IV. Pastoral Presence (availability to students, outreach and relationships with faculty and staff, connections to college or university committees and organizations, building presence, campus presence, other);

V.   Community Building (Newman Club, social activities, hospitality, leadership development, ecumenism, other);

VI. Facilitating Justice and Peace Awareness (service opportunities, justice and peace activities and programming, other);

VII. Relationship with Parishes/Archdiocese (links with neighboring parishes and parishes of students, involvement with diocesan committees, programs, activities, other);

VIII. Team Building/Team Relationships (meetings, decision-making process, mutual support, prayer, communication skills, including confrontation on occasion, other);

IX. Fiscal Responsibility/Administration (income, expenditures, staff supervision, building maintenance, other); and

X.   Personal and/or Team Qualities that make you particularly effective in your campus ministry.

Colleague Consultation Process and Procedures

A *Service Offered by the Catholic Campus Ministry Association*

Colleague Consultation is a service offered by the Catholic Campus Ministry Association to its members and groups associated with them. Based upon the goal of the requesting individual, trained consultors assist the local campus minister or diocesan director with listening, reflecting, questioning, evaluating, and developing a vision for the future of their ministry. The Colleague Consultation process consists of five parts: (1) site request; (2) selecting consultor team; (3) information gathering; (4) site visitation; and (5) consultation report. Each part is completed in accordance with the confidentiality policy of the association. The goal and procedures of each part follow:

Site Request—Goal: To establish a written agreement between requesting individual (requestor) and director of the Colleague Consultation program.

1. Requestor sends a letter, stating purpose and goal of consultation.
2. Colleague Consultation director reviews with the requestor the consultation process; procedures; and program costs, which include a $200 CCMA fee, consultor travel, food, and lodging.
3. Program director acknowledges the arrival of the site's consultation goal and CCMA fee.
4. Colleague Consultation director sends a letter to campus ministry diocesan director (or president of Catholic college, where applicable) and all staff members on site informing them of the upcoming consultation.

Selecting Consultor Team—Goal: To select two or three consultors whose backgrounds and expertise will enable the consultation to meet site's goal. Geographic proximity is preferred.

1. Director confers with requestor on appointing consultors and the appointment of one consultor as chair.
2. Chair contacts selected consultors and requestor identifying consultors.
3. Dates of site visitation are agreed upon among chair, director, and requestor.

4. Letter from chair is sent to requestor and program director, confirming agreed-upon goal of consultation, dates, and arrival/departing times.

Information Gathering—Goal: To assemble a written profile of the site and give it to the consultors for review prior to their arrival.

1. By receiving written information prior to the site visitation, consultors can begin to assemble a profile of the campus ministers and the campus ministry program. It is recognized that most sites do not have all the materials listed below. The following list has been prioritized to help the requestor in the gathering process. Requestor should send duplicate copies of as much information as possible to *each* consultor, as well as to the program director.
   a) campus ministry mission statement, including goals and objectives;
   b) all job descriptions;
   c) campus ministry annual report;
   d) campus ministry budget and overall university budget, if the consultation is for a Catholic college;
   e) campus ministry program brochures, flyers, and publications;
   f) program and staff evaluations;
   g) on-site evaluation conducted by chaplains/faculty/staff/students reviewing strengths and weaknesses of staff and/or program (see, e.g., "Ohio Catholic Conference—Campus Ministry Self Report," *Campus Ministry Guidelines* [Washington, D.C.: USCC, 1976], pp. 15-24);
   h) staff meeting minutes or summary statements;
   I) statements that profile the ministry/parish;
   j) college or university catalog with institutional Mission Statement;
   k) all governance documents, such as Newman Center or student organizational constitution, parish council guidelines, board of trustees constitution, and so forth; and
   l) diocesan correspondence or documentation related to diocesan structure or diocesan site evaluation.

Site Visitation—Goal: To spend two to three days of quality time on-site in order to gain firsthand information from campus ministers, programs, and associated individuals in an effort to assist the requestor in reflecting, questioning, evaluating, and planning for the future.

Preliminary Tasks (Prior to Arrival):
1. Chair reconfirms goals and objectives about the visitation through a clearly written statement based upon initial goal from site and a review of site materials.
2. Consultors and requestor agree on process and time schedule of on-site interviews.
3. Consultors review all materials sent from campus ministry site.
4. Consultors tentatively agree on individual responsibilities and format of final written report.

On-Site Tasks:
1. Chair convenes consultors and campus ministry staff to review goals and objectives, process, and schedule.
2. Individual consultations with all parties directly involved with campus ministry program (e.g., staff, auxiliary staff, diocesan director, parish council, musicians, peer ministers, volunteers), as well as those university/college personnel responsible for (or associated with) the program.
3. Consultors meet periodically during consultation to share, clarify, confirm, and plan.
4. Consultors attend worship/program/events of the campus ministers where possible.
5. Consultors meet before and after general session with the campus ministry requestor and/or staff to prioritize recommendations and clarify writing process of the final report.
6. Chair convenes consultors and requestor for preliminary verbal report and opportunity for further clarification or additions. Presence of local campus ministry staff is optional.

Consultation Report—Goal: To document on-site consultation findings and recommendations as related to agreed upon visitation goal.

1. Consultors return to home city and chair writes first draft, or consultors divide up the initial draft and chair assembles parts.

2. Completed first draft sent to all consultors by chair for corrections/additions.
3. Chair corrects and edits final draft and sends it to requestor for signature and brief response/reaction.
4. Copies of final consultation document sent to requestor, consultors, and director within one month of visitation.

Follow-Up (Optional)—Goal: To revisit the recommendations of the consultation; review the implementation process, new developments, and current successes/failures; and to give new insights into possible solutions, where applicable.

The process for follow-up can take many forms (e.g., telephone discussion with requestor, conference call with consultors and team, or revisitation of site by chair/consultor team). The requestor will need to take the initiative for implementation of this optional stage.

Rev.
Vincent
Krische

Fund Raising for Campus Ministry

As we prepare to enter the new millennium, the Church is re-discovering the gospel meaning and value of stewardship. Rather than simply looking to the need for fund raising and continuing the concern over finances, we are called to develop the faith of the people wherein their Catholicism becomes a way of life expressed in a living relationship with Christ and his Church. This way of life invites one to become personally involved, to deepen the understanding of their faith, and to promote the reign of God through sharing their gifts.

Using stewardship as a gospel foundational principle in developing and strengthening the Church is, to my thinking, a radical new approach to ministry. As campus ministers, we are privileged to serve students during their critical years when they are solidifying their faith foundation. In helping them to become good stewards, we will be forming a stronger community of faith and a more effective instrument and sign of the kingdom. Stewardship requires us to look at the totality of our gifts and calls us to make a return on all of these gifts.

A look then at funding for campus ministry is grounded in stewardship and becomes the framework for all that is to be said in this chapter. Stewardship is always an invitation to which a free and generous response is elicited. As we seek to strengthen campus ministry, exercising the principles of stewardship will serve us well. In fund raising, we talk about much more than finances, for we believe that healthy finances are the result of a healthy faith. Faith-consciousness raising will flow over into fund raising.

There is today a distinction between "fund raising" and "development." Briefly, fund raising refers to the annual operations budget, appeals to the donor's income, and is repeated annually. Development refers to planned giving, including endowments, charitable lead trusts, charitable remainder trusts, wills, estates, and insurance, and it appeals to the donor's assets. A planned gift is given only once and is for long-term financing. People will begin giving at lesser levels, usually to the annual appeal, and as they become more convinced of the value of the ministry and actually establish a relationship with the ministry, their gifts will increase. Eventually, maybe twenty years or more, a major gift may be offered. For this chapter, I will be writing primarily on fund raising.

Fund raising begins with the students in our Catholic centers today. The benefit that they receive from our ministry will pay off years down the road when they will have some disposable income. In this sense, we find ourselves sowing seeds of effective ministry, which will reap a harvest some years in the future. As we teach them to know the Lord Jesus as he lives, teaches, heals, and serves in and through his Church, and as we call them to love him deeply in his Church and to serve him faithfully in all our brothers and sisters, we will be guaranteed a great future for campus ministry.

In the spring of 1995, through the generosity of a grant from the Lilly Foundation, CARA undertook a study of how campus ministry is funded. I would recommend that you get a summary of the results from CCMA, for it will help you in understanding the great need to involve yourself in fund raising. Among the many interesting facts discovered, I will point out only a few. The report states

> While fund raising does take time that might otherwise be spent in other forms of ministry, there are numerous advantages. Chief among these are

▲ Fund raising is ministry.

▲ It forces the articulation of a vision if you have to contain it in a one-page letter.

- It gets students involved and helps them take responsibility and hence increases ownership of the campus ministry program.
- It broadcasts information about the program to those on the outside.
- It forces the minister to keep up contacts with graduates, faculty, staff, and other friends of the institution and the ministry.
- It allows the minister to tell the local churches how young people are responding to the Church.
- It allows you to help people outside become knowledgeable and involved.
- Because you are selling something, it forces you to be very clear about it—people will not buy a product if it is not presented well.

Keep in mind that fund raising requires

- A personal belief in the value and importance of the ministry in the Church.
- A deep love and concern for the Church and recognition of the needs of the Church for the present and next generation.
- A superb gift of patience, acknowledging that it takes time, effort, and commitment to get a substantial gift from someone.
- A vision of what the ministry can be if it had all the finances it needed.

- A willingness to plant the seeds trusting that someone else may reap the harvest.
- An openness to invite many people into the leadership role of the ministry and a humility to carefully discern and follow their advice.

Fund raising/development requires a clear and concise mission statement. It is important to state in two or three sentences the essence of your particular ministry. A very common question people ask is, "What do you do?" or "What is your ministry?" To briefly and candidly answer these questions will assist the donor in making a positive decision to offer a gift.

Being familiar with key statistics is also important (e.g., how many students you serve, your annual budget, how much the students contribute in the Sunday collection, and the strength of your alumni/ae support). Knowing these facts and others you believe to be important will work positively on your behalf.

An effective fund raising/development program requires (1) efficient organization, (2) strategic planning, (3) careful selection of capable and effective volunteers, (4) thorough follow-up, (5) accurate recording of donations, (6) notes for improvement, and (7) appropriate thank-you's.

Fifteen years ago, if anyone had told me that a major part of campus ministry would be involved in fund raising, I would have denied it vehemently! I was never interested in raising money; I never considered it to be one of my "gifts." I always thought I should spend my time doing what I thought I could do best, and I firmly believed that the financial responsibility for campus ministry belonged to someone else: *the diocese*. The annual diocesan drive was to include donations for campus ministry. I would simply receive the quarterly check from the bishop's office, add to that whatever small amount would be placed in Sunday collections, and maybe send an annual letter to parents requesting some help.

But, this approach put me in another bind—a bind that I did not like: the insecurity of whether or not our proposed budget would be funded each year kept the whole campus ministry on edge; the knowledge that at any time our budget could be cut, allowing no recourse for us (which has happened far too many times in this country); the uneasiness of having to appear annually before a diocesan board to defend the budget, while most board members did not know or understand campus ministry needs as much as we did; the fear of having to establish a community of full-time employed persons who would make us dependent upon them financially; and the awareness that our ministry would never be able to develop or grow significantly.

Components to Successful Fund Raising Within a Campus Ministry Setting

1. Building a Base of Donors—Identification

Because campus ministry is associated with institutions of higher education, it has several natural sources of funding. Natural constituent groups include the following:

▲ Catholic students currently enrolled

▲ Parents of current students

▲ Catholic faculty, staff, and administration

▲ Catholic alumni

▲ Friends

▲ Home parishes of currents students

▲ Vendors

This list is not exhaustive. It can be a logical starting point for building a solid foundation for financial support. Successful fund raising involves large numbers of people who believe in the ministry. It is important to build lists of names of potential donors from among many groups. Potential donors and current non-donors are found close to home: staff, volunteers, committee members, and so forth. The individuals can become major donors over time.

Current donors (or future donors) were once small donors. The largest gifts to institutions usually occur when a well-organized approach has been taken to the fund raising process. Large gifts will emerge after time and after careful, meaningful approaches have been taken.

Building a list of donors can be done in different ways. Those just starting could look over the lists of board members of different university/college organizations. A good place to begin would be the boards of alumni, endowment, and athletic associations. Undoubtedly, there will be some Catholic people serving in those areas. They are already committed to the university and value its importance. Through an educational process, the campus ministry can show them the role that the Catholic Church can play as a partner with the university in providing services for students. From these names, a committee can be formed. Once a strong committee is established, the list building begins. Committee members will know others, who will know others, and so on.

A close relationship with the alumni association will help to uncover specific data.

Another important way to build a list is to gain parents' names, addresses, and telephone numbers from the students when they register with campus ministry. Once they begin to support campus ministry, leave their name on the list even after their son or daughter graduates, unless they ask to be removed. Most of them will continue supporting the program if they believe it was of benefit to their daughter or son.

This list management is a part of a comprehensive program known as donor acquisition or identification, and it requires persistence, research, and networking. A computer is essential for filing, storing, and updating donor information. The development office of your diocese or institution could help you find the appropriate software program that would fit your needs.

Detailed, accurate, and current gift records are extremely important. It is helpful to know how much a person gives and to what causes they will give. A thorough record-keeping system can track some of these items: gift dates, gift amounts, largest gifts, areas of interest, number of gifts given, and cumulative totals. Personal details are important as well: birthdays, anniversaries, and any important dates learned from the donor.

2. Public Relations—Information

Good communications and public relations go hand in hand with a successful fund raising program. It is indeed a self-generating system of accomplishments and announcements. Campus ministry programs are too often well-kept secrets. It is difficult, if not impossible, for individuals to support a program about which they know little or nothing.

It is recommended that you be in touch with your donors six times a year. Strategies for effective public relations as part of the total information picture include the following items:

▲ Newsletters (parents, students, alumni, and so forth)

▲ Diocesan and local newspapers

▲ Christmas, Thanksgiving, Easter cards

▲ Monthly letters to priests

▲ Letters of "congratulations" to parents, students, and so forth

▲ Special event announcements

▲ Personal telephone calls, letters, and visits

If your budget cannot currently support a qualified public relations person, consider a for-credit arrangement with the college/university's school of journalism. Try to arrange to have several students cover events, write feature stories, give interviews, or do whatever it takes to get the real message (and mission) out to various groups and supporters during a quarter or a semester.

Beyond this, many campus ministers learn how valuable, capable, and dedicated volunteers can be. Students themselves can put together a newsletter for parents and alumni. It does not have to be a "slick" production, but it should be professional. Articles for campus or diocesan newspapers could be written by faculty members, addressing issues at stake in their disciplines. Free space in campus newspapers and community-service radio announcements may be utilized to publicize events. It is also important here to recognize that the constituents of campus ministry are far beyond the geographical confines of the campus and extend throughout the country and beyond.

Campus ministry can never do too much public relations, and no matter how hard it tries, there will always be people who have "never heard of campus ministry."

This phase of the total program is known as information. Once the audience has been identified, they will need information about the program before they can ever be approached for support.

3. *Structures to Facilitate Leadership— Involvement*

There is one basic element that is a common thread to all successful endeavors: leadership. For any organization to succeed with collective long-range plans (as outlined in *Empowered by the Spirit*) and to become well-positioned nationally, qualified leadership is mandatory.

This leadership should be developed from among the people who are served; be representative of the various constituencies; be people who are already recognized in their local communities as well as in the university; be capable of substantial financial support themselves; believe in young people and in the importance of campus ministry; share a vision of what the ministry can become; and be convinced that their time and ideas can make a great difference in the ministry and produce good fruits. People who are leaders want to see results!

Effective leadership will flow from a well-structured board or council. This group should meet on a regular basis, usually quarterly, at the campus ministry site. It is important that they become very familiar with the ministry and with the people who are involved.

Those who agree to serve on a fund-raising board or council should bring these three Ws to their service:

Wisdom,

Wealth,

Work . . .

and for all of us to be successful, let us look for one more: *Wallop!*

Traditionally, governing/advising bodies (board or council) are built around natural constituent groups. It is wise to engage the assistance of people who know the institution and who are willing to work on behalf of campus ministry. If they are willing to serve in such a role but are somewhat new to the institution, an orientation session can be very helpful to them and perhaps even to long-time committed members.

Once campus ministry finds a supporter who knows the political, operational, and mechanical workings of the college (a key alum for example), a staff member needs to ask his/her help in moving the ministry program ahead. Perhaps cooperative arrangements with the endowment, alumni, or foundation boards to encourage matching gifts from alumni can be pursued by an influential alum.

Involving key people with the fund raising effort is the most valuable step in the fund raising process. It is more important than information, because information can easily be ignored. Involvement and leadership are real.

4. *Getting Gifts—Inclination*

With any fund raising endeavor, the groundwork that is done is the key to success. A sizeable part of the campus ministry effort must be spent studying the market, the constituents, and the donor pool.

It is imperative that one knows how people feel about the ministry being done, knows about their perceptions (or misperceptions), and is able to ask the questions, "How are we doing? What do you think are our strongest points? Our weakest points?" and be open to their responses. This gives valuable information about ministry performance but perhaps more important, involves others while sharing ownership and leadership.

When campus ministry asks for a gift, someone is being invited to join a very significant group of people: leaders of your governing board, university officials, college deans, major corporate chairpersons, community leaders—all people who enjoy the respect of others. Giving to a successful program is a community project, and many donors are needed to make a successful ministry.

As one progresses in fund raising, one realizes that the work takes on a life of its own and present results will determine future direction. This happens when people become involved as volunteers in this important endeavor. They will appreciate how much they are needed and will be thrilled by the success their involvement engenders. Being a volunteer gives them great leverage in asking others for involvement and gifts, and it provides needed credibility for the ministry. It offers them an opportunity to deepen their own faith and love in the Church.

The best givers will be the ones who know and see the mission in action. The largest gifts come from those closest to the ministry—alumni, parents of students who appreciate the assistance their son or daughter received, and friends—because they feel good about the ministry and want it to be strengthened.

It is very helpful to have a broad base of support: many people giving smaller amounts is better than a few giving larger amounts. In fund raising, the least important result is the actual money received; the most important is what happens to those who give and how they can become ambassadors for the ministry.

Keeping a history of giving will enable the campus minister gradually to ask people to upgrade their level of giving. If someone gave $50 a year for five years, they could be asked to increase it to $75. They also feel good about this because they know you remember and their gift is appreciated.

Evaluating large donors ($10,000 and more) can be done in various ways:

examine their history of giving to other organizations; meet with their peers and ask them to evaluate a person's capacity to give; meet with the prospect many times, trying to discern his or her areas of interest in the ministry. A great deal of time and effort must be spent in "courting" a potentially large donor.

The campus minister is now only one small step away from a total program; campus ministry has identified, informed, involved, and determined inclination; now it is ready for the next step.

5. Communicating the Need— Asking for an Investment

I am excited about our programs, our facility, our students, our alumni, our mission, and our impact. And I am excited about our ever-growing endowment, our increasing plate collection, our major-capital campaign gifts, and the list goes on. In asking a donor to give, I communicate my excitement and invite him or her to become a part of our mission.

Asking for a gift is very simple. Once the campus minister has provided people with adequate information about the ministry, they are asked to join this worthy effort through their prayers, moral support, and financial support. It is best to always ask for a specific amount, whether $50 or $1 million. The candidate must feel good about being part of the ministry by "buying into it." Be careful not to ask for a gift that might be too small. Asking for a significant gift confirms the belief of the campus minister in what he or she is doing, and the minister's belief in his or her capacity to assist. People are usually complimented, not offended, when asked for a significant gift. They may sometimes act "shocked," but they appreciate the fact that they have been asked for something significant.

People will join others in supporting winning programs. One of the reasons universities with large endowments continue to raise huge funds is because people want to be identified with success. People like strong, exciting visions and well-run operations.

If the campus minister has done a good job with identification, information, involvement, and inclination, then donors will feel good about a gift because they will see it as an investment. As stewards of their investment, the campus minister has an obligation to build with their generosity and to keep them well-informed about the good that happens through their gifts.

6. Overview and Review

A fund raising program has the following goals: (1) to strengthen the faith of individuals in Jesus Christ and his Church; (2) to enable them to acknowledge that all they have is a gift from God; (3) to inspire them to be good stewards in their gifts for the glory of God and extending his reign on earth; (4) to cultivate friends in the faith; (5) to raise the funds for the ministry. Accomplishing these goals is the creative part of the process and involves the five "I"s:

▲ **Identification:** building the list of persons who could provide support.

▲ **Information:** informing people about the programs, the people involved, the needs, and the dreams.

▲ **Involvement:** inviting people to join the team and become part of making something significant happen.

▲ **Inclination:** being very specific in asking for a special gift, about which they will feel good.

▲ **Investment:** waiting for their decision and appreciating their response. (Acknowledge their investment within a week so that they know that the campus minister appreciated the gift and sincerely needed their help. It is also good to recognize them in the newsletter or in other materials sent to supporters.)

Once the campus minister has gone through all the steps with a donor and secured a gift, the process begins all over again at a new level. People move from potential donors to first-gift givers, to renewable gifts, to larger gifts, to capital gifts, and finally, to bequests and deferred gifts. It is hoped that the people will move up the ladder by increasing their gifts. They may spend several years on each level, but the more they see happening with their gifts, the easier it will be to interest them further. Remember that every gift is an investment, and it says something about the donor's openness to campus ministry.

Successful Fund Raising Programs

Fund raising should be an essential component of every campus ministry program. Many good results accrue from a healthy fund raising program. By becoming involved in fund raising, it is possible to discover new gifts within oneself; to strengthen campus ministry in ways never considered possible; to provide for the campus ministers who are to come later; to state in a very fundamental and profound way the belief that campus ministry is the most important ministry in the Church today; and to achieve great satisfaction in strengthening people's faith in Christ and his Church, and to enable them to serve Christ in this way.

Stewardship

The list of fund raising ideas is almost limitless. There are many clever ideas that others have successfully used.

▲ **Pledge Sunday.** The success of any program is determined by those who are closest to the program and benefit directly from it. For this reason, it is important that students and permanent community (faculty, staff, and university administrative personnel) be asked to pledge to the ministry each year. This invites them to grow in their faith and express their love in service. Students will be asked, on the first Sunday after Labor Day, to pledge $2 per week or $30 per semester by completing and signing a commitment card. It is also good to accustom them to the habit of giving to the Church. Encourage the permanent community to tithe five percent of income. They, too, sign a commitment card.

▲ **Phonathon.** Each year, a national telephone campaign can be conducted by calling parents and alumni asking them for a gift for the ministry. The students can do the telephoning, and the ministry can enjoy many fringe benefits. When students are willing to get on the phone to call people and ask for a donation, they believe in campus ministry.

▲ **Check Levels of Giving.** This is geared for people who have a capacity to donate a larger amount for the annual operating budget. Level 4 = $2,500; Level 3 = $1,000; Level 2 = $500; and Level 1 = $300. We also give special attention to them by listing their name in our publications. One can celebrate a Mass for their intention each year on the anniversary of their birth and, if married, on their wedding anniversary.

▲ **Auctions.** There are people among our constituents who are in a position to help in a special way. Perhaps an alum or parents of a student are in a business that can provide a fund-raiser (e.g., a student's parent is president of a chocolate candy company and can get retailers to donate candy for an auction). The event can be built around a nice meal and evening of entertainment with the auction in-between. Other types of auctions can also be considered.

▲ **Book Week.** This is a simple project which requires very little work on the part of the staff. You simply ask each student at the end of each semester to donate one of their textbooks to the campus ministry. In order for them to associate their faith and education, they are asked to bring the book to the chapel and place it near the altar. Having beforehand worked out an arrangement with the manager of the university book store to purchase these books from the Catholic center, at the end of final exams you call and ask them to pick up the books. They then offer you the check according to the value of the used books.

▲ **Golf Tournament.** Many parents and alums love to play golf. Organizing a tour-

nament for parents and alums can be a very successful fund-raiser. Finding help and expertise in how to organize such an event is easy. Many non-profits sponsor such tournaments and are willing to advise others on how to sponsor a successful tournament.

▲ **Parents/Family Weekend Event.** Providing a dinner, dance, barbecue, or some such event on this special weekend can provide a nice money-raiser. Perhaps a parent or alum who may have a catering or some similar business may be willing to sponsor or co-sponsor the event, thus enabling the campus ministry to be free of any major expense and yield more income for the center.

▲ **Garage Sales.** Each spring at the close of the semester, ask students who are graduating and moving to donate any furniture (e.g., sofas, beds, tables, desks, dishes, and typewriters). When school begins in the fall, have a huge "garage sale" and attract other student buyers. This is a very labor-intensive project, in that it involves someone picking up items from those who would have no way to get them to you; organizing and pricing the items; and obtaining storage space for them during the summer. The pay-off is that there is not much overhead, and the project does show a profit.

▲ **Yogurt Sunday.** This is an interesting idea that requires only volunteers. A local yogurt shop might allow your students to work at the shop for a Sunday afternoon. They then give a percentage of the profits for the time worked. This is a great advantage for the shop owner, because it generates much publicity. We try to urge students to come to the shop for yogurt. It promotes fun and builds community. This same idea can be tried with hamburger stands, ice cream shops, restaurants, and so forth.

▲ **T-Shirt Sales.** You can order t-shirts with the logo or name of your student organization and sell them to students. It may be helpful to take pre-orders so that the ministry has an idea of how many are needed. This publicizes the center as the students wear the t-shirts.

- ▲ **Oktoberfest and Mardi Gras.** It is possible to have a good fund raiser at a time that coincides with another university event, when many parents and alumni are in town. Sporting events are excellent times; it is possible to have a Oktoberfest after a football game and a Mardi Gras celebration after a basketball game. An event coinciding with homecoming can also be very successful. These can be major fund raising events, perhaps $10,000 or more. They require a lot of publicity, invitations to parents and alumni, fun events, and strong committee leadership.

- ▲ **Other events.** Care packages at the semester's end, old book sales, art events, and many other ideas are appropriate fund raising. Although most of these events will not bring in huge dollars, their value is in getting people involved and volunteering for the ministry. This is of tremendous benefit and will always strengthen the belief in and love for our young people involved in campus ministry.

Conclusion

It is good to keep in mind always that fund raising/development involves a sacred trust. When people support your ministry, they trust that you will exercise the best stewardship. The more Spartan your administration, the more impressed people will be. The trust that donors place in your administration is a real gift.

Fund raising can be one of the most rewarding undertakings of campus ministry. It will always enhance the ministry by enabling it to become better and better. It will help to expand the vision of the Church's ministry to higher education. It will secure the ministry for the future and continue to garner the gifts and talents of people of faith in the services of the Lord, Jesus Christ. What more could one desire?

Resources for Fund Raising for Campus Ministry

Books/Articles

Broce, Thomas E. *Fund Raising, 2d Edition.* Norman, Okla.: University of Oklahoma Press, 1979. Thoughout this well-written book on fund raising is a philosophy that encourages positive approaches to the science and art of fund raising. It is a good reference for "how-to" projects and programs that are just beginning their operation.

Panus, Jerold. *Mega Gifts: Who Gives Them, Who Gets Them.* Chicago: Pluribus Press, 1984. Well-written accounts, from a donor's perspective, on the process of acquiring major gifts of $1 million or more. Emphasizes the importance of strong, exciting programs. Available from Pluribus Press, Inc., 160 E. Illinois, Chicago, Illinois 60611.

Piquet, Leo A. *Fund Raising: A Primer for Campus Ministers.* Newton Center, Mass.: The National Institute for Campus Ministries, Inc., 1979. An excellent start-to-finish document that gives clear examples of procedure, letters, budgets, envelope designs, offertory or special collection efforts.

Religious Literacy and College Students: The Promise of Campus Ministry, A Symposium for Catholic Bishops and Campus Ministry Leaders. Dayton, Ohio: The Catholic Campus Ministry Association, September 10, 1995. This reference contains an exclusive summary entitled "The Ministry Association," as well as several excellent talks on the importance of ministry. It is available from CCMA at 513-229-4648.

Seymour, Harold J. *Designs for Fund Raising, 2d Edition.* Ambler, Pa.: Fund Raising Institute, 1966. Considered one of the most accurate and insightful texts in the field. This book is used by thousands of development officers throughout the nation as a guide for annual funds and/or capital campaigns.

Dimensions of Campus Ministry

Introduction

Rev. James
J. Bacik

The campus ministry pastoral, *Empowered by the Spirit*, moves logically from a brief look at the persons who serve on campus to a longer examination of six aspects or distinct ministerial functions, which constitute the work of the Church in the academic community. This section of the handbook gives greater precision to the whole discussion by exploring various dimensions of campus ministry. The metaphor *dimension*, borrowed from theologians and other scholars, directs our attention to general characteristics that should pervade all aspects of campus ministry. Attention to these dimensions suggests a whole realm of ministerial activity.

All campus ministry, for example, should have a *spiritual dimension*. A healthy spirituality is not confined to a few pious exercises each day but, rather, pervades all aspects of life. Campus ministers need to develop a spirituality that is workable within the framework of busy and demanding schedules. All particular programs and activities should aim, in one way or another, at helping people to become more attuned to the will of God, to be better disciples of Christ, and to be more responsive instruments of the Spirit.

Likewise, campus ministers, who bring an *interfaith dimension* to their work, maintain a general and abiding concern for dialogue and cooperation among various religious traditions. Such a sustained positive attitude helps shape the general approach and direction of campus ministry programs. It also makes it easier to promote particular activities, such as common services and joint efforts on behalf of justice.

Finally, thinking of *evangelization as a dimension* of campus ministry prevents the faith community on campus from retreating into a private self-contained enclave. It encourages the local church to be an attractive welcoming community with an abiding concern for humanizing the culture and reaching out to others. With this outlook firmly in place, church members can attend to the concrete task of personally inviting honest searchers and unaffiliated believers, as well as inactive Catholics, to participate in the life of the faith community.

By including a section on dimensions, this handbook encourages a broad and holistic approach to campus ministry.

*Sr. Mary
Johnson,
SNDdeN
Ph.D.*

The Challenge of Generations

We who are engaged in ministry to the people of God in the United States are called to perform two distinct tasks in our relationship with the newer generations in the U.S. population. The first task is to tear down the barriers that hinder us from meeting and listening to, learning from, and teaching younger people. The second is to build new kinds of bridges capable of spanning the subtle—and sometimes not so subtle—generational chasms which exist within our Church so that God's action within those generations can be more clearly discerned and we can more easily hear the voices of newer generations define their reality and their vision.

Do these tasks confront only Catholic campus ministers? Not at all. In fact, within the last few years many Catholic, Protestant, Jewish, and non-mainline religious organizations have displayed keen interest in the question of how to engage newer generations. Several popular and scholarly works deal with this issue from a variety of perspectives. Two recent sociological studies have dealt with the religious and spiritual lives of the U.S. baby-boom generation. They are *A Generation of Seekers* by Wade Clark Roof and *Vanishing Boundaries* by Dean Hoge, et al. An edited collection by Roof, Carroll and Roozen, *The Post-War Generation and Establishment Religion*, looks at baby boomers in Europe and Australia as well. Finally, a study of the religious involvement of "Generation X" in the United States is now underway.

So generational categories are being used to analyze religious activity across wide populations, and the cultural characteristics of each generation are being described and contrasted across generations. Various religious organizations are also determining how they include or exclude newer generations from either the population served or the population that serves. For instance, within the Catholic community in the United States, retreat houses, parishes, and a myriad of voluntary associations are grappling with the question of which generations are being served.

Let me introduce a concept that is more helpful here than "generation," since that term is often used in an historical sense and is presumed to mean a twenty- to twenty-five-year period.

The more helpful sociological concept for our purposes is "generational cohort." A generational cohort is a group of people born during a certain period, sharing a similar social location and shaped by significant social forces during its members' coming of age (i.e., their early adulthood). Those who use cohort analysis, based on the theory of Carl Mannheim, use the years 17-25 as the indicator of the coming of age.

We are seeing, however, that the coming of age can include social traumas like the Kennedy assassination for the baby boomers and the Challenger explosion for Generation X, which happened for some in their childhood or adolescence. Mannheim argued that those social, political, and economic forces leave a distinct imprint upon the cohort which can affect people's attitudes and behaviors for the rest of their lives.

What the social forces were, how strong they were in their shaping power, how sweeping they were, or how brief or long their duration determines the length of that generational cohort. It could be as long as twenty years or as short as five. Let me give you some example of social forces that can create a cohort and thus examples of the length of some cohorts.

Three examples of social forces that have shaped three cohorts are the Depression, the Vietnam War, and the escalation of violence in the homes, schools, and streets of the United States.

Sometimes the consequences of the shaping power of the seemingly more blatant social forces are easier to analyze. For instance, we can see that those individuals who came of age during the Depression hold attitudes about thrift and savings that are not held by younger people reared during periods of greater affluence.

Similarly, the cohort that came of age during the Vietnam War holds very different attitudes about authority, the role of the federal government, and patriotism than do men and women who came of age during the Second World War.

I believe that the concept of generational cohort can serve as an effective tool for campus ministers. I would suggest that you gather a group of faculty, staff, and/or students and ask which of the following cohorts each person falls into, which social forces shaped them in society and in the Church, and what their understanding is of God, faith, religion, and spirituality because of this generational location. Meaningful and rich discussions often flow from these categories.

Demographers divide the U.S. population into six distinct cohorts labeled Depression (born 1912-21), World War II (born 1922-27), Post-War (born 1928-45), Boomers I (also known as the Older Boomers born 1946-54), Boomers II (also known as the Younger Boomers born 1955-65), and Generation X (born 1966-76 and known by a variety of names, most of them pejorative: slackers, the MTV generation, and the Lost Generation, to name just a few).

Missing from the schema are the approximately four million people who were born before 1912 and the more than 68 million people born after 1976. From the point of view of market researchers, the pre-Depression cohort is quite small and the post-Generation X population has not yet come of age and therefore, not yet been shaped into one or more distinct cohorts. For the purposes of discussions, however, it is important to include the younger students and probe key shaping influences with them.

The Spiritual Dimension of Campus Ministry

Dr. Michael Galligan-Stierle

To be effective, ministers must attend to their own spiritual development. Campus ministers who are serious about their prayer life and can speak openly about their relationship to God will be able to direct others. Ministers who have wrestled with the great questions of meaning, purpose, and identity can offer helpful guidance to other genuine searchers. (ES, 27)

Introduction: An Experience of Love

On February 25, 1987, a campus ministry colleague and a close personal friend died of cancer at the age of thirty-eight. I have never experienced anyone who lived a life of love more visibly than my friend, Joe Ruperto. His welcoming personality, loving disposition, and gentle words knew no boundaries. Joe always greeted another with a hug. At Joe's funeral, friends spoke of how he had changed their lives, how he had touched the deeply spiritual in them, and how his love for them made God's love real. Everyone who came that evening embraced, young and old, for we knew that God's love was being passed on in our simple embrace.

Every campus minister, now and again, has been absorbed in the joy and pain of friendship and intimacy. Such encounters influence and change one's life. They shake one's very core of being and identity, often evoking feelings and emotions previously unknown.

A careful look at a love relationship reveals attraction, accessibility, discovery, depth, commitment, honesty, everydayness, brokenness and reconciliation, celebration, inclusion and exclusion of others, and a sense of awe. Whether human love or divine love, the characteristics are the same.

1. A Love Relationship with God

If I invite God, the perfect lover, as my partner, I discover God's presence and abiding love in my life and in the world. I desire to probe and deepen this intimacy. I commit to faithfulness in life's day-to-day events. I resolve to ask forgiveness for infidelity, and I seek recommitment to a life style of holiness. I have the ability to celebrate this

relationship. I yearn to share the beauty of this relationship, inviting others into it. I stand in awe of God's greatness and generous giving. I am consumed without fear or loss. Prayer is my constant companion for entering this ecstasy and all its ramifications. In this pursuit, I also achieve human (w)holiness.

This personal relationship with God is the heart of a spiritual life. This relationship is one of God's first gifts to us. This heart is enlivened and energized with a love for others. Generative by nature, love cries out to be shared. Initiated by the supreme Lover, it reaches out to other lovers, echoing the famous Judeo-Christian maxim, "We must love God and love our neighbor as ourselves."

2. God's Love Exists in Love of Self and the World Around Us

Healthy self-awareness and self-esteem are essential to any balanced love relationship. Respect and care for body and spirit affirm the sacredness (wholeness) of our entire self. Working hard, recreating well, developing meaningful relationships, appreciating the world of art, nurturing good eating habits, exercising regularly, and setting aside times for study and solitude all maintain, refresh, and replenish the person. Self-care, reflected in a balanced life, becomes a gift we offer to those we love—both God and neighbor.

Beyond the self and our earthly sisters and brothers, we embrace the universe, the earth, the animals, and the plants as part of God's creation. They are offered as a sign of God's love and an embodiment of the sacred, the arena of life. All life is sacred. The love relationship between people and God does not exist in a vacuum. Love relationships among people and with God are part of the integrated larger system of the universe of life. Consequently, awareness of and care and respect for creation are an extension of our personal self-awareness and self-esteem. Thus, creation care, too, is an important part of any love relationship.

3. *The Message of Jesus*

Jesus, as the embodiment of God's love for us, described the essence of a spiritual life as loving God and loving neighbor as oneself. This contradicted the prevailing wisdom, which identified the spiritual life as the fulfillment of the Torah—the Law. Others simplified this message by summarizing the components of the spiritual life as the 613 precepts. Jesus, a sage within the wisdom tradition, selected two lines from the Scriptures to describe the essence of a spiritual life: Deuteronomy 6:5 (i.e., love of God) and Leviticus 19:18 (i.e., love of neighbor).

The genius of Jesus' approach consisted in his simplified formula: love God and love neighbor as oneself. He was not interested in beginning a new religion; he was interested in focusing the essence of the spiritual journey—a relationship—between God and God's people. His followers have been trying to learn and to live this "simplicity" ever since.

4. *Enabling Love*

Prayer and the care of others are the best ways of developing this relationship. Prayer can be described as opening one's heart to God's influence and sharing all of one's life with God. Care is made real by feeding the hungry, giving drink to the thirsty, clothing the naked, visiting the imprisoned, sheltering the homeless, visiting the sick, and burying the dead. One can also extend this loving concern to others by comforting, teaching, advising, correcting, forgiving, being patient, and praying for them. A study of Jesus' life reveals his love lived out in these practical ways.

Just as Jesus faced the challenge of focusing spiritual truths for his day, today's students face a similar challenge. Numerous spiritual paths are offered: the New Age, cults, biblical fundamentalism, mainline denominational options, and a multifaceted Catholic tradition. If one is to return to the roots of the Catholic tradition, one needs to reclaim Jesus' clarity: love God and love

neighbor as oneself. Students, faculty, and staff need to hear and to see the campus minister speak and live this basic Christian principle. It must become the measure of the campus minister's lifestyle and activities. It is the core of Jesus' message. Can people identify the campus minister's life and ministry as the love of God and the love of neighbor in action? If not, the campus minister must revisit the basics of the tradition: the life and message of Jesus.

5. *Programing the Spiritual Dimension*

Today, students and faculty have a new thirst for spiritual matters. Their combined needs of identity, intimacy, generativity, and integrity have put enormous pressure on their vocational and moral life choices. The alienation experienced by our larger society is keenly felt by young adults, as well as by the older adults who now comprise about 50 percent of the campus population. Consequently, many students and faculty members want to draw closer to God, to others, and to the world around them.

Quality opportunities for spiritual growth can be offered, opportunities that are numerous and varied. While the student services office actively presents a wide variety of personal growth topics, it is up to campus ministers to give optional study and exposure to unfolding the spiritual and ethical richness of our tradition. Selections from each of the six aspects of *Empowered by the Spirit* can illuminate the multifaceted giftedness of Roman Catholicism.

Furthermore, campus ministry can be an evangelization vehicle within higher education. For example, a campus minister can enrich the campus community by promoting gospel values. By proclaiming the holiness of life and creation, campus minis try contributes to the institution's and the

The campus ministry center sponsored a canoe trip, but the outing was not the best canoe trip that year. The center sponsored a dance, but it was not the finest dance that year. The chaplains sponsored a career night, but it was not the finest career fair ever sponsored. However, at each of these events, the spiritual component was clearly recognized and celebrated. The time devoted to hospitality, a meaningful time of prayer, a recognition of the sacred, the affirmation that God is pleased when people enjoy one another's company, and the encouragement to choose a profession wherein one can contribute to the betterment of society manifested the spiritual component of life. In addition, whenever the chaplains offered a program that specifically focused on faith development, it was excellent.

individual's spiritual growth. Offering appropriate guidance and programming reflects this mission. Finally, if the program reaches its goal, then the participants are better equipped to find and to celebrate the spiritual dimension of the world when they return to daily campus activities.

6. *Specifying the Spiritual Dimension*

The spiritual dimension of any campus ministry program is contingent on three key factors: (1) the explicit spirituality of the campus minister; (2) the articulation of a specific spiritual component within each campus ministry activity; and (3) the ability of the participants to share visibly the excitement of their spiritual journey. Good planning gives the program's spiritual component visibility and integrity from the beginning.

First, the spirituality of the campus minister is vital because the community looks for spiritual guidance through the words and deeds of its leaders. No one has completely incorporated the spiritual dimension into one's entire lifestyle, but the campus minister can provide an honest living witness as a Christian who is intentionally developing one's spirituality.

Second, it is necessary to articulate the spiritual dimension of the most mundane activities. In this way, the community members discover the sacredness of the ordinary in daily life. While the campus minister may recognize this sacred character more quickly than most, many might never notice without the chaplain's actually naming it. Campus people—students, faculty, administrators, and staff—look to campus ministers to be spiritual leaders in a campus community. They do not look to the campus minister to be the campus specialist in the social, educational, or career areas, although these skills can enrich the academic community. People look to the campus minister to help

the community name and celebrate the spiritual dimension of the world.

Third, when someone is in love, most friends and relatives quickly learn the partner's attributes through a variety of words and feelings, usually with a great deal of emotion and excitement. Often, however, this same person may be mute when it comes to proclaiming the glories of the Catholic community or the love of God. Most Catholics are not accustomed to proclaiming this enthusiasm in verbal and nonverbal ways. The campus minister here faces the challenge of leading the Catholic student to experience God's love and the love of the community, as well as empowering the student to use love's enthusiasm in expressing and sharing it.

Summary

Because Joseph Ruperto took the first step to love others, people he touched were moved to care for others. God, having first loved us, enables us to a loving relationship with others. This article encourages that freshness and newness in our love relationship with God.

The spiritual dimension of campus ministry will become real when first, the campus minister models a love of God, a love of neighbor, and a love for all creation; second, all campus ministry programs consciously contain a spiritual dimension; and third, the community members enthusiastically proclaim the message of love in word and deed.

In her autobiography, *Story of a Soul,* Therese of Lisieux admitted:

> . . . I am going to stammer some words even though I feel it is quite impossible for the human tongue to express things which the human heart can hardly understand. (p. 187)

May we be as brave and loving in our stammering.

The Spiritual Dimension of Campus Ministry Continued: An Inventory

Dr. Michael Galligan-Stierle

Introduction

The spiritual dimension of campus ministry can be clarified by a review of three factors: (1) *minister*, (2) *programs*, and (3) *participants*. Using the six aspects of campus ministry, examined in *Empowered by the Spirit*, three sets of questions probe the spiritual reality of the chaplain, campus ministry activities, and campus ministry participants. By exploring these questions, the minister and the ministry will deepen, expand, and enrich the vitality of the Church on campus.

Forming the Faith Community

Establishing bonds of love within the Catholic community.

Minister: Is your love for individuals, as well as for the larger campus Catholic community, visible and easily identifiable? Do you demonstrate this love through actions of hospitality?

Programs: What are the spiritual components you use in your community building activities? Which ones are most effective?

Participants: How do the members of the community share their enthusiasm for the community with other members of the college? Do they believe in the value of the community enough to invite others to participate actively?

Appropriating the Faith

Passing on the biblical and theological richness of the Catholic tradition so that these concepts can become living realities within an individual.

Minister: How are you updating yourself theologically and integrating these concepts into your life? What was the last class or book that helped you in this area? How does your reading of theology help your relationship with God and neighbor?

Programs: How are you programming the theological richness of our tradition in your ministry? How are the participants integrating these theological concepts into their daily school activities and their prayer life?

Participants: In the last year, how have the members of the Catholic community developed their faith life and shared their enthusiasm for the essentials of the faith with others? Have they learned how to communicate their past/current struggles and their methods of resolving/living with their conflicts?

Forming the Christian Conscience

Using gospel values to refine one's value system and subsequent actions.

Minister: What is one value related to conscience formation that the campus community can easily identify in you? What is one area that you are currently working on in your life?

Program: How have you developed the consciences of your Catholic community in the last six months? Does your community have an understanding of the need for theological reflection or social analysis process in conscience formation? What church documents have you used in this year's programming?

Participants: How have community members shared their values with others in word and deed?

Educating for Justice

Engaging in justice-oriented learning/activities based on the conviction of the holiness of creation and Jesus' preferential option for the outcast.

Minister: Do your actions and value system reflect a lifestyle of justice and a consistent ethic of life? How might this be improved and integrated into your spirituality?

Programs: Does your justice programming contain a reflective component to enable participants to grasp the connection between helping the needy and one's spirituality?

Participants: How do individuals in your community encourage one another to be people of justice? How might they verbalize the spiritual component of their volunteer work?

Facilitating Personal Development

Choices related to career and educational opportunities, as well as leisure time activities, are grounded in a relationship with God.

Minister: How can you develop a spirit of thankfulness to God concerning your educational and leisure time activities? What do you do to feed your spirit and stretch your boundaries? How might a spiritual companion help you to trace your growth and develop a healthy self-concept/spiritual deepness?

Programs: What is one campus ministry activity in the personal development area that you sponsor that has an explicit spirituality component? How can you promote this component in a creative and meaningful way?

Participants: Do many community members see their educational and leisure time activities as a chance to respond to God's call? How might they develop their concept of self as a temple of the Holy Spirit?

Developing Leaders for the Future

Developing a self-concept wherein one believes and acts as a steward of one's gifts for the Christian community, as well as for the larger world community.

Minister: What is one way you model Christian leadership and good stewardship of your personal gifts in the community? What is one way you might improve the spiritual component of your leadership in the community?

Program: How do you incorporate the spiritual aspect of leadership in your training of students? What is your best development program for student leadership, and how is spirituality included?

Participants: Do your college-age student leaders identity their gifts as God-given? How do they encourage others to use their gifts?

Resources for the Spiritual Dimension of Campus Ministry

by Mary Beth Lamb

Books

Brock, Rita Nakashima. *Journeys by Heart: A Christology of Erotic Power.* New York: Crossroad, 1988. Erotic power is not what you think! Brock defines it as the fundamentally ultimate reality of human existence; the power of our interrelatedness; the power that heals our brokenhearted society created by dysfunctional patriarchal family structures. Her interpretation of the Gospel of Mark will challenge and provoke. Recommended for anyone seeking to reinterpret Christ for today.

de Mello, Anthony. *Sadhana, A Way to God: Christian Exercises in Eastern Form.* St. Louis, Ill.: The Institute of Jesuit Sources, 1978. A classic in the literature, these spiritual exercises are helpful for one's personal prayer and for leading others into the prayer of awareness and contemplation.

Fox, Matthew. *Original Blessing: A Primer in Creation Spirituality.* Santa Fe, N.M.: Bear and Company, 1983. Fox has rediscovered the venerable tradition of creation spirituality as explicated by the medieval mystic, Meister Eckhart. This book is thematic in approach, playing out the themes of befriending creation, darkness, creativity, and transformation. Great for group discussions or for meditations on a theme. The catalog of Bear and Company is also recommended for videos, books, and the meditation series.

Groeschel, Benedict J. *Spiritual Passages: The Psychology of Spiritual Development.* New York: Crossroad, 1988. A well-balanced contribution to the dialogue between spirituality and psychology. In a stimulating and challenging way, Groeschel writes for Christians trying to take their own spiritual development seriously and for those hoping to assist others in their spiritual journey.

McFague, Sallie. *Models of God: Theology for an Ecological Nuclear Age.* Philadelphia, Pa.: Fortress Press, 1987. McFague sees triumphalist, imperialistic, patriarchal metaphors for God as not only oppressive but as working against the continuation of life on this planet. She experiments with remythologizing the relation between God and world through the metaphors of mother, lover, and friend.

Miles, Margaret. *Practicing Christianity: Critical Perspectives for an Embodied Spirituality.* New York: Crossroad, 1988. Miles surveys traditional Christian spiritual practices and analyzes these for values regarding body, community, earth, women, and social justice. She develops a critical method for constructing a contemporary practice for Christians. Useful for evaluating the Christian practices we promote.

Nouwen, Henri. *In the Name of Jesus: Reflections on Christian Leadership in the Future.* New York: Crossroad, 1989. A reflection on his own life experience, Nouwen challenges major current perceptions of leadership and describes temptations leaders face in the desire to be relevant, popular, and powerful. Intended to be a source of inspiration and renewal, this is just one of many books by this widely published spiritual guide.

Peck, M. Scott. *The Different Drum: Community Making and Peace.* New York: Simon and Schuster, Inc., 1988. This book has become the manual for many groups seeking to develop community life and commitment. Peck correlates the small community's journey with the individual's spiritual search and with the larger society in the institutions of the Christian Church in the United States, the U.S. government, and the U.S. arms race.

Perkins, Pheme. *Love Commands in the New Testament.* Ramsey, N.J.: Paulist Press, 1982. This short but packed book is a study of New Testament ethics in its cultural setting. A biblical scholar, Perkins shows how the early Christian community's behavior sprang from the way in which it viewed itself in relation to God and creation. The key to this relationship was love with a "critical edge." The book contains study questions at the end of each chapter.

Roof, Wade Clark. *A Generation of Seekers: The Spiritual Journeys of the Baby Boom Generation.* San Francisco: Harper, 1993

Whitehead, Evelyn Eaton and James D. *Seasons of Strength: New Visions of Adult Christian Maturing.* Garden City, N.Y.: Doubleday and Company, 1984. The Whiteheads have published many books in the area of education and ministry, bringing together the social sciences and Christian theology. This one focuses on Christian adulthood, re-envisioning the patterns of power, confidence, and loss that shape maturity through vocation and virtue. The reflective exercises at the end of

each chapter are helpful in integrating the material on a personal level.

Periodicals

Creation: Earthy Spirituality for an Evolving Planet is published by Friends of Creation Spirituality. [Subscriptions: *Creation*, 160 E. Virginia Street, #290, San Jose, California 95112.] *Creation* explores connections among science, mysticism, art, and current issues in our culture in order to heal the split between spirit and matter, body and soul, man and woman, God and world. It also includes columns on liturgy, art as meditation, and ritual.

Human Development: The Jesuit Education Center for Human Development. [Subscriptions: *Human Development*, Box 3000, Dept. HD, Denville, New Jersey 07834.] This journal is designed for those involved with religious leadership and formation, spiritual direction, pastoral care, and education to foster their personal growth and those they serve. It features current knowledge from the fields of psychology, psychiatry, medicine, and spirituality.

Praying: Spirituality for Everyday Living. [Subscriptions: *Praying*, P.O. Box 419335, Kansas City, Missouri 64141.] This bimonthly journal from the National Catholic Reporter Publishing Company offers fresh and integrating views on various practical aspects of spirituality using well-known down-to-earth writers and approaches.

The Way: Review of Contemporary Christian Spirituality. [Subscriptions: *The Way*, Subscriptions Department, 114 Mount Street, London, England W1Y 6AN.] Each issue centers on a theme in spirituality (e.g., RCIA process, spiritual direction, Ignatian spirituality, creation spirituality, community) and offers several book reviews.

Weavings: A Journal of the Christian Spiritual Life. [Subscriptions: *Weavings*, The Upper Room, 1908 Grand Avenue, P.O. Box 189, Nashville, Tennessee 37202.] This journal explores different themes around such issues in spirituality as prayer, woundedness, liturgy, education, and body. It contains excellent articles and book reviews from ecumenical contributors.

The Ecumenical and Interfaith Dimension of Campus Ministry

Rev. Francis Colborn

We affirm the development of ecumenical and interfaith relationships. . . . Mutual trust has grown as members of various religious traditions work together on common programs. . . . We commend this ecumenical and interfaith progress and give full support to greater and more creative efforts in this direction. Catholics who are deeply rooted in their tradition and who maintain a strong sense of identity with their religious heritage will be better prepared to carry out this mission. (ES, 8)

Introduction

Campus ministers work in a variety of settings that offer different opportunities for interaction with other religious traditions. Nevertheless, they share some common concerns, principally, the need to find an approach to interfaith ministry appropriate for the present and the future.

Ministry on college campuses frequently involves collaboration among campus ministers of different faiths and takes many diverse forms. In an unusual instance, Protestant, Catholic, and Jewish clergy are employed full-time as official college chaplains. More frequently, one or more chaplains are employed by a private college, while others are more or less "officially" recognized. There are many campuses where clergy and lay ministers of different faiths work together de facto. In some of these cases, facilities are available on campus for religious activities, while in others, campus ministers must locate their activities off campus.

A Critique of Liberal Ecumenism

Since the situations are so diverse, the activities that can be done cooperatively vary tremendously from one campus to another. Often, a number of realities exist over which there is little or no control. But campus ministers can control their attitude toward working with people of different beliefs. What is the general understanding of interfaith ministry on campus? What is the vision? What are the goals?

In an earlier era, ministers of different religions worked in the same setting without much contact or even much friendliness. A preconciliar mentality painted the others as rivals, even enemies. The Second Vatican Council's statements on the Church, on ecumenism, and on non-Christian religions promoted a different approach. The Church came to see ecumenism as a search for understanding of "our separated brothers and sisters." Even those who were not Christians could somehow be seen, in the words of the Council, as "related to the Body of Christ." Campus ministers looked for opportunities to dialogue about theology. They set about building coalitions to work for peace and justice.

Soon enough, this "Vatican II" approach was challenged by another, more liberal, view of interreligious dialogue. Differences among Christian denominations seemed to be diminishing. Differences among Jews and Christians seemed less important than a shared "Judeo-Christian tradition." Indeed, all the great religions of the world seemed to be about the same thing: promoting the spiritual development of the individual.

One campus minister described her view of ministry thus:

> All religious expressions are like the welling up, in different spots, of one great underground stream of spirituality. The minister's role is to help people get in touch with the stream and express it in whatever way seems best to the individuals in question.

Practically, this meant de-emphasizing religious teaching and traditional ritual. Openness to all forms of religious expression, however idiosyncratic, became normative.

Recently, this "liberal" view has come under criticism. This individualistic notion of spirituality seems to have roots in what Ernst Troeltsch called the "mystical" form of religion and seems to be related to those traditions that emphasize justification by interior religious experience. Such a view certainly accords well with the modern culture of individualism but may be difficult to reconcile with the Catholic understanding of "community."

Furthermore, some Jews protest talk of "Judeo-Christian tradition" as a subtle attempt to deny them their distinctive Jewish heritage by submerging them in a liberal version of Christianity. Is the modern liberal approach, then, a kind of religious-cultural imperialism? More philosophically, is the "modern" view of religion a form of Kantian rationalism? In other words, is religion to be reduced to a religion of "pure reason"? And if so, who will define what is rational—a liberal middle-class elite?

Finally, is the modern view of relationships among diverse religions simply an ideology in service of the powers that be? Religious particularism and traditionalism may be obstacles to international commerce. Multinational corporations need, not religious fanatics, but rational agents who are moved by the calculations of self-interest. The military-industrial complex is best served by people who regard religion as a private affair, not by passionate partisans of moralistic politics.

Postmodern Ecumenism

What is a postliberal view of interreligious ministry? How would campus ministry look in a postmodern view of the world? To begin with, it would address the modern world—the dominant institutions of society, including educational institutions—with a real desire to understand and to communicate. No retreat to the preconciliar mentality; no withdrawal to the cultural ghetto of premodern Catholicism.

In a postmodern frame of mind, people rediscover their roots in tradition and in the importance of their religious and cultural communities. Catholics can affirm strongly their own Catholicism, while affirming just as strongly the pride of others in being Jewish or Hindu or whatever. What is sought is understanding of others who are different, precisely because they are different, rather than some illusory consensus of "what all reasonable people must see."

Some people see this as the road to agnosticism. If all knowledge is an expression of particular traditions and values, is truth possible? Christian ecumenism over the last twenty-five years sheds some light on this question. By listening to others, people can really learn something about their own tradition. They are not less Catholic because they have learned from Protestants, but they have changed in their understanding of Catholicism.

One postmodern approach to interreligious work, then, is not to seek least-common-denominator consensus nor to abandon the search for religious truth as hopeless, but to seek mutual enrichment and shared learning by comparing differences. This approach may give campus ministers some basis for a concerted address to the issues of justice and peace that affect us all.

Since the "modern" worldview is still dominant, the meaning of a postmodern worldview must remain sketchy and incomplete. Moreover, any such view must imply that a multitude of worldviews will continue to coexist; in other words, the theory predicts that not everyone will accept it. Some will continue to approach campus ministry with premodern views of the Church and the world, while others will find the modern, liberal worldview perfectly acceptable. A postmodern approach, as described above, has some advantages. It corresponds with historical and cultural influences emphasized by many postmodern thinkers. It allows for an open-minded tolerance toward people of different beliefs—or of no belief.

> To go beyond the modern, liberal view of things means to enter into critical dialogue with that view, rather than simply to embrace it. On issues of war and peace, of life and death, of economic justice, of sexual ethics, and of many others, postliberal thinkers may find themselves holding minority opinions. To be a minority, to dissent from the views held by the majority of modern academics, does not necessarily mean to be wrong. Of course, it does not automatically mean being right, either. The arguments have to be waged in terms other than those of "scholarly consensus" or "as we all know. . . ."

At the same time, it enables us to give clear witness to our own convictions as ministers of the Gospel.

Structuring Ecumenism on Campus

Where there is no preexisting structure for cooperation, campus ministers will have to reach out to others to establish networks for communication and sharing. At one large state university, representatives from different denominations agree to meet monthly to share ideas on helping students and on the approaches to ministry of differing religious traditions. At another college, the campus ministers have formed a "United Campus Ministry" board, with officers, by-laws, and committees for social, spiritual, and service activities. In other cases, the structure of "chaplaincy" is inherited, and what remains is for the persons involved to develop positive working relationships.

Where there is some sharing of concerns and joint planning, more serious conversation (dialogue) follows. A Jewish and a Catholic chaplain have, for example, cosponsored a discussion of Catholic-Jewish relations at a time of some tension over papal policies toward issues of concern to Jews. Campus ministers have joined with international student groups to invite experts to talk about the diverse religions and cultures of the world. Panels of speakers on sexuality, on spiritual expression through music, on diverse interpretations of Scripture, and on women in ministry have addressed these and other issues from the perspective of various religious traditions. In addition to programs for students, there are, in some places, opportunities for campus ministers to engage in ongoing dialogue with theologians of other religions.

Beyond dialogue or, perhaps, accompanying these conversations, campus ministers may engage in joint action for service to others. Some campus ministers have cosponsored, with other religious and secular groups, volunteer programs in which students engage in community service. "Witness for Peace" is another area that offers opportunities for interfaith cooperation. In some settings, it is possible for campus groups with religious inspiration to join neighborhood community organizations to work for justice in local communities. All such activities promote cooperation, not only with people of other religions, but with those of no religion who care about serving the world.

Sharing in prayer and religious celebration may be the ultimate step, or at least the most delicate one, in interreligious ministry. Obviously, great sensitivity is needed to allow people to pray together without imposing one set of ideas on others. Nevertheless, there are some good examples of such interfaith spiritual sharing. In one place, Protestants and Catholics could join together in an Ash Wednesday service. In another, the December holidays could provide an occasion for celebrating a "Festival of Lights": lighting of candles, blessing of a decorated tree, a festive dinner, and explanation of Christmas and Hanukkah as a feast of light. Thanksgiving is another occasion for coming together, either simply to express thanks to God or to share a turkey dinner (kosher, of course). The Jewish celebration of Sukkoth can be a time for Jews and Christians to pray for peace together. Experience has shown that campus ministers can find opportunities for this kind of sharing.

Realism demands some mention of the difficulties that interfaith cooperation can encounter. The basic need, after centuries of mistrust, is for people to approach "the others" with sensitivity and respect. Catholic campus ministers may encounter two different kinds of difficulties. On the one hand, there are fundamentalist Christian groups who are still reluctant to acknowledge Catholics as real Christians. They may engage in hard-sell proselytism directed at Catholics. They may or may not be willing to enter into dialogue to promote mutual understanding. On the other hand, some more liberal groups may not only disagree with particular teachings of the Catholic Church, but may even resent what they see as Catholic intransigence on some issues. Disagreement, if not accompanied by respect, can lead to hostility toward campus ministers who represent the Catholic Church.

Empowered by the Spirit addressed such problems: "To those who demonstrate less tolerant attitudes, we extend an invitation to join in the dialogue" (ES, 8). Perhaps this is an implicit reminder to Catholic campus ministers of their essential purpose. God has not sent them onto the campus to win all arguments or to solve all problems or to make everyone like them. Their ministry is one of service. While faithfully witnessing to their tradition and beliefs, they are called to listen respectfully to others. Where they meet reciprocal willingness to engage in interfaith cooperation, they can enhance their ministry. Where campus ministers do not find such willingness, they are called to persevere in their invitation to dialogue. If no one else benefits from their effort, at least they themselves may learn something.

It may be helpful to bear in mind two slogans taken from very different sources. One is "No pain, no gain." Another, more profound one is "God does not call us to be successful but to be faithful." The success of interreligious ministry, as of everything else, is in God's hands.

Programs for Interfaith Ministry

1. "Talk It Out"—Interfaith Dialogue

This program is the center of the Campus Interfaith Ministry at Wilkes University. It is a weekly program that brings together students from a wide variety of faith traditions (Catholic, Protestant, Jewish, Muslim) to dialogue on a variety of subjects etc. The program has a few core elements:

1. A paper each week from a different faith tradition;
2. A meal prepared by one or two students to be shared by all. The meal is usually an expression of the students' tradition (e.g., a Jewish student prepared a meal of falafel);
3. Discussion around a variety of subjects—relationship, stress, to prayer, and beyond. The goal is to see where faith traditions are similar and to be open to the differences. Out of these sharings comes service work through various projects and social gatherings.

Contact:
Mary Hession
Wilkes University
134 S. Washington St.
Wilkes Barre, Pennsylvania 18701
Tel. 717-831-5904

Place: Wilkes University

2. Interfaith Thanksgiving Service

A kosher turkey dinner can be prepared by the kosher dining room staff on campus. Chaplains and students participate in the readings and blessings. The meal is served after the significance of each part has been explained.

Contact:
Margaret Ann Landry, RSHM
SUNY-Stony Brook, Humanities 158
Stony Brook, L.I., New York 11794
Tel. 516-632-6562

Place:
SUNY-Stony Brook University

3. Holiday Celebration: Festival of Lights

The program brings together Christian and Jewish students to celebrate the December holidays. A ceremony can be developed that includes music, lighting of candles, lighting and blessing of a fir tree, and an explanation of Christmas and Hanukkah as festivals of light, as well as a festive dinner.

Contact:
Rev. Robert J. Lord
108 Fifth Avenue
Milford, Connecticut 06460-1297
Tel. 860-874-3184

Place:
Central Connecticut State University

4. Interfaith Holy Week Celebrations

Two important Holy Week celebrations for the Christian and Jewish communities are a Good Friday prayer service and the Seder meal. The Hillel and Catholic student groups come together to share a Seder meal. This is led by the Jewish group. The Christian groups on campus cosponsor a Good Friday service. This always includes a contemporary/dramatic retelling of the passion account by the faculty and students.

Contact:
Dr. Michael Galligan-Stierle
Wheeling Jesuit College
Wheeling, West Virginia 26003
Tel. 304-243-2385

Place: Wheeling Jesuit College

5. Ash Wednesday Service

By hosting a Christian Ash Wednesday service with Catholic and Protestant chaplains, university people of various Christian religions can share the beginning day of Lent in prayer together. The Ash Wednesday service is created by the campus chaplains who presided.

Contact:
Dr. Michael Galligan-Stierle
Wheeling Jesuit College
Wheeling, West Virginia 26003
Tel. 304-243-2385

Place: Wheeling Jesuit College

6. *Religious Diversity Day*

A one-day exhibit in the Student Union building could include representatives of Roman Catholic, Episcopalian, Presbyterian, Methodist, Lutheran, Greek Orthodox, Jewish, and other denominations. Display tables can be set up and handouts provided for those interested in learning about the various traditions. Videotapes about Judaism and Orthodoxy could be shown. A panel discussion on sexuality in different religious traditions could conclude the day.

Contact:
Margaret Ann Landry, RSHM
SUNY-Stony Brook, Humanities 158
Stony Brook, L.I., New York 11794
Tel. 516-632-6562

Place: SUNY-Stony Brook University

7. *"Religious Workers Association" Dialogue*

A panel of six people, representing six different traditions (e.g., Christian mainline Church, Christian evangelical, Jewish, Moslem, Bahai, and so forth), convene monthly to discuss different topics and to explain what each tradition holds as "teaching" or doctrine on those topics. The program helps participants to get to know and respect each other. It is an opportunity for speakers to set aside religious differences and work on understanding the religious goals of each tradition. The topics should be varied, such as the religious concerns of students or the nature of our ministry.

Contact:
Rev. David Turner, OSB
5700 College Road
Lisle, Illinois 60532
Tel. 708-960-1500/4088

Place:
University of Illinois at
Urbana-Champagne

8. *Lecture Series on Religious Diversity*

A Newman Association lecture series includes speakers from Catholic, Anglican, Protestant, Jewish, Hindu, and other perspectives.

Contact:
Sr. Madeleine Tacy, OP
856 Tucker Rd.
N. Dartmouth, Massachusetts 02747-3531
Tel. 508-999-8872

Place:
University of Massachusetts - Dartmouth

9. *Interreligious/Intercultural Speaker Series*

This program promotes knowledge of world religions and their cultural contexts. The Catholic chaplain and the director of the International Student Center meet with a student committee to formulate plans. Since the center on our campus has a popular Thursday Luncheon Program, it was decided to incorporate the series on Religions and Cultures of the World into that program. An appropriate time can be selected for your particular campus. It is best to begin with the less well-known Asian religions and to ask each speaker to discuss the relationship between his or her tradition and "justice and peace." Attendance at our luncheons averaged about 200 at each of the four events. Presentors included an excellent Hindu speaker, a Buddhist speaker (who drew the largest crowd), an expert on African religions, and a Christian-Jewish-Muslim "trialogue."

Contact:
Sr. Candace Introcaso, CDP
919 N. Columbia
Claremont, California 91711
Tel. 909-621-8825

Place: The Claremont Colleges

10. *Interreligious Retreat*

The Protestant, Catholic, and Jewish chaplains at a private college campus recruit a small group (no more than fifteen) of Christian and Jewish students to take part in an overnight retreat. The starting assumptions are first, our differences are real and important; second, we can understand each other best by sharing stories of personal experiences; third, we can benefit from tackling hard questions. Students and chaplains, too, share their responses to these questions: What have been your best experiences of God within your own religious tradition? and What are the things you find most difficult about other people's religious traditions? This type of a retreat offers the opportunity for a deep, serious, and, perhaps, difficult experience of unity and diversity and of the presence of God among us.

Contact:
Sr. Candace Introcaso, CDP
919 N. Columbia
Claremont, California 91711
Tel. 909-621-8825

Place:
The Claremont Colleges

Resources for the Ecumenical and Interfaith Dimension of Campus Ministry

Books/Articles

Griffin, David Ray. "A Theology of Religious Pluralism: A Postmodern Approach," in *Ailanthus* (Summer 1990): 1-26. Explains what a postmodern approach might be from the standpoint of process theology. Originally given at a campus ministers' convention (NACUC).

Hagan, Charles H. "The Challenge of Jehovah's Witnesses" in *The Living Light* 31 (Spring 1994): 66-72.

Nelson, J. Robert. "The Ecumenical Challenge of Ethical Issues," in *Origins* 18:45 (April 20, 1989): 762-770. Good overview and analysis of issues, with potential for collaboration and/or controversy.

Ojo, Benedict Bimbola. "When Sects Threaten Your Parish", in *The Priest* (January 1996): 8-10.

Parsonage, Robert R., ed. *Invitation to Dialogue: The Theology of College Chaplaincy and Campus Ministry*. New York: Education in the Society, National Council of the Churches of Christ in the USA, 1986.

Rankin, Robert, ed. The Recovery of Spirit in Higher Education: Christian and Jewish Ministries in Campus Life: New York: Seabury Press, 1980.

Rausch, Thomas. "Ethical Issues in Ecumenism," in *America* 160:2 (January 21, 1989): 30-33. Report on an ecumenical discussion of issues of concern to campus ministers and others.

The Evangelization Dimension of Campus Ministry

Rev. Carl B. Trutter, OP

The goal is an adult appropriation of the faith that fosters personal commitment to Christ and encourages intelligent witness in the world on behalf of the Gospel. (ES, 58)

Introduction

Assisting people on campus with their faith development is a primary task for campus ministers. This task is best understood in light of the gospel mandate to evangelize. Catholic evangelization, however, must be distinguished from the specific recruitment practices of other religious groups on campus. Moreover, the depth and breadth of Catholic evangelization have unique challenges and opportunities within the university environment. Paul VI spoke to the heart of Catholic evangelization in 1975, when he wrote:

> For the Church, evangelizing means bringing the Good News into all the strata of humanity, and through its influence transforming humanity from within and making it new: "Now I am making the whole of creation new." (*On Evangelization in the Modern World*, 18)

Any discussion of Catholic evangelization within the university milieu must take into account four realities:

1. Students between the ages of eighteen and thirty are experiencing a period of significant change in their religious attitudes, values, beliefs, and practices.
2. There are other religious groups on campus willing and able to address the religious search of college students. Some of these groups may use questionable recruitment practices.
3. The university has standards on behavior, rhetoric, and discussion that define credible public intercourse and debate.
4. Catholics, in any context, have deeply held values and convictions to share: belief in a loving God, a relationship with Jesus Christ, a human and historical Church that responds to the needs of others, and a commitment to reason and education.

A closer look at these four realities will provide a framework for Catholic evangelization on campus and suggest some practical ways campus ministry can fulfill the gospel mandate to "make disciples of all nations" (Mt 28:19).

Religious Change Among Students

College students often live in an in-between time of religious conviction and practice. They have usually left behind the fairly stable patterns of their nuclear family. They have not yet identified their own careers, value systems, or lifestyles. During these in-between years, students gradually alter their feelings and beliefs about God, organized religion, and morality; they may significantly change the way they live out their feelings and beliefs.

Although it is difficult to articulate the many dimensions of religious change, the most visible behavior is their absence at Sunday Mass. Studies verify this, and certainly campus ministers experience it.

David Roozen claims that "about 42 percent of Catholics drop out of church attendance for two years or longer sometime in their lives. Over half the dropping out occurs in the teen years and early twenties, and the more highly educated young people tend to drop out relatively more often. Of the dropouts, the majority return sometime in their lives" (Roozen, 1980).

Other common patterns of change for Catholic students include the following:

▲ adopting a personalized, individualized religion that is separated from organized religious life;

▲ investigating and joining a para-church or fundamentalist group, often through the invitation of other students;

- entering another Christian denomination on the occasion of marrying a person of that denomination; and
- becoming agnostic or atheistic because of bad experiences of church, through the influence of anti-religious professors or through their own studies of philosophy, religion, or history.

The reason that students change their attitude about religion, and especially why they drop out, is a mixture of many factors. Dean R. Hoge, et al. identify the following nine factors that significantly influence the student's religious belief and practice:

1. freedom in making decisions after leaving or rebelling against earlier support groups (e.g., friends, family);
2. academic, social, and athletic activities occupying their attention;
3. problems with or objections to the Church, its teachings, its members, its leaders;
4. moving from the family parish and not being drawn into religious life on campus;
5. the Church's lack of help in providing meaning and purpose to life or the perception that church activities are boring and uninteresting;
6. the person's lifestyle incompatibility with participation in church life, especially sexual practices that are contrary to official sexual mores of the Church;
7. professors and academic pursuits that challenge previous views on religion and Church;
8. pressure from peers with a diversity of attitudes and practices concerning religion; and
9. organized proselytizing by evangelical, fundamentalist para-church groups or cults that convince an individual to abandon his or her former religious beliefs (Hoge, et al., p. 11).

To respond faithfully to these factors in student lives, campus ministers must remember that Catholic evangelization is always first and foremost the proclamation of the Gospel to those who are Catholic. It is the attempt to present the Good News in ways to rekindle in the hearts of believers, however weak or strong their faith may be, a life of faith.

Other Religious Groups on Campus

John Butler argues that "religion is quantitatively and qualitatively more diverse and more present on campus than it ever has been" (Butler, p. 15). Any dean of students can quickly list the various religious groups that are officially organized on campus and those that are unofficially active.

These religious groups can be broken down into a number of categories: (1) mainline Christian denominations; (2) other religions (e.g., Jewish, Islam); (3) para-church Christian organizations (e.g., Inter-Varsity, Campus Crusade, Navigators); (4) independent church groups (e.g., the Boston Church of God); and (5) new religious movements (e.g., the Unification Church, New Age, neo-pagan groups).

The relationship between and among these groups vary from campus to campus, as can their day-to-day working relationship with the university. Many campuses enjoy excellent ecumenical and interfaith relations and open, positive, and mutually supportive relationships with the university. There are some campuses, however, where either no cooperation exists among religious groups or there is hostility within the groups against one or more of them. Also, some university administrations are very reluctant to work with religious groups on campus.

The outreach of these various religious groups may range from a passive form of hospitality to a very aggressive recruitment drive. The local Lutheran campus ministry may have an "all are welcome" notice on their worship announcements, whereas a fundamentalist group may pursue students to the extent that they harass them in their classes and in their homes. The continuum of techniques include an open-door policy, invitations, visiting, deception, and harassment.

Catholic evangelization within this pluralistic context must be extremely sensitive to the beliefs and practices of other religious groups without minimizing the value of the Catholic tradition.

Credibility with the University

The university is founded on the lofty goals of truth, education, and service to humanity. It values critical thinking and the unbridled search for knowledge. It has established, through its search of history, testing of different methods, and assimilation of various philosophies, a set of standards for behavior, argumentation, discussion, and debate.

The university will not tolerate religious organizations and activities that fail to recognize and support either its goals or methods. Many administrators dismiss religious persons or groups that do not follow campus guidelines. Faculty may challenge claims of various religious ideologies in their courses. Student personnel administrators may focus exclusively on the behavior of students and challenge religious activities and practices.

In this context, Catholic evangelization must be credible in the eyes of the university. The Church must acknowledge the common history it shares with higher education and rightfully claim its rich tradition of support. Campus ministries need to be aware of the mission, purpose, and goals of the university and seek to reflect them in their activities. Campus ministers must be willing and able to argue for the role the Church plays on campus. Students and campus ministers need to be able to engage faculty openly on the religious and moral implications for their disciplines. Student personnel administrators also need the benefit of a value perspective that transcends specific behavioral concerns.

In many ways, the standards of the university define the rules for Catholic evangelization. These rules are to be freely and faithfully embraced by the local campus ministry as invitations to demonstrate the perennial power of the Gospel.

Faith on Campus

Once a Catholic student or a faculty member places one's foot on university soil, the Church is on campus. Due to the large number of Catholics on campus today, it is impossible to deny the impact that Catholicism is having, and will have, on the university.

These Catholics on campus bring with them a distinct religious heritage, varying degrees of church involvement, and a wide variety of spiritualities. Nevertheless, all

these people are Catholic and will draw from their understanding of their religious tradition as they teach or attend their classes, conduct their research, debate policy, and organize campus life.

Campus ministry is the official presence of the Church on campus, which is responsible for gathering the faithful on campus to nurture their own faith lives, to support the development of the university, and to attend to the needs of others. Catholic evangelization permeates all these responsibilities. The Church on campus need not be apologetic about its beliefs or shy about its convictions. Interesting and exciting campus activities are important ways to evangelize. Campus ministers can, however, design explicit programs to impact the Catholic community on campus, the university, and others.

Conclusion

Catholic evangelization is one dimension of campus ministry. It seeks to enrich the faith life of Catholics, respect the religious traditions of others, embrace the standards of the university, and share the Catholic faith with others. Catholic evangelization is characterized by a deep reverence for the unique activity of God in the life of the individual and avoids any techniques that hinder individual freedom and conscience. Campus ministries have developed a wide variety of programs that intentionally reach out to Catholics on campus, to the university, and to others interested in the Catholic faith.

Programs for Catholic Evangelization

1. *The Evangelization Team*

This is a select group of students who volunteer to be trained in the spirituality, goals, and methods of Catholic evangelization. They become a living witness so others can be encouraged to share their faith with their peers. An excellent example of this approach is the Catholic Commission, a movement of Catholic college students founded at the University of Arizona Newman Center, Tucson, in 1985. Their focus is to reach out to the college students of America with the goal of proclaiming the message of Jesus Christ to the world.

2. Small Communities

These are small groups formed around common interests, ministries, or peer associations. Examples could be a peer ministry group, liturgical choirs, volunteer groups, and retreat groups. The gatherings of these groups may include all or some of the following five elements: (1) informal sharing of their personal faith stories; (2) discussion of Scripture or current topics; (3) participation in a common project, such as working in a soup kitchen or planning a campus retreat; (4) sharing prayer and song; and (5) inviting a guest presenter followed by an open discussion. These small faith communities are formed with the purpose of supporting and enabling the personal growth of the group members.

3. Individual Evangelization

Active Catholic students can be encouraged to share their faith by good example, by talking with friends about their beliefs and practices, and by inviting friends to campus ministry activities (e.g., socials, liturgies, and discussion groups). Campus ministers can reach active Catholic students through talks with leaders, well-prepared homilies and liturgies, newsletters, and campus ministry bulletins.

4. RCIA

The Rite of Christian Initiation of Adults is an ideal model for the process and ritual of evangelization. The RCIA, with roots in the early centuries of Christianity, is a parish-based approach to evangelization and will require some adaptation. Any campus setting, either a large residential school or a small commuter campus, can use the RCIA. Incorporation into the Catholic Church, through regular faith-sharing sessions and the rites of acceptance, election, and the sacraments of initiation at the Easter Vigil, is the end result of this dynamic process.

5. Retreats

Weekend retreats or days of renewal serve as an excellent way to deepen a person's faith. Some campus ministries use a definite model, such as "Search"; others will use retreat professionals or a student team. Retreats and days of renewal use a blend of the following elements: (1) time away from the academic setting; (2) the opportunity to develop a small community of faith; (3) the opportunity to hear, to reflect, and to discuss the various aspects of Catholic living; and (4) the chance to pray and play in an informal way.

6. Religious Affairs Committees

Many times, a university will encourage the development of a religious affairs committee that monitors the religious groups on campus and provides a liaison between these groups and the university. Many of these committees, like the one at the University of Nebraska, write a code of ethics to govern the recruitment techniques used by religious groups on campus. These committees are an excellent way to establish a good working relationship among different religious groups and with the university's administration.

7. Public Discussion

There are many opportunities to engage different disciplines within the university in a public exploration of current issues. Campus ministers can sponsor a lecture series; cosponsor an ethics seminar with other religious groups; participate in a university- or student-sponsored presentation; volunteer as a panelist for different symposiums; and be available for guest lecturing. All these events give the campus minister a public opportunity to say what the Church believes and how that belief is relevant to the world today.

Resources for the Evangelization Dimension of Campus Ministry

Books

Bohr, David. *Evangelization in America.* New York: Paulist Press, 1977. A lengthy study dealing with proclaiming the Good News, living the Good News, and past and current history of evangelization in the Catholic Church in the United States.

Butler, John, ed. *Religion on Campus.* San Francisco, Calif.: Jossey-Bass, Inc., 1989.

Gallup, George, Jr. and Jim Castelli. *The People's Religion.* New York: MacMillan Publishing Co., 1989. The shape of American faith for the 1990s, resulting from years of research and polling of people about, among other things, their attitudes toward separation of church and state, abortion, gun control, communism, premarital sex, and education.

—. and David Poling. *The Search for America's Faith.* Nashville, Tenn.: Abingdon Press, 1980. A fascinating book that links current sociological facts (e.g., on the yearnings of youth, on positive aspects of the Catholic Church in the United States) with projections for the future as already unfolding in the United States.

Hoge, Dean R., Kenneth McGuire, CSP, and Bernard F. Stratman, SM, eds. *Converts, Dropouts, Returnees: A Study of Religious Change among Catholics.* Washington, D.C.: United States Catholic Conference, 1981. Descriptions about who converts, dropouts, and returnees are in the United States, with statistical typologies of converts, dropouts, and returnees. Includes an Appendix, by Alvin A. Illig, CSP, that gives concrete suggestions to stimulate creative planning.

Rauff, Edward A. *Why People Join the Church.* Washington, D.C.: Glenmary Research Center, 1979. An exploratory study based on personal interviews in diverse sections of the United States, with chapters on "Evangelizing and Being Evangelized" and "Implications for the Church."

Documents

Ad Hoc Committee on Biblical Fundamentalism, National Conference of Catholic Bishops. *A Pastoral Statement for Catholics on Biblical Fundamentalism.* March 26, 1987. English-Spanish Edition. Washington, D.C.: United States Catholic Conference, 1987. This statement discusses how fundamentalism "is typified by unyielding adherence to rigid doctrinal and ideological positions" and discusses the Catholic response as a community of faith, which is the Lord's Church with a living tradition that presents God's word across the centuries.

Paul VI. *On Evangelization in the Modern World.* Apostolic Exhortation. December 8, 1975. Washington, D.C.: United States Catholic Conference, 1976. An elaborate consideration of the basic contemporary church teaching on Catholic evangelization, including the Church as evangelizer, description, content, methods, beneficiaries, workers, and spirit of evangelization.

Synod of Bishops. *Declaration on Evangelization.* Rome: Synod of Bishops, October 25, 1974. This declaration contains the seminal statement that "the mandate to evangelize all constitutes the essential mission of the Church" and addresses young people in evangelization, difficulties to evangelization, and the relation between liberation and evangelization.

Booklets

Princeton Religion Research Center. *Faith Development and Your Ministry.* Princeton, N.J.: Princeton Religion Research Center, 1985. A report based on a Gallup Survey for the Religious Education Association. The report has valuable sections (e.g.,"Styles of Faith"; "Personal Experience and Faith Change"; and ten suggested steps for "Faith Development").

Trutter, Carl B., OP. *Faith on Campus: An Emerging Agenda.* Dayton, Ohio: Catholic Campus Ministry Association, 1989. An essay on the nature and purpose of Catholic evangelization on campus. A good discussion starter.

—. *Sharing Our Faith: A Manual for Catholic College Students.* Dayton, Ohio: Catholic Campus Ministry Association, 1987. A practical guide that campus ministers can use with students to empower them to share their Catholic faith with other students. Contains chapters on attitudes, six steps for sharing one's faith journey, and ministry in the Christian community.

Articles

Roozen, David A. (Hartford Seminary Foundation). "Church Dropouts: Changing Patterns of Disengagement and Re-entry," in *Review of Religious Research* 21:4 (Supplement, 1980): 427-450. A sociological study that suggests that dropping out of church life is a temporary stage in a person's life. Dropping out occurs most frequently during teen years, and the reasons often are moving into a new community or time schedule. Up to 80 percent of religious dropouts re-enter active church involvement, and the re-entry rate is greatest among those between twenty-five and thirty-four years of age.

Trutter, Carl B., OP. "Young Adults Can Share," in *The Catholic Evangelist* II:6. Insight into the culture of young adults, especially college students, which describes five main difficulties to and four positive steps for evangelization by Catholic young adults.

——. "Sharing Faith at the University," in *Process: The Journal of the CCMA* V:3. A description of concrete models for evangelization on college campuses, especially through support groups of students as peer ministers.

Rev. J.
Friedel

Vocation Ministry on Campus

The dreams of college students are poised for greatness—the dream to master a field of study; to have the perfect, fulfilling job; to make a difference in the world; or to be a phenomenal teacher, doctor, biologist, or cellist. Some of these dreams have been minutely detailed, intricate with tiny features; others have been painted with only the broadest of strokes, waiting for more to unfold. Where do the dreams come from, and how do they become clearer for the dreamer?

The task of ministry is the naming of the mystery as it plays itself out in our lives. Each dream, which comes from God and ends in God, is a mysterious call that invites our response. God calls each of us to greatness in fulfilling our own unique dream. Many on our campuses are still searching for their dreams. Others are trying to make sense of the dreams they've been given. As campus ministers we are vocation ministers, for part of our task is assisting our students and the university community in discerning the ways in which they are called to respond to their individual dreams from God.

How then do we go about the business of helping people to discern their dreams? How do we invite members of our campus community to consider all of the various options available to them as members of the faithful—religious life and priesthood, as well as single life and marriage? How do we maintain an awareness of the equal dignity of each particular vocation, yet make certain that we give adequate exposure to the vocations of service in the Church?

To be "sign and instrument of the kingdom" on our campuses, we must take our responsibility as vocation ministers seriously. We must examine our own attitudes toward vocation ministry, raise awareness of the necessary search for the dream in each member of the faithful, and actively recruit individuals to seriously consider service in the Church as lay ministers, priests, and brothers and sisters.

Examining Our Own Attitudes

The attitude of the campus minster is key to any type of vocation ministry on campus. It seems clear that assisting members of the campus community to recognize and follow their dreams fits in very easily with our stated vision of campus ministry, especially when we speak of "Forming Faith Communities," "Facilitating Personal Development," and "Developing Leaders for the Future." It is crucial that we begin to see that campus ministry is vocation ministry.

Two major stumbling blocks often threaten the positive promotion of vocation ministry on campus. The first concerns the relationship between vocation ministers and campus ministers. Real or perceived, ministers of both groups have stated that the "other" has simply not been supportive of their efforts. Let us remember that there is no "other" in the Body of Christ; we are working toward the same purpose and goal! We need to understand and appreciate one another, and this will happen only through honest conversation and active, patient cooperation on common endeavors. Let the "brainstorming" and "collaboration" begin!

The other difficulty centers on those working in campus ministry whose experiences make it difficult for them to positively support or invite others in particular vocation choices. The prophetic words of Cardinal Joseph Bernardin in his address to the Catholic Campus Ministry Association national convention in January 1989 seem an appropriate response:

> At this time in our history, it might seem foolhardy to some, and outrageous to others, that I propose, for example, that women working in campus ministry invite young men whom they esteem to think about the possibility of diocesan priesthood. But that is part of what I am

suggesting. I am also recommending that campus ministers invite and encourage young men and women to consider religious life and other Christian lifestyles and ministries.

The choice before us is clear. We can live with the Church we have, and love it and seek to build it up from within even as we work for renewal and conversion. Or we can retreat from it and let it decline or be directed by voices other than our own.

Raising Awareness

Whether we speak of our actions as being proactive, intentional, or purposeful, the bottom line is that vocation ministry must be explicitly and implicitly woven into the fabric of campus ministry. We need to raise awareness that the search for an individual's personal response to God's call to holiness is a necessary step of any Catholic's maturity. We further need to recognize that this process takes place within the context of the community of the Church. The Church, then, has an obligation to support the discernment process of each individual and uphold the dignity of each vocation discerned.

The first step in heightening our awareness will be to change the way we think. Vocation ministry must stop being equated with religious life and priesthood only. We must speak openly and regularly about all the ways a person can fulfill his/her dream. It is vital that the different options be placed before our campus communities in a consistent manner, lest we give the impression that any one vocation is superior to any other.

Once we begin to change the way we think, additions/changes to our programming will follow. There are many suggestions and resources listed at the end of this article; however, these represent just a few of the many excellent programs that have been developed around the country. Networking is invaluable to creative programming in any area, and vocation awareness is no exception.

It is also important to remember that relationships and example are key to our life in the Church. If we want to model good marriages, we need to ensure the presence of happy, healthy couples in our ministries. If we want to model various forms of religious life, we need to be sure to invite dedicated, life-filled religious to our campuses on a regular basis. The principle holds true for singles and priests, as well.

Active Recruitment

Only if we have done our work in the above areas do we dare begin the process of actively recruiting those who might be called to a life of service in the Church. It will be interpreted that these are the only dreams we care about supporting, however, unless we have laid the groundwork. We can actively recruit for priests only if we have likewise promoted marriage.

There are many dreamers out there waiting for their dreams to unfold. We need to make sure that all members of our campus community have been invited to consider the possibility of a role of service in any of its varied forms. If we encounter a student who shows an aptitude for ministry, we have an obligation as vocation ministers to encourage that student to consider priesthood, religious life, or lay ministry.

The Church needs good ministers. Our campus ministries are staffed with dedicated lay ministers, both single and married, religious and priests. Do we find our lives rewarding enough to invite others to do the same? Hopefully, like those we serve, our dreams are poised for greatness.

Programs and Resources for Vocation Ministry

Vocation Discernment Groups

Various groups have been formed on campuses across the country to support and encourage students who are discerning a possible call to service in the Church. Some of these groups limit themselves to those who are examining the call to religious life and priesthood; others are designed to include those who wish to pursue professional positions as lay ministers. Some of the groups are highly structured, featuring outside speakers and formal programs; others gather for simple prayer and informal discussion. Some meet monthly; others, bi-monthly; still others, weekly. The key to all groups is the creation of a safe, visible forum in which students can explore the possibility of a call to service.

Contacts:
Rev. Dean Wilhelm
St. Mary's Catholic Center
Texas A & M University
103 Nagle Street
College Station, TX 77840
Tel. 409-846-5717

Rev. Ray May
St. Lawrence Center
University of Kansas
1631 Crescent Road
Lawrence, KS 66044
Tel. 913-843-0357

Student Peer Ministry

This program employs post-graduate students who have shown a capacity for ministry to serve the campus community. Working under the supervision of the campus minister, students serve as peer ministers in the areas of retreats, liturgy, and community outreach. Many peer ministers have moved on to the Archdiocese of Washington's "Channel" Program, which invites its participants to do a period of volunteer service, living in community, working in areas of education, social, or parish ministry. Students who feel a possible call to ministry have the opportunity to test that call in an actual role of service.

Contact:
Shirley Osterhaus
Shalom Center
Western Washington University
102 Highland Drive
Bellingham, WA 98225
Tel. 206-733-3400

On-Campus Retreats

This retreat format provides many solutions to retreat programming on campus. The cost is minimal (as vocation ministers volunteer their time as retreat directors), scheduling takes place around other campus activities and classes, and the retreat design couldn't be simpler! Participants gather for orientation on Sunday evening and are assigned to a director. For the next four days, retreatants meet with their director at a mutually agreed upon time and commit themselves to thirty minutes of additional prayer with the Scriptures each day. Perhaps some shared activity among participants is

scheduled in the evening, sharing insights and experiences on the last evening. Through connection with students, vocation ministry is promoted in an implicit way without it being the focus of the retreat experience. Pioneered at Louisiana State University in 1988, this retreat phenomenon is being implemented on numerous campuses across the country.

Contact:
Rev. Pat Mascarella
Catholic Student Center
Louisiana State University
P.O. Box 25131
Baton Rouge, LA 70894-5131
Tel. 504-344-8595

LifeQuest—A Retreat for Discernment

In November 1992 the Diocese of Springfield-Cape Girardeau and the Vincentian Priests and Brothers of the Midwest Province sponsored the first LifeQuest Discernment Retreat. Since that time, there have been several such retreats at various locations throughout the Midwest. LifeQuest is for any Catholic woman or man between the ages of eighteen and forty who is unmarried, curious about religious life or priesthood, and open to the questions of others who are searching. LifeQuest is not considered a "recruitment tool" for any particular group; those who volunteer their time see themselves in a role of service to the larger Church by helping men and women explore the possibility of sisterhood, brotherhood, or priesthood.

Contact:
Rose Jean Powers, OSU
Campus Ministry
Brescia College
717 Frederica Street
Owensboro, KY 42301-3023
Tel. 502-686-4334

Vocation Mass

A special Mass is held monthly to pray for young people who are still exploring which particular way God is calling them to live their lives. Surrounding parishes from the region are invited to participate with the university community, fostering a supportive environment between the campus and the larger Church. Those considering vocations of service in the Church feel the encouragement from regular, visible prayer, and all are reminded of the dignity of every particular vocation.

Contact:
Rev. J. Friedel
Catholic Campus Ministry
Southeast Missouri State University
512 N. Pacific
Cape Girardeau, MO 63701
Tel. 314-335-3899

Vocation Directors and Campus Ministers Co-Op

The purpose of this group from Northern California is to bring campus ministers and vocation directors together regularly to collaborate on various activities. Recent successes include an inter-collegiate retreat, a pilgrimage to Taize, a vocation and volunteer resources fair, facilitation of lunch/Scripture groups on campuses by vocation ministers, and compilation of a resource directory of these ministers with their particular gifts to share with each other. It would seem that this group has broken the barrier between their "worlds" and is reaping the benefits of shared ministries.

Contacts:
Ritzi Centano Faust
Campus Ministry Office
University of San Francisco
2130 Fulton
San Francisco, CA 94117-1080
Tel. 415-666-6582

Your own diocesan vocation office
or National Conference of Diocesan
Vocation Directors
P.O. Box 1570
Little River, SC 29566
Tel. 803-280-7191

Religious vocation ministers in your area
or National Religious Vocation Conference
1603 S. Michigan Avenue, #400
Chicago, IL 60616
Tel. 312-663-5454

"Vocation Ministry on Campus"—A Workshop

This one-day workshop, offered through the Catholic Campus Ministry Association, helps campus ministers explore vocation ministry as an integral part of spreading the Gospel on campus. Relying on the ideas of Sharon Parks, the workshop examines the many misconceptions about the nature and purpose of vocation ministry and demonstrates how an intentional vocation ministry enhances and strengthens our mission of campus ministry.

Contact:
Don McCrabb
Catholic Campus Ministry Association
300 College Park Avenue
Dayton, OH 45469-2515
Tel. 513-229-4648

Print Resources

Alliance for Vocation Ministry on Campus. *Follow Me: A Pastoral Planning Process for Vocation Ministry on Campus, Revised Edition.* Dayton, Ohio: Catholic Campus Ministry Association, 1994. Brief pamphlet articulating the need for collaboration between vocation ministers and campus ministers. Common ground, goals, and challenges are discussed, including a format for beginning dialogue between these two groups.

National Conference of Catholic Bishops. *A Future Full of Hope: A National Strategy for Vocations to the Priesthood and Religious Life in the Dioceses and Archdioceses of the United States.* Washington, D.C.: United States Catholic Conference, 1995. This document outlines intentional vocation ministry as a necessity for the continued growth of the church in the United States.

Dan Rauzi, SDB. *God Grant Me a Discerning Heart: A Manual for Vocation Discernment.* Chicago: National Religious Vocation Conference, 1995. Resource materials for assisting young people in the process of discernment. Fourteen separate components, usable for both individuals and groups.

Vocation Resource Catalogue. Chicago: National Coalition for Church Vocations. Catalogue of various vocation promotion materials: posters, prayer cards, brochures, workbooks, etc.

Volunteer Opportunities

Connections: A Directory of Volunteer Opportunities. Washington, D.C.: St. Vincent Pallotti Center for Apostolic Development. Published annually. 202-529-3330.

Opportunities: An Annual Volunteer Service Handbook. Evanston, Ill.: Berry Publishing Services. Published annually. 800-274-9447.

Response: Volunteer Opportunities Directory. Washington, D.C.: Catholic Network of Volunteer Service. Published annually. 800-543-5046.

Religious Life/Priesthood

A Guide to Religious Ministries for Catholic Men and Women. New Rochelle, N.Y.: Catholic News Publishing Company. Published annually. 914-632-1220.

Vision: The Annual Religious Vocation Discernment Handbook. Chicago: National Religious Vocation Conference. Published annually. 312-663-5454.

Your Choice: A Handbook for Catholic Young Adults Seeking Their Place in a Lifetime Ministry. Chicago: National Religious Vocation Conference. Published semi-annually. 312-663-5454.

Aspects of Campus Ministry

Forming Faith Communities

Sr. Kathleen Dorney, CND

The call to form communities of faith flows both from the very nature of the Gospel itself and from the pastoral situation on campus. . . . Today, the Church on campus is challenged to be a credible sign of unity and a living reminder of the essential interdependence and solidarity of all people. (ES, 36 and 37)

The challenge and the responsibility before all campus ministers are to foster and sustain vital communities of faith. Many campus ministers believe this to be at the heart of the ministry. Most of the talents and energies of a campus minister are directed toward forming genuine communities; communities shaped and formed by the gospel message of Jesus; communities also influenced by the cultural milieu of the society, as well as the specific environment of the campus where the campus ministers serve.

As residents of the United States, campus ministers and students have been conditioned by a strong sense of the importance of the individual. Robert Bellah, et al., in *Habits of the Heart*, have presented an excellent study on the role and the effects of individualism in the culture. Madonna Kolbenschlag adds another dimension to this study, when she uses the metaphor of the "spiritual orphan" to describe the alienation experienced by many in today's society. There is in the culture a tremendous need for a sense of belonging, for a place or a space where one can be "at home." Added to this is the alienation many students feel

when they enter higher education. "Campus ministers who listen well know that there is a genuine hunger for community in the academic world . . ." (ES, 35).

Our individualistic culture needs functioning models that demonstrate the value of cooperative efforts for common goals. Healthy Christians need a community in which they can develop and utilize their talents and gifts. Alienated individuals need a place where they are known by name and can share with others who share their true values and beliefs. Even persons happily involved in many forms of communal activity need a community of faith to focus their values, reinforce their beliefs, and energize their efforts in the world (Bacik, p. 24).

The chief assets a campus minister has in forming faith communities are the people who come together for the eucharist. The people are vital to the eucharist, and the eucharist is central to a community of faith. All who assemble for the eucharist must strive to be part of a welcoming community, offering hospitality to all peoples. The attitude of the campus minister, as well as the attitude of the members of a faith community, speaks volumes to all in

the academic community. The faith community must echo a presence that is both warm and welcoming.

The community comes together as a people of God to celebrate the central event of the eucharist. "Prayerful liturgies enable us to praise God with full hearts and create a sense of belonging, as well as nourish people for a life of service" (ES, 37). Careful planning is essential for prayerful liturgies. The planning itself can be an experience of community, as well as a means of having the community take ownership of liturgical celebrations. Planning committees that include people from various aspects of the community will help ensure that liturgy is a celebration of all the people. Involvement by the members of the community as lectors and eucharistic ministers adds to the celebration of the eucharist. A balance of male and female ministers together at the altar gives a visible sign of a Church striving to be inclusive. Other forms of worship—liturgy of the hours, scripture services, communion services, thematic prayer services—add another dimension to a faith community. Various styles of participation and of leadership in the prayer life of the community enrich the faith of the people.

As communities of hospitality, campus ministers need to be aware of the many people who bear the added burden of feeling alienated from the Church because of their sex, their race, or their sexual orientation. A welcoming community makes a conscious effort to be inclusive in language, in images of God, and in action. Communities need an openness that both welcomes these people and accepts their experiences, talents, and gifts as vital to community. International students, commuters, older students, and the physically challenged also need special words and gestures of welcome. Campus ministry aspires to a model of Church that is "a visible sign of unity of the whole human family and an instrument of reconciliation for all" (ES, 36).

Campus orientation at the beginning of an academic year is an excellent place to make one's presence known. Involvement in and presence at these various functions give the campus minister immediate visibility. Numerous social events at the beginning of the academic year are invitations to new people to get to know the community and to join in the various activities. How campus ministers first meet and greet people often sets the tone for the community's vitality the rest of the year.

> **M**y experience in campus ministry has confirmed my belief that the heart of our worship and our ministry is eucharistic. The group Biblical Explorers is only one example of this. Weekly, we gather together around God's work. Each and every time we gather, we take and bless, we break and share. We come to God's word with faith and break open that word. In doing this, we break open the words that are our lives. We eat. We drink. We remember. We are filled with thanksgiving.
>
> **Michael Moynihan, SJ**
> **Santa Clara University**

Suggestions for Student Orientation

1. Send a letter of welcome to new students during the summer. Include an invitation to the first few events you sponsor that semester. Often, a list of Catholic students can be obtained from the registrar's office, student services, or the chaplain's office. If no religious preference cards are available, you might want to start a process of having them included in new students' information packets.

2. Sponsor an open social event as soon as possible when the academic year begins (e.g., cookouts, dinners, and so forth). Invite all community members as well as new students, new faculty. new staff, and their families.

3. Have specialized events for specified groups of people (e.g., new students' Mass and dinner, graduate students' dinner, faculty cocktail hour, couples' potluck dinner).

4. Provide outdoor events in prominent places (e.g., volleyball game near student center or residence hall).

5. Use orientation packets of the university and/or your own to distribute pens, key chains, or some other handouts that have your center's name, schedule, and phone number on them.

6. Welcome all—especially new students and their parents—as they move into the residence halls. Provide refreshments, a helping hand, a listening ear.

7. Advertise with all other groups and clubs during student fairs and other similar campus activities.

Sr. Kathleen Dorney, CND
Wheeling Jesuit College

Social events are good for fostering and celebrating community. The "food ministry" is among the most valuable ministries on campus. Coming together over a meal is a natural setting for students, faculty, and staff to mingle with one another. The planning, cooking, serving, and cleaning surrounding a meal afford excellent opportunities for people to work together and to get to know one another. Community often happens around the table and in the kitchen.

Students with numerous time commitments find it more convenient to gather around a meal. Sometimes campus communities gather together after Sunday eucharist to share a meal. The local pizza place, a table in the college dining hall, or a homemade meal at the center all provide a setting for nourishing community. Sports events, discussion groups, evening classes, drama presentations, and dances present opportunities for bringing people together and forming community in nonthreatening ways. Working together at a soup kitchen, a shelter, or in other social outreach programs not only reinforces the participants' commitment to a ministry outside themselves, but also provides a great setting for community to happen. "For where two or three are gathered together in my name, there am I in the midst of them" (Mt 18:20).

"Can I be a Catholic and an intellectual?" Such a question focuses the struggle many young adults face as they enter into a critical, questioning academic setting. A strong faith community supports, sustains, and encourages people in their quest for a deeper, more meaningful faith life. Honest informal exchanges between Catholic faculty and students provide students with faithful Catholic witness. Catholic faculty and staff presence at worship enhances the meaning of a faith community in higher education. These experiences reveal intellectuals who are believing, practicing adult Catholics.

Group processes around faith sharing and faith development are invaluable means of fostering a deep faith community. RCIA and RENEW are ongoing programs that have been adapted to campus ministry settings. RCIA, especially, continues to enliven the community and gives students an opportunity to make a firm faith commitment.

Candidates and their sponsors journey together toward the reception of the sacrament of baptism and/or confirmation. The witness of faith and the bonding that is experienced affect the whole community.

Retreats, whether evening, day, or weekend, are significant community-forming events. Careful planning and commitment are necessary ingredients for all retreat programs. A variety of styles in content, format, and presenters addresses different needs of people and broadens one's sense of prayer, faith, and the holy. Several campuses within a geographic area often combine resources in offering retreats.

Residential colleges and universities have the opportunity to organize "communities" around living areas. Newman Centers and designated residence halls sometimes provide actual experiences of living in households of faith and provide viable options for experiencing community.

Baptism calls all people to be ministers of the community. In all that campus ministers do, including structures of government, church workers need to model the Church as a community of ministers. The gifts and talents of all community members must be a factor in shaping the Church. "All are co-responsible for the well-being of the faith community. This model also suggests that the members are called to minister to one another and that there is a mutuality of giving and receiving between leaders and other members of the Church" (Bacik, 1988).

The challenge of a campus minister is exciting and life giving. The responsibility is awesome. The campus minister strives to foster vital communities of faith so that the gospel message may be lived and proclaimed to the world.

The experience of Christian community on campus is important to the life of the whole Church. Students who have such a

When I arrived at a campus parish as an incoming student, I found that I was being told that we are all part of the Church; in fact, we *are* the Church, and this meant that the Church needed my gifts and talents. As a member of this community, that responsibility was something I could not ignore.

I feel that campus parishes and Catholic centers should be places that challenge and encourage the faith of the students so that their understanding of being Catholic is stretched and examined. I hope that there are places in which students come to experience their faith, touching all aspects of their lives.

Becky Bacon
Purdue University

positive experience and are taught their responsibilities to the larger Church will continue to be a very valuable resource for family, parish, and diocesan life when they leave school. (ES, 43)

Presence is the one thing that made campus ministry at Georgetown University a success for me. Of course the ball is always in the student's court when it comes to participating in anything, but they were visible enough that at least we all knew where the courts were. Opportunities for becoming involved were many, but no rigid structure of fixed activities was imposed on the students. The campus ministers listened to our needs, involved us in the planning of things, and encouraged student leadership. During my four years at Georgetown, I perceived the campus ministers to be a group of diverse and creative people who offered a constant source of support while tapping individual students' gifts for the benefit of the community.

Programs for Forming Faith Communities

1. *Resident Life Communities*

Small groups of men or women live in the same wing or floor of a residence hall. They share prayer, fellowship, and social events. Some basic elements needed are a student coordinator, an outside advisor, a household agreement, a faith statement, and a written commitment from each participant.

Contact:
Mrs. Cathy J. Heck
Christ the King Chapel
Franciscan University
Steubenville, Ohio 43952
Tel. 614-283-6506

Place:
Franciscan University of Steubenville

2. *Student Volunteer House/Hall Contacts*

The student volunteer is involved in peer ministry to reach out actively to others in the service of the Church. They are to contact personally all Catholic students in their area, registering them with the Newman Center, holding regular meetings to inform and discuss activities at the center, and keeping ministry staff aware of student needs.

Contact:
Rev. Vincent Krische
1631 Crescent Road
Lawrence, Kansas 66044
Tel. 913-843-0357

Place: University of Kansas

3. *Caring Community*

In order to build a loving faith-filled community, a group of thirty-five to seventy people share their faith experience in small groups of six or seven for two hours a week. It takes fifteen weeks to train a core group and another fifteen weeks for the program. By promoting thoughtful relationships with others, it fosters a way of living that provides a meaningful and practical connection between faith and life.

Contact:
Rev. Charles Mocco
Ecumenical Center, UWGB
2420 Nicolet Dr.
Green Bay, Wisconsin 54311-7001
Tel. 414-465-5133

Place:
University of Wisconsin

4. *RENEW for Campus Ministry*

This program offers an opportunity to form community, to integrate Scripture with one's life story, and to develop a social justice commitment. A year is needed to prepare RENEW campus leaders. There are five six-week sessions that are held over a two-and-one-half year period. This program uses Sunday liturgy, home materials, large-group activities, and small-group faith sharing.

Contact:
National Office of RENEW
1232 George Street
Plainfield, New Jersey 07062
Tel. 201-769-5400

Places:
Princeton University
   (Princeton, New Jersey)
Rider College (Lawrenceville, New Jersey)
American University (Washington, D.C.)
Marywood College
   (Scranton, Pennsylvania)

5. *Retreat Programs*

Various themes for retreats occur during the scholastic year. Mini-retreats are one-day sessions. New-student retreats can be held in July with a follow-up in October. Lenten-Focus retreats fill the spring and Lenten season. Renewal Week begins with a Sunday liturgy, followed by four evenings of different liturgical themes. A liturgical ministers' training retreat occurs at the beginning and the end of the academic year. The faculty retreat invites faculty members to participate in a Holy Thursday retreat offered specifically for university faculty, staff, and their spouses. Pre-Cana retreats are offered for engaged couples who are students, alumni, or of the associate parish. Handicapped Encounter Christ is a service retreat with and for the physically disabled, which helps the disabled and able-bodied students to build community.

Contact:
John Lozano and Linda Jaczynski
Campus Ministry Office
Villanova, Pennsylvania 19085-1699
Tel. 610-519-4083

Place:
Villanova University

6. Student-Led Retreat

This is a retreat given by a few students for a group of fifteen to twenty students. The subject of the retreat is the result of brainstorming with the students who are giving the retreat. This allows the retreat to meet the immediate spiritual needs of the group.

Source:
"Retreats: Experiences of Transformation" in *Prepare the Way of the Lord* CCMA (1988): 112-114

7. Encounter with Christ Program

"Community" is the theme of the weekend. It is achieved by allowing students to encounter themselves, Christ, the Church, and the community. Most of the presentations are given by students who have previously been participants. The time commitment is from Thursday evening to Sunday morning.

Contact:
Bro. Cosmos Rubencamp, CFX
Diocesan Director of Campus Ministry
811 Cathedral Place
Richmond, Virginia 23220
Tel. 804-359-5661

Place:
Diocese of Richmond

8. St. Clare's House

This facility provides "Augustine's" ideal of communal hospitality. It is to be used by individuals who need overnight accommodations, groups who need space for meetings, reflection, and community building activities.

Contact:
Ms. Barbara Haenn
Campus Ministry Office
Villanova, Pennsylvania 19085-1699
Tel. 610-519-4080

Place:
Villanova University

9. RCIA

Candidates and their sponsors journey together toward the reception of the sacraments of baptism and/or confirmation. This is a list of campuses where RCIA is adapted to the college setting:

Places:
Loyola University (Chicago, Illinois)
University of Rhode Island
    (Kingston, Rhode Island)
University of Scranton
    (Scranton, Pennsylvania)
Georgetown University
    (Washington, D.C.)
St. Thomas More House, Yale University
    (New Haven, Connecticut)
Newman Canter, Drexel University
    (Philadelphia, Pennsylvania)
Barry University (Miami, Florida)

10. Friday Night Faith Alive: A Christian Coffeehouse Experience

All Christian campus ministry groups can organize an open-mike coffeehouse once a semester. This uses a pre-scheduled program that is flexible. On occasion, individuals may share or sing or read a poem, even if they were not on the schedule. All who want to perform first obtain permission from their campus minister. The coffee house is held in the union building with small tables and candles on the table. Coffee, tea, punch, and snacks are provided free of charge.

Contact:
Ms. Theresa D. Miller
Lock Haven University
445 W. Main St.
Lock Haven, Pennsylvania 17745
Tel. 717-748-8592

Place:
Lock Haven University

11. University Mass and
   Student Liturgy Committee
   Creativity and participation will
enhance the campus Mass when students
are invited to take responsibility for "their
Mass." A core group of a chaplain, students,
a musician, and faculty make up the committee. A weekly planning session, training
days, and a seasonal planning workshop
enable students to become knowledgeable
and committed to a meaningful worship
experience for planners and participants
alike.

   Contact:
   Ms. Barbara Humphrey
   113 Healy Hall
   Georgetown University
   Washington, D.C. 20057-1037

   Place: Georgetown University

12. Liturgical Ministers Program
   This is a highly coordinated program in
which all ministers of liturgy are trained, commissioned, build community, and are encouraged to be responsible within the area of service to which they are called. Each group has
its own campus minister directing it.

   Contacts:
   Shawn Tracy, OSA (Presiders)
   Beth Hassel, PBUM
      (Eucharistic Ministers)
   Noreen Cameron and Barbara Haenn
      (Lectors)
   Gary Stegall (Pastoral Musicians)
   Shawn Tracy, OSA (Hospitality)
   Campus Ministry Office
   Villanova, Pennsylvania 19085-1699
   Tel. 215-645-4080

   Place: Villanova University

13. Guidelines for Music Ministry
   This program for organizing music ministry on campus divides the responsibility of
ministry into two areas: planning and organizing; and talent in performing. This program also acknowledges that both the coordinator and music leader can be the same
person.

   Contact:
   Kathleen Kanavy
   University of Scranton
   Scranton, Pennsylvania 18510
   Tel. 717-941-6152

   Place: University of Scranton

Non-Eucharistic Liturgy Preparation Worksheet Guide

Adapted from Frank J. Lewis Campus Ministers Institute 1987

Patterns

Liturgy of the Hours
Introduction (Song)
Psalm(s)/Canticle
Proclamation
Praise (Gospel Canticle)
Intercessory Prayer
Conclusion (Prayer, Blessing)

Liturgy of the Word
Introduction (Song/Prayer)
Proclamation
(with Psalm Response)
Response
(Prayer, Action)
Conclusion (Blessing)

A. What to Celebrate

1. Who are we—this community as Body of Christ?
    - What is there to celebrate?
    - strengths and gifts
    - weaknesses and needs

2. Here and now:
    - What is special about today in our faith-journey?
    - heritage/today's feast
    - contemporary events

3. What in Scripture can speak to us here and now?
    - Choose reading(s)/psalm(s)

4. What is this Scripture saying to us here and now?
    - Formulate theme

B. How to Celebrate

1. Structure: Overall script?

2. Ministries: Resources available/needed

3. Particulars:
    a. Presider: who, vestments, and so forth
    b. Proclamation: lector(s), lectionary, Bible, and so forth
    c. Music: leader(s), instruments, songs, songbooks, tape player, cassettes, and so forth
    d. Assembly: participation aids, and so forth
    e. Environment: where, set-up, who is responsible, and so forth
    f. Ritual: who and what
    g. Art: who and what
    h. Movement, dance: who and what
    i. Prayer texts: written or improvised; who and what

Eucharistic Liturgy Preparation Worksheet Guide

Adapted from Frank J. Lewis Campus Ministers Institute 1987

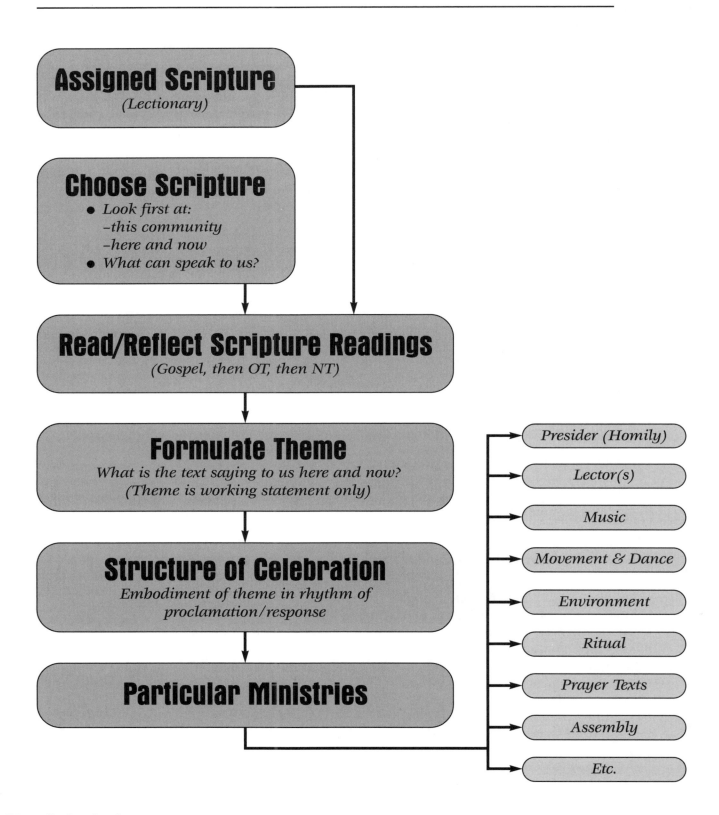

Assigned Scripture
(Lectionary)

Choose Scripture
- *Look first at:*
  –this community
  –here and now
- *What can speak to us?*

Read/Reflect Scripture Readings
(Gospel, then OT, then NT)

Formulate Theme
What is the text saying to us here and now?
(Theme is working statement only)

Structure of Celebration
Embodiment of theme in rhythm of
proclamation/response

Particular Ministries

Presider (Homily)

Lector(s)

Music

Movement & Dance

Environment

Ritual

Prayer Texts

Assembly

Etc.

Resources for Forming Faith Communities

Community

Bacik, James J. "Achieving Community: Culture, Theology, and Leadership," in *Church* (Summer 1988). Bacik not only gives us insight into the cultural influences, theology, and the type of leadership needed in achieving community, but he has a gift for unifying these dimensions in a way that challenges us to create dynamic communities in our church settings.

Bellah, Robert N., et al. *Habits of the Heart: Individualism and Commitment in American Life.* New York: Harper and Row, 1985. Bellah et al. trace the conflict between individualism and the need for community/commitment in today's world.

Gallagher, Maureen. *Ministry of Hospitality.* Mahwah, N.J.: Paulist Press, 1982. A filmstrip explaining the rationale and means to welcome newcomers to a parish and worship. A significant portion of the material is aimed at helping ushers, welcomers, and greeters do an effective job.

Hug, James, ed. *Tracing the Spirit.* New York: Paulist Press, 1983. Reflects on smaller communities that are engaged in the struggle for justice.

Kolbenschlag, Madonna. *Lost in the Land of Oz: The Search for Identity and Community in American Life.* New York: Harper and Row, 1988. The spiritual orphan is the metaphor that Kolbenschlag uses to describe the alienation in today's American society. She probes not only what is but offers a vision for connectedness in the future.

McKenna, Megan. "Base Communities in North America," in *Pax Christi* (Winter 1987). An interview with Dr. McKenna on implementing the base community movement in the USA.

Moynihan, Michael, SJ. "Forming the Faith Community," in *Prepare the Way of the Lord.* Dayton, Ohio: CCMA, 1988. Through the power of story, personal insights, and practical applications, the author elucidates what he believes to be fundamental to developing faith communities: sharing of story, meal, and light.

Mulvaney, Mary. "Paul's First Letter to the Campus Ministers: A Model for Building Small Christian Communities," in *Prepare the Way of the Lord.* Dayton, Ohio: CCMA, 1988. The author suggests the development of small communities around issues that are significant for the college community (e.g., liturgy, social justice, community service, catechesis, and social activities). These communities are not "committees because they actively develop themselves in these five areas: share faith, mutual support, prayer, continued learning, and outreach."

Peck, M. Scott, M.D. *The Different Drum: Community Making and Peace.* New York: Simon and Schuster, 1987. Challenging as well as practical ways to move from individual growth to small-group community to a more global notion of community; the story of "The Rabbi's Gift" is an excellent image for community.

Whitehead, Evelyn Eaton and James D. *Community of Faith.* New York: Seabury Press, 1982. The Whiteheads present the essential elements needed for the building of Christian communities.

Liturgy/Prayer

Baker, Thomas and Frank Ferrone. *Liturgy Committee Basics: A No-Nonsense Guide.* Washington, D.C.: The Pastoral Press, 1985. This book is filled with practical directions for forming a liturgy committee, planning and running meetings, as well as building blocks for good liturgy.

Johnson, Laurence J. *The Mystery of Faith: The Ministers of Music.* Washington, D.C.: National Association of Pastoral Musicians, 1983. Johnson provides a comprehensive presentation of the various expressions of the Church's ministry of music—cantor, choir, instrumentalists, organists, as well as assembly, deacon, presider, composer, and dancer. Each ministry is explored through historical background, liturgical documentation, reflections, and suggested questions.

Lee, Bernard J., SM, ed. *Alternative Futures for Worship.* Vol. 3. *The Eucharist.* Collegeville, Minn.: The Liturgical Press, 1987. "We are happy to offer our work as a small part of the search for forms of worship that are faithful to the Christ event and respectful of the cultural configuration of the daily lives we lead" (p. 15). Intentional Christian communities are seen as the building blocks of church life.

Retreats

Conlee, Mary Beth. "Retreats: Experiences of Transformation" in *Prepare the Way of the Lord*. Dayton, Ohio: CCMA, 1988. An extremely practical resource for anyone planning a retreat.

de Mello, Anthony. *Wake Up! Spirituality for Today: A Way to God for Today*. Videotape. Tabor Publishing, One DLM Park, P.O. Box 7000, Allen, Texas. This video is perfect for a retreat experience wherein you have a process person, but you need to import a speaker.

Pax Christi USA. *Retreat Packet*. National Catholic Peace Movement, 348 E. 10 Street, Erie, PA 16503; Tel. 814-453-4955. Pax Christi can provide numerous written materials applicable for community building retreat experiences.

United Nations. *Sabbath: Environmental Earth Rest Day*. United Nations, Two U.N. Plaza, New York, NY 10017. This environmental program packet includes an interfaith compilation of prayers and activities.

Appropriating the Faith

A truly liberating and elevating education is incomplete without the study of theology or religion. (ES, 51)
A Christian faith that fails to seek a more mature understanding is not faithful to its own inner dynamism. A culture that is unaware of its religious roots and substance is impoverished and weakened. (ES, 53)

Mr.
Michael
Nachman

Introduction

Assisting in the process of appropriation of faith is similar to being a midwife. Campus ministers coach and support, but above all, they accompany another on the journey toward new life. It is the challenge of all who work with young adults to assist in the birthing of mature faith. This central responsibility is vital if the young person is to begin the lifelong process of integrating faith and life in creative ways. This process is characterized by a clarification of basic Catholic values and meanings, deepened by Scripture, and enriched by our tradition. In a campus atmosphere, which offers many engaging and attractive contrary lifestyles, students often flounder because of their lack of basic knowledge of religion in general and of Catholicism in particular.

Appropriating faith is best served by approaches that model hospitality, openness, and tolerance while maintaining a clear Catholic identity. Recognizing the important role of models and mentors is the first requirement. Such persons model not perfection, but a struggle to live faithfully in a complex and unfinished world.

Campus life reflects our culture in fostering an atmosphere where one is tempted to accept easy answers to complicated personal and social problems. In fact, church members are often unaware of the real questions. The ability to reflect on personal experience and integrate the fruits of that reflection with Scripture and tradition, while remaining open to new possibilities, is the challenge faced by all who work with young adults.

Religious Illiteracy on Campus

While religion—along with sexuality and jobs—is a frequent and often intense topic of discussion among students, these exchanges often fail to go beyond the sharing of ignorance and misunderstanding. Students lack basic factual information about religion. But more important, they are unaware of the resources that religion provides for living life to the fullest measure. Catholic students often perceive the Church as an oppressive parent or an irrelevant institution and, too often, disregard the riches of generations of experience (see Olson, 1988).

Without an integrating focus, students are often tempted by simple answers in emotionally laden packages. It is easier to accept blindly than to live in the tension of the open questions and struggle toward a complex solution. For the past decade, students have become increasingly motivated by vocationalism, rather than by the need to develop an integrated philosophy of life.

The activity of fundamentalist groups and cults on campuses indicates the ever present struggle for meaning (see LaVerdiere, 1983). This irrepressible need can be ignored only at great cost. Those who journey with young adults are privileged to be part of the awakening of a struggle that, with some guidance, can lead to the richness of adult faith.

Faith Development

The central task of young adulthood is to discover and fashion a faith that will shape their relationship between self and the world. The developmental space between adolescence and adulthood is the area where identity and commitment are shaped. Sharon Parks, in *The Critical Years: The Young Adult Search for a Faith to Live By*, explores the development of self-identity that is not-yet-adult and the growing awareness of the need to find an appropriate social role. The young adult's probing commitment requires mentors who anchor a vision of a

> In business class, I learned how to earn money; at church, we learned how to share it.
>
> In management, I learned how to allocate resources; at church, we learned to be good stewards of the earth.
>
> In anthropology, I learned where humans come from; at church, we learned where we're going.
>
> In physics, I learned how small the world is; at church, we learned that it is sacred.
>
> In poly. sci., I learned who our national enemies are; at church, we were told to love them.
>
> In geography, I learned to recognize borders; at church, we were taught to see through them.
>
> In history, I read the perspective of the victors; at church, we developed solidarity with the poor.
>
> In computer science, I learned to manipulate information; at church, we learned to seek the truth.
>
> In advertising, I was taught to sell an idea; at church, we were challenged to be honest.
>
> In school, I was taught to succeed; at church, we were called to help those who fail.
>
> *Scott Suma*
> *Rockford, Illinois*

possible self. They will listen to the voices of invitation from those perceived as having the desired qualities they can incorporate into their new vision of themselves. They respond less to heroes and more to persons (peer and adult) who openly share their struggle to bring faith and life together.

Parks offers challenges for professors to be "spiritual guides," to be the ones who provide insight into the world of meaning and significance. A syllabus can become a confession of faith that opens new vistas and challenges previously held beliefs. As mentors, professors will require models of how they can share their faith with students. Assisting faculty in seeing their vital role in this area can make an important impact on many students, as well as enriching the faculty and challenging the academic atmosphere of the institution (see Palmer, 1983).

A Deeper Call

The movement toward adult faith for the young adult takes place in an environment of subtle forces that form persons at a non-conscious level. In this respect, campuses reflect the materialism, individualism, and relativism of our culture. The allure of status and money are powerful forces that lead students toward lives of quantity and shallowness and away from quality and depth. Their sense of service is dulled as they strive to fulfill cultural expectations.

Deep within themselves, students often sense a deeper call (see DeCoster, 1987). The spiritual longing for significance and meaning surfaces, causing disarray to carefully laid career plans. Providing students with experiences of service in multicultural, poverty, and foreign environments can assist them in rooting their lives in a deeper appreciation of the mystery of the ordinary and the simple. They require models of hope in a world easily disposed to despair. Campus ministers can assist them in developing the courage to face the future creatively while living deeply each moment.

Strategies

Facilitating a growing and deepening faith is best done by exposing students to peers, faculty, and other adults who are developing an integrated faith. Hearing and seeing people in the process is a core strategy that can take many forms to fit specific circumstances (e.g., a Catholic lawyer sharing with law students; recent graduates sharing their initial career experiences).

People can only grow toward what they can imagine. While mentors and models assist in the formation of an adult vision, people also need the critical dimension of theological reflection to bring the light of Scripture and the richness of tradition to bear on current personal and social struggles. This type of reflection can take place in conjunction with any type of event. Combined with journal writing, its effectiveness is enhanced. Pausing to reflect theologically on the meaning of a recycling drive, a service trip to the inner city, or a tutoring program raises basic questions and forms a closer bond among faith, action, and understanding. Once students have learned the power of such reflection to transform their lives, they will not return to blind acceptance or simple rejection as means of dealing with complex issues.

Any opportunity campus ministers can give students to tell their story is a valued time, filled with possibilities. Whether as part of a bible-sharing group, a theological discussion series, a counseling session, or a committee meeting, each occasion has the possibility of deepening reflection and offering opportunity to interface and integrate faith and experience. Learning that life is an ongoing adventure with wonderful twists and turns can only happen if students practice imagining the world of possibilities. The faith-sharing model also works well with faculty and staff and can provide a needed form outside the academic environment for person-to-person exchanges.

Hospitality and invitation are two basic approaches that go hand-in-hand in creating a welcoming atmosphere. At their heart, are openness and honesty that stand for solid values and create a vulnerability that can thrive in an atmosphere of rigorous dialogue and questioning. Campus ministers need to think and act inclusively, avoiding the routine traps of either/or thinking. When students experience this openness, they will be better disposed to hear the challenging messages of Scripture. Whether gathered for social, liturgical, or service purposes, each provides an opportunity to nurture the hunger for knowledge of faith.

Those who have the advantage of working with a department of Theology or Religious Studies are challenged to form alliances to assist students in furthering and deepening their integration. This can happen through formal classes or informal programs. Campus ministers or others of their choosing can offer numerous types of educational programming that are not necessarily part of an accredited program or formal academia. Such programs might include seminars, panels, study groups, short courses or semester-long programs in theology, social justice, personal development, liturgy, ethics, and so forth. Students, faculty, and staff are all potential participants and beneficiaries of educational offerings by campus ministers.

The many catechisms and introductions to Catholicism now in print, along with the fine audio cassettes and videotapes available, provide rich resources for a wide variety of needs and settings. Use of these media can provide the needed expertise often unavailable on campus.

Programs for Appropriating the Faith

by Ms. Barbara Humphrey

1. Beginning Today

This program is aimed at giving baptized and confirmed Catholics an "update on their Catholic Christian heritage." Offered for a brief duration during the semester, each session offers a mixture of content and process. Group members choose their meeting site. Participants, in groups of five to twelve students, sign a covenant with their group members, agreeing to attend faithfully each meeting.

Contact:
Mr. Peter McCourt
203 Otey
Blacksburg, Virginia 24060-7415
Tel. 703-957-0032

Place: Virginia Tech

2. Bible Sharing and Pizza

A weekly meal-time informal sharing period is followed by an hour bible-sharing program using *Share the Word*. This gathering enables students to delve deeper into the Scriptures, to apply Christian principles to their lifestyles, and to develop a sense of Christian community.

Contact:
Ms. Alice L. Redding
Gettysburg College
Box 427
Gettysburg, Pennsylvania 17325
Tel. 717-337-6284

Place: Shippersburg University

3. Directed Retreat

Twenty-four students, six spiritual directors, a cook, and a retreat director gather for a weekend experience. Prayer and meals are shared together. Spiritual direction is accomplished one-on-one (four retreat participants for each spiritual director). Each spiritual director meets with his or her students five times over the weekend, guiding the students on a path of spiritual growth. Students are encouraged to continue the process with their director after the weekend.

Contact:
Ms. Barbara Humphrey
113 Healy Hall
Georgetown University
Washington, D.C. 20057-1037

Place:
Georgetown University

4. Spiritual Directors Pool

A list of spiritual directors is offered to students who inquire about spiritual guidance. Special care is taken to recruit a variety of spiritual directors. An in-depth initial interview with the student enables a good director/directee match.

Contact:
Maureen McGrath
6925 N. Sheridan
Chicago, Illinois 60626
Tel. 312-508-2200

Place:
Loyola University at Chicago

5. Brothers and Sisters in Christ (BASIC)

Through small co-lead student groups of seven to twelve members meeting weekly, BASIC aims to deepen the understanding and commitment of its participants to the Christian faith and the Catholic Church, to promote prayer and reflection, and to provide meaningful fellowship.

Contact:
Mr. Jefferey Piccirilli
St. Mary's Church
111 E. High Street
Oxford, Ohio 45056
Tel. 513-523-2153

Place:
Miami University

6. Last Lecture Series

Well-known faculty and administrators are invited to offer a 30-minute "Last Lecture," as if it were their very last opportunity to communicate the values and convictions that have motivated them throughout life. The six speakers are asked to distribute one promotional flyer to all of their classes (designed and photocopied by the chaplain), listing all six professors, titles, and dates.

Contact:
Dianne DeMarco, RSM
Lakewood, New Jersey 08701
Tel. 201-364-2200

Place: Georgian Court College

7. Faculty-Student Dialogue

Students are paired with faculty members in a one-on-one dialogue that last the semester. These sharing sessions enrich and support the students in their personal and spiritual development.

Contact:
Mr. Tom Gorman
P.O. Box 677
Bowling Green, Ohio 43402
Tel. 419-352-7555

Place: Bowling Green State University

8. Theologian-in-Residence

With a theologian-in-residence, campus ministry can offer courses in religion or theology and make available college credit through a Catholic college or university. This enables students to study Catholicism and transfer credits into the state university they are attending.

Contact:
Thomas Ryba, Ph.D.
St. Thomas Aquinas
535 State Street
West Lafayette, Indiana 47906
Tel. 317-743-4652

Place:
Purdue University

9. Religious Studies Curriculum

By working in conjunction with the university administration, a Religious Studies program can be established. This is a long-term project, interfaith oriented, but is a key structural change within the university.

Contact:
Rev. John C. Weimer
1219 Elmwood Avenue
Buffalo, New York 14222
Tel. 716-882-1080

Place:
State University College at Buffalo

Resources for Appropriating the Faith

Books/Articles

Cunningham, Lawrence. "New Catechism: A First reading" in *Commonweal*, 120 (1993): 8-12.

DeCoster, David A. "On the Campus: The Blind Spot Extended: Spirituality," in *Journal of College Student Personnel* 28 (May 1987): 274-276. Three state university educators/administrators argue that persons "should be afforded the same privilege and extended the same opportunity to attain spiritual development as they are given in all other areas related to student development in the college years." Personal development goes hand-in-hand with the academic study of religion.

"Fundamentalism" in *New Theology Review* 1:2 (May 1988). This special issue is devoted entirely to the topic. Solid analysis, with good bibliographic references. Essential reading for an in-depth response to the many challenges that fundamentalism presents: origins, eschatology, political, and Catholic forms of fundamentalism.

Hudson, Deal W. "Teach Our Faith Convincingly" in *Christian World*, 39 (1994): 36-43.

LaVerdiere, Eugene, SSS. *Fundamentalism: A Pastoral Concern.* Collegeville, Minn.: The Liturgical Press, 1983. This short pamphlet sketches the scope of the problem under the categories of theological, pastoral, social, and personal. A good place to start in planning a response for your particular campus situation.

Ludwig, Robert A. *Reconstructing Catholicism for a Generation.* New York: Crossroad, 1995.

Marthaler, Berard L. Ed. *Introducing the Catechism of the Catholic Church.* Mahwah, N.J.: Paulist Press, 1994.

Olson, Wayne C. "Campus Ministry as Remedial Religion: A Personal Perspective," in *Christian Century* (April 13, 1988): 381-382. A personal perspective on the challenges of working with students at a public college who know little about their faith, need to unlearn narrow attitudes, and need to be challenged to think deeper about the interfaces of Church and society. Assisting students to internalize a meaningful and personal faith is the joy and frustration of every campus minister.

Palmer, Parker J. *To Know as We Are Known: A Spirituality of Education.* New York: Harper and Row, 1983. Palmer presents a wealth of thoughtful challenges in stimulating us to bring together our educational and spiritual understandings. This book will be useful in opening a dialogue with faculty on what they are doing as educators. Focuses on search for truth.

Parks, Sharon. *The Critical Years: The Young Adult Search for a Faith to Live By.* San Francisco: Harper and Row, 1986. Parks outlines the specific faith development stage of a young adult by developing the territory between James Fowler's stage three (Synthetic-Conventional Faith) and his stage four (Intuitive-Reflective Faith), as well as by expanding and deepening the insights of Sam Keen and Carol Gilligan. Parks presents some challenging concepts: professors as "spiritual guides"; a syllabus as a confession of faith; and the role of imagination in facilitating the transition to adult faith. "Review Symposium" in *Horizons* 14:2 (Fall 1987): 343-363. Provides four critical perspectives on Park's book. James Fowler is one of the respondents, and his comments help place Park's contribution in the context of his own.

Catechism (Basic)

Catechism of the Catholic Church. Washington, D.C.: United States Catholic Conference, 1994.

Chilson, Richard. *Catholic Christianity.* Mahwah, N.J.: Paulist Press, 1987.

Cunningham, Lawrence. *The Catholic Faith: An Introduction.* Mahwah, N.J.: Paulist Press, 1987.

Hellwig, Monica. *Understanding Catholicism.* Mahwah, N.J.: Paulist Press, 1980.

Kung, Hans. *On Being a Christian.* New York: Doubleday and Company, 1976.

McBrien, Richard. *Catholicism.* St. Paul, Minn.: Winston Press, 1980.

Pennock, Michael F. *This is Our Faith: A Catholic Catechism for Adults.* Notre Dame, Ind.: Ave Maria Press, 1989.

Faith Inventory Instrument

The Catholic Faith Inventory. Mahwah, N.J.: Paulist Press. This inventory is especially helpful with RCIA candidates or individuals interested in discovering their developed and undeveloped faith areas.

Forming the Christian Conscience

Campus ministry has the crucial task of assisting in the formation of Catholic consciences so that individuals who will continue to face very complex ethical issues throughout their lives are prepared to make good moral judgments according to gospel values. (ES, 63)

Rev. Robert Aaron, OMI, and Mr. Donald R. McCrabb

Introduction

College students need conscience formation. They face many questions, challenges, and pressures that did not even exist ten years ago. During their college years, students make moral decisions that shape their vision of themselves, of others, and of God for the rest of their lives.

Without sound moral principles or clear values, students often become paralyzed when faced with a moral decision. According to the USCC Department of Education, the number of Catholic high school students receiving no formal religious education rose from 1.5 million (36.5 percent) in 1965 to more than 3 million (61.4 percent) in 1974.

The campus ministry challenge is to help college students learn and apply the basics of moral theology. This is particularly crucial for young adults who, as Sharon Parks says in her book *The Critical Years*, are on a journey away from home. This physical, emotional, and psychological departure from home is the first step toward adult meaning making.

Older students and faculty, too, face similar questions of meaning, morality, and ethics. Although they have more experiences than young adults, they also must confront a wide variety of moral questions within their personal and professional lives. Their personal and professional integrity demands an informed and developing conscience.

Understanding Conscience

Catholic moral theology usually understands the conscience as *before the act*, whereas conscience in daily conversation is usually referred to *after the act*. Frequently, campus ministers hear the phrase "my conscience is bothering me" rather than "I am educating my conscience." There are three facets to conscience: (1) It is a human faculty; (2) it is an ongoing process; and (3) it is an event.

People have the unique *human faculty* to decide. They can choose right from wrong. "The human capacity for self-direction equally implies a human responsibility for good direction" (O'Connell, 1990, 110). Conscience, then, is a human characteristic.

This faculty evokes the human ability to search and reason. Consequently, conscience is also a *process* of reflection, discernment, discovery, discussion, and analysis. People ponder which action is right or wrong and which choice is better. They search for ways to understand their own behavior. Lawrence Kohlberg's and Carol Gilligan's research in moral development demonstrates how people arrive at moral decisions at different times in their lives. Gilligan has been especially helpful in showing the unique ways women reach moral decisions. As a process, conscience is a fragile reality that grows and develops over time.

Finally, conscience is also *an event*; the concrete judgment of a person in time and space. In this sense, conscience is supreme. People must act, and they will do so based on conscience. There is no alternative. Their action reveals their conscience.

Beyond Sin to Virtue

Sin is the human failure to love and serve God. *Sin* is a religious term that points to a reality about the relationship between persons and God. Human beings are separated from the fullness of divine life, love, and will. This separation puts all human beings, prior to any particular act, into a state of sin. In Catholic theology, this is called *original sin*.

Much of Catholic moral theology since the Middle Ages focused on sin as *an act*, secondarily, on the *agent*. If the act was grave (such as, murder), then the agent was in a mortal (deadly) state of sin. If the act was light (such as, profane language), then the person was in a venial (easily pardoned) state of sin.

This two-dimensional view of sin (act and agent) does not adequately account for motive or development. For an act to be understood as truly sinful, the maturity of the person, as well as the person's motives, needs to be considered.

Frequently, people focus on whether or not the act is objectively evil (no one gets hurt). They fail to consider their intention and the life direction the act reveals. "No one gets hurt," it is often said, if a person drinks heavily in the privacy of one's own home. But if the intention is to avoid responsibility, perhaps then drinking is a sure sign of a sinful attitude toward self, others, and God.

The challenge of the Christian life is not only to avoid evil but also to do good. It is not enough to stop ourselves from doing what is wrong (e.g., lying, stealing, murder). God invites the person to do good to the best of one's ability, given one's situation. The virtuous person is someone confronting the complexities of the situation and making the best possible decision for the greatest good.

"Conscience has to do with the relationship of our whole self, our whole life, to God. . . . In every moment and every choice, God calls me, and I should seek to act in every situation so as to respond to God's call" (Lohkamp, 1982, 88). Conscience is one aspect of the human quest for integrity and the Christian quest for holiness.

Elements of an Informed Conscience

The conscience needs to be formed and can be formed. It is a religious obligation of the Christian to seek such formation. What are some of the elements of an informed conscience?

1. *The Christian conscience must be gospel based.* While Jesus did not address many of today's ethical issues, his teachings do reflect basic values that the Christian must consider essential in making moral decisions.

2. *The Christian conscience must be formed through study and reflection.* The individual needs to learn discernment of a given act as right or wrong and why. Studying moral principles helps a person be more objective about one's decisions. Through reflection, a person learns from one's own experience and that of others' experience. Two extremes need to be avoided: a legalistic approach to one's moral code and a laxity toward the formation of conscience. These extremes have similar results: the individual surrenders responsibility for one's moral choices.

3. *The Christian conscience must be guided by the teachings of the Church.* The Church has a rich heritage of moral teachings, discernment, and discussions. The person facing moral problems will find a great deal of support, guidance, and insight into a particular problem by careful examination of the Church's teachings.

4. *The Christian conscience must be aided by prayer.* Ultimately, the person must follow the dictates of one's conscience. Prayer can deepen and expand the significance of a moral issue and a particular course of action.

5. *The Christian conscience must rely on the community of faith.* The individual must make moral decisions alone but is not alone in making moral decisions. The Church is populated, both past and present, with wisdom figures. Their stories can educate, comfort, and challenge.

Cardinal John Henry Newman once wrote, "Conscience does not repose on itself, but vaguely reaches forward to something beyond itself and dimly discerns a sanction higher than self for its decisions, as is evidenced in that keen sense of obligation and responsibility which informs them" (as quoted in ES, 63).

Forming the conscience is a lifelong endeavor for the Christian. Every decision is an opportunity for the good, for giving life, for love.

Methods of Forming the Christian Conscience

There are five basic "methods" one can use to form a Christian conscience: (1) worship, (2) education, (3) pastoral counseling, (4) advocacy, and (5) modeling.

The sacrament of reconciliation, offered individually or during retreats and penance services, provides occasions of conscience formation. Homilies are regular opportunities to underscore the gospel values Jesus proclaimed and to apply those values to contemporary ethical issues. The other sacraments also provide opportunities for the examination of conscience and moral reflection. The liturgical year enriches these opportunities with special seasons and feasts.

A course in moral theology is the best systematic way to assure moral education. Students may not be able to commit to a regular course, so mini-courses, telecourses, seminars, or self-directed studies can be viable alternatives. Other educational opportunities include guest lectures, panel discussions, and university-wide ethics seminars. A curriculum in moral theology, with bibliography and a lending library are good resources for a campus ministry to have easily accessible.

Pastoral counseling sessions can help the person achieve a greater sense of moral responsibility for one's own actions, a deeper sense of one's own motives, and a more profound sense of the call of God in one's life. A person coping with the grief of a parent's death does not need a lesson in medical ethics. Rather, conscience formation through pastoral counseling needs to respect the specific needs of the person seeking counseling.

The faith community actively forms the conscience of its own members when it advocates for justice and calls the university to its lofty goals of truth and service. Advocating for justice is more than justice education, which seeks to inform the faith community about the body of Catholic social thought. Rather, advocacy occurs when the community discerns and actively seeks a particular good. This prophetic role extends into the very heart of the university when the Church raises a concern for ethics and values.

Leaders in the faith community influence conscience formation by example. Campus ministers need to be aware of their community's strengths and weaknesses in conscience development. Personal morality

may be a strength in some communities, but social concerns are very weak. Another community may be very concerned about environmental issues, but lax in personal morality. Campus ministers can actively develop their own understanding of moral theology and gently call the larger community to a keener sense of moral responsibility.

Programs for Forming the Christian Conscience

1. Newman Lecture Series

A noon-time brown bag lecture series for students, using the faculty, on topics relevant to the college student today. Topics can range from personal faith testimonies by faculty (modeling) to a lecture on a particular moral issue (education).

Contact:
Sr. Madeline Tacy, OP
856 Tucker Road
N. Dartmouth, Massachusetts 02747-3531
Tel. 508-999-8872

Place:
University of Massachusetts, Dartmouth

2. The Color of Our Skin

To establish a campuswide forum to examine the reality of racism and to engage in social analysis, leading to action on issues affecting the campus. A steering committee was established, composed of students and two campus ministers; fifteen topics and speakers were selected, and a color brochure was printed to advertise the forum.

Contact:
Scott Rains, Campus Ministry
Illinois Benedictine College
5700 College Road
Liste, Illinois 60532-0900
Tel. 708-960-1500

Place:
Illinois Benedictine College

3. Week on Violence

A forum to examine the roots of violence and the need for personal and social transformation. Based on the insights of Rosemary Haughton, *Transformation of Man* (Template Publishers, 1967, 1980), the program looks at ways of transforming the violence in our society's approach to the environment, minority relations, and international relationships.

Contact:
Frances Nosbisch, OSF
Brian Cliff College
3303 Rebecca Street
Sioux City, Iowa 51104
Tel. 712-279-5485

Place: Brian Cliff College

4. Peace Conference

An annual conference, with a different focus each year, aimed at raising awareness about peace and developing skills for peace-making and conflict resolution. An interdisciplinary steering committee of students, faculty, and campus ministers plan the conference, select topics and speakers, and advertise the program through campus and local newspapers.

Contact:
Union Plaza Interfaith Center
3801 West Temple Avenue
Pomona, California 91768
Tel. 909-869-3608

Place:
California State Polytechnic University

5. Ash Wednesday Night Watch

A three-hour evening of reflection for people to consider what the season of Lent means for them. The evening begins with liturgy and then opens up into a variety of activities: meditation in the chapel with music; a variety of videotapes and audiotapes; a mini-lecture on journaling; an opportunity for the sacrament of reconciliation; a mini-bookstore for people to browse through; and a place for refreshments. The evening ends with a simple closing prayer in the chapel.

Contact:
Charlene Fontana, SSJ
1219 Elmwood Avenue
Buffalo, New York 14222
Tel. 716-882-1080

Place:
State University College at Buffalo

6. Faculty Ethics Forum

An ongoing forum for faculty to discuss ethical topics. A core group, developed around lunch (the center supplies soup and sandwiches), meets several times a month. The core group directs the programs, selects topics, and continually invites other faculty to join.

Contact:
Rev. Jack Weimer
1219 Elmwood Avenue
Buffalo, New York 14222
Tel. 716-882-1080

Place: State University College at Buffalo

7. Ethics Seminars for University Administrators

This program has been sponsored for several years by the Illinois Catholic Conference's Campus Ministry Department and targets upper-level administrators of the colleges and universities throughout the state. Presidents, vice presidents for academic affairs/provosts, and vice presidents for student affairs or their equivalents are invited to a presentation and discussion on various ethical issues in higher education. Topics have included "Ethical Trends on Campus"; "Ethical Issues within Institutional Change"; "Institutional Conscience Formation"; and "Ethical Issues in Intercollegiate Athletics."

Contact:
Rev. Stephen Potter
512 Normal Road
DeKalb, Illinois 60115
Tel. 815-758-6667

Place: Northern Illinois University

8. Course: Human Sexuality and Sexuality Morality

While such a course focuses on sexuality issues, it affords an excellent opportunity for instruction and discussion of general conscience formation and development skills.

Contact:
Ms. Jan Slattery
Archdiocese of Chicago
700 S. Morgan
Chicago, Illinois 60607
Tel. 312-829-0670

Place: Archdiocese of Chicago

9. Justlife Study Group

Ten students gathered and shared their insights from the *Justlife/90 Study Guide*. *Justlife/90* provides information and analysis on the nuclear arms race, economic justice, and abortion. It includes an "Abortion Alternatives Petition: A Call for the Right to Life with Economic Justice." *Justlife/90* is published by a Catholic-Protestant coalition, committed to the protection of all life.

Contact:
Justlife Education Fund
10 Lancaster Avenue
Philadelphia, Pennsylvania 19151
Tel. 215-645-9388

10. Pro-Life Programs

Rev. Michael Mannion, a national speaker and author on healing abortion-related experiences, recommends two types of programs. These programs are most effective when presented by a medical doctor, a therapist, a spiritual leader, a person who has had an abortion, and a local campus minister.

a) Understanding the Reality, Impact, and Fallout from Abortion

This program focuses on educating the college community about the facts on abortion from an interdisciplinary perspective. Information from genetics, fetology, psychology, and theology help to educate the student. For scientific data and further information, contact Dr. Vincent Rue at the Institute for Abortion Recovery and Research; Tel. 603-431-1904.

b) Project Rachel

Directed to women who have had an abortion, this program recognizes that God as the author of life is the only one who can heal the wound created by the loss of life. Based on Jeremiah 31:15 and Rev. James Burtchaell's book *Rachel Weeping* (Harper and Row, 1984), this program invites individuals to healing and to a renewed commitment of human life. For further information, contact the National Office of Post-Abortion Reconciliation and Healing; Tel. 414-483-4141.

Contact:
Rev. Michael Mannion
Catholic University of America
620 Michigan Avenue
Washington, D.C. 20064
Tel. 202-319-3575

Place: Catholic University of America

Resources for Forming the Christian Conscience

Books/Articles

Badia, Leonard F. and Roland A. Sarino. *Morality: How to Live It Today.* New York: Alba House, 1979. Information on the five basic elements of an informed conscience.

Gilligan, Carol. *In a Different Voice: Psychological Theory and Women's Development.* Cambridge, Mass.: Harvard University Press, 1989. Taking Lawrence Kohlberg's theories as the basis of her analysis, Gilligan asserts that morality includes considerations of care, compassion, and personal responsibility overlooked in Kohlberg's emphasis on justice. Furthermore, Gilligan forwards the idea that women reach moral decisions differently than men. Gilligan contends that women are more oriented toward a morality of care and men toward a morality of justice.

Kohlberg, Lawrence. *Essays on Moral Development: The Philosophy of Moral Development.* Vol. 1. San Francisco: Harper and Row, 1981. This is one of the numerous books and articles authored by Kohlberg. Kohlberg extends and revises Piaget's theory of moral development by proposing six moral development stages. Understanding his thoughts is essential to any discussion of moral development today.

Lohkamp, Nicholas, OFM. *Living the Good News: An Introduction to Moral Theology for Today's Catholic.* Cincinnati, Ohio: St. Anthony Messenger Press, 1982. An easy-to-read introduction to Christian morality and the functioning of the conscience.

O'Connell, Timothy E. *Principles for a Catholic Morality.* Revised Edition. New York: Harper and Row, 1990. A well-accepted textbook on Catholic moral theology that clearly articulates the history of moral theology, the new developments within moral theology and their effects, and concerns for the future.

Pilarczyk, Daniel E. *Twelve Tough Issues: What the Church Teaches and Why.* Cincinnati, Ohio: St. Anthony Messenger Press, 1988. A series of reflections on twelve contemporary moral issues.

Whitehead, Evelyn Eaton and James D. *A Sense of Sexuality: Christian Love and Intimacy.* New York: Doubleday and Company, 1989. A clear, compassionate, Christian, and mature attitude toward the problems that face ordinary people.

Educating for Justice and Peace

Dr. Kathleen Maas Weigert

Campus ministry is called to be a consistent and vigorous advocate for justice, peace, and the reverence for all life. All the baptized should understand that "action on behalf of justice is a significant criterion of the Church's fidelity to its missions. It is not optional, nor is it the work of only a few in the Church. It is something to which all Christians are called according to their vocations, talents, and situations in life". (ES, 73)

Introduction

The above excerpt is both a call and a challenge. In light of *Empowered by the Spirit*, this article is developed as both a celebration and a prod: rejoicing over current good efforts and urging all to work creatively toward a more just and peaceful world. Let us begin with an examination of the context of justice and peace work and then move to the challenges and possibilities.

On college and university campuses, what is the atmosphere for justice education in which campus ministers work? In 1985, *Empowered by the Spirit* noted "a great deal of apathy is in evidence on campus today," as well as "a strong current of individualism that undercuts concern for the common good and eclipses the urgency of social concerns" (ES, 72). Certainly, this has been a theme for at least a decade. The first step in establishing justice and peace education efforts is an understanding of the national and local campus community.

National characteristics of college students are made available in a "Fact File," published by the *Chronicle of Higher Education* in the early months of each year. It is reported that

> a record number of 1989 freshmen, 44.1 percent, said influencing "social values" was very important to them. In addition, almost one-quarter of the freshmen said participation in community-action programs was very important (Dodge, January 24, 1990).

Local information about the student body, faculty, administration, and staff could be provided by locating a campus resource center that gathers such data. Given data from both these sources, the campus minister will be in a better position to design different programs to meet the gospel call and the varied experiences and attitudes of the campus constituency.

It is not unusual for institutions—both public and private—to have mission statements that identify a "sense of justice" or "consciousness of our common humanity" as a desired characteristic of graduates. Where the mission statement articulates such a vision, justice and peace education is a response to and an extension of that mission. It can also be used in searching out allies who share that same commitment and who will be, therefore, more ready to participate in the effort. One way to find such allies is to hold an evening session for various constituencies on "Justice and Peace in the College or University's Mission: What Can/Should Be Done?"

Numerous colleges and universities respond to the call for justice and peace by providing a variety of programs to enable students to do community service; some are making such service part of graduation requirements (see Dodge, June 6, 1990). States, too, reflect this focus, as seen in the Illinois legislation that requires the state's twelve public four-year colleges and universities to encourage students to participate in thirty hours of community service a year. Catholic colleges are deeply involved in service projects as well. A recent survey of the 226 Catholic colleges and universities in the United States yielded 165 responses, of which 114 said campus ministry was involved in justice and peace studies programs, and 104 said their programs included service projects (see Carey, 1990). Finally, the growth of such national student organizations as Campus Compact and COOL

(Campus Outreach Opportunity League) attests to the importance of service to the larger community. Thus, in the area of service, it is clear that a national consensus is building around the importance of student involvement in community service. Justice and peace education efforts can draw strength from this growing trend and can obtain concrete suggestions from the work already succeeding.

Elements of Education for Justice and Peace

Empowered by the Spirit presents four areas of justice and peace that need the attention of a campus ministry program: (1) philosophy of educating for justice and peace; (2) internal policies and practices of the college or university; (3) goals of justice programming; and (4) possible justice and peace projects and programs.

Philosophy of Educating for Justice and Peace

On one level, the whole pastoral on campus ministry presents a *philosophy of education* that relates to justice and peace efforts. The particular section on "Educating for Justice" specifies some ideas that need to be pondered. First, the life of Christ and his redemptive ministry "taught us the essential unity between love of God and love of neighbor" (ES, 74). Therefore, Christians are called to "action on behalf of justice. . . . It is not optional . . ." (ES, 73). This wording echoes the statement made by the bishops in their 1983 pastoral letter *The Challenge of Peace: God's Promise and Our Response*, "Peacemaking is not an optional commitment. It is a requirement of our faith. We are called to be peacemakers, not by some movement of the moment, but by our Lord Jesus" (Peace, 333). The combination of these two statements provides a powerful guide for peaceful living and justice programming.

Since there is both a personal and a structural element involved in such work, one cannot do the personal without the structural: "The Gospel he proclaimed and the Spirit he sent were to transform and renew all of human existence, the social and the institutional dimensions, as well as the personal" (ES, 74). This theme is carried out quite forcefully in the bishops' 1986 document *Economic Justice for All: Pastoral Letter on Catholic Social Teaching and the U.S.*

Major Lessons in Catholic Social Teaching

Any list of "major lessons" of Catholic social teaching is difficult to draw up (there is such a large body of church teaching) and dangerous to publish (what about all the important items that are left out?). Offered with all due caution, therefore, is the following list of key emphases that characterize Catholic social teaching today, with some suggested documents that demonstrate these points particularly well.

1. Religious and Social Dimensions of Life Are Linked (see *Church in the Modern World*, no. 39)

2. Dignity of the Human Person (see *Peace on Earth*, nos. 8-26)

3. Option for the Poor (see *Call to Action*, no. 23)

4. Love and Justice Are Linked (see *Justice in the World*, nos. 16, 34)

5. Promotion of the Common Good (see *Christianity and Social Progress*, no. 65)

6. Political Participation (see *Christmas Message*, 1944)

7. Economic Justice (see *On Human Labor*)

8. Stewardship (see *On Human Labor*)

9. Global Solidarity (see *Progress of Peoples*)

10. Promotion of Peace (see *Peace on Earth*)

(Source: Henriot, Peter J., SJ, Edward P. DeBerri, and Michael J. Schultheis. Catholic Social Teaching: Our Best-Kept Secret. Maryknoll, N.Y.: Orbis Press, 1987. Pp. 13-14.)

Economy, where they call us to a vision of a new order: "Love implies concern for all—especially the poor—and a continued search for those social and economic structures that permit everyone to share in a community that is a part of a redeemed creation (Rom 8:21-23)" (Justice, 365). Finally, the Church has a rich tradition that shapes this effort, namely, the body of Catholic social thought: "It is especially important for Catholics on campus to assimilate these teachings and to use them in their work for justice" (ES, 75).

In summary, many elements help shape the parameters for justice and peace education efforts undertaken by the campus minister. They can be used as reference points when the campus minister is trying to decide on particular programs and offerings. A variety of resources to further explore these ideas can be found in "Resources for Educating for Justice and Peace," at the end of this article.

Shaping the Internal Policies and Practices of the University

As each college/university determines its own internal policies and practices, campus ministers and others interested in justice and peace education have the opportunity to question, challenge, and help shape university policies that affect all members of the college/university community. Policies that do not guarantee freedom from racial, sexual, or handicapped discrimination and harassment need to be critiqued and changed. Admissions policies and hiring practices are two other areas needing attention. Needless to say, this same scrutiny must be given to the campus ministry offices:

> . . . the Church on campus should remember that "any group which ventures to speak to others about justice should itself be just, and should be seen as such. It must, therefore, submit its own policies, programs, and manner of life to continuing review." (ES, 76)

The Goals of Peace and Justice

Campus ministers involved in this work "have the responsibility of keeping alive the vision of the Church on campus as a genuine servant community dedicated to the works of justice, peace, and reverence for life, in all stages of its development"

(ES, 73). In addition, the aim of student involvement is an enablement of students to do the works of justice and peace: "Christians must learn how to empower individuals and groups to take charge of their own lives and to shape their own destinies" (ES, 75). Furthermore, all education efforts must result not in what some call "the paralysis of analysis" but in effective action: "As the faith community carries on this educational task, it must remember that the goal is not learning alone, but constructive action to eradicate injustice and to transform society" (ES, 76). As *Economic Justice for All* reminds us, we are called to "conversion and common action, to new forms of stewardship, service, and citizenship" (Justice, 27). After all, what all campus ministers strive to develop is "lifelong seekers after justice" (ES, 79).

Understanding Justice and Peace Projects and Programs

Empowered by the Spirit suggests a variety of opportunities to deepen faith, to raise consciousness, and to become involved in service projects and programs:

> Since the struggle for social justice demands involvement and not simply objective analysis, the Church on campus should provide ample opportunities for all of its members to work directly in programs and projects designed to create a more just social order in which peace and reverence for life are possible. (ES, 79)

There are three implications to this statement. First, programs should have an action component. This idea builds on *The Challenge of Peace*, where the bishops stated: "To be a Christian, according to the New Testament, is not simply to believe with one's mind, but also to become a doer of the word, a wayfarer with and a witness to Jesus" (Peace, 276). Second, programs must be available for all members of the community: students, faculty, administration, and staff. Third, programs must provide opportunities to reflect on the experiences "in the light of the Gospel and the social teachings of the Church" (ES, 79). Just doing things is not sufficient unto itself; reflection is integral.

The Pastoral Circle: A Reflective Model for Identifying Injustices and Life-Giving Strategies

by Michael Galligan-Stierle, Ph.D.

The reflective model of the pastoral circle offers an individual and/or a community a vehicle for analyzing the key forces at work in deciding issues of justice/injustice. The pastoral circle invites the participants to move from their lived experience to social analysis, to theological reflection, to pastoral planning and action.

Insertion (lived experience). The individual/community is invited to identify clearly the issue to be investigated. Thoughts and feelings related to the issue are identified.

Social Analysis. The important influential elements of a particular situation (e.g., institution, issue, problem, event) are analyzed though a series of questions related to history, structures (e.g., economic, political, social, and cultural); connections between structures, values (e.g., motivation, hopes, dreams); project outcome; and conclusions, based upon this new learning.

Theological Reflection. Through theological reflection, the individual/community prays for the light of discernment; reads relevant scripture passages and church social encyclicals; clarifies gospel values being upheld and destroyed; examines the realism of church practices and the possible role of the Church; and identifies key points brought to light when one most felt the working of the Spirit. This theological reflection is brought to bear on the results of the first two stages.

Pastoral Plan and Action. Those participating in the pastoral circle design a pastoral plan in which new ways of acting are based upon the previous analysis. New action is inaugurated by the individual/community.

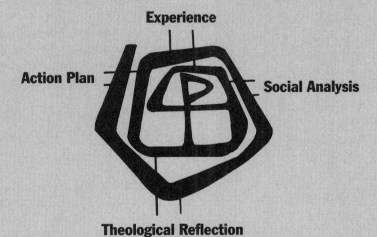

Experience

Action Plan

Social Analysis

Theological Reflection

(The pastoral circle model is summarized from Holland, Joe and Peter J. Henriot, SJ. *Social Analysis: Linking Faith and Justice.* Maryknoll, N.Y.: Orbis Books, 1983. Design concept for the Pastoral Circle is adapted from Hofbauer, Rita, GNSH, Dorothy Kinsella, OSF, and Amata Miller, IHM. *Making Social Analysis Useful.* Washington, D.C.: Leadership Conference of Women Religious, 1983.

Programs and Service Projects for Educating for Justice and Peace

A. Programs to Raise Money and Educate about Hunger

1. CROP Walks

The name given to local community hunger-education and fund-raising events sponsored by Church World Service (an international relief, development, and refugee resettlement agency of thirty-two Protestant and Orthodox communions in the United States). With the anthem call, "We walk because they walk," CROP Walkers ask people in their communities to "sponsor" them for some amount of money; the money goes to local (25 percent) and global (75 percent) needs of the hungry and the poor.

Contact:
CROP Walks
Church World Service, P.O. Box 968
Elkhart, Indiana 46515
Tel. 219-264-3102

2. Hunger Awareness Week

Several colleges set aside a particular week to educate about local and global hunger; some include in this the actual raising of funds for hunger relief, development, and advocacy. The activities may involve faculty, students, and local community. Some examples of the range of possibilities include a 5k run, auctions, talent shows, discussion groups, films, and fact sheets.

Contact:
Nancy Bramlage, SC
Office of Campus Ministry
300 College Park Drive
Dayton, Ohio 45469-0408
Tel. 513-229-2576

Place: University of Dayton

Contact:
Fran Glowinski, OSF
6525 N. Sheridan Road
Chicago, Illinois 60626
Tel. 312-508-2200

Place: Loyola University of Chicago

Contact:
Rev. Ray Jackson, OSA
Villanova, Pennsylvania 19085
Tel. 610-519-4484

Place:
Villanova University

B. Programs Linking Worship and the Needs of the Poor and Hungry

1. Lenten Program

Beginning with a "Fast Feast!" the program sponsored by the Office of Campus Ministry and the Center for Social Concerns encouraged participants to donate money to the homeless, the hungry, and the missions; homiletic themes related to these needs were suggested for the final three Sundays of Lent.

Contact:
Coordinator for Service/
Social Action Groups
Center for Social Concerns
Notre Dame, Indiana 46556
Tel. 219-239-7862

Place:
University of Notre Dame

Contact:
Steve Newton, CSC
Office of Campus Ministry
Notre Dame, Indiana 46556
Tel. 219-239-6536

Place:
University of Notre Dame

C. Programs to Raise Awareness about Social Concerns

1. An Evening of Prayer

This evening should promote an awareness and an understanding of the many opportunities for peacemaking in our world through discussion, challenge, and prayer. Many diverse groups gather to hear speakers or a panel discussion, followed by an event such as a procession, a prayer, or a reception.

Contact:
Mary Pliska
3410 W. Campus Drive
Wichita Falls, Texas 76308
Tel. 817-692-9778

Place:
Catholic Campus Ministries at
Midwestern State University

2. Friday Forum for Faculty and Staff

Three to four times each semester, faculty and staff are invited to a forty-five-minute "talk-discussion" by a faculty member on an area of social concern. Each semester has a "theme," for example, "Racism and Sexism in the Classroom." A simple $1.00 lunch is served.

Contact:
Dr. Kathleen Maas Weigert
Faculty Liaison/
Academic Coordinator
Center for Social Concerns
Notre Dame, Indiana 46556
Tel. 219-239-5142

Place:
University of Notre Dame

3. *Thirty-Hour Fast*

The purpose of this fast is to raise the consciousness of all those at the university and locally about world hunger and to raise funds for local and world hunger programs. Friends and family should sponsor a person's fasting (e.g., at ten cents an hour), and funds can be donated to various food organizations. At the end of their fast, all fasters are invited to a meager meal of soup and bread, followed by a presentation and discussion.

Contact:
Rev. William McGuirk
1200 Oakland Avenue
Indiana, Pennsylvania 15701
Tel. 412-463-2277

Place:
Indiana University of Pennsylvania

D. Programs to Involve Students in Local Community's Needs

1. *Christmas in April*

In April each year, the University of Notre Dame and different agencies and individuals in the city of South Bend collaborate to link student volunteers with skilled and unskilled laborers for the purpose of improving the housing stock of low-income people in the neighborhood adjacent to the university. This "town-gown" collaboration brought "Christmas in April" to many needy families. From forty-seven homes with a total value $500,000 of labor and materials, it has grown to sixty homes with a total value estimated at $750,000, performed by some 3,000 volunteers.

Contact:
James A. Roemer
Director, Community Relations
310 Main Building
Notre Dame, Indiana 46556
Tel. 219-239-6614

Place:
University of Notre Dame

2. *Pulse, The BC Social Action Agency*

Begun in 1970, this Boston College program offers more than 200 undergraduates the opportunity to combine supervised social service or social advocacy field work with a study of philosophy, theology, and other disciplines.

Contact:
Richard Carroll Keeley
Director
McElroy 117
Chestnut Hill, Massachusetts 02167
Tel. 617-552-3495

Place: Boston College

3. *Visitors to the Aged*

The students are given the opportunity to appreciate the aging process and its difficulties; to offer their gifts and receive the blessings of older people; and to build leadership, commitment, and friendship.

Contact:
Sr. Mary R. Pellegrino, CSJ
1200 Oakland Avenue
Indiana, Pennsylvania 15701
Tel. 412-463-2277

Place:
Indiana University of Pennsylvania
(Newman Center)

E. Semester Break/Summer Opportunities

1. *Semester Break Programs*

A number of colleges use their fall and spring breaks to involve students in service/awareness activities throughout the country. Some go to Appalachia; some go to Washington, D.C.; some go out of the country. Some work with troubled teenagers; others attend sessions with justice and peace lobbying groups. Some are tied in with academic credit; some are not. Some involve just students; others include faculty, staff, and alumni.

Contact:
Michael Affleck
Coordinator for Justice and Peace
Programming
Center for Social Concerns
Notre Dame, Indiana 46556
Tel. 219-239-7943

Place:
University of Notre Dame

Contacts:
Barbara Haenn and
Rev. Ray Jackson, OSA
Villanova, Pennsylvania 19085-1699
Tel. 610-519-4080

Place:
Villanova University

Contact:
Rev. Stephen Hornat, SSE
Office of Campus Ministry
Winooski Park
Colchester, Vermont 05439
Tel. 802-654-2342

Place:
Saint Michael's College

2. *Summer Service Projects*
Since 1980, the Notre Dame Summer
Service Project has placed Notre Dame students in service projects in cities where there
are alumni clubs, thus serving the needs of
the poor in these cities; providing an opportunity for alumni-student discussions of social
concerns; and contributing to the continuing
value education of the students, the alumni,
and the total Notre Dame community.

Contact:
Sue Cunningham
Center for Social Concerns
Notre Dame, Indiana 46556
Tel. 219-239-7867

Place: University of Notre Dame

F. Post-Graduate Opportunities

1. *ACCESS: Networking in the Public Interest*
A national nonprofit organization that
provides information services to the nonprofit sector and whose aim is "to further
strengthen the sector's ability to serve the
public," which it does in two main ways: catalogs of available job openings in nonprofit
organizations and a comprehensive database
of organizational profiles.

Contact:
ACCESS National Office
67 Winthrop Street
Cambridge, Massachusetts 02138
Tel. 617-495-2178

2. *Alternatives to the Peace Corps: Gaining
Third-World Experience*
Revised and Updated Edition, 1986, by
Becky Buell. Answers common questions
about work abroad and provides a resource
guide to service organizations, work
brigades, study tours, and alternative
travel.

Contact:
Food First Books
Institute for Food and Development
Policy
145 Ninth Street
San Francisco, California 94103
Tel. 415-864-8555

3. *Connections: A Directory of Lay Volunteer
Service Opportunities*
Provides helpful information on choosing a program, as well as specific information about graduate programs arranged by
topic (e.g., agricultural economics; ethnic
studies; women's studies). An annual directory of lay opportunities is available free of
charge.

Contact:
St. Vincent Pallotti Center for Apostolic
Development, Inc.
715 Monroe Street, N.E.
Washington, D.C. 20017
Tel. 202-529-3330

4. *Education for Action: Graduate Studies
with a Focus on Social Change*
1987 Edition by Andrea Freedman, with
Kim Berry and Mary Crain. Provides helpful information on choosing a program, as
well as specific information about graduate
programs arranged by topic (e.g., agricultural economics; ethnic studies; women's
studies).

Contact:
Food First Books
Institute for Food and Development
Policy
145 Ninth Street
San Francisco, California 94103
Tel. 415-864-8555

5. *Invest Yourself: The Catalogue of Volunteer Opportunities*

By Susan G. Angus, Editorial Coordinator. Published annually, this guide provides the largest available listing of full-time voluntary service projects and individual placement opportunities through North American organizations.

Contact:
Commission on Voluntary Service and Action, Inc.
New York, New York

6. *The Overseas List: Opportunities for Living and Working in Developing Countries*

1985 Edition by David M. Beckmann, Timothy J. Mitchell, and Linda L. Powers. A tool for those looking for a job or scholarship that would take them to the Third World; provides statistics, names, addresses.

Contact:
Augsburg Fortress Publishers
426 So. Fifth Street
Minneapolis, Minnesota 55440
Tel. 612-330-3300

7. *The Response: Lay Volunteer Mission Opportunities*

An annual directory of information on lay mission opportunities in the United States and abroad; distributed free of charge.

Contact:
International Liaison of Lay Volunteers in Mission
4121 Harewood Road, N.E.
P.O. Box 29149
Washington, D.C. 20017
Tel. 202-529-1100

8. *Volunteer! The Comprehensive Guide to Voluntary Service in the U.S. and Abroad*

1988-1989 Edition, by Marjorie Adoff Cohen. A guide to the "basics" of voluntary service; information on agencies and organizations needing volunteers, as well as on workcamps, here and abroad.

Contact:
Council on International Educational Exchange
Commission on Voluntary Service and Action, Inc.
New York, New York

Resources for Educating for Justice and Peace

Books/Articles

Benestad, Brian and Francis J. Butler, eds. *Quest for Justice: A Compendium of Order, 1966-1980.* Washington, D.C.: United States Catholic Conference, 1981. Bishops' statements on a variety of social issues, from domestic and foreign policy to capital punishment and race relations.

Carey, Loretta, RDC. *Development in Peace Education in U.S. Catholic Colleges and Universities, 1981-1990.* An analysis of survey data gathered by Sr. Carey, at the request of the United States Catholic Conference, for the Akademie Loccun Conference, "Peace Education: Task of the Churches," June 14-17, 1990. For more information, write Sr. Loretta Carey, RDC, Lincoln Center Campus, Fordham University, 113 W. 60th Street, New York, NY 10023.

Dodge, Susan. "Colleges Urge Students to Do Community-Service Work; Some Even Require It." *The Chronicle of Higher Education* (June 6, 1990): A6, A30. Discusses the growing number of colleges making a "formal commitment to community service by encouraging their students to sign up for local volunteer projects."

——. "More Freshmen Willing to Work for Social Change and Environmental Issues, New Survey Finds." *The Chronicle of Higher Education* (January 24, 1990): A31-A32. Provides an overview of the data for more than 200,000 students who enrolled in colleges and universities in the academic year 1989-1990.

Evans, Alice Frazer, Robert A. Evans and William Bean Kennedy. *Pedagogies for the Non-Poor.* Maryknoll, N.Y.: Orbis Books, 1987. A stimulating book that presents eight case studies of "models of transformative education" for the nonpoor; includes a section of reflections on such education, one being a conversation with Paulo Freire.

Fahey, Joseph and Richard Armstrong, eds. *A Peace Reader: Essential Readings on War, Justice, Non-Violence and World Order.* New York: Paulist Press, 1987. A selection of readings from the classical to contemporary; includes summaries of each and questions for discussion.

Fenton, Thomas P. and Mary J. Heffron, eds. *Third World Resource Directory: A Guide to Organizations and Publications.* Maryknoll, N.Y.: Orbis Books, 1984. A guide to "resources about the Third World and United States involvement in the affairs of Third-World nations and peoples," organized by areas of the world, as well as by issues (e.g., food; human rights; militarism; transnational corporations; and women).

Gremillion, Joseph. *The Gospel of Peace and Justice: Catholic Social Teaching since Pope John.* Maryknoll, N.Y.: Orbis Books, 1976. Collection of major documents from 1961 to 1975, with excellent introductory essay on themes; detailed index.

Hamilton, John Maxwell. *Entangling Alliances: How The Third World Shapes Our Hirees.* Washington, D.C.: Seven Locks Press, 1990. Explores "the ties that bind everyday people in the United States with those in seemingly distant developing lands."

Haughey, John, ed. *The Faith That Does Justice.* New York: Paulist Press, 1977. Various statements on key issues in social change from a Christian perspective.

Henriot, Peter J., SJ. *Opting for the Poor: A Challenge for North Americans.* Washington, D.C.: Center of Concern, 1990. Drawing on his own personal experiences, Henriot "helps us understand who the poor are, why they are poor, and the response necessary to 'stand with the poor' in their demand for justice and the restructuring of society."

Holland, Joe and Peter J. Henriot, SJ. *Social Analysis: Linking Faith and Justice.* Revised/Enlarged Edition. Maryknoll, N.Y.: Orbis Books, 1983. A helpful examination of the "pastoral circle" (or "circle of praxis"), with its four elements: insertion, social analysis, theological reflection, and pastoral planning; includes a concise "Social Analysis: A Practical Methodology."

Hollenbach, David, SJ. *Nuclear Ethics: A Christian Moral Argument.* New York: Paulist Press, 1983. An important treatment of the major positions regarding nuclear policy, with special emphasis on the developments within the Catholic community.

Honnet, Ellen Porter and Susan J. Poulsen. "Principles of Good Practice for Combining Service and Learning," in *Wingspread Special Report.* Racine, Wis.: The Johnson Foundation, October 1989. Report based on consultation with more than seventy organizations interested in service and learning; conducted by the National Society for Internships and Experiential Education (NSIEE).

Johnson, David M., ed. *Justice and Peace Education: Modes for College and University Faculty.* Maryknoll, N.Y.: Orbis Books, 1986. An examination of concrete justice and peace education attempts by faculty in the humanities, social sciences, professional disciplines, and interdisciplinary courses at various Catholic colleges/universities.

Kendall, Jane C. and Associates. *Combining Service and Learning, A Resource Book for Community and Public Service.* Three Volumes. Raleigh, N.C.: National Society for Internships and Experiential Education, 1990. Vol. I contains principles, theories, research, and so forth. Vol. II contains practical issues and ideas for programs and courses that combine service and learning. Vol. III is an annotated bibliography (see Luce entry, below).

Lopez, George, ed. "Peace Studies: Past and Future," in *The Annals of the American Academy of Political and Social Science* (July 1989). A series of articles examining the current state of "the substantive and pedagogical diversity" characterizing university-level peace studies.

Luce, Janet, ed. *Service Learning: An Annotated Bibliography for Linking Public Service with the Curriculum.* Raleigh, N.C.: National Society for Internships and Experiential Education, 1988. A resource that provides a wealth of information on service-learning from the definitional issues to the practical attempts to do it.

McCrabb, Donald R. "Volunteer Activities at Catholic Colleges and Universities," in *CCMA Newsletter* XV:10 (June 1989): 1, 6. A brief look at the results of interviews with representatives of fifteen Catholic colleges and universities on their efforts in volunteer activities.

Merton, Thomas. *Faith and Violence.* Notre Dame, Ind.: Notre Dame Press, 1968. A series of essays examining how Christians should respond to conflict and violence.

Murnion, Philip J., ed. *Catholics and Nuclear War: A Commentary on "The Challenge of Peace."* New York: Crossroad, 1983. Series of essays examining the various issues of the bishops' pastoral letter on war and peace.

National Conference of Catholic Bishops/United States Catholic Conference. *Building Economic Justice: The Bishops' Pastoral Letter and Tools for Action.* Washington, D.C.: United States Catholic Conference, 1987. Contains the bishops' economic pastoral; discussion questions; some ideas for how the Church and the local parish could respond; and a helpful "Scripture Guide to Justice."

Network Education Program. *A Call to Build Society on Earth: The Catholic Social Justice Tradition.* 1989. Includes a chart of the key social issues raised in encyclicals, synodal statements, and by Vatican II, as well as articles discussing various ideas found in the tradition.

O'Brien, David J. and Thomas A. Shannon. *Renewing the Earth: Catholic Documents on Peace, Justice and Liberation.* Garden City, N.Y.: Doubleday/Image Books, 1977. Contains major social teachings of John XXIII, Paul VI, the Second Vatican Council, and the World Synod of Bishops; some statements of U.S. Catholic bishops and helpful commentaries.

Schultheis, Michael J., Edward P. DeBerri and Peter J. Henriot, SJ. *Our Best Kept Secret: The Rich Heritage of Catholic Social Teaching.* Washington, D.C.: Center of Concern, 1987. A clear, compact guide to the major documents of the Church's social teaching; provides historical background and study guide.

Sivard, Ruth Leger. *World Military and Social Expenditure.* Thirteenth Edition. Washington, D.C.: World Priorities. Tel. 202-965-1661. Since 1974, this annual resource presents data on the use of the world's resources for social and for military purposes.

Sweeney, Duane, ed. *The Peace Catalog.* Seattle, Wash.: Press for Peace, 1984. Provides information and perspectives on a number of topics, including the arms race, military spending, empowerment, violence, and non-violent action.

Thomas, Daniel C. and Michael T. Klare, eds. *Peace and World Order Studies: A Curriculum Guide.* Fifth Edition. Boulder, Co.: Westview Press, 1989. An essential resource for those looking for curricular assistance on peace studies; includes information on professional associations, undergraduate academic programs, and graduate and professional academic programs.

Periodicals

America. A weekly magazine published by North American Jesuits, featuring articles on religion, politics, economics, literature, and the arts. 106 West 56th Street, New York, NY 10019.

Christianity and Crisis. A Christian journal of opinion (politics, social justice, theology, ethics, international affairs) directed by an ecumenical board and published biweekly. 537 West 121st Street, New York, NY 10027.

Commonweal. A biweekly journal of opinion, published by Catholic laity, dealing with religion, world and national politics, literature, and the arts. 15 Dutch Street, New York, NY 10038.

Maryknoll Justice and Peace Office News Notes. Published every other month, this newsletter gives concise reports on justice/peace issues around the world, church actions and statements, and so forth. Maryknoll Justice and Peace Office, 3700 Oakview Terrace, N.E., Washington, D.C. 20017.

Salt. A social justice magazine, with articles and action ideas about justice/peace issues. Articles show how individuals, parishes, and so forth do the work of justice and peace; provide ethical and scriptural background; offer concrete action ideas. Claretian Publications, 205 West Monroe, Chicago, IL 60606.

Sojourners. Monthly publication of Sojourners Community, an evangelical Christian group committed to community life and to working for justice and peace. Provides articles on a variety of scriptural, theological, justice, peace, and community-life issues. *Sojourners*, 1321 Otis Street, N.E., Box 29272, Washington, D.C. 20017.

Audiovisual Resources

Catalog of Audio-Visual Materials. March 1989 Edition. An annotated guide to over 500 titles in the lending library which are available for ordering. The Nuclear Age Resource Center, Interim Building—Eastern Campus, Cuyohoga Community College, 4250 Richmond Road, Cleveland, OH 44122; Tel. 216-987-2224.

Local Heroes, Global Change. A four-part PBS series that tells "how villagers and international bankers, politicians, and scholars have searched and struggled in their own ways and found viable solutions. This can help the U.S. faith community understand more clearly the hope for ending hunger." Cassettes and special study materials developed by the Interreligious Coalition for Breakthrough on Hunger are available from Alternatives Coalition, P.O. Box 429, 5263 Bouldercrest Road, Ellenwood, GA 30049; Tel. 406-961-0102.

The American Profile Poster: Who Owns What, Who Makes How Much, Who Works Where, and Who Lives With Whom. Stephen J. Rose, 1986 (Social Graphics). A multicolored 21" x 32" chart and accompanying book vividly capture key aspects of American society. Available from Educational Department, Pantheon Books, 28th floor, 201 East 50th Street, New York, NY 10022.

The International Human Suffering Index (1987). A brightly colored 18" x 24" index that statistically rates living conditions in 130 countries. Order from *The Human Suffering Index*, Population Crisis Committee, 1120 19th Street, N.W., #550, Washington, D.C. 20036; Tel. 202-659-1833.

The World Bank Atlas 1988. Twenty-First Edition. Using the Eckert IV projection for all maps, this atlas presents, in three languages, data on economic and social indications for 185 countries and territories. International Bank for Reconstruction and Development—The World Bank, 1818 H Street, N.W., Washington, D.C. 20433.

College/University Organizations

ACCU Advisory Council on Justice and Peace Education. Founded in 1977, the Advisory Council is dedicated to promoting campus-based justice and peace education programs. Association of Catholic Colleges and Universities, Suite 650, One Dupont Circle, Washington, D.C. 20036; Tel. 202-457-0650.

Campus Compact: The Project for Public and Community Service. "A coalition of 230 college and university presidents committed to fostering public service opportunities for students and to integrating service experiences with the undergraduate curriculum." Newsletter available. Campus Contact, P.O. Box 1975, Brown University, Providence, RI 02912; Tel. 401-863-1119.

COOL (Campus Outreach Opportunity League). Mission is "to strengthen, through service and in an environment of diversity, the capacity of students for thoughtful action and to create a student voice in the community to address the challenges we face as a society." National Office, 386 McNeal Hall, University of Minnesota, St. Paul, MN 55108-1011; Tel. 612-624-3018.

COPRED (Consortium on Peace Research, Education and Development). Founded in 1970, COPRED is an organization of scholars, teachers, and community activists committed to taking "a leadership role in the development of peace and conflict resolution education, research, and practice." Center for Conflict Resolution, George Mason University, 4400 University Drive, Fairfax, VA 22030; Tel. 703-323-2806.

NSIEE (National Society for Internships and Experiential Education). A voluntary association of institutions, organizations, and individuals "committed to fostering the effective use of experience as an integral part of education, in order to empower learners and promote the common good." NSIEE, 3509 Haworth Drive, Suite 207, Raleigh, NC 27609; Tel. 919-787-3263.

The Peace Studies Association. An independent federation of college and university peace studies programs, designed to complement the work of existing organizations by addressing the needs of emerging and existing peace studies programs. Conflict and Peace Studies Program, Campus Box 471, University of Colorado, Boulder, CO 80309-0471; Tel. 303-492-7718.

Amnesty International. A human rights organization working for the release and freedom of people imprisoned anywhere in the world for their conscientious beliefs, as long as they have not advocated or committed acts of violence. Amnesty International, 322 Eighth Avenue, New York, NY 10001; Tel. 212-633-4200.

Bread for the World. A Christian citizens' movement focusing on hunger issues and working for government policies that provide adequate nutrition for people in this country and other countries. Bread for the World, 802 Rhode Island Avenue, N.E., Washington, D.C. 10018.

Campaign for Human Development. An annual collection throughout the country that provides financial resources to low-income self-help groups and offers a variety of educational materials and other resources to educate the nonpoor about economic justice and our responsibility. Campaign for Human Development, 3211 Fourth Street, N.E., Washington, D.C. 20017-1194; Tel. 202-541-3210.

Catholic Church Offices. Your own (arch)diocesan office probably has resources on justice and peace. There may also be a council of churches and synagogues in your city or state that has such resources.

Catholic Relief Services. To provide resources and educational materials on hunger and its related issues throughout the world, and to provide numerous materials in educational experiences on a variety of global issues. Catholic Relief Services, 209 West Fayette Street, Baltimore, MD 21201; Tel. 301-625-2220.

Center for Global Education at Augsburg College. Provides educational programs in Latin America, designed to explore the history of political change, the dynamics of social justice, and the role of the Church in Latin America. Center for Global Education, 731 21st Avenue South, Minneapolis, MN 55454; Tel. 612-330-1159.

Center of Concern. "An independent, interdisciplinary team engaged in social analysis, theological reflection, policy advocacy, and public education on issues of peace and justice." Center of Concern, 3700 13th Street, N.E., Washington, D.C. 20017; Tel. 202-635-2757.

Fellowship of Reconciliation. Founded in 1914, by people of faith who sought ways other than violence to deal with international conflict, the Fellowship works throughout the world for peace, justice, and reconciliation. It has various denominational affiliates, including the Catholic Peace Fellowship. Fellowship of Reconciliation, Box 271, Nyack, NY 10960.

Food First: Institute for Food and Development Policy. Founded in 1975, this center for research and education for action has a special focus on hunger, core public values, and democracy. Publishes Food First News four times a year. Food First, 145 Ninth Street, San Francisco, CA 94103; Tel. 415-864-8555.

The Hunger Project. An international not-for-profit organization committed to ending world hunger by the turn of the century through programs including communication and education, strategic global initiations, and support of on-the-ground projects. Global Office, 1 Madison Avenue, New York, NY 10010; Tel. 212-532-4255.

Institute for Peace and Justice. Publishes resources designed to educate for justice and peace; provides analysis of important issues. 4144 Lindell, #122, St. Louis, MO 63108; Tel. 314-533-4445.

National Catholic Conference on Interracial Justice (NCCIJ). To implement the teaching of the Catholic Church on issues of cultural and racial justice and to promote its vision of a multicultural, multiracial understanding, mutual respect, and collaboration for an inclusive Church and society. NCCIJ, 3033 Fourth Street, N.E., Washington, D.C. 20017; Tel. 202-529-6480.

Network. A Catholic social justice lobbying group, it attempts to make Congress more responsive to the needs of all people, particularly the poor, the powerless, and the marginalized. Network, 806 Rhode Island Avenue, N.E., Washington, D.C. 20018; Tel. 202-526-4070.

Oxfam America. An international agency, founded in England in 1942, funds self-help development projects and disaster relief in poor countries in the Third World; also prepares and distributes educational materials for people in the United States on the issues of development and hunger. Oxfam America, 115 Broadway, Boston, MA 02116; Tel. 617-482-1211.

Pax Christi USA. United States section of the international Catholic peace movement; its primary objective is "to work with all people for peace for all humankind, always witnessing to the peace of Christ." Publishes a quarterly magazine, several resources, and educational projects. Pax Christi USA, 348 East 10th Street, Erie, PA 16503; Tel. 814-453-4955.

Peace with Justice Week. Focuses on the powerful linkages between social justice and peace; scheduled the week between World Food Day and World Disarmament Day, it reaffirms the growing faith commitment to a global vision of justice, peace, and the integrity of creation. Provides resources, organizing suggestions, and programs. Peace with Justice Week, 777 U.N. Plaza, 12th Floor, New York, NY 10017; Tel. 212-682-3633, ext. 36.

Project Equality. An ecumenical research and training organization that concentrates on urban ministry, focusing principally on congregationally based community organizing. Project Equality, 5700 South Woodlawn Avenue, Chicago, IL 60637; Tel. 312-271-7070.

Religious Task Force on Central America. Started in 1980, the Task Force does education and coordination among the faith community (greater strength in the Roman Catholic community) on Central America. Religious Task Force on Central America, 1747 Connecticut Avenue, N.W., Washington, D.C. 20009; Tel. 202-387-7652.

Sierra Club. A national environmental organization, with the stated goal to preserve, protect, and enjoy the wild places of the earth. Sierra Club, 530 Bush Street, San Francisco, CA 94180; Tel. 415-776-2211.

World Food Day, National Committee for World Food Day. October 16 is World Food Day, a day to focus attention on the importance of maintaining a balance between development and the protection of the environment. World Food Day, 1001 Twenty-Second Street, N.W., Washington, D.C. 20037; Tel. 202-653-2402.

Facilitating Personal Development

When campus ministry brings the light of the Gospel to the educational process, the search for personal development leads to a Christian humanism that fuses the positive values and meanings in the culture with the light of faith. (ES, 88)

Sr. Jody O'Neil, SP

Higher education attracts women and men from varying ages for a multitude of reasons. A vocational/career pursuit may be uppermost for many traditional-aged students. Nontraditional-aged students might enter academia to complete an unfinished degree or to prepare for a second career. Students may be enticed by the important skills afforded them through a liberal education (e.g., critical thinking, writing, and analyzing).

Regardless of their primary motivation, students entering higher education open wide the doors of personal development. Campus ministry is present actively assessing student needs. More importantly campus ministry is there to meet students where they are, walk with them and challenge them to grow in personal development.

Spirituality

Students exhibit a deep and genuine spiritual hunger. This spiritual hunger might be manifested quite differently from the religious practices of their parents. Many do not consider Mass attendance an obligation; God the Judge has been replaced by "God who loves me regardless of my sins." Christ is Healer and is identified with the marginalized. Sacraments and sacramentals are viewed as nurturance for continued growth and conversion, and consequently, students receive them as they feel the need. The response to faith-sharing groups, bible study programs, and the like grow when personal needs for support, deep sharing, and community are met.

Some academic circles judge it to be uncool to be religious in any overt sense. Candor about practicing religion in these circles could further provoke hostility.

Somewhat acceptable is the personal redefining of religious tradition as "I have spiritual values" or "I have faith but not in institutional religion."

Campus ministry provides an arena for responsible dialogue and education on spiritual issues—an environment that is conducive to conversion. Catholic students participate and benefit from eucharistic and other liturgical prayer experiences within a supportive faith community in which they can deepen and share their own faith.

On January 8, 1988, in his address entitled "Campus Ministry in the Church of Today and Tomorrow," Cardinal Joseph Bernardin made note of the fact the college years are often the first time students are away from home:

> [So this] offers a unique opportunity for them not only to "go to church" passively or, perhaps, reluctantly, but to be the Church really and truly. By establishing a climate of welcome and a forum for sharing, campus ministries help prepare them to be the faithful Church of the future.

Psychological/Emotional

During the campus turmoil of the 1960s, most colleges gladly surrendered their parental role. American campuses changed overnight. Coed dorms, unregulated hours, meager law enforcement, and less-structured academic requirements all happened at once. Michael Hunt, in his book *College Catholics*, claims that the American campus needs to devise ways of getting control of itself and its problems. Assessment of the emotional and social maturity of the eighteen-year-old shows that they are not ready to be so totally on their own. One way this is evidenced is through campus newspapers where numerous accounts of illegal and anti-social behavior of students are cited.

In his book *Youth and Dissent*, Kenneth Keniston theorizes that a new stage in development has emerged, which he calls "post adolescent." Persons in this stage are caught in the ambivalence between adolescence and adulthood. Most university students fall into this group and, thus, have gone through adolescent individuation from their family of origin, and a new sense of self has emerged. This new self is not yet a full participant in the adult world. Keniston says that this person has not "settled questions whose answers once defined adulthood: questions of relationship to the existing society; questions of vocation; questions of social role and style" (1990, p. 6).

Sharon Parks, in her book *The Critical Years*, uses these observations of Keniston to add to the faith development theory of Fowler, a new developmental stage that she calls the "young adult." She feels this is not merely a transition between adolescence and adulthood, but a real stage of its own developmental task: to discern a fitting relationship between self and society; to move from the dependence of adolescence to the interdependence of adulthood.

These developmental tasks are not easy ones. Simply living with ambivalence causes much stress. In addition, university life today is both mobile and transient. The resident student living away from home for an extended period of time and the commuter student spending a significant amount of time traveling demand major adjustments for both students and their families. The cost of higher education also requires many students to work while attending school. In the process of balancing academic demands with personal needs, roommate allowances, and job and family pressures, the beginning days of settling-in can be quite stressful. Support systems must be built. It takes time to make friends, especially in the huge state schools and on largely commuter campuses. Students do get homesick, feel embarrassed, make mistakes, and worry about measuring up to academic standards. Dealing with stress also can uncover dysfunctional family issues.

Campus ministry attempts to bridge the college/university and church experience to provide a welcoming presence for the campus community. Campus ministry provides an environment to enable students to find meaning in their lives. Community-building activities and small faith-sharing groups are planned throughout the year to give students opportunities to make friends with those who share similar values. Peer ministry is an effective process affording students the opportunities to reach out and minister to one another. Students involved in peer ministry learn helping skills in their ministry training that can be valuable assets in their later careers. Campus ministers who are trained in counseling or who elicit the assistance of the counseling department on campus can organize peer support groups. Campus ministers serve as adult models who often lend a listening ear to those in need. With students' heightened desire to be of service, organized service groups provide a broader awareness of human need and outreach opportunities.

Relationships/Sexuality

Deep within everyone is the need to be loved. Love grounds an individual and gives personal identity. Students value the warmth and intimacy of relationships, yet they often lack the ability to articulate their innermost needs. Thus confusion and miscommunication compound the difficulties of forming relationships. Furthermore, one of the problems of growing up within a dysfunctional family is the lack of clear personal boundaries leading to problems of enmeshment or dependency.

Healthy relationships are energizing and fulfilling. Unhealthy relationships can manifest themselves in an inordinate emphasis on power, ambition, and subtle forms of violence, such as sexism, substance abuse, overeating, workaholism, co-dependency, and busyness that precludes reflectiveness. True growth impels everyone to harness the energies of love. Like nuclear energy, the power of love can be used to enhance or to destroy life.

Campus ministry sponsors presentations and discussions on intimacy needs, married and celibate love, and the intricate role of God in our human spiritual journey. Campus ministers can provide programs dealing with the enhancement of self-esteem, since self-esteem is necessary for healthy relationships with others. Support groups can provide a safe space for students to explore issues, share fears and support one another in the growth process.

Self-Fulfillment in the Academic World

Higher education, once a luxury, has become a necessity for those who want to follow a career. Today's society and culture have been highly blessed with material resources. Students often speak of pursuing the most lucrative job following graduation, but the reality is that few students will achieve a higher standard of living than their parents. Universities sometimes intimate that a degree practically guarantees economic success and social recognition. For many, vocational interests far outweigh personal development or self-fulfillment. Graduation, however, would be a hollow achievement if, in fact, the learning process terminated with the exclusive attainment of merely vocational goals.

"To be a young adult is to search for the stuff in which to ground an emerging self and out of which to form a vision of the promise of life" (Parks, 1986, 150). Students need to ask what their acquired subject matter means in light of lived experience. People of faith provide the best answers to those questions, because faith leads believers to make meaning in their world, to fuse their acquired knowledge with their beliefs into a harmonious whole.

Campus ministry is one of the few places in the modern university where students and faculty are encouraged to leave behind the narrow specialization of their major discipline and integrate what they know with what they believe. Campus ministers provide the setting in which students and their professors interact and share what it means to be a believer in the modern world. In this interchange, students are enlivened by new levels of understanding, and self-fulfillment will be enhanced while faculty are given the chance to see students as whole persons rather than as disembodied minds.

Campus ministers can set the stage for student personal development during the college years. Each student's individual journey, despite all its challenges, is supported by the unfathomable grace of God—a grace that frees each person to embody the Gospel and form the Church of the future.

Significant efforts are made by the university to aid students in their transition from campus life to the real world. Likewise campus ministry needs to assist students' transition from our campus faith communities to the larger church. Michael Hunt, in his book *College Catholics*, suggests ten guidelines to help young people deepen their faith after college. (1) Find a parish. (2) Learn more about your faith. (3) Prepare for marriage (or other life commitment). (4) Join or form a small Christian community. (5) Deepen your prayer life. (6) Unlock the riches of the bible. (7) Expand your knowledge of Christian culture. (8) Be involved in social justice concerns. (9) Become a volunteer. (10) Become a witness in the world.

Programs for Facilitating Personal Development

Emotional Health and Healing

This series of programs offered through campus ministry focuses on helping people deal with emotions and emotional dysfunction. Several components are included: a ten-week credit course, Emotional Health and Healing (through the Mental Health Technology Department—three academic credits or audit status); evening programs on dealing with emotions; in-service programs for student services personnel on campus; various ten-week support groups; days of reflection and weekend retreats that focus on personal emotional growth and healing. These programs identify the normal healthy emotional cycle of energy and the process necessary to return to health after developing patterns of dysfunction, as well as provide support for persons to actually deal with feelings. Critical to these programs is a referral system in the community for further counseling and support services.

Contact:
Jane Steinhauser
Sinclair Campus Ministry
444 West Third Street
Dayton, Ohio 45402
Tel. 513-226-2768
E-mail: jsteinha@sinclair.edu
Place:
Sinclair Community College

Outreach Programs

A variety of programs is offered for students in residence halls and fraternity/sorority houses each semester. RAs schedule programming provided by Newman Center staff. Topics are selected according to student interest: intimacy; friendship; conflict management; stress and time management; substance abuse; occult activity; and so forth.

Contact:
Rev. Steve Knox
512 Normal Road
De Kalb, Illinois 60115
Tel. 815-758-6669

Place:
Newman Catholic Student Center,
Northern Illinois University

Support Groups

1. *Hand in Hand* is a program of care and concern for single, pregnant women at the University of Dayton. Women in the program are offered assistance in the decision process needed early in the pregnancy by a skilled, non-judgmental woman or man who will keep complete confidentiality and the utmost respect for the beliefs of the student. A mentor is likewise provided, an understanding faculty or staff person who has experienced pregnancy. In maintaining a relationship with her mentor, the single pregnant woman can find support in her fears, needs, and joys. The *Hand in Hand* program can also help students with practical issues such as housing, academic difficulties, counseling, pregnancy testing, and emotional support.

Contact:
Mary Louise Foley, FMI
300 College Park
Dayton, Ohio 45469-0408
Tel. 513-229-2093
E-Mail: Foley@Trinity.udayton.edu

Place:
Campus Ministry, University of Dayton

2. *B-GLAD* is a peer-led support group for students dealing with issues related to sexual orientation. *B-GLAD* seeks to provide a supportive and affirming environment for open discussion and education regarding issues of sexual orientation. *B-GLAD* affirms confidentiality, sensitivity, and understanding without judgment.

Contact:
Kathleen Rossman, OSF
300 College Park
Dayton, Ohio 45409-0408
Tel. 513-229-3310
E-Mail: Rossman@Trinity.udayton.edu

Place:
Campus Ministry,
University of Dayton

Women's Spirituality Groups

Women on campus and women in the community gather to share their spirituality with one another. Groups (limited to nine women) meet weekly for one to two hours. Sharing consists of exploring faith journeys, concerns, meditation, ritual, and so forth. Members make a commitment to participate, agreeing to keep shared information confidential. An evaluation is done at the end of each quarter.

Contact:
Shirley Osterhaus
Shalom Center
102 Highland Drive
Bellingham, Washington 98225
Tel. 360-734-5176

Place:
Western Washington University

Care Packages

This program promotes a stronger relationship among students, parents, and the Catholic Church on campus. A month prior to final exams, the Catholic center sends a letter and order form to all parents of registered Catholic students. Parents respond with completed order forms and money. Baskets and contents are purchased, assembled, and made available for student pick-up.

Contact:
Jenny Bagby
1631 Crescent Road
Lawrence, Kansas 66044
Tel. 913-843-0357

Place:
St. Lawrence Catholic Campus Center

Resources for Facilitating Personal Development

Books

Corey, Marianne Schneider and Gerald. *Becoming a Helper.* Pacific Grove, Calif.: Brooks/Cole Publishing Company, 1989. A good basic resource for anyone interested in any dimension of the helping profession. This text comes with faculty handbooks with a wide variety of useful information, programs, and process ideas. Write the publisher for a desk set with instructor's guides.

——. *I Never Knew I Had a Choice.* Monterey, Calif.: Brooks/Cole Publishing Company, 1986. This text comes with faculty handbooks with a wide variety of useful information, programs, and process ideas. Write the publisher for a desk set and instructor's guides.

Daniels and Horowitz. *Being and Caring.* Palo Alto, Calif.: Mayfield Publishing Company, 1976. This is a textbook used for personal development courses. This text comes with faculty handbooks with a wide variety of useful information, programs, and process ideas. Write the publisher for a desk set and instructor's guides.

Hunt, Michael J. *College Catholics: A New Counter Culture.* New York: Paulist Press, 1993. This book is an exploration of the processes through which college students grow, mature, and enter into adulthood. A significant contribution to the world of campus ministry are the author's ten practical suggestions for enhancing the faith life of students as they move from college life to the "real world."

Keniston, Kenneth. *Youth and Dissent: The Rise of a New Opposition.* New York: Harcourt Brace Jovanovich, 1960. In this collection of essays, Keniston discusses the ambivalence and vulnerability that characterize the post-adolescent stage that he terms simply "youth." He portrays the "radical" campus activist in a more positive light, as bright and idealistic rather than dumb and resentful.

May, Gerald G. *Addiction and Grace.* San Francisco: Harper and Row, 1988. The author outlines addictive behavior in all areas—alcohol, eating, sexuality, co-dependency, gambling, work—and discusses adult children of alcoholics, organizations, and so forth. He states that our fundamental disease is not a sign of something wrong, but of something more profoundly right. "It is God's song of love in our soul."

Parks, Sharon. *The Critical Years: The Young Adult Search for a Faith To Live By.* New York: Harper and Row, 1986. The author explores the studies of faith and moral development and expands them to include a new stage: young adulthood. She broadens the concept of faith from its religious domain to the role of meaning-making in life. She stresses the role of higher education in the personal development of young adults.

Riso, Don. *Personality Types: Using the Enneagram for Self-Discovery.* Boston: Houghton Mifflin Co., 1987. The Enneagram is an extraordinary framework for understanding more about ourselves. No matter from which point of view we approach, we discover fresh connections of new and old ideas. This is highly suggestive of the possibility that the Enneagram is a universal, psychological symbol, something discovered rather than invented.

Schaef, Ann Wilson. *When Society Becomes an Addict.* San Francisco: Harper and Row, 1987. Rather than focusing on addictions to such substances as alcohol, drugs, or food or to processes such as gambling, sex, or work, this interesting and unusual treatise uses the concept of relationship addiction. The symptoms associated with relationship addiction provide telling insights into why we have a dysfunctional society.

Strauss, William and Neil Howe. *Generations.* New York: William Morrow and Company, 1991. This text provides facts on characteristics of the 13ers.

Pamphlets/Articles

Bernardin, Joseph Cardinal. *A Challenge and a Responsibility: A Pastoral Statement on the Church's Response to the AIDS Crisis.* Chicago: Chicago Catholic Publishing Company, 1986. Cardinal Bernardin calls upon the members of our faith community to join him in reaching out to and caring for those suffering with AIDS, as well as their families and friends. He calls upon civic, governmental, religious, and community leaders to work collaboratively.

Flynn, Eileen. *AIDS: A Catholic Call for Compassion.* Kansas City, Missouri: Sheed and Ward, 1985. The author concentrates on the American homosexual patient population and presents a report on the impact of AIDS on its victims and caregivers, as well as on the general public. Her aim is to facilitate a careful and compassionate response to AIDS.

Nelson, James. *The Intimate Connection: Male Sexuality, Masculine Spirituality.* Philadelphia: Westminster Press, 1988. Spirituality and sexuality are so intimately connected that attempts to separate or minimize their relationship result in insidious and detrimental personal and cultural consequences.

Developing Leaders for the Future

From the perspective of faith, the Scriptures present a distinctive understanding of leadership. Jesus told his followers, "You are the light of the world . . . your light must shine before all so that they may see goodness in your acts and give praise to your heavenly father" (Mt 5:14-19). This suggests that all the disciples of Jesus carry the responsibility of offering personal witness in order to make a difference in the world and of using their influence to bring others to a greater appreciation of the goodness of God. (ES, 96)

Ms. Kathleen Kanavy

Introduction

Developing leaders in and for the Roman Catholic Church in the United States is an exciting and explosive aspect of campus ministry. Three dynamics are occurring simultaneously.

First, the Church has deepened its understanding of the Christian call to minister in the contemporary world (see McBrien, 1987). As stated in *Empowered by the Spirit:*

> The nature of Christian leadership can also be understood from the viewpoint of the vocation we all receive from God. Through baptism, "all the faithful of Christ of whatever rank or status are called to the fullness of the Christian life and to the perfection of charity" [*Dogmatic Constitution on the Church*, 40]. (ES, 98)

An emerging theology of ministry since the Second Vatican Council supports and develops this perspective:

> If Christian ministry is rooted in baptism, then all maturing believers are called to express their faith in action; everyone has a vocation that includes a witness to Christian values and service to others. (Whiteheads, 1986, 159)

This understanding permeated the preparations and analyses of the 1987 Synod on the Laity and *Vocation and Mission of the Laity in the Church and in the World.*

Second, the number of Catholic parishes with nonordained pastors steadily increases. This necessitates the development of new styles of leadership and ministry that no longer depend solely upon ordained priests. Peter Gilmour, in *The Emerging Pastor:*

Non-Ordained Catholic Pastors, states that ". . . this emerging phenomenon is not taking place solely because of the decline in priests. It is emerging also because of a developing consciousness about what it means to be Christian and Catholic . . ." (Gilmour, 7-8).

The data support this point of view. Dean Hoge, in *Future of Catholic Leadership: Responses to the Priest Shortage*, shows how "the shortage of priests is an institutional problem, not a spiritual problem" (Hoge, vii). What is most exciting for campus ministers is that

> Today's Catholic college students want broader opportunities to participate in church leadership. . . . Many students, 70 percent among those active in Catholic campus ministry, are interested in lay ministry careers. . . . This means that in the total Catholic population, the pool of people interested in full-time, paid lay ministries is about fifty times as large as that of people interested in vocations—priestly or religious life. (Jones, 1986, 1, 4-5)

Third, the Church's understanding of ministry as the privilege of a few is undergoing significant change.

> Rooted in a common baptism, ministry is portrayed as a shared imperative. . . . The differences among us in ministerial callings arise not from the presence or

absence of a "real" vocation, but from specific gifts we find among us. . . . Ministry is not meant to be delivered to a passive and docile community of believers. Ministry arises from within the community itself (Whiteheads, 1986, pp. 159-160).

Given these dynamics within the Church today, how are campus ministers to train leaders for the future? *Empowered by the Spirit* outlines three areas: (1) identifying potential leaders on campus among students, faculty, and staff; (2) nurturing leadership skills in the Christian perspective; and (3) developing strategies for forming Christian leaders.

Potential Leaders

Currently, the number of potential leaders is encouraging. The bishops' pastoral letter states that "campus ministry has the great opportunity to tap the immense pool of talent in our colleges and universities and to help form future leaders for society and the Church" (ES, 93). Many young, ambitious students will someday hold prominent positions in secular and religious communities. International students will return to their countries carrying skills and knowledge capable of furthering development in those countries and closer interrelationships in the global community.

Recent studies reveal an increase in the number of students willing to become involved. A 1990 survey, conducted by the Higher Education Research Institute at the University of California, Los Angeles and the American Council on Education, shows that more freshmen are willing to work for social change and environmental issues. Compared with the last ten incoming classes, fewer students are concerned with making a lot of money; more students are concerned with community-action programs.

Many campus ministers rely on the "self-identification" method to surface potential leaders, that is, students who are interested in particular campus ministry programs, activities, or services volunteer their time and slowly emerge as leaders in those areas. Other methods include registration forms, questionnaires, and a general "call for help." Some campus ministers recruit leaders by personal invitation, recognizing a special talent in the student or faculty member.

There is a tremendous richness of talent in the university that is available to campus ministry. Once potential leaders have been identified, however, how can campus ministry nurture "Christian" leaders?

A Christian Perspective on Leadership

The Gospel is the basis of a Christian perspective on leadership:

. . . In the Christian community, genuine leadership is based not on coercive power or high status, but on loving service that leads to the empowerment of others (Mk 10:42-45). Thus, the clear teaching of Scripture is that gifts and talents are not given simply for personal advantage; they are to be used generously for the benefit of others and for the good of society and the Church (ES, 96). . . . From the perspective of faith, it is clear that effective leadership in the contemporary world is connected both with a sense of loving service and with a more mature development in self-knowledge. (ES, 97)

Writing to the secular community, Robert K. Greenleaf echoes similar leadership virtues by proposing the image of servant leader:

If a better society is to be built, one more just and caring . . . , the most effective and economical way . . . is to raise the performance as servant of as many institutions as possible by . . . committed individuals—servants. (Greenleaf 1973, 112)

Many problems and possibilities await those who train students for a Church that is still emerging and for a society that has not yet realized a practice of Christian leadership in the world. Evelyn and James Whitehead offer a focus for the Christian leader. The use of prestigious titles can "distract both the leader and the community from the unique leadership of God" (Whiteheads, 1986, 13) and can position the leader above others. The style Jesus urges is clear: "Anyone who wants to become great among you must be your servant, anyone who wants to be first among you must be an attendant to all" (Mk 10:43-44).

Strategies for Developing Christian Leaders

What are the strategies for campus ministers in forming Christian leaders?

The bishops' pastoral urges us (1) to identify the gifts of those within our communities and to use them for the common good; (2) to encourage students to exercise their influence in other groups and activities; (3) to help students discern and prepare for their vocations in life; (4) to offer faculty members and administrators opportunities and training for leadership in the faith community (see ES, 99-102).

Practically, how does this occur? Three approaches seem to emerge: (1) leadership development as an integral component of campus ministry experiences; (2) specified training to develop leaders; and (3) peer ministry.

It is clear that the training of leaders occurs in each aspect of campus ministry. On-the-job training appears to be the most effective method of training leaders. Peer ministers develop their listening skills. Student representatives to the Campus Ministry Council or Advisory Board learn decision making and planning skills. Students in the choir learn how to plan a meaningful prayer experience, sharpen their musical abilities, and develop organization and evaluation skills. Every aspect of campus ministry is essentially a leadership practicum.

More formal leadership training programs will help students practice developing skills and complement their previous leadership training. Most college students have had some workshops on the basics in leadership: how to introduce yourself to others, awareness of personal gifts, awareness of other's gifts, and communication. Students may need more help with skills such as decision making, problem solving, planning, group facilitation, conflict management, and evaluation. Everyone—students, faculty, and campus ministers —can benefit from "refresher" classes in these areas.

In addressing the specific skills needed for a leader, what is important is not only the training programs or leadership workshops/retreats that are used, but also the images of leadership, power, authority, community, and stewardship that underlie our language and praxis. Excellent insights are found in the works of Evelyn and James Whitehead, Robert K. Greenleaf, James Bacik, and Gerald Foley, and in the writings

and speeches of John Paul II. Model programs follow in the areas of leadership training, vocations, marriage preparation, liturgical training, and a powerful dimension for the emerging Church: peer ministry.

As students mature in their leadership skills and develop a competency in their chosen major, they will begin to discern their career direction. Campus ministry needs to be present to students—through spiritual direction, small groups, liturgy, and special programs—to help students discern where and how they can best live out their Christian vocation.

Programs for Developing Leaders for the Future

1. Ministry Awareness Program (MAP)

The Ministry Awareness Program is a four-phase program that provides young adults with a "map" to help them discern and chart a possible career in the Church. The first phase is to invite men and women—identified by pastors, campus ministers, and others—to a regularly scheduled dinner and discussion gathering. Next, people explore the spiritual and theological traditions of the Church with an emphasis on personal spiritual growth. Third, the students commit themselves to a specific ministry in the local area for ten to twenty hours a month over several months. Finally, after graduation, the Office of Church Vocations follows up on participants to see how their interest in ministry has developed.

Contact:
Rev. Michael P. Shugrue
Catholic Student Center
Box 99057
Durham, North Carolina 27708-9057
Tel. 919-684-8959

Place: Duke University

2. Peer Ministry Archdiocesan Leadership Program

This leadership program seeks to empower student peer ministers throughout the archdiocese to reflect on the personal development required of a peer minister. The program consists of four reflections, followed by a series of personal discernment questions/ statements: (1) Being Real; (2) Being Present and Available; (3) Stretching Toward Realness; and (4) Prayer. Some of the questions/statements include "What does being real mean to you?" "What makes you feel real?" "What allows you to be present to another?" "Name three people you admire"; "Recall three people who have challenged you to stretch"; "In your own words compose a prayer that reflects you."

Contact:
Ms. Barbara Humphrey
113 Healy Hall
Georgetown University
Washington, D.C. 20057-1037
Tel. 202-687-4731

Place: Georgetown University

3. *Student Peer Ministers*

This program employs three students who are placed under the supervision of the Catholic campus minister for one year. Students work ten hours a week (at $5.00 an hour), with office hours and regular in-service. Positions include Peer Minister for Liturgy, for Retreats, for Parish/Community Outreach.

Contact:
Shirley Osterhaus, OSF
102 Highland Drive
Bellingham, Washington 98225
Tel. 206-733-3400

Place: Western Washington University

4. *Toward Marriage Program*

This Friday evening (7:00 to 10:00 p.m.) and Sunday afternoon (12:30 to 6:00 p.m.) program prepares engaged couples for marriage. There are three large group presentations: "Communication"; "Intimacy in Marriage"; "Faith Dimension Within Marriage." Mini-Sessions include "How Do You Feel about Money?"; "Say What You Mean"; "Two Faiths, One Love"; "The Good News Called NFP (Natural Family Planning)"; "The Blessing of Parenthood!"; "The First Year or Two—What's It Really Like?" The day concludes with a brief ceremony and a social.

Contact:
Director
Toward Marriage Program
6 Madbury Road, P.O. Box 471
Durham, New Hampshire 03824-0471
Tel. 603-868-5514

Place:
Christian Life Center

5. *Lay Liturgical Presiders*

This program seeks to train lay men and women to preside at noneucharistic liturgies, that is, prayer services celebrating the liturgy of the word and the communion rite. It has been most appealing to students already active as liturgical ministers (reader, eucharistic minister, minister of hospitality, acolyte). The training includes two evening sessions of one and one-half hours each. Beginning in Advent, student-led non-eucharistic services are scheduled weekly.

Contact:
Honora Werner, OP
Georgian Court College
900 Lakewood Ave.
Lakewood, New Jersey 08701-2697
Tel. 908-364-2200, Ext. 680

Place:
Georgian Court College

6. *Liturgical Musicians Training Program*

The objectives are to train interested music ministers in the various skills used in a parish liturgical music program and to develop leadership skills. Student coordinators—volunteer or invited—lead other students working in one of the following areas: planning liturgies; daily liturgies; programs; library; cantoring; instrumentalists; workshops; social involvement; set-up; new members; administrative; and assistant leaders. The training includes weekly hands-on experiences, under the supervision of the director or another experienced student coordinator, and regular organizational meetings to discuss the structure and effectiveness of the experiences.

Contact:
Kathleen Kanavy
Director of Liturgical Music
Scranton, Pennsylvania 18510-4676
Tel. 717-961-6152

Place:
University of Scranton

7. *New Exodus*

This is a comprehensive lay leadership training program. There are eight two-hour segments, each with a forty-five-minute videotape featuring Cynthia Thero. Workbooks for participants and a facilitator's manual include group and personal exercises for reflection and sharing, background materials on each topic, and opening and closing prayer services. The sessions include "The Growing Importance of Lay Leadership in the Church"; "Making Church Leadership a Constructive Experience"; "Communication Skills: Key to Successful Leadership"; "The Cutting Edge of Excellence: Productive Interpersonal Skills"; "Effective Decision Making for Parish Leaders"; "Making Meetings Work for You"; "Working through Parish Problems and Conflicts"; "Looking Toward the Future of Church Lay Leadership."

Contact:
New Exodus
1370 Pennsylvania Street, Suite 330
Denver, Colorado 80203
Tel. 303-832-4181

8. *Ministry to Young Adults Program*

A team from the Center for Human Development offers this training program for young adults. Eighteen meetings are possible, with further opportunities for two weekends away. Audio, video, and written materials are supplied and discussions of the real concerns to young people follow. The training program includes these components: Retreats with Facilitator and Ministry Team Formation; Ongoing Formation; Walking with Each Other (One-to-One Support Groups); Formation of Young Adult Ministry Team; Retreat/Social Weekend; Meetings with and Support from Other Groups; Social/Recreation; Facilitators' Gathering; Agreement of Young Adult Facilitators to Initiate the Program in Their Campus Ministry; and Presentation of Program in Campus Setting.

Contact:
Center for Human Development
P.O. Box 4557
3027 Fourth Street, N.E.
Washington, D.C. 20017
Tel. 202-529-7724

9. *Graduate-Student Internship Program*

This program is designed for the young adult student who desires practical ministry experience to complement theological studies. It offers financial support, graduate tuition, and various types of living arrangements. In addition, most programs include

an orientation and training; a nine- or ten-month work experience for two years; a mentor or reflection group; an annual evaluation; professional meetings; and an annual retreat.

Contact:
Fran Glowinski, OSF
6525 N. Sheridan Road
Chicago, Illinois 60626
Tel. 312-274-3000

Place:
Loyola University of Chicago

Contact:
Sr. Jody O'Neil, S.P.
300 College Park Avenue
Dayton, Ohio 45469-0408
Tel. 513-229-3339

Place:
University of Dayton

Contact:
Rev. Edward Blackwell, Jr.
16400 N.W. 32nd Avenue
Miami, Florida 33054
Tel. 305-628-6525

Place:
St. Thomas University

Resources for Developing Leaders for the Future

Books/Articles

Bacik, James. "Achieving Community: Culture, Theology and Leadership," in *Church* 4 (Summer 1988): 23-27. Introduces "committed-openness" as a leadership style for pastoral ministers, based on the sociology of Robert Bellah, et al. in *Habits of the Heart* (University of California Press, 1985) and a model of the Church as sacrament of the Spirit.

——. "Peer Ministry: Leadership and Services on Campus," in *Community and Social Support for College Students*. Norman S. Giddan, ed. Toledo, Ohio: University of Toledo, 1988. This article explores significant aspects of peer ministry: community building; liturgical participation; formation; working for justice; and service to the academic world. The author's campus ministry experiences, theological studies, and straightforward writing make this article a prime resource.

Cowan, Michael A., David N. Power, OMI, Evelyn Eaton Whitehead, James D. Whitehead and John Shea, eds. *Alternative Futures for Worship.* Vol. 6. Collegeville, Minn.: The Liturgical Press, 1987. Vol. 6 of this seven-volume series explores "Leadership Ministry in the Community." "It is a conversation about leadership, power, and ministry in the contemporary Christian community—a conversation whose partners include Christian tradition, social psychological theory and research, the developmental psychology of adulthood, and liturgical and pastoral theology" (Cowan). The Whiteheads, David Power, and John Shea dialogue by examining these facets of leadership. A presentation of several rituals concludes this challenging volume.

Foley, Gerald. *Empowering the Laity.* Kansas City, Mo.: Sheed and Ward, 1986. The author emphasizes our call to be Church all week long. He explores the theology of work, spirituality, leisure, politics, religion, and "embodying the dry bones." Of particular interest is "The Lay Ministry Explosion."

Gilmour, Peter. *The Emerging Pastor: Non-Ordained Catholic Pastors.* Kansas City, Mo.: Sheed and Ward, 1986. What happens when a parish no longer has a resident priest-pastor? The author examines the challenges this reality poses through interviews and stories of emerging pastors and their parishioners. Each chapter concludes with provocative questions for reflection, discussion, and research.

Greenleaf, Robert K. *The Servant as Leader.* Newton Center, Mass.: Robert K. Greenleaf Center, 1970 and 1973. This essay examines leadership qualities: listening, understanding, finding one's optimum, acceptance and empathy, prescience, persuasion, conceptualizing. A leader is a servant who changes herself or himself first. The implications for power, authority, and the future are hopeful and visionary.

Hoge, Dean. *Future of Catholic Leadership: Responses to the Priest Shortage.* Kansas City, Mo.: Sheed and Ward, 1987. This book is a summary of research (1983-1986) on the priest shortage compiled by Hoge and a group at The Catholic University of America, supported by a grant from the Lilly Endowment. Hoge summarizes the research and proposes options for action for future leadership at the parish level. Data collected from Catholic youth and young adults and its implications are particularly noteworthy.

Jones, Arthur. "College Students Want Church Role," in *National Catholic Reporter* (February 7, 1986): 1, 4-5. This article, the first in a three-part series, highlights some of the key findings in Dean Hoge's 1983-1986 research study, "Future of Catholic Leadership." It emphasizes data from Catholic students on their attitudes toward vocations.

McBrien, Richard P. *Ministry: A Theological, Pastoral Handbook.* San Francisco: Harper and Row, 1987. What is ministry? How has ministry evolved? What qualities do ministers need? What is ministerial spirituality? The author addresses these questions through a theology of ministry and pastorally practical guidelines. Summaries, discussion questions, and suggested readings conclude each section. "Called and Gifted: The American Catholic Laity" comprises the appendix.

Power, David N. *Gifts That Differ: Lay Ministries Established and Unestablished.* New York: Pueblo Publishing Company, 1980. Three dimensions of lay ministry are examined. "The Present" looks at the documents, facts, and the theology for this postconciliar development. "The Tradition" looks at the ministerial roles within the Church through history, with emphasis on New Testament understanding. "The Ongoing Present" discusses implications for the Church and for liturgical ministers.

Swain, Bernard F., Patricia Dunn, James Gorman and William Kondrath. *Liberating Leadership: Practical Styles for Pastoral Ministry.* San Francisco: Harper and Row, 1986. Clear principles and concrete illustrations of four pastoral leadership styles (sovereign, parallel, semimutual, and mutual) make this book a valuable source for campus ministers to understand, evaluate, and choose a recipe for a productive campus ministry leadership style.

Whitehead, Evelyn Eaton and James D. *The Emerging Laity: Returning Leadership to the Community of Faith.* New York: Doubleday and Company, Inc., 1986. The authors reexamine some inherited notions about Christian leadership and its two crucial elements: power and authority. The images of power, authority, and community in the Scriptures and the ongoing wisdom of the Christian tradition are the criteria. The authors conclude that the Catholic Church must seek to develop more adequate roles of formal leadership in the Church. The conclusion discusses education and skills training for ministry, which includes a model for training and resources. A bibliography is also included.

———. *Method in Ministry: Theological Reflection and Christian Ministry.* New York: The Seabury Press, 1980. Effective ministry combines reflection and action. This book proposes a model and a method for theological reflection in ministry and discusses education for ministry. Practical applications and bibliography are included.

Other

Chambers, Thomas, CSC. *ISLI (International Student Leadership Institute),* 1974. ISLI is designed to provide knowledge and skills in leadership and membership roles in small task-oriented groups. During training conferences, participants observe the growth of a group, leadership styles, dimensions of leadership behavior, brainstorming, positive communication, development motivation, problem-solving, and action planning. The program is particularly directed toward college-age and high school students.

Support Organizations and Their Resources

Introduction

Mr. Donald R. McCrabb

Support organizations are vital to the well-being of any ministry. Such organizations provide resources, services, and programs that assist campus ministers and campus ministries at different stages of their development. Moreover, these organizations provide a rich network among all those in campus ministry for mutual support, encouragement, and discernment.

Four types of national organizations are listed: (1) Catholic campus ministry organizations; (2) Catholic organizations that may be helpful to campus ministry; (3) other campus ministry organizations; and (4)

higher education associations. Special emphasis is given to the four Catholic campus ministry related organizations. In addition to these national organizations, there are a number of regional and statewide associations that meet on a regular basis for campus ministry in-service and professional support.

The good news for everyone in campus ministry today is that help—with a particular problem, developing a program, reaching out to faculty, setting up a student organization, designing a retreat, or organizing an ethics seminar—is only a phone call away.

Catholic Campus Ministry Association (CCMA)

Mr. Donald R. McCrabb

We encourage campus ministers to take responsibility for their own personal and professional development. . . . Membership in appropriate professional organizations . . . can provide motivation and direction for improving their performance. (ES, 29)

The Catholic Campus Ministry Association (CCMA) is a professional organization for Roman Catholic campus ministry in the United States of America. CCMA provides the personal and professional support network of those engaged in campus ministry and works within the Church and society to promote the mission of the Church in higher education.

CCMA was organized in 1969. It is a direct outgrowth of the National Newman Chaplains Association, which provided for the professional needs of many Catholic campus ministers through the 1950s and 1960s. The association reconstituted itself in 1969 to better address the needs of all Catholic campus ministers. CCMA summarizes its purpose in the following mission statement:

> The Catholic Campus Ministry Association is a national voluntary organization of individuals and groups of campus ministers who associate to foster their theological and professional growth and to promote the ministry of the Catholic Church in higher education. CCMA, in dialogue with others, articulates a vision for this ministry and develops its human and financial resources to further this mission. The association promotes active leadership and participation by its constituents at national, regional, and local levels in planning, implementation, and education.

Professional Services

Campus ministers need to be recognized as competent representatives of the Church on campus. CCMA addresses this need by developing professional standards for campus ministers and a certification process for campus ministers.

There are times when campus ministers need an objective review of their program or assistance in developing their ministry. CCMA provides consultation services that can help assess problem areas, develop long-range plans, and evaluate programs.

The personnel services provided by CCMA are based on the belief that campus ministers are professionals, with rights to due process. The association develops personnel policies, advocates equitable and professional personnel practices in campus ministry, and provides mediation or arbitration services.

In order to facilitate the placement of qualified campus ministers, CCMA offers a position referral service that publishes position openings in the CCMA newsletter, keeps position announcements and resumes on file, and provides limited career counseling.

Finally, CCMA realizes the need for research in any profession. The association has conducted a study of salaries, assessed the needs of its members, and is exploring ways to assess the effectiveness of the ministry.

Publications

In order to link the ministry together on a regular basis, CCMA publishes a monthly newsletter, *Crossroads*. Feature articles focus on developments within the ministry, program ideas, higher education news, and association news. Book reviews, position announcements, and a calendar of events are also published.

Many topics and issues in campus ministry require in-depth explanation. To do this, the association publishes a professional journal twice each academic year.

People are the heart and soul of the association. To facilitate ongoing personal and professional interaction, CCMA annually co-publishes the *Campus Ministry Directory* with the National Association of Diocesan Directors of Campus Ministry (NADDCM). The directory provides organizational and membership information on CCMA and NADDCM. Information on the National Catholic Student Coalition (NCSC) and other related groups is also included.

Campus ministry is a growing ministry within the Church and society. To respond to the changing needs of the ministry, CCMA stocks a full range of publications that can be ordered from the national office. These resources include books published by the association, as related to campus ministry, audiocassettes and videotapes, and ministry aids.

Educational Services

Campus ministers need ongoing professional development. CCMA responds to the educational needs of campus ministers through a host of unique programs. CCMA sponsors a national convention every two or three years. Study weeks are offered to explore in depth a particular theme related to campus ministry. Special workshops are offered to assist campus ministers in the development of their pastoral skills.

In addition to providing professional enrichment, CCMA supports national efforts to educate new campus ministers. CCMA co-sponsors with other organizations the Campus Ministry Mentoring Program and supports the Frank J. Lewis Institute in Campus Ministry.

All education is costly in terms of time and money. To assist in these areas, CCMA provides limited scholarships for some educational and degree programs. To recognize the time involved in professional enrichment, CCMA sometimes provides continuing education units for campus ministry programs.

Resource Library

New book releases are available to CCMA members through the Book Review Library. Members select the book of their choice, review it for the CCMA newsletter, and keep the book for their efforts. CCMA also has a small permanent library that is available on a limited basis.

The audio and videotape library has a growing number of listings gathered from CCMA conventions and other programs, specialized areas of interest, and general ministry aids.

CCMA also maintains an up-to-date resource file on specific campus ministry programs and topics (e.g., peer ministry, leadership development) and maintains the campus ministry archives.

Advancement

Through the process of evaluation, consultation, and leadership, CCMA attempts to "read the signs of the times" and respond appropriately through special projects. CCMA has already conducted special projects on evangelization, vocations, and the future of Catholic education.

Through its public relations efforts, CCMA promotes the mission of the Roman Catholic Church in higher education, encourages a wider participation in this ministry, strengthens the credibility of campus ministers, and invites others to support the work of the association.

Membership

CCMA is a membership organization. Full membership is reserved for campus ministers—those officially responsible for this ministry—and grants constitutional rights, access to services, and membership privileges. Associate membership is available to those interested in campus ministry and is limited to services and some membership privileges. Corporate memberships are available for those companies and organizations that service campus ministry.

Complete membership information is available from Membership Services, Catholic Campus Ministry Association, 300 College Park Avenue, Dayton, Ohio 45469-0407; Tel. 513-229-4648.

National Association of Diocesan Directors of Campus Ministry (NADDCM)

Edited by Ms. Linda Furge

[The diocesan director of campus ministry] is the usual liaison with the bishop and the local diocese. The director can help facilitate their [campus ministers'] personal growth, call for a proper accountability and possible diocesan-wide programming. As the diocesan bishop's representative, the director encourages the interaction among campus ministers in the diocese who serve on public, Catholic and other private campuses. (ES, no. 32)

One hundred years after the beginning of American Catholic campus ministry, a group of diocesan directors of campus ministry established the National Association of Diocesan Directors of Campus Ministry (NADDCM) on November 10, 1983, in Madison, Wisconsin, to support and facilitate the development of campus ministry.

NADDCM assists diocesan directors in ministering to higher education institutions by raising crucial and legitimate questions facing the educational system. It encourages its members to bring the rich heritage of the Church and the values of the Gospel to the public, Catholic, and private institutions of higher education in the United States.

NADDCM is committed to the implementation of *Empowered by the Spirit* and works with other groups of like mind to accomplish the following:

▲ to promote campus ministry at all institutions of higher education within each diocese through the leadership of diocesan directors

▲ to offer support and enrichment to the membership through regional and national structures

▲ to respond to the ministerial and administrative needs of diocesan directors

▲ to collaborate with the national Conference of Catholic Bishops and the United States Catholic Conference in matters of ministry in higher education

▲ to support regular communication between diocesan directors and local bishops

▲ to serve as advocate for campus ministry in areas pertaining to its effectiveness and growth

▲ to consult and to maintain liaison with individuals, organizations, and those institutions involved in the promotion of mutual interests

▲ to foster a planning process for future dimensions of campus ministry

Structure

A volunteer board of directors consists of a president, vice president, secretary/treasurer, four regional representatives, and two ex-officio members representing the United States Catholic Conference (USCC) Department of Education and the Catholic Campus Ministry Association (CCMA). The officers are elected by the membership at the annual convention. Regional representatives are elected at the same time by the individual regions. The board of directors conducts the daily business of the association.

Membership

All diocesan directors of campus ministry, diocesan coordinators, diocesan liaisons, or diocesan contact persons are considered members. Each diocese has one vote. Only those who have paid the annual dues are eligible to vote, hold office, or carry on the business of the association. Associate membership is open to representatives of national organizations who relate to campus ministry or state organizations of campus ministers.

Networking

NADDCM has official links with the USCC Committee on Education, the Catholic Campus Ministry Association, and the National Catholic Student Coalition.

Services

An annual convention is held, offering speakers and workshops, as well as an opportunity to conduct association business. Regional representatives encourage the formation of local campus ministry structures and officially appointed diocesan directors/liaison/contacts for the sake of strengthening campus ministry on local, regional, and national levels.

NADDCM collaborates with CCMA in publishing an annual campus ministry directory, supports both the campus ministry mentoring program and the Frank J. Lewis Institution in Campus Ministry, participates in the Alliance for Vocation Ministry on Campus, and endorses professional certification of Catholic campus ministers.

For information, contact NADDCM president, Joe Kiesel-Nield, 706 N. Sprague, Ellensburg, WA 98926. Phone/FAX: 509-925-3043.

National Catholic Student Coalition (NCSC)

Mr. David
Klopfenstein

*The goal is an adult appropriation of the faith that fosters personal commitment to
Christ and encourages intelligent witness in the world on behalf of the Gospel. (ES, 58)*

T he National Catholic Student
Coalition (NCSC) is a national organization of Catholic students from
colleges and universities in the
United States. NCSC's vision parallels the
bishops' statement that the goal of campus
ministry is to "foster personal commitment
to Christ . . . in the world."

The NCSC came into being in the early
1980s because students, campus ministers,
and the International Movement of Catholic
Students wanted to reestablish a U.S. national Roman Catholic student organization. The
earlier national student organization, the
National Federation of Newman Clubs, dis-
solved in 1968. In March of 1982, NCSC was
officially founded. Seven months later, the
statement of vision was created to identify in
words what NCSC is and hopes to become.
This vision underlies NCSC's structure and
action.

Statement of Vision

Called by name to share in the priesthood
of Jesus Christ by virtue of our baptism, we
are committed to fidelity in living the
Gospel. We see Christ as the embodiment of
all that it is to be human, acknowledge the
dignity of all creation, and rejoice in our
responsibility as servants and stewards. We
recognize the global vision of the Gospel
which calls us to a change of heart expressed
through word and action in solidarity with
the struggle for justice and the commitment
to love.

The purpose of the National Catholic
Student Coalition is to serve Christ by living
the Gospel in the modern world. The coalition provides a national framework to unite
existing Catholic student regional groups
and hopes to serve as an inspiration and

support to incipient and floundering regional networks. The strength in coalition provides a collective platform from which
Catholic students can speak out on issues of
peace and social justice, and it encourages
students to take a role in overturning the
institutionalized evil of our day and redefining the milieu. We recognize the responsibilities of student life and attempt to integrate
a commitment to Christian activism and lay
ministry with the student's lifelong vocation. We recognize the value of the campus
minister's/chaplain's involvement in pre-
serving organizational continuity, and assert
that campus ministers/chaplains must take
a supporting role to allow for development
of a truly lay and student ministry. The
coalition commits itself to the free exchange
of successful campus ministry programs
among member organizations, as this will
enrich the religious life of its member students. Lastly, the coalition asserts that
although it is ecumenical and non-
exclusionary in outlook, it is primarily a
Catholic student organization in concord
with the spirit and tenets of the Second
Vatican Council.

In order to effect the creation of a better
world order, the NCSC is challenged

▲ to assume a role as active participant in a
collegial response to the Church;

▲ to maintain open dialogue with other
groups who further espouse the purposes
and causes we espouse;

▲ to be sensitive to issues that face society
and humanity today and encourage a
forum for discussion; and

▲ to support the fellowship of youth and
young adults in the growth of the Catholic
community.

The NCSC is made up of all who agree to the challenges set forth in the vision statement and pay the appropriate annual membership fee. These fees are used to promote communication through various mailings including the *Catholic Collegian*, the official newsletter of the NCSC; resource materials; international information; and all other resources of the NCSC. Membership is open to individual college students, Catholic campus groups, and Catholic campus ministry organizations. Benefits that members can receive from supporting the NCSC include the following:

▲ Opportunities for students to take leadership roles in the Church in the United States.

▲ A formal way for students to speak with the bishops of the United States.

▲ Opportunity for students to identify with the universal Church and her mission.

▲ Opportunity to develop enthusiasm in a group of students who have a sense of belonging. This contagious spirit contributes to the growth and development of the local community.

▲ Communication and networking among campus ministries on the student level.

▲ A vehicle of communication, the *Catholic Collegian*, the official NCSC newsletter.

▲ Promotion of the development of specific campus programs such as Hunger Clean-Up and Pax Christi groups.

▲ Outreach to colleges and universities with no organized ministry programs and provision of the resources and encouragement to create one.

The NCSC is student administered. Leadership is provided by an elected national team of six university students, two campus ministers, and two invited members—one an episcopal advisor and the other a representative of the United States Catholic Conference.

The NCSC is organized into five geographical regions. Students of each region meet during the national leadership conference, held each year between late December and early January, to select five regional representatives who encourage networking among students in the states of the region. The regional meetings also nominate candidates to run for the National Team. All proposed legislation is discussed in the regional meetings before it is voted on by the general assembly. This process provides real leadership training opportunities for the participating students.

NCSC is a nonprofit corporation, listed in *The Official Catholic Directory*. Funding is based on membership fees, donations, and grants.

To contact current NCSC leaders or to find out about the national leadership conference, write

NCSC, 300 College Park Avenue, Dayton, Ohio 45469-2515; Tel. 513-229-3590.

National Church Structures Relating to Campus Ministry

Sr. Lourdes Sheehan, RSM

We bring to the attention of the whole Church the importance of campus ministry for the future well-being of the Church and society. (ES, 6)

Campus ministry finds a significant official and national church presence in three ways:

1. In 1985 the U.S. Catholic bishops published a significant reflection on campus ministry in their pastoral letter, *Empowered by the Spirit: Campus Ministry Faces the Future.*
2. Along with other educational ministries, campus ministry is represented on and considered by the Bishops' Committee on Education. This group of designated bishops, clerics, religious, and lay people advises the national body of bishops and the USCC Department of Education staff on various issues and concerns relating to education.
3. The USCC representative for higher education and campus ministry, under the supervision of the secretary for education, deals directly with national organizations, issues, and programs relating to campus ministry.

What follows is a more detailed description of these important national church structures.

NCCB

The National Conference of Catholic Bishops and the United States Catholic Conference are a permanent institute (cf. *Code of Canon Law*, c. 447), composed of the Catholic bishops of the United States of America, in and through which the bishops exercise in a communal or collegial manner the pastoral mission entrusted to them by the Lord Jesus of sanctification, teaching,

and leadership, especially by devising forms and methods of apostolate suitably adapted to the circumstances of the times. Such exercise is intended to offer appropriate assistance to each bishop in fulfilling his particular ministry in the local Church; to effect a commonality of ministry addressed to the people of the United States of America; and to foster and express communion with the Church in other nations within the Church universal, under the leadership of its chief pastor, the pope.

The National Conference of Catholic Bishops deals principally with matters connected with the internal life of the Church.

USCC

The United States Catholic Conference deals principally with affairs involving the general public, including social concerns, education, and communications, on the national level and in support of efforts at the regional and diocesan levels.

Every three years, the bishops approve goals and objectives that guide the NCCB/USCC staff in developing plans and programs (cf. *NCCB/USCC Handbook*, February 1989).

USCC Department of Education

The Department of Education exists primarily "to assist the bishops . . . in fulfilling their roles as teachers of the faith community." Working closely with the Committee on Education, the staff helps establish and implement the Conference's policies and programs for all areas and levels of Catholic education.

Special emphasis is given to providing leadership

▲ for the betterment of Catholic educational institutions and for the promotion of ongoing faith development through catechesis and related ministries, and

▲ for actualizing the vital roles of parents and pastors in Catholic education.

Other objectives include:

▲ fostering maximum participation in programs of federal assistance;

▲ representing the Catholic voice in the educational community;

▲ encouraging the continued Catholic identity of institutions of higher education;

▲ providing guidance on issues of public policy;

▲ developing catechetical guidelines and materials related to leadership formation, doctrinal content, programming, and multicultural concern; and

▲ engaging in ecumenical and interreligious dialogue and cooperation.

The representative for higher education and campus ministry works as a team member within the Department of Education at the United States Catholic Conference, is responsible to the secretary for education, and works collaboratively with the following:

▲ national organizations such as the Association of Catholic Colleges and Universities (ACCU) in the implementation of the bishops' pastoral on Catholic higher education;

▲ the offices of the NCCB/USCC in providing research and in developing positions that the bishops might espouse in responding to documents on higher education, issues of culture and education from the Holy See; and

▲ NADDCM, CCMA, and NCSC on behalf of Catholic campus ministry, especially in the implementation of the bishops' pastoral on campus ministry.

In addition, the representative

▲ oversees the eastern and western Frank J. Lewis Institutes for new campus ministers and the Campus Ministry Mentoring Program;

▲ represents the NCCB/USCC with the national organizations in American higher education; and

▲ represents the NCCB/USCC with international organizations in higher education, such as the International Federation of Catholic Universities (IFCU).

Other Catholic Ministry Organizations

1. Association of Catholic Colleges and Universities (ACCU)

A network for the presidents of Catholic colleges and universities. Publishes a newsletter and a journal.

Contact:
ACCU
One Dupont Circle, N.W., Suite 650
Washington, D.C. 20036
Tel. 202-457-0650

2. Catholic Relief Services (CRS)

Supports a Global Education Office, with a special concern for campus outreach. Publishes a quarterly newsletter.

Contact:
Global Education Office, CRS
209 West Fayette Street
Baltimore, Maryland 21201-3403
Tel. 410-625-2220

3. The Mexican American Cultural Center (MACC)

Specializes in preparing ministers to work in the Hispanic community. Offers a number of programs on language and culture.

Contact:
MACC
3019 W. French Place
San Antonio, Texas 78228
Tel. 512-732-2156

4. National Association of Church Personnel Administrators (NACPA)

Offers a number of programs and publications on personnel matters, such as performance appraisals, due process, collaboration, and personnel policies.

Contact:
NACPA
100 E. Eighth Street
Cincinnati, Ohio 45202
Tel. 513-421-3134

5. National Association for Lay Ministry (NALM)

A membership organization of people who are professionally committed to, and involved in, the development of laity in ministry. Activities include an annual conference, a newsletter, networking, advocacy, and research.

Contact:
NALM
80 W. 78th Street
Chanhassen, Minnesota 55317
Tel. 612-949-9242

6. National Association of Pastoral Musicians (NPM)

A membership organization to support liturgical musicians. Offers publications and educational programs.

Contact:
NPM
225 Sheridan Street, N.W.
Washington, D.C. 20011
Tel. 202-723-5800

7. National Catholic Educational Association (NCEA)

Provides publications and programs of interest to Catholic educators.

Contact:
NCEA
1077 30th Street, N.W., Suite 100
Washington, D.C. 20007
Tel. 202-337-6232

8. National Center for the Laity (NCFL)

Its purpose is to promote the vocation of the laity in and to the world. Founded in 1978, it provides a newsletter, conferences, printed and audio resources, work-support groups and retreats, and a speakers bureau.

Contact:
NCFL
1 E. Superior Street, Suite 311
Chicago, Illinois 60611
Tel. 312-271-0289

9. National Conference of Diocesan Vocation Directors (NCDVD)

Offers publications and programs to support diocesan vocation efforts.

Contact:
NCDVD
Box 1570
Little River, South Carolina 29566
Tel. 803-280-7191

10. National Federation for Catholic Youth Ministry (NFCYM)

Offers publications and programs to support diocesan youth ministry efforts.

Contact:
NFCYM
3700 Oakwood Terrace, N.E.
Washington, D.C. 20017
Tel. 202-636-3825

11. National Religious Vocation Conference (NRVC)

Offers publications and programs to support the vocation efforts of men and women religious orders.

Contact:
NRVC
1603 S. Michigan Avenue, Suite 400
Chicago, Illinios 60616
Tel. 312-663-5454

12. North American Forum on the Catechumenate (The Forum)

Sponsors programs to train people in the Rite of Christian Initiation of Adults.

Contact:
The Forum
7115 Lessburg Pike, Suite 308
Falls Church, Virginia 22043
Tel. 703-534-8082

13. Pax Christi, USA

Offers publications and programs to support the national Catholic peace movement. Has a special outreach to college students.

Contact:
Pax Christi, USA
348 E. 10th Street
Erie, Pennsylvania 16503
Tel. 814-453-4955

Other Campus Ministry Organizations

1. **American Baptist Campus Ministers Association**
   The Baptist House
   2117 West Petty Road
   Muncie, Indiana 47304
   Tel. 317-284-5735

2. **Associates for Religion and Intellectual Life (ARIL)**
   Publishes a journal that examines the relationship between all religions and the intellectual life.
   Contact:
   ARIL
   College of New Rochelle
   New Rochelle, New York 10805
   Tel. 914-654-5425

3. **Association of Coordinators of University Religious Affairs (ACURA)**
   The professional organization for persons hired by the university to coordinate the religious affairs on campus.
   Contact:
   ACURA
   Janet Cooper Nelson
   President
   University Chaplain
   Brown University
   Box 1931
   Providence, Rhode Island 02912
   Tel. 401-863-2344

4. **Association of Hillel and Jewish Campus Professionals (AHJCP)**
   Professional association for those serving Jewish students on campus.
   Contact:
   AHJCP
   Hillel International Center
   1640 Rhode Island, N.W.
   Washington D.C. 20036
   Tel. 202-857-6557

5. **Baptist Student Union**
   Contact:
   National Student Ministry
   127 Ninth Avenue North
   Nashville, Tennessee 37234
   Tel. 615-251-3634

6. **Campus Ministry Women (CMW)**
   A personal and professional support network for women of all denominations and faiths who work in campus ministry.
   Contact:
   CMW
   Sherri Bohjanen
   Lutheran Campus Ministry
   Northern Michigan University
   N5 Hunt Hall
   Marquette, Michigan 49855

7. **Council for Ecumenical Student Christian Ministry (CESCM)**
   An interdenominational organization on the executive level that promotes ecumenical campus ministry and student conferences.
   Contact:
   CESCM
   Clyde O. Robinson, Chair
   7407 Steele Creek Road
   Charlotte, North Carolina 28217
   Tel. 704-588-2182

8. **Episcopal Society for Ministry in Higher Education (ESMHE)**
   The professional organization for Episcopalian campus ministers.
   Contact:
   ESMHE
   Julia Easley, Episcopal Chaplaincy
   University of Iowa
   26 East Market Street
   Iowa City, Iowa 52245
   Tel. 319-351-2211

9. **Higher Education Ministries Arena (HEMA)**
   Contact:
   Donald G. Shockley, Chair
   Campus Ministry Section
   P.O. Box 871
   Nashville, Tennessee 37202
   Tel. 615-340-7404

10. **Intercollegiate Pentecostal Conference International (IPCI)**
    A support organization for campus ministers in the Pentecostal tradition.

Contact:
IPCI
100 Bryan Street, N.W.
Washington, D.C. 20001

11. *National Association of College and University Chaplains and Directors of Religious Life (NACUC)*

This is the professional organization for chaplains hired by the college or university—usually a private, church-related school—to serve the students of the host denomination and to coordinate the religious activities of all denominations.

Contact:
NACUC
John Patrick Colatech
President
Office of Chaplain
Allegheny College
Box 14
Meadville, Pennsylvania 16335
Tel. 814-332-2800

12. *National Campus Ministry Association (NCMA)*

An ecumenical professional association for campus ministers.

Contact:
NCMA
Phil Harden, President
633 SW Montgomery Street
Portland, Oregon 97201
Tel. 503-226-7807

13. *National Council of Churches (NCC)*

Sponsors an office on Education in Society.

Contact:
Education in Society, NCC
475 Riverside Drive, Room 710
New York, New York 10115
Tel. 212-870-2277

14. *United Methodists in Campus Ministry*

Contact:
Beth Scott, Chair
United Campus Ministry
101 Northwest 23rd Street
Corvalis, Oregon 97330
Tel. 503-753-2242

15. *United Ministries in Higher Education*

Contact:
Linda Danby Freeman
7407 Steele Creek Road
Charlotte, North Carolina 28217
Tel. 704-588-2182

16. *World Student Christian Foundation*

Contact:
5, Route des Morillons
1218 Grand-Saconnex
Geneva, Switzerland
Tel. 41-22-798-8953

Mr. Donald R. McCrabb

Higher Education Associations

1. *American Association of University Professors (AAUP)*

The leading advocacy organization for university professors.

Contact:
AAUP
1012 14th Street, N.W., Suite 500
Washington, D.C. 20005
Tel. 202-737-5900

2. *American College Health Association (ACHA)*

Provides publications and programs on campus health-related issues. Co-sponsored, with the U.S. Centers for Disease Control, HIV/AIDS Prevention Workshops for college staff and campus ministers.

Contact:
ACHA
P.O. Box 28937
Baltimore, Maryland 21240
Tel. 410-859-1500

3. *American Council on Education (ACE)*

Conducts research into the status of education in the United States and holds conferences for leaders in education.

Contact:
American Council on Education
One Dupont Circle, N.W., Suite 800
Washington, D.C. 20036
Tel. 202-939-9310

4. *National Association of Student Personnel Administrators (NASPA)*

The national organization for student-life professionals. Has written professional standards for various positions within the student-life area. Provides publications and conferences.

Contact:
NASPA
1875 Connecticut Avenue, N.W., Suite 418
Washington, D.C. 20009
Tel. 202-265-7500

5. *Special Resources*

A number of higher education associations have very focused purposes. *The Higher Education Directory*, published annually by Higher Education Publications, Inc., has all the higher education associations listed.

Contact:
Higher Education Publications, Inc.
6400 Arlington Boulevard
Falls Church, Virginia 22042
Tel. 703-532-2300

Annotated Bibliography

Mr. Raymond
R. Lagesse

Books

Alden, Betsy and Helen Neinast, eds.
Church and Campus Calling: A Collection of Resources for Ministries in Higher Education.
Nashville, Tenn.: United Ministries in Education, 1985. This volume describes the contemporary context of ministry, theological reflections on the Church's mission, and a variety of campus ministry programs. It represents a range of perspectives in its contents. It is designed primarily for the practitioner but also keeps other interested constituencies in mind. A study guide, a list of additional resources, and suggested application tools are included.

Brummet, Barbara. *The Spirited Campus: The Chaplain and the College Community.*
New York: Pilgrim Press, 1990. Brummet identifies and explores some of the personal, ministerial, theological, and ethical issues in the evolution of a college chaplaincy in a small liberal arts college. Two essential questions are raised and addressed: How do we, as ministers, deal with institutional and social structures in the establishment of college chaplaincy? and, How do positions, such as chaplaincy, evolve? The narrative style involves the reader in the decision-making process.

Butler, John, ed. *Religion on Campus.* San Francisco: Jossey-Bass Inc., 1989. This is a source book for student-services personnel on the relationship between the campus and different religions. It examines the current situation, gives a preview of faith development, reviews the legal implications, and advocates a positive working relationship between the university and religions. A solid basis for dialogue with the university.

Campus Ministry Communications. *What's the Big Idea? Plug into 627 Campus Ministry Programming Ideas.* Chicago, Ill.: Campus Ministry Communications, 1982. A "cookbook" of campus ministry programs organized under twenty recipes: from the Arts to Worship. References are given where to find additional information.

Commission on Campus Ministry of the College and University Department, National Catholic Educational Association. *Guidelines for Campus Ministry at Catholic Colleges and Universities.* Washington, D.C.: College and University Department, National Catholic Educational Association, 1974. Based on statements from the *Catholic University in the Modern World*, the Second Congress of Catholic Universities of the World, this short guide outlines the current situation of the university and the social *milieu* of the mid-1970s; defines the nature of campus ministry; lists the functions of campus ministry; gives guidelines for the status of campus ministry at Catholic campuses; and comments on campus ministry in settings beyond the Catholic institution.

DeMan, Thomas. *Dominican Campus Ministry: 1908-1988.* Marysville, Wash.: Tulali Bay Press, 1988. A brief history of the twenty-four universities and colleges served by the Order of Preachers. The text also introduces the reader to the state of campus ministry, the persons involved, the history of the Dominican presence on campus, and the particular charism of Dominican campus ministry.

Evans, John Whitney. *The Newman Movement: Roman Catholics in American Higher Education, 1883-1971.* Notre Dame, Ind.: University of Notre Dame Press, 1980. A historical perspective by a knowledgeable author, this work gives a detailed historical narrative of the people, the beginnings, and the evolution of Catholic campus ministry. This text is suited to those seeking a foundational understanding of campus ministry.

———. *An Evaluative Study of Institutional Guidelines for Campus Ministry.* Research Report No. 2. Cambridge, Mass.: National Center for Campus Ministry, February 1973. This report seeks to give chaplains and administrators a clearer sense of identity, function, and status of campus ministry. It gives a historical perspective on the guidelines and evaluation, conclusions and recommendations, and outside perspectives on Catholic campus ministry. The report is well documented.

Galligan-Stierle, Michael, ed. *Prepare the Way of the Lord: Biblical People as Models for Campus Ministry.* Dayton, Ohio: Catholic Campus Ministry Association, 1988. The proceedings of the 1988 CCMA Eastern Study Week with the keynote addresses of Eugene LaVerdiere, Martha Ann Kirk, Roland Murphy, Marie Carol Hurley, and Michael Moynihan. Twenty-four workshop lectures and five prayer experiences are also given.

Gribbon, R. T. *Students, Churches, and Higher Education: Congregational Ministry in a Learning Society.* Valley Forge, Pa.: Judson Press, 1981. The results of workshops with clergy and lay leaders, this work provides an ecumenical guide for involving a congregation in campus ministry; it is a useful guide for engaging faculty. Various possible forms of ministering to college students by a local community are presented through stories, analysis, and exercises.

Hassel, David J., SJ. *City of Wisdom: A Christian Vision of the American University.* Chicago, Ill.: Loyola University Press, 1983. Based on a historical reflection of American universities, which produces a creative synthetic vision of higher education, this book gives challenging focus for campus ministry work. The author helps to situate the vision of campus ministry into a larger institutional context.

Murphy, Lawrence T. and John Whitney Evans, eds. *Perspectives for Campus Ministers.* Washington, D.C.: Division of Higher Education, United States Catholic Conference, 1972. This short work examines some aspects of work and institution that shape the identity and response of campus ministers. Ways of looking at campus ministry by those engaged in it are the central points of the work.

National Conference of Catholic Bishops. *Empowered by the Spirit: Campus Ministry Faces the Future.* Washington, D.C.: United States Catholic Conference, 1986. This pastoral letter speaks particularly to those working at non-Catholic institutions, yet the theme is equally applicable to all who work in higher education. Campus ministry is defined; the people who serve on campus are described; and six aspects of campus ministry are discussed at length. This is an essential document for anyone working in campus ministry.

———. *Catholic Higher Education and the Pastoral Mission of the Church.* Washington, D.C.: United States Catholic Conference, 1980. This statement of the U.S. Catholic bishops details the identity and mission of Catholic higher education as a pastoral ministry and focuses on dimensions of curriculum, Christian formation of teachers, constituencies served, and support for Catholic education. Campus ministry is described and affirmed as one aspect of that identity.

Parsonage, Robert R., ed. *Invitation to Dialogue: The Theology of College Chaplaincy and Campus Ministry.* New York: Education in Society, National Council of the Churches of Christ in the USA, 1986. This unique theological reflection on the Church's mission and ministry in higher education is the product of a broad ecumenical effort. Four sections give theological insights into campus ministry from Protestant, Roman Catholic, and minority perspectives. The last section is a study guide for initiating dialogue among campus ministers.

Rankin, Robert, ed. *The Recovery of Spirit in Higher Education: Christian and Jewish Ministries in Campus Life.* New York: Seabury Press, 1980. Three areas relative to campus ministry are assessed: (1) the discovery and nature of the spirit; (2) contemplation and action in higher education; and (3) the ministries of faith communities. This collection of essays addresses the religious events happening within colleges and universities and the religious communities that have been formed within them. Articles treat perspectives from Jewish, Roman Catholic, Evangelical, and mainline Protestant traditions.

Shaw, P. Gerard, OSA, ed. *Empowered by the Spirit: Campus Ministry Faces the Future—A Commentary.* North Andover, Mass.: Merrimak College Press, 1986. The twelve articles comment on the campus ministry pastoral letter from the perspective of different people engaged in higher education and in ministry: bishops, university administrators, professors, campus ministers, and pastors. The articles enhance an understanding of the bishops' pastoral, *Empowered by the Spirit*.

Shockley, Donald G. *Campus Ministry: The Church Beyond Itself.* Louisville, Ky.: Westminster/John Knox Press, 1989. This philosophical reflection advocates the renewal of campus ministry for the global mission of the Church. It is a "why-to" rather than a "how-to" book. It examines the past history of campus ministry and the leadership of the mainline denominations in order to carve a vision for the future.

Student Ministry Department. *Baptist Student Ministry Guide Book.* Nashville, Tenn.: Sunday School Board of the Southern Baptist Convention, 1988. This is the latest revised edition of the Southern Baptist handbook for campus ministers of this denomination. It is a how-to book. It describes methods for organizing and developing a campus ministry program. It is divided into sections on Individual Christian Growth and Christian Outreach in terms of evangelization and social action.

Underwood, Kenneth. *The Church, The University and Social Policy: The Danforth Study of Campus Ministry.* Vol. I, II. Middletown, Conn.: Wesleyan University Press, 1969. This research project is the foundational opus for information about campus ministry in the United States. Campus ministry's influence and relationship to the university and the structure and forces of the ministry in the social environment are covered in detail. It limits discussion to the Protestant perspective at public institutions. "Policy Research" or prophet inquiry is a dominant theme.

The United States Catholic Conference. *Campus Ministry Guidelines for Diocesan Directors and Campus Ministers.* Washington, D.C.: Department of Education, United States Catholic Conference, 1976. The predecessor of this current handbook. It contains chapters on the role of the diocesan director,

evaluation instruments for campus ministry, a selection of statements about campus ministry, job descriptions, contracts, and a resource directory of campus ministry-related associations.

———. *National Survey of Campus Ministries.* Washington, D.C.: United States Catholic Conference, 1979. Commissioned by the United States Catholic Conference, The Catholic University of America, and Illinois Benedictine College, this national survey attempted to establish a database of information about campus ministry that covers topics on models of ministry; the setting of ministry; training and characteristics of the campus ministers; campus ministry programs; and the relationship of campus ministry to the particular campus and to the local Church. Results are discussed, findings are summarized, and recommendations for future research are listed.

———. *The Status of Campus Ministry Today.* Washington, D.C.: Department of Education, United States Catholic Conference, 1977. This short report gives a brief history of the origins and growth of the Newman Apostolate, discusses the crisis in higher education in the mid-1970s, and includes campus ministry's response. The report catalogs factors and forces that affect campus ministry and then discusses present challenges to that ministry. It closes with a vision for the future of campus ministry.

Westerhoff, John H., ed. *The Church's Ministry in Higher Education.* Papers and responses to a conference at Duke Divinity School, January 27-29, 1978. New York: United Ministries in Higher Education, Communication Office, 1978. This volume reassesses the Danforth Study of Campus Ministries ten years later. It focuses on campus ministry in the southern United States and emphasizes African Americans. The broad spectrum of respondents discuss inclusive policy and program decision making. Part I explores the conflicts involved in doing campus ministry, and Part II explores the desired future for campus ministry in higher education.

Articles/Journals

Association of American Colleges, Commission on Religion in Higher Education. *The Role of Institutionally Appointed Campus Professional Religious Leadership.* Washington, D.C.: Association of American Colleges, 1972. This position paper addressed to college administrators describes the university or college chaplain as one who performs a complex role in the arenas of decision making, unifying campus factions, reconciling and healing in the institution, and revealing the moral and spiritual resources of the religious traditions. The special skills needed to perform this task are discussed.

Bernardin, Joseph Cardinal. "Campus Ministry in the Church of Today and of Tomorrow," in *Origins* 18:34 (February 2, 1989): 553-556. This sharp and inspiring address to campus ministers reflects on the Church of the future, gives campus ministers five formal objectives to implement, presents correlating attitudes that influence these objectives, and concludes with two concerns for the future.

Braxton, Edward K. "Catholic Students and Secular Universities," in *America* 150 (April 28, 1984): 315-19; and 151 (June 2, 1984): 428. The article focuses on the difficulties Catholic students encounter at secular universities in adjusting their faith experience to the pluralism experienced on campus. Forces that influence a student's shift in understanding of religion are discussed, including the influence—both positive and negative—of the faith community.

————. "The Church and the University: Ministry on Campus," in *Origins* 14:47 (May 9, 1985): 763, 765-770. Braxton delivered this paper at the Seattle Study Week of the Catholic Campus Ministry Association. It uses themes from the first draft of the bishops' 1987 pastoral on campus ministry. It discusses the Catholic student at a secular university, student faith development, the practical structures for ministering to students, and the relationship between Church and university.

Burden, Susan. "Lay Catholic Campus Ministers: Data, Analysis, Interpretation," in *Process* 4:2 (Spring 1978): 5-8. This report explains the results of a Catholic Campus Ministry Association-sponsored survey of lay campus ministers. It describes the target group in detail and reports on issues of support and resistance, accountability, and salary/benefit packages.

Elsesser, Suzanne. "Full-Time Lay Ministers in the Church," in *Origins* 10:10 (August 14, 1980): 145, 147-151. This report discusses campus ministers among various categories of lay ministers in the Church. Issues of role description, job advancement, support structures, and employment practices are treated in detail.

Evans, John Whitney, ed. "A Theme Issue: The Campus Minister," in *Counseling and Values* 16:2 (Winter 1972): 78-141. This entire issue is devoted to the topic of campus ministry in higher education: J. Evans, "Campus Ministry Today: Some Projections"; J. Morin and R. Nelson, "Campus Ministry: A Celebration of Hope"; A. Kelley, "Women in Pastoral Ministries"; R. Sullivan, "Campus Ministry on the Secular Campus: Perspectives and Problems"; J. Blumeyer, "Campus Ministry in Jesuit Colleges and Universities"; P. O'Neill, "The Contemporary Campus Ministry: Youth and Drugs"; H. Nouwen, "Training for Campus Ministry"; R. Devor, "Training for Campus Ministry: Another View"; and J. Evans, "Documentation: Campus Ministry Guidelines for Catholic Colleges."

Harshbarger, Luther H. "The Role of Professional Religious Leadership in Colleges and Universities, an Occasional Paper." Washington, D.C.: Association of American Colleges, 1972. This short paper is a useful dialogue guide for exploring the relationship of campus ministry at secular institutions. Harshbarger's incisive thesis is that the university has a responsibility to incorporate religious leadership on campus as a definitive dimension of an academic environment.

Hemrick, Eugene F. "The Need to Define Roles: Church Ministries," in *Origins* 10:10 (August 14, 1980): 151-4. This report draws from three national surveys on church ministers: campus ministers, directors of religious education, and permanent deacons. It underlines the problems derived from lack of job descriptions for church ministers and suggests areas for improving and empowering ministry leadership.

Inman, David A. "Issues in Governance for Campus Ministry," in *NICM Journal* 5:4 (Fall 1980): 71-81. This discussion on governance builds from Underwood's monumental study. There are three major parts: (1) the historical development of governance, based on Underwood's study; (2) a discussion of present strategies in governance; and (3) suggestions for the future challenge in campus ministry leadership.

Jones, George W., ed. "Campus Ministry," in *Counseling and Values* 20:2 (February, 1976): 52-104. This entire issue is devoted to the topic of campus ministry in higher education: G. Dahl, "Ministry in a Learning Society: Toward a New Symbiosis of Faith, Learning, and Power"; R. Rankin, "The Urgent Need for Ministry in Higher Education"; N. Malone, "Case Studies and the Campus Ministry"; P. Palmer, "Campus Ministry and Its Publics: Some Reflections on Accountability"; D. McGown, "Evaluation in Protestant Campus Ministry"; Y. Lander, "The Process of Evaluation as Developed by College Chaplains"; T. Gumbleton, "A Diocesan Approach to Accountability in the Roman Catholic Church"; D. Hazelwood, "Campus Ministry at Community Colleges"; R. Rose, "Roots, Issues, and the Campus Ministry"; and G. Jones, "Social Change Ministries: A Feasibility Study of Campus Religious Affairs Centers."

Krump, John. "Newman Centers: Are College Catholics Making the Grade?" in *U.S. Catholic* 47 (September 1982): 31-35. This article covers Newman Centers across the nation in order to give a profile of their activity, the people who frequent the centers, and the success campus ministers have in their work. The article paints a favorable picture of campus ministry.

Madden, Lawrence J., SJ. "The Role of Campus Ministry in the Catholicity of the College or University," in *Occasional Papers on Catholic Higher Education* 1:1 (July 1975): 12-4. At Catholic institutions, campus ministry has important roles in the academic,

pastoral, liturgical, and social conduct of the school. The character and training of the campus minister and the organizational aspects of the campus ministry team are discussed in this article.

——, ed. "Renewal and New Directions in the Church on Campus," in *Occasional Papers on Catholic Higher Education* 2:2 (Winter 1976). Washington, D.C.: National Catholic Educational Association, College and University Department. This collection of essays focuses on three themes: understanding "Church" as a network of people; awareness of the shared responsibility and leadership for ministry by all Christians; and spirituality of campus ministry. Discusses leadership roles of president and faculty, lay minister, and models of spiritual direction.

McCarthy, Edward. "The Ministers Needed on Campus," in *Origins* 15:34 (February 6, 1986): 561-562. This pastoral letter on campus ministry by the Archbishop of Miami addresses the urgent need for more ministers on campus. Sufficient priests are not available; therefore, support of and involvement in campus ministry on the part of college faculty, staff, parents, and students are stressed.

Rankin, Robert. "Revolution in the Campus Ministry: The Evangelical Challenge," in *NICM Journal* 2:1 (Winter 1977): 153-76. This article helps to understand changes in campus ministry development. Rankin's thesis is that the evolution in campus ministry follows a process parallel to the evolution of scientific thought; he discusses the "conversion" element in both paradigms.

Secretariat for the Laity and Family Life, National Conference of Catholic Bishops. "Youth Ministry in the United States," in *Origins* 18:32 (January 18, 1989): 518-528. This informative report examines how the Catholic Church ministers to the needs of young people based on survey results from bishops and national groups connected with youth work. It reports that youth are influenced by relationships, seek a spirituality, and are affected by fundamentalism. The detailed overview of organizations and movements in youth ministry is a good directory resource for campus ministers.

Toohey, William. "Campus Ministry at Catholic Universities," in *Process* 4:1 (Winter 1978): 1-6. The author reflects on the vision of campus ministry for a Catholic university. Based on gospel principles, this article comments on leadership, team models of ministry, outreach to university constituencies, programming, and suggestions for the future.

van Beeck, Frans Jozef. "The Role of Colleges and Universities in Preparing Leadership and Ministries in the Church of the Future," in *Occasional Papers on Catholic Higher Education* 4:1 (Summer 1978): 4-10. Ministry and leadership renewal in the Church require personal and communal faith and experience. Examples of faith-sharing communities within the framework of the Church are cited. Areas of action are suggested for those who share any responsibility for ministry in higher education.

Vatican Congregation for Catholic Education and the Pontifical Council for the Laity. "The Pastoral Ministry on the University Campus," in *Origins* 6:13 (September 16, 1976): 197, 199-204. This report is the result of a five-year joint study; it gives an outline of problems and trends in campus ministry. It describes the particular needs and qualifications of university chaplains, details changes in contemporary university life that affect campus ministry, and gives detailed pastoral action recommendations.

Vatican Congregation for Catholic Education and the Pontifical Councils for Culture and for the Laity. "The Church and University Culture," in *Origins* 18:7 (June 30, 1988): 109-112. This is a synthesis of the responses to a Vatican questionnaire sent out in April 1986 concerning pastoral work in the university. Of particular emphasis was the encounter of the Church with the university culture. The article first sets the scene of the university and then discusses the problems inherent in that scene. Some possible approaches are examined as a response to the problems and the needs of this focus of concern to the entire Church.

Waters, Brent P. "Campus Ministry as the Church's Phoenix," in *NICM Journal* 7:3 (Summer 1982): 64-71. This article discusses the problem of campus ministry identity and then suggests a transition from playing roles to providing resources to higher education. The four principal resources of memory, conscience, spirituality, and vision are effectively presented.

Whitehead, Evelyn Eaton. "Models of Ministry in Higher Education," in *NICM Journal* (Winter 1976): 14-22. Explores the common values shared by ministry in higher education. Based on these values, it identifies three models of ministry with and to higher education: (1) ministry over against the values of higher education; (2) ministry to and through the values of higher education; and (3) ministry alongside the values of higher education.

Dissertations

Costin, June Meredith. "Catholic Campus Ministry with Commuter Students: Assessing Needs and Developing Strategies." D.Min. diss., St. Mary's Seminary and University, 1988. This study explores commuter needs and the strategies for meeting them. The four models of ministry of the Danforth Study of Campus Ministry were translated into ministerial activities of counseling, worship, discussions, and participation in church leadership. Student responses indicated that most seek spiritual guidance, support, and community. Theological models of small groups apply rather than models of large church communities.

Gohm, Robert, SJ. "A Catholic Response to Evangelicalism on Campus." D.Min. diss., St. Mary's Seminary and University, 1988. This study is useful as an orientation for understanding and dealing with the impact of fundamentalist groups on Catholic students. It treats approaches to presenting a Catholic counterpoint to evangelical influences.

Hadrick, Mary Emma. "The Actual and Ideal Leadership Role of the Campus Minister in Selected Public Community Colleges as Perceived by the Ministers, the Administration, the Faculty and the Students." Ph.D. diss., The Catholic University of America, 1985. An analysis of actual leadership roles compared with ideal roles is the focus of this study. A list of recommendations indicates seven needs of campus ministry ranging from role definition to personnel selection and training for those working in the community college setting.

Lagesse, Raymond Richard. "A Descriptive Profile of Campus Ministry Personnel at American Jesuit Colleges and Universities." Ph.D. diss., Saint Louis University, 1989. This study constructs a detailed, descriptive profile of campus ministers at Jesuit colleges and universities and relates the description to an attitudinal profile of their satisfaction with organizational style. Preferred models of ministry are discussed along with many descriptors useful for understanding campus ministers at Catholic institutions.

Lanagan, Margaret Ann. "The Distribution of Catholic Campus Ministers' Time among Work Components Established by the United States Catholic Conference and the National Catholic Educational Association." Ph.D. diss., The American University, 1979. Studies the distribution of campus ministers' time spent among eight ministry work components derived from two Catholic guideline documents. Includes descriptive characteristics of campus ministers, along with the time analysis of campus ministry activities.

McDermott, Neal W. J. "A Modified Framework for Doing Campus Ministry in Roman Catholic Institutions of Higher Learning." D.Min. diss., Candler School of Theology at Emory University, 1984. A review of official Roman Catholic church documents on ministry in the Church are addressed to a framework for campus ministry at Catholic institutions. The framework is critiqued in light of recent theological writings. A sociological survey of Catholic institutions is also provided.

Norris, David John. "Rites of Passage: The Relationship of Ritual to Faith Development in Young Adults." D.Min. diss., St. Mary's Seminary and University, 1988. This study examines types of liturgical style and background interests of congregants and seeks the relationship between a person's faith development and how that person perceives ritual activity in the Mass. Young adults have specific musical needs and wish to give input. The dissertation makes a significant statement of the present status of liturgy in the Roman Catholic Church.

Other

Two sources of pertinent campus ministry literature contain items too numerous to annotate in this bibliography. They are identified below for the interested researcher.

Catholic Campus Ministry Association. Established in 1969. Dayton, Ohio: University of Dayton. Since 1974, CCMA has published a journal about campus ministry. From 1974 to 1981, the journal was called *Process* (vol. 1:1—7:1). In 1986, it was renamed the *Journal of the Catholic Campus Ministry Association* (vol. 1:1—). CCMA also publishes a monthly newsletter. This literature is available from the national office of CCMA.

Center for the Study of Campus Ministry. Established in 1974 (no longer operational). Valparaiso, Ind.: Valparaiso University Library. From 1974 until its demise in 1987, CSCM published a campus ministry series of papers, yearbooks, summer seminar proceedings, study conference proceedings, and newsletters. This literature is now available through the Valparaiso University Library.

Program Reply Sheet

Do you have one or more programs that have been especially successful? If so, please photocopy this program reply sheet and complete one for each program that you would like to share with colleagues. Mail your complete and concise program reply sheet(s) to: CCMA National Office, 300 College Park, Dayton, OH 45469. The national office will make available these programs to any requesting individual. Thank you for participating and for being a continuing resource for campus ministry.

Name of Project/Program:

(Please duplicate for each individual project or program)

School:

Contact Person:

Address:

(City)   (State)   (Zip Code)

Phone: (   )

Objective(s):

Target Group(s):

Describe the Steps

1. Planning:

2. What actually happened?

3. Evaluation:

4. Resources Used:

Please attach samples of materials used: for example, outlines, posters, flyers, handouts, articles, evaluation form, and so forth.

About the Authors

REV. ROBERT AARON, OMI, is an instructor in pastoral studies and spirituality and director of the Intern Program at the Oblate School of Theology (San Antonio). He was formerly the director of campus ministry at the University of Minnesota (Duluth) and at the College of St. Thomas (St. Paul). Fr. Aaron has also worked extensively in the retreat field throughout the Midwest. He holds an M.Div. from Oblate College of the Southwest (San Antonio) and an M.Chr.Sp. as well as a B.A. in philosophy from Creighton University (Omaha). He was the recipient of the Distinguished Service Award from the College of St. Thomas.

REV. JAMES J. BACIK is a priest of the Diocese of Toledo and is serving as campus minister and adjunct professor of humanities at the University of Toledo. Previously, he taught at Mt. St. Mary's Seminary (Cincinnati) and served as campus minister at Bowling Green State University. Fr. Bacik holds an S.T.D. from the University of Oxford (England). He is the author of a number of books, among which are *Apologetics and the Eclipse of Mystery* and *Contemporary Theologians*. In addition, he served as writer for the editorial committee that produced *Empowered by the Spirit: Campus Ministry Faces the Future*.

REV. EDWARD BRANCH is director of the Atlanta University Center. He previously served as director of campus ministry at The Catholic University of America.

REV. FRANCIS COLBORN is pastor of Holy Name of Jesus Church, Los Angeles, California, and former Catholic chaplain at the Claremont Colleges (California). He has previously served as professor of theology at St. John's Seminary (Camarillo) and as associate pastor of St. Alphonsus Parish in Los Angeles. Father Colborn holds both an S.T.L. and an S.T.D. from the Gregorian University (Rome). He is the author of *Living as a Catholic Today*, as well as numerous articles on theology.

DR. JUNE MEREDITH COSTIN is the director of campus ministry and faculty member at Kansas Newman College, Wichita, Kansas. She is the former associate diocesan director of campus ministry for the Diocese of Wilmington (DE) and prior to that position was a diocesan campus minister for the Diocese of Richmond (VA). She is also adjunct faculty member of Loyola (New Orleans) in the Institute for Ministry (LIMEX) and has served as facilitator in that program. She holds a D.Min. from St. Mary's Seminary and University, Baltimore, an M.A. in colonial history from the College of William and Mary, Williamsburg, and an A.B. in economics from Bryn Mawr College, Bryn Mawr, PA. She is the recipient of the Status of Women—Recognition Award from Old Dominion University, Norfolk, and the Role Model Award at Goldey-Beacom College, Wilmington, DE.

SR. KATHLEEN DORNEY, CND, is a campus minister at Wheeling Jesuit College. She was formerly campus minister at Yale University and at the University of Bridgeport and has also taught at the high-school level in both New York and Connecticut. Sr. Dorney holds an M.A. in pastoral studies from Loyola University (Chicago) and an M.A. in mathematics from Columbia University. She has devoted much of her professional years to counseling, ministry, education, and theology.

DR. CAROL FOWLER is the director of the Department of Personnel Services for the Archdiocese of Chicago. Previously, she served as director of ministry in higher education for the archdiocese, as a campus minister at Michigan State University, and as a coordinator of campus ministry for the Diocese of Lansing. Dr. Fowler holds a D.Min. from St. Mary's Seminary and University (Baltimore); an M.A. in counseling psychology from Alfred Adler Institute (Chicago); and a B.A. in social science, with secondary teaching certificate from Michigan State University. She has served as past president of the NADDCM.

REV. JAY FRIEDEL has served as director of campus ministry at Southeastern Missouri State University in Cape Girardeau, Missouri, since 1992.

DR. MICHAEL GALLIGAN-STIERLE is the director of campus ministry at Wheeling Jesuit College. Previously, he served in that capacity for the Archdiocese of Miami, Florida Atlantic University (Boca Raton), the University of Maryland (Baltimore), and Loyola College (Baltimore). Dr. Galligan-Stierle holds a Ph.D. in Scripture as well as an M.A. in theology from St. Mary's Ecumenical Institute (Baltimore); an M.A. in psychology from Loyola College; and a B.S. in philosophy and theology from St. Mary's University (San Antonio). He is the recipient of the Charles Forsyth Award for Outstanding Leadership in Campus Ministry and an Excellence in Leadership Award from the Archdiocese of Miami.

REV. CHARLES H. HAGAN is the representative for higher education and campus ministry in the Department of Education at the United States Catholic Conference in Washington, D.C. He has served as the director of the Newman Center at the University of Pennsylvania and as assistant professor of theology at Immaculata College. Fr. Hagan holds an S.T.D. from the Gregorian University (Rome) and is a doctoral candidate in higher education at the University of Pennsylvania (Philadelphia). He is the author of *Sacred and Secular, New Hope for Healing*.

SR. JOAN HARTLAUB, CSJ, was the associate director of the Office for Campus Ministry in the Archdiocese of Los Angeles, as well as the director of the Campus Ministry Mentoring Program. She has been a campus minister since 1977. During the years 1986-1987, Sr. Hartlaub was co-director of the Frank J. Lewis Institute, West (Seattle). She holds a master's in theology from the University of Notre Dame, in addition to her undergraduate studies.

MS. BARBARA HUMPHREY is a campus minister at Georgetown University, Washington, D.C. and director of the Campus Ministry Mentoring Program. She has previously served as campus minister at the

University of Miami, Florida International University, the University of Missouri, and Kent State University. Ms. Humphrey has a B.A. in telecommunications from Kent State University.

SR. MARY JOHNSON, SND, is assistant professor of Sociology at Emmanuel College, Boston, Massachusetts.

MS. KATHLEEN KANAVY is the director of liturgical music and a campus minister at the University of Scranton. Her previous work in the Diocese of Scranton includes being a team member in the Office of Music and a liturgy consultant in the Office of Religious Education. Ms. Kanavy holds a B.M. in music education from Marywood College (Scranton) and is currently completing a M.Chr.Sp. from Creighton University (Omaha). She has served as coordinator for the campus ministry division of the National Association of Pastoral Musicians (NPM); as liturgy coordinator for the 1989 CCMA Conference; and as a speaker for numerous regional and national NPM Conferences. She has authored several articles in *Pastoral Music* and *The Catechist*, as well as a music education resource for catechists.

MS. MARY ANNE KASAVICH was the diocesan director of Newman campus ministry for the Diocese of Cleveland. She previously served as a Newman campus minister at Case Western Reserve University (Cleveland) and as a part-time lecturer in the Religious Studies Department of John Carroll University (Cleveland). Ms. Kasavich obtained a B.A. in humanities from Rosary College (River Forest), an M.A. in religious studies from John Carroll University, and has done doctoral coursework in New Testament at the Divinity School of The University of Chicago.

MR. DAVID ROBERT KLOPFENSTEIN was the executive administrator of the National Catholic Student Coalition (NCSC) in Dayton, Ohio. Previously, he served as the external secretary of the NCSC. Mr. Klopfenstein holds a B.A. in English from Wake Forest University (Winston-Salem).

REV. VINCENT E. KRISCHE is the director of St. Lawrence Catholic Campus Center at the University of Kansas. He has served on the USCC National Advisory Council for Campus Ministry, the CCMA Executive Board, the Editorial Committee for the U.S. Bishops' Pastoral on Campus Ministry, and the USCC Committee on Education. In addition, he was founding president of NADDCM. Fr. Krische holds an M.A. in religious studies and a B.A. in philosophy from St. Thomas Theological Seminary, and a B.S.T. from The Catholic University of America. He is the recipient of the Archbishop Hallinan Award for Membership on the Editorial Committee for the Pastoral Letter, as well as the Archbishop Hallinan Award for Excellence in Campus Ministry.

MR. RAYMOND R. LAGESSE was the assistant dean for the College of Arts and Sciences at Saint Louis University, as well as the associate campus minister for the Newman Center at Southern Illinois University (Edwardsville). Previously, he was the director of campus ministry at Parks College of Saint Louis University, chairperson of the Modern Language Department of Bishop Connolly High School, and both a member and chairperson of the CCMA Executive Board. Mr. Lagesse holds a Ph.D. in higher education administration from Saint Louis University; an M.Div. from Weston School of Theology; an M.A. from Fordham University; a Ph.L. from Weston School of Philosophy; and an A.B. from Boston College. He is listed in *Who's Who in the Midwest* and in *Who's Who in American Education.*

REV. F. STEPHEN MACHER, CM, was a campus minister for the Law School of St. John's University (New York City). He holds a D.Min. from Drew University (Madison, N.J.), having completed his doctoral project on Parish-based Young Adult Ministry. In addition, he has earned master's degrees in both theology and counseling. Fr. Macher has served on the CCMA Executive Board and was instrumental in the formation of the Colleague Consultation Program. In addition, he has facilitated six Frank J. Lewis Campus Ministry Training Institutes and is the author of several articles on campus and young adult ministry.

MR. DONALD R. MCCRABB is currently the executive director of the CCMA. He has served as a professional lay minister in the

Church as both a campus minister and a pastoral associate. Mr. McCrabb holds an M.A. in theology from the University of Dayton, in addition to his undergraduate work. He is the author of numerous articles on campus ministry.

MR. MICHAEL J. NACHMAN is associate director of the Ministry Formation Department for the Diocese of Toledo. He has served for twenty years at Christ the Teacher University Parish at Northern Illinois University (DeKalb), where he directed the Loyola University (Chicago) Extension Program in Theology, coordinated the Pre-Marriage Education Program, and, for five years, served as parish administrator. Mr. Nachman holds an M.A. in theology from the Aquinas Institute of Theology (Dubuque) and an M.S. in family studies from Northern Illinois University. He is a former treasurer and member of the CCMA Executive Board, as well as a member of the Department of Campus Ministry of the Catholic Conference of Illinois.

SR. JODY O'NEIL, SP, is assistant director of campus ministry, directing Residence Life Ministry and the Graduate Assistantship Program at the University of Dayton. Prior to that she directed the Newman Center for the University of Evansville, served as campus minister at Rockford College and Rock Valley Community College, Highland Community College, and Sauk Valley Community College. In addition, she served as assistant director and co-director of diocesan campus ministry for the Diocese of Rockford. She has served as both secretary and chair for the Department of Campus Ministry of the Catholic Conference of Illinois. Sr. Jody holds campus ministry certification, an M.A. in religious studies from Mundelein College, and a B.A. in art education from St. Mary-of-the-Woods College. She has done graduate work in spiritual guidance at Alban Institute.

SR. SHIRLEY OSTERHAUS, OSF, is the Catholic campus minister at Western Washington University (Bellingham). She has served as a rape crisis counselor and as a director of religious education in Pueblo (Colorado), Eugene (Oregon), and Dubuque

(Iowa). Sr. Osterhaus holds an M.Ed. (religious studies focus) from Boston College and a B.A. in theology from Briar Cliff College (Sioux City). During the past five years, she has participated in three delegation trips to Central America. Sr. Osterhaus is the recipient of the Alumna Distinguished Service Award (Briar Cliff College) and the Inter-American Peace Award for her work with Central American Refugee Assistance (CARA).

SR. JOANN PLUMPE, OP, was the director of campus ministry at Miami University (Oxford, Ohio), a position she has held for the past five years. Prior to that time, she served as campus minister at Utah State University (Logan). In addition, she has taught high school mathematics in the Detroit area. Sr. Plumpe holds an M.A. in religious studies from Fordham University; an M.A. in mathematics from the University of Montana; and a B.S. in mathematics from Siena Heights College in Adrian (Michigan).

SR. JUDITH A. RINEK, SNJM, was the Catholic campus minister at the University of La Verne, an interdenominational school in southern California. During her fourteen years in the field of campus ministry, she has served at California State Polytechnic University (Pomona), St. Mary's College (Moraga), and Holy Names College (Oakland). Sr. Rinek holds an M.A. in theology from the Graduate Theological Union (Berkeley) and an M.A. in biology from Perdue University. Her theological thesis formed the foundation for two keynote presentations on teamwork given at the CACCM Meeting in Santa Cruz (1987) and at the Frank J. Lewis Institute at Santa Barbara (1989).

MR. JOHN A. RIVERA was the campus minister at Incarnate Word College (San Antonio) and served as acting director of campus ministry at the same institution. He has been a Catholic campus minister at both Miami-Dade Community College and Florida Memorial College. In addition, he has served as director of campus ministry at Abilene Christian University, Hardin-Simmons University, and McMurry University. Mr. Rivera holds an M.A. in pastoral ministries from St. Thomas University (Abilene); an

M.B.A. from Hardin-Simmons University (Abilene); and a B.S. in civil engineering from the University of Texas (Austin).

SR. MAUREEN SCHAUKOWITCH, OSF, was the director of campus ministry at Santa Clara University. Prior to that, she served as associate campus minister at St. Mary's College (Winona). Before moving into the field of campus ministry, Sr. Schaukowitch taught junior high school in Milwaukee for ten years. She holds an M.A. in religious education from Fordham University and a B.A. in history and sociology from Cardinal Stritch College. Currently, she is pursuing a doctorate in private school administration from the University of San Francisco.

REV. GEORGE M. SCHROEDER is the pastor of Holy Name Church, Steamboat Springs, Colorado and was the director of campus ministry for the Archdiocese of Denver. He has served as Catholic campus pastor at the University of Minnesota (Duluth), as both chairman and member of the CCMA Executive Board, and as president of the NADDCM. Ordained from St. Paul Seminary in 1962, Fr. Schroeder holds an M.A. in communicating arts from the University of Wisconsin (Superior). He is the recipient of the National Charles Forsyth Award from the CCMA.

MR. P. GERARD SHAW, was vice president for student life at Merrimack College (North Andover). Prior to that, he served as director of campus ministry at Biscayne College (Miami). Mr. Shaw holds a Ph.D. in higher education administration from Boston College; an M.A. in systematic theology from Washington Theological Union; an M.S. in human relations from Biscayne College; and a B.S. in accounting from Villanova University. He was editor of *Empowered by the Spirit: Campus Ministry Faces the Future—A Commentary.*

SR. LOURDES SHEEHAN, RSM, is the director of the Alliance for Catholic Education at Notre Dame University and former secretary for education at the United States Catholic Conference in Washington, D.C. A member of the Sisters of Mercy, Province of Baltimore, she has served as a Catholic school teacher, a principal, a superintendent of schools, and a director of Christian education. Prior to joining the USCC in 1990, Sr. Sheehan was executive director of the National Association of Boards of Education at the National Catholic Educational Association. She holds an Ed.D. in educational leadership from Virginia Tech; an M.A. in colonial history from the University of Pennsylvania; and a B.A. in history/education from Mount Saint Agnes College (Baltimore).

REV. CARL B. TRUTTER, OP, is socius and vicar provincial of the Dominican community and former director of campus ministry for the Archdiocese of San Antonio. Previously, he served as director of field education for the Aquinas Institute of Theology; as a campus minister at the University of Illinois, at the University of Houston, and at Vanderbilt University; as chair of the Texas Catholic Campus Ministry Association; and as promoter of university ministry for the Southern Dominican Province. Fr. Trutter holds a doctorate in religion from the Chicago Theological Seminary, with studies at the Aquinas Institute of Theology, Emory University, St. George's College (Jerusalem). He has served on the executive boards of the CCMA and the NADDCM. In addition, he is the author of *Sharing Our Faith: A Manual for Catholic College Students* and *Faith on Campus: An Emerging Agenda*.

MS. KATHLEEN MAAS WEIGERT is the faculty liaison/academic coordinator at the Center for Social Concerns, a concurrent associate professor in American studies, and a faculty fellow in the Joan B. Kroc Institute for International Peace Studies at the University of Notre Dame. Prior to joining the Center for Social Concerns in 1983, Ms. Weigert was an assistant dean in the College of Arts and Letters at Notre Dame. She holds a Ph.D. in sociology from the University of Notre Dame and an M.A. and a B.A. in international relations from the University of Minnesota. She is the co-designer of the undergraduate Concentration in Peace Studies and co-recipient of a three-year Lilly Endowment grant for the Gender Studies Concentration.

REV. THOMAS WELBERS is pastor of Our Lady of the Assumption Church, Claremont, California, and former director of the Office for Campus Ministry in the Archdiocese of Los Angeles. He has served as director of the Newman Center at California State University (Long Beach). Rev. Welbers has spent many years in the field of parish ministry, in both teaching and writing on the liturgy. He holds a Licentiate in Sacred Liturgy from the Pontifical Liturgical Institute (Rome).

Appendix

Empowered by the Spirit:
Campus Ministry Faces the Future

A Pastoral Letter on Campus Ministry
Issued by the National Conference of Catholic Bishops, November 15, 1985

INTRODUCTION

1. "I pray that he will bestow on you gifts in keeping with the riches of his glory. May he strengthen you inwardly through the working of his Spirit. May Christ dwell in your hearts through faith and may charity be the root and foundation of your life" (Eph 3:16-17). For over a century, Catholic campus ministry in our country, empowered by the Spirit, has been forming communities of faith which witness to the presence of the risen Christ. Now we are at the beginning of a new era filled with opportunities to build up the faith community on campuses and to promote the well-being of higher education and society as a whole. In this pastoral letter addressed to the Catholic Church in the United States and especially to the Church on campus, we offer our prayerful support, encouragement, and guidance to the men and women who are committed to bringing the message of Christ to the academic world. In preparing this letter, we have consulted with many of them and have come to a deeper appreciation of their dedication and achievements, as well as their concerns and frustrations. This new era, which is filled with promise, challenges campus ministry to respond creatively to the promptings of the Spirit for the well-being of the Church and higher education.

2. Our 1981 statement on Catholic higher education concluded by noting "the excellent intellectual and pastoral leadership of many Catholics engaged as teachers, administrators, and campus ministers in the colleges and universities which are not Catholic."[1] We said at that time that "we hope for a future opportunity to speak of their invaluable contribution to the intellectual life of our country."[2] In this pastoral letter, we fulfill that hope and turn our attention primarily to the ministry of the Church on these public and private campuses, where each year millions of Catholics are being prepared as future leaders of society and Church.[3] We are mindful of our previous comments on the crucial importance of Catholic higher education, especially the distinctive task of campus ministry on Catholic campuses to call the total institution to spread the Gospel and to preserve and enrich its religious traditions.[4] In addition, the suggestions for this document made by those who serve at Catholic institutions affirmed that all who minister in the world of higher education have certain common concerns and similar desires for cooperation. Collaboration among all colleges and universities within a diocese enhances the Church's ministry to higher education. Mutual support, joint sponsorship of programs, and sharing of resources improve the total efforts of campus ministry. Many of the perspectives, suggestions, and directions in this pastoral letter should be helpful to those who serve so well in our Catholic institutions of higher education.

3. Campus ministry is best understood in its historical, sociological, and theological context. Thus, the first section discusses our hopes for the Church on campus in the light of its previous history. The next section locates campus ministry within the relationship between the Church and the world of higher education, highlighting the need for renewed dialogue. Campus ministry derives its life from the persons who bring the Gospel of Christ to the academic world. Therefore, the third section focuses on the members of the Church on campus, emphasizing the call of all the baptized to collaborate in the work of the Church, as well as the special responsibility of professional campus ministers to empower others for this task. The fourth section examines six aspects of campus ministry that flow from the nature of the Church and the situation on campus. Here we state principles and suggest strategies for carrying out this ministry. The epilogue notes our own responsibilities as bishops to serve the Church on campus and calls the Church to an exciting new phase in the history of campus ministry in our country.

I. History and Current Opportunities

A. HISTORY AND CONTEMPORARY DEVELOPMENTS

4. The Church's response to current opportunities on campus will benefit from an awareness of the history of the Newman Movement in the United States.[5] This ministry began in 1883 at the University of Wisconsin with the founding, through lay initiative, of the Melvin Club which was designed to keep Catholics on campus in touch with their religious heritage. A decade later the first Newman Club was established at the University of Pennsylvania, with much the same purpose. It was named after John Henry Cardinal Newman, who was the English leader in the nineteenth-century intellectual renewal in the Church and later was chosen the great patron of campus ministers in our country. During this initial stage, farsighted leaders recognized that the growing number of Catholic collegians attending public institutions needed support and instruction in their religious heritage. They responded by establishing clubs for Catholic students, with their own chaplains and residence halls.

5. In 1908, the second stage began with the establishment of the first association of Catholic clubs in state universities. What would become the National Newman Club Federation replaced this first effort about the time of World War I. This phase, which lasted until 1969, was often characterized by a defensive and even hostile attitude on the part of Catholic students and their chaplains toward the academic world, which was perceived as dominated by a secularist philosophy. During this period, many students and chaplains in the Newman Movement felt estranged from the rest of the Church and decried the lack of support from the hierarchy.

6. The third stage, begun in 1969 in response to the Second Vatican Council and continuing until the present, has produced some healthy new developments. First, the Church as a whole has grown in appreciation and support of campus ministry. It is true there are still problems: some colleges and universities lack officially appointed campus ministers and many others are understaffed and suffer from financial problems. At times, there are misunderstandings between the Church on campus and local parishes and diocesan offices. However, progress has clearly been made in integrating campus ministry into the life of the Church. Today, there are over two thousand Catholics ministering on campuses throughout the country—a significant increase over a couple of decades ago. There is an increased commitment to providing well-trained campus ministers who appreciate the need for continued professional and theological development. Student groups at all levels collaborate with official representatives of the Church. Diocesan directors of campus ministry help keep campus concerns before the whole Church. More Catholics appreciate the importance of campus ministry and support diocesan funding of this work. Through this pastoral letter, we affirm these positive developments and pledge to work with others to build on them. We bring to the attention of the whole Church the importance of campus ministry for the future well-being of the Church and society. Our goal is to foster a closer relationship and a greater spirit of cooperation between campus ministry and the rest of the local Church. Campus ministry is an integral part of the Church's mission to the world and must be seen in that light.

7. Second, we endorse the improving relationship between the Church on campus and the academic community. While problems remain, Catholics have developed a greater understanding of the positive values and legitimate concerns of higher education. Many campus ministers have established good working relationships with administrators, faculty, and staff. There is greater appreciation of the way the Church benefits from the teaching, research, and service carried on by colleges and universities. Similarly, many administrators view campus ministry as an ally in the common effort to provide an integrated learning experience for the students. Faculty members frequently value the presence of campus ministers who demonstrate an appreciation of the spiritual life and can articulate their Catholic heritage. In our consultations, we found that many leaders in the academic community welcome a word from the Church on matters of mutual concern.[6] Our hope in this letter is to build on this fund of good will and to heal any wounds which linger from past mistakes and misunderstandings. With respect for the freedom and autonomy of the academic community, we believe it is time to foster a renewed dialogue between the Church and higher education, to the benefit of society as a whole.

8. Third, we affirm the development of ecumenical and interfaith relationships. There are, of course, problems in resolving longstanding differences, and at some colleges and universities dialogue and cooperation have been difficult to establish and maintain. However, on many campuses, the Catholic community and other religious groups who share a common vision of ministry and who are interested in ecumenical and interfaith cooperation have developed strong working relationships. This occurs especially with other Christian Churches, with whom we share a common commitment to Jesus Christ, and with the Jewish community, with whom we hold a common heritage and shared Scriptures. In some situations, Catholic campus ministers share an interfaith center and collaborate in some ministerial tasks. In other places, the Catholic community cooperates with other religious groups through regular meetings, joint study, and shared prayer. Mutual trust has grown as members of various religious traditions work together on common programs, such as projects to promote social justice. We commend this ecumenical and interfaith progress and give full support to greater and more creative efforts in this direction. Catholics who are deeply rooted in their tradition and who maintain a strong sense of identity with their religious heritage will be better prepared to carry out this mission. We appreciate the contributions and cooperative attitudes of most of the various religious communities on campus. The Catholic community on campus might also seek to engage those who are concerned with human ethical values of our society but do not directly relate their concerns to a faith tradition. To those who demonstrate less tolerant attitudes, we extend an invitation to join in the dialogue. In this pastoral message, we address the Catholic campus community and discuss its particular challenges and opportunities. While we will not treat directly the ecumenical and interfaith dimensions of campus ministry today, we hope that the Catholic communities on individual campuses will be prompted by this letter to renewed dialogue and collaboration in serving the common good.

9. Finally, this third stage in the history of the Newman Movement has produced a remarkable diversity of legitimate styles and approaches to campus ministry, designed to match available resources with the unique situations at particular colleges and universities. These creative responses range from well-organized teams serving the needs of a large university parish to an individual ministering part time in a small community college. The styles include ministries that are primarily sacramental and those that rely mainly on the ministry of presence. Some campus ministers work on Catholic campuses where they can influence policy decisions, while others serve in public institutions where they have little or no access to the centers of power. In some situations priests are working full time, while in others the ministry is carried out almost entirely by members of religious orders and lay people. Ministers on residential campuses can offer many set programs for students, while those who serve on commuter campuses must be attentive to the creative possibilities demanded by such a fluid situation. Most serve on one campus, although some are responsible for several colleges and universities. While we cannot discuss in detail all styles of ministry, we will offer principles and strategies designed to encourage all those concerned with the Church on campus to make vigorous and creative applications to their own situations.

B. CURRENT CHALLENGES AND OPPORTUNITIES

10. We believe this is the opportune time to address a challenging word to the Church on campus. Catholics are attending colleges and universities in numbers that far exceed their percentage of the general population.[7] It is crucial that these emerging leaders of Church and society be exposed to the best of our Catholic tradition and encounter dedicated leaders who will share their journey of faith with them. Thus, the time is right to encourage campus ministers to renew their own spiritual lives and to facilitate the faith development of the Catholics on campus.

11. Today, there is a growing interest among many Catholics in various ministries. On campus, there is a great reservoir of energy and talent that could be utilized in the service of the Church and the world. Therefore, the time is right to challenge faculty members, administrators, support staff, and students to contribute their time and gifts to the common effort to help the academic community achieve its goals and to build up the Church on campus.

12. The academic world is in the midst of an important debate on how to improve the quality of higher education in our country.[8] Fundamental questions about the purpose, methods, and direction of higher education must be addressed, as colleges and universities continue to define their mission and to improve their performance. Therefore, the time is right to encourage Catholics on campus to participate in these local debates and, thus, to contribute their insights and values to this crucial national discussion.

II. Campus Ministry and the Relationship Between the Church and Higher Education

A. HISTORY

13. Campus ministry is an expression of the Church's special desire to be present to all who are involved in higher education. Throughout its history, the Church has been instrumental in cultivating the intellectual life. During the period of the Fathers, great centers of learning at Antioch and Alexandria instructed the faithful and promoted the integration of faith and culture. The Church contributed her resources to the task of forming medieval universities and founded many of them, including the great schools of Bologna, Paris, Oxford, and Cambridge. In the modern world, government increasingly has taken over the responsibility for higher education, with a resulting split between the Church and the university. This has occurred in our own country with the establishment of a massive system of public higher education that has its own autonomy. Shortly after 1900, it was evident that enrollments in this system were growing faster than those in the Catholic and Protestant colleges, which for so long had constituted higher education in the United States. From the perspective of faith, Christians often detected in public institutions a growing secularism that celebrated the autonomy of reason and left little room for consideration of religious questions or moral values. This situation intensified after World War I, and the Church responded not only by increasing her traditional commitment to higher education, but also by trying to protect Catholic students from the antireligious elements perceived on public campuses. During this period, the Church and higher education experienced a good deal of mutual misunderstanding. Some people in the academic world feared that the Church would try to reassert, in more subtle ways, its control over higher education. On the other side, members of the Church, at times, regarded secular higher education as a threat to the Christian way of life. The time has come to move beyond these misunderstandings and to forge a new relationship between the Church and higher education that respects the unique character of each. We remain convinced that "cooperation between these two great institutions, Church and university, is indispensable to the health of society."[9]

B. THE CONTRIBUTION OF HIGHER EDUCATION

14. We respect the autonomy of the academic community and appreciate its great contributions to the common good. Higher education benefits the human family through its research, which expands our common pool of knowledge. By teaching people to think critically and to search for the truth, colleges and universities help to humanize our world. The collegiate experience provides individuals with attitudes and skills that can be used in productive work, harmonious living, and responsible citizenship. Since higher education in the United States has taken on public service as one of its tasks, society has received significant assistance in solving human and technical problems. The Second Vatican Council placed this contribution in a personal context when it said that people who apply themselves to philosophy, history, science, and the arts help "to elevate the human family to a more sublime understanding of truth, goodness, and beauty and to the formation of judgments which embody universal values."[10]

15. The Church, as well as society as a whole, benefits from the contributions of higher education. The members of the Church hold a common faith in Jesus Christ, a faith that seeks understanding. When the academic world produces new knowledge and encourages critical thinking, it assists Christians in the process of deepening and articulating their faith. When higher education fosters fidelity toward truth in scientific research and collaborative efforts to improve the quality of life in our world, it helps to prepare for the acceptance of the gospel message."[11]

16. There is no doubt that the world of higher education has its own problems that must be addressed and dehumanizing practices that must be challenged. Fidelity to the Gospel demands critical judgment, as well as affirmation. It is, however, vital that campus ministry maintains a fundamental appreciation of the contributions made by higher education to society and the Church.

C. THE CONTRIBUTION OF THE CHURCH

17. The Church brings to the dialogue with higher education its general mission to preach the Gospel of Christ and to help the human family achieve its full destiny.[12] Thus, the Church seeks to help higher education attain its lofty goal of developing a culture in which human beings can realize their full potential.[13] In providing this assistance, the Church joins its voice with others in promoting the ideal of educating the whole person. From our perspective, this means keeping the dignity and worth of human beings in the center of our reflections on the purpose of higher education. Education is the process by which persons are "assisted in the harmonious development of their physical, moral, and intellectual endowments."[14] It aims at the formation of individuals who have a sense of ultimate purpose and are moving toward greater freedom, maturity, and integration. At the same time, genuine education nurtures a sense of responsibility for the common good and provides skills for active involvement in community life.

18. We think that it is important to keep the problems of higher education in a larger societal and educational context. Thus, family life must be seen as central to the process of educating the whole person, since "the family is the first and fundamental school of social living."[15] Moreover, improvement in the quality of higher education is dependent on primary and secondary schools doing a better job of cultivating the intellect, passing on the cultural heritage, and fostering constructive values. If students are better prepared by a healthy family life and solid primary and secondary education, institutions of higher learning can attend to their primary purpose, "the passionate and disinterested search for the truth," which makes human beings free and helps them achieve their full humanity in accord with their dignity and worth.[16] The search for truth should also include the ability to handle ethical issues and to achieve a harmonious integration of intellect and will.

19. The Church also brings to the dialogue its traditional understanding of wisdom. We believe that the faith community and the institution of higher learning are involved in a common pursuit of the life of wisdom.[17] There are various interpretations of wisdom, but we agree with those who hold that its pursuit includes discovering the highest principles that integrate all knowledge; uncovering the deepest secrets that constitute human nature; and achieving a personal synthesis in which knowledge and love are ultimately united. For us, the mystery of human existence is fully revealed in Jesus Christ. He reminds us of our profound dignity and our immense potential. He provides us with perspective and teaches by example how love illumines knowledge. The wisdom that we learn from Christ includes the cross, which confounds the wisdom of the world (1 Cor 1:18-24). From the perspective of the cross, we are called to challenge the limitations and contradictions of the world (1 Cor 3:18-23). At the same time, our wisdom tradition includes an understanding of God's mysterious plan to bring all things in the heavens and on earth into unity under the headship of Christ (Eph 1:9-10). The risen Lord has poured out his Spirit on all creation and so we are moved to celebrate truth, goodness, and beauty wherever they are to be found. Since no single community can monopolize the gift of wisdom, the Church joins with the university and others in the search for wisdom. But, when the quest for wisdom is forgotten or diminished, then the Church must keep the ideal alive for the good of society. When the so-called wisdom of the world is employed in support of injustice, the Church must proclaim the wisdom of the cross, which challenges all oppressive structures. In the Church, the practical wisdom enunciated by the Hebrew sages is celebrated; the traditional philosophical wisdom is remembered; and the integrating wisdom of faith is proclaimed. For Christians, this whole quest for wisdom finds its summation and final fulfillment in Jesus Christ, who is the wisdom of God (1 Cor 1:24). We are convinced that the Christian wisdom synthesis, merely sketched out here, is a valuable resource in the continuing dialogue between the Church and higher education.

20. In a new relationship, the Church can work with higher education in improving the human community and establishing a culture that enables all human beings to reach their full potential. While admitting our failures in the past, we are concentrating on the future and a new era of cooperation. In the dialogue, we expect to learn and benefit from the work of higher education and will contribute our support, experience, and insights.

D. CAMPUS MINISTRY DESCRIBED AND DEFINED

21. Campus ministry is one of the important ways the Church exercises her mission in higher education. Its goals include promoting theological study and reflection on the religious nature of human beings "so that intellectual, moral, and spiritual growth can proceed together; sustaining a Christian community on campus, with the pastoral care and liturgical worship it requires; integration of its apostolic ministry with other ministries of the local community and the diocese; and helping the Christian community on campus to serve its members and others, including the many nonstudents who gravitate toward the university."[18] Campus ministry gathers the Catholics on campus for prayer, worship, and learning in order that they might bring the light of the Gospel to illumine the concerns and hopes of the academic community. All the members of the Church on campus are called, according to their own gifts, to share in this ministry, guided by the professional campus ministers. "The work of campus ministry requires continual evaluation of traditional methods of ministry and also new approaches which are licitly and responsibly employed. These latter can be highly appropriate in the campus setting, where there exists an audience receptive to the kind of sound innovation which may in the future prove beneficial to the larger Catholic community."[19] Such creativity has produced great diversity in organization, style, and approach, as campus ministers strive to form a searching, believing, loving, worshiping Catholic presence on campus. With this diversity in mind, campus ministry can be defined as the public presence and service through which properly prepared baptized persons are empowered by the Spirit to use their talents and gifts on behalf of the Church in order to be sign and instrument of the kingdom in the academic worlds. The

eye of faith discerns campus ministry where commitment to Christ and care for the academic world meet in purposeful activity to serve and realize the kingdom of God.

III. Persons Who Serve on Campus

A. THE BAPTIZED

22. The Church carries out its pastoral mission to the academic world both through its communal life and through the Christian witness of its individual members. "The baptized by the regeneration and the anointing of the Holy Spirit are consecrated as a spiritual house and a holy priesthood" (cf. 1 Pt 2:4-5), in order that through all their works they may "proclaim the power of him who has called them out of darkness into his marvelous light."[20] All the faithful on campus, by virtue of their baptism, share in the task of bringing the humanizing light of the Gospel to bear on the life of the academic community. They are called to live out Christian values while engaging in the teaching, learning, research, public service, and campus life that constitute the academic world. They are united with other believers in this work but make their own unique contributions, according to their personal talents and specific circumstances. "As generous distributors of God's manifold grace, put your gifts at the service of one another" (1 Pt 4:10). The Second Vatican Council further specified this scriptural teaching: "From the reception of these charisms or gifts, including those which are less dramatic, there arise for each believer the right and duty to use them in the Church and in the world for the good of [humankind] and for the upbuilding of the Church."[21] Thus, all the baptized members of the academic community have the opportunity and the obligation, according to their unique talents and situations, to join with others to help higher education reach its full potential.

23. The faithful are called not only to bring Christian witness to the academic world, but also to exercise their baptismal prerogatives by helping to build up the Church on campus. While many persons today generously contribute their time, talent, and experience to the faith community, Catholic faculty, staff, and administration

have a unique opportunity and calling to lead and direct campus ministry programs, according to their gifts. These individuals are particularly needed on the many campuses throughout the country where no campus ministry programs presently exist. This contribution is enhanced when individuals take time to prepare themselves through prayer and study for this work. In section four of this letter, perspectives and strategies will be enunciated to build the various aspects of campus ministry. We hope that students, including the large number of older students,[22] administrators, faculty members, and all who are concerned with higher education will be able to make creative applications to their own situations based on the conviction that the Spirit moves among all the People of God, promoting them, according to their own talents, to discern anew the signs of the times and to interpret them boldly in the light of the faith.[23]

B. PROFESSIONAL CAMPUS MINISTERS

24. Some members of the Church on campus are called to lead the faith community. Ideally, these men and women are professionally trained and exercise the kind of leadership that serves and empowers others. As officially appointed campus ministers, they are sent to form the faith community so that it can be a genuine sign and instrument of the kingdom. Their task is to identify, call forth, and coordinate the diverse gifts of the Spirit possessed by all the members of the faith community. Their challenge is to educate all the baptized to appreciate their own calls to service and to create a climate where initiative is encouraged and contributions are appreciated. One of the most important functions of campus ministers is to provide a vision and a sense of overall direction that will encourage and guide the other members to contribute to the well-being of the academic community and the Church on campus. If they understand their own family relationships in a faith perspective, they will be able to help others who are trying to improve the quality of their family lives. Setting up programs that embody this vision is a concrete way of encouraging others and of demonstrating what can be done with cooperative efforts. The goal of this style of leadership is to multiply the centers of activity and to unleash the creative power of the Spirit so that the community of faith can be an authentic sign and instrument of the kingdom.

25. Some professional campus ministers exercise the universal priesthood based on baptism, and others are ordained priests or deacons through the sacrament of holy orders. It is a sign of hope that a growing number of lay people serve as leaders in the faith community on campus. We commend members of religious orders who continue to make important contributions by gathering and encouraging the faithful. It is of historical significance that women "who in the past have not always been allowed to take their proper role in the Church's ministry"[24] find greater opportunities on campus to exercise their leadership abilities. Deacons often possess special talents and important life experiences that enhance their leadership skills. We encourage the priests who help form the faith community in a great variety of ways. Their prayerful celebration of the eucharist, which invites active participation and manifests the unity of the congregation, as well as their compassionate celebration of the sacrament of reconciliation are especially important. All those officially appointed to lead the Church on campus have a great responsibility to form vibrant communities of faith and an exciting challenge to bring forth the gifts of individual believers.

26. In order to meet these challenges, campus ministers often form teams that provide a broader base of leadership to the faith community. Individual members bring their unique personalities and gifts to the team and work cooperatively to set direction and carry out some programs. The team members are coresponsible for the well-being of the faith community and accountable in their own areas of activity and competency. At the same time, they have the support of their colleagues when needed. Praying together helps the men and women on the team to keep in mind the true source and goal of their mission and to experience a sense of solidarity. We encourage the formation of such team ministries, which serve

as models of ministry and community for the rest of the Church.

27. There are certain general challenges faced by all campus ministers. To be effective, ministers must attend to their own spiritual development. Campus ministers who are serious about their prayer life and can speak openly about their relationship to God will be able to direct others. Ministers who have wrestled with the great questions of meaning, purpose, and identity can offer helpful guidance to other genuine searchers. Those who have appropriated the faith and mined the riches of the Catholic heritage will be in a better position to invite others to join the faith community. If they genuinely care about the weak and oppressed, they will inspire others to work for social justice. Finally, campus ministers who have achieved an integration of faith and culture will naturally serve as role models for students and faculty members who are trying to achieve a similar synthesis. In summation, the leaders of the faith community must be perceived as persons who know the struggles of life and who are working to develop themselves spiritually.

28. Campus ministers are also called to empower the faith community and its individual members in the task of helping their colleges or universities to reach their full potential. Ministers who have a genuine respect for academic life and for institutions of higher education will see clearly the importance of this work and find creative ways to respond. A healthy self-confidence will enable them to relate openly with faculty members and administrators and to empathize with students who are struggling with their personal growth. By gaining the respect and confidence of the various members of the academic community, they will find many ways to get involved on campus and promote human values in the institution. Campus ministers with solid training and good credentials will have more opportunities to enter into the mainstream of academic life on campus. Today, it is clear that campus ministers must not remain on the margins of the academic community but must accept the call to bring the light of the Gospel to the very center of that world.

29. To prepare for meeting all these challenges, we encourage campus ministers to take responsibility for their own personal and professional development. Clear contractual arrangements that include carefully defined expectations and procedures for accountability and evaluation help to set a proper framework for their personal enrichment. Membership in appropriate professional organizations, participation in activities on diocesan, regional, and national levels, involvement in support groups with other campus ministers, and regular interaction with a spiritual director can provide motivation and direction for improving their performance. If campus ministers are to remain flexible in response to the rapidly changing needs of the campus community, they need to study contemporary developments in Scripture and theology while deepening their knowledge of the Christian tradition. Attaining an advanced degree or achieving competency in a particular area not only contributes to professional development, but helps gain respect in the academic world. Today, skills in counseling and spiritual direction, as well as knowledge of family systems and life cycles, group dynamics, and adult education are especially valuable for leaders of the faith community. An understanding of the nature and dynamics of the academic world enables campus ministers to apply Christian teachings and values more effectively.

30. In addition to these common challenges, campus ministers find that the unique situations of their particular campuses create their own concerns and opportunities. For example, campus ministers at community colleges must respond to the needs of students who live at home and have jobs. They often need assistance in defining their roles and responsibilities in the home. Many students are married and are present on campus only for their classes. Some ministers have been able, in these situations, to form small faith communities around shared prayer or social action projects. At these two-year colleges, the ministry of presence is especially important, as is securing the support and active involvement of interested faculty members. These institutions are often open to the addition of religion courses into the curriculum. Skills in marriage and career counseling are especially valuable. It is important for these campus ministers to maintain close relationships with neighboring parishes because that is where many students will find their primary faith community.

31. It is possible also to identify other particular challenges. Campus ministers on private denominational campuses must be especially attentive to the ecumenical dimension. Those who work primarily with minority students, including recently arrived immigrants, refugees, and international students, must be in touch with their cultural background and family experiences, as well as the unique challenges they face in the academic world. Large state schools produce logistical problems for campus ministers in handling so many students. On commuter campuses, making contact with students is difficult in itself. All of these particular challenges represent opportunities for creative ministry.

32. Professional campus ministers are crucial to the work of the Church on campus. They bear the heavy responsibility of guiding the faith community and empowering others to assist in the task of helping higher education reach its full potential. The extent and intensity of these demands remind them that they must gather others to assist them. They should expect support and guidance from the diocesan director of campus ministry, who is the usual liaison with the bishop and the local diocese. The director can help facilitate their personal growth, call for a proper accountability, and possible diocese-wide programming. As the diocesan bishop's representative, the director encourages the interaction among campus ministers in the diocese who serve on public, Catholic, and other private campuses. We recognize our responsibility as bishops to offer all campus ministers moral support, to provide financial assistance to the degree this is needed and possible, and to help them achieve the competency they need to be effective witnesses of the Gospel.

IV. Aspects of Campus Ministry

33. After situating campus ministry in the relationship between the Church and higher education and discussing the persons who perform this service, we now turn our attention to six aspects of campus ministry. These ministerial functions reflect the general mission of the Church on campus and the distinctive situation of higher education today. In her ministry, the faith community on campus must be faithful to the essential teachings of the Church and, at the same time, read the signs of the times and accordingly adapt the message of the Gospel to meet the needs of the academic community.[25]

A. FORMING THE FAITH COMMUNITY

1. Community and Alienation on Campus

34. Campus ministry attempts to form faith communities in an academic environment that knows both a healthy sense of solidarity and a good deal of alienation. Ideally, colleges and universities gather teachers and students together into a community of shared values and common dedication to the pursuit of truth. In fact, on campuses there is a good deal of collaborative effort. Organizations abound, close friendships are formed, interest groups gather the like-minded. Many administrators, faculty members, and students move easily in this world and find that it satisfies their needs for companionship and involvement. Many Christians freely gather into communities of faith in which they share their strengths and gifts with others.

35. On the other hand, lonely voices on campus cry out for intimacy, and mildly estranged individuals express a desire for more personal interaction. Students who leave home and come to large universities often feel lost in the vast impersonal world. The world of research and scholarship can seem cold and demeaning to graduate students. Commuter students who are on campus only briefly for classes do not have the opportunity to form close bonds with others. Some sense of alienation seems inevitable for international students who must cope with a new culture. Recently arrived immigrant and refugee students experience the isolation and loneliness of being separated from family and homeland. Older students worry about fitting in and being accepted and, at times, have the added complication of marital and family pressures. Even

students in small private colleges can experience a lack of depth in their relationships and a consequent sense of estrangement. Complaints are also heard from faculty members about the superficiality of their relationships with close colleagues and the lack of opportunities for interaction with those in other departments. Some feel cut off from the centers of power as important academic decisions are made without their input. The difficulty of gathering students for anything except social events and concerts is a continuing problem for student affairs leaders. Administrators speak openly about the fragmentation of campus life and search for ways to overcome it. The voices of estrangement are many and varied. Campus ministers who listen well know that there is a genuine hunger for community in the academic world, as well as a strong sense of solidarity.

2. The Importance of Christian Community

36. The call to form communities of faith flows both from the very nature of the Gospel itself and from the pastoral situation on campus. Christianity is ecclesial by its very nature. The communal character of salvation is already clear in the Hebrew Scriptures: "It has pleased God, however, to make [human beings] holy and save them not merely as individuals without any mutual bonds, but by making them into a single people, a people which acknowledges him in truth and serves him in holiness."[26] This truth was exemplified in the life of Jesus Christ who, led by the Spirit, gathered together a community of followers. The twelve served as official witnesses of his saving mission and symbolic representation of the new People of God. Through his striking parables and miraculous signs he proclaimed the kingdom in which all human beings, animated by the Spirit, were to live in peace and harmony. The death and resurrection of Jesus brought a new outpouring of the Spirit which "makes the Church grow, perpetually renews her and leads her to perfect union with her Spouse."[27] Under the influence of the Spirit, the Church remembers the prayer of Jesus that "all may be one, Father, as you are in me and I am in you, so that the world may believe" (Jn 17:21). All the baptized, empowered by the Spirit, share responsibility for forming the

Church into a genuine community of worship and service. Guided by the Holy Spirit, the Church is called, with all of its limitations and sinfulness, to wend its way through history as the visible sign of the unity of the whole human family and as an instrument of reconciliation for all.[28]

37. Today, the Church on campus is challenged to be a credible sign of unity and a living reminder of the essential interdependence and solidarity of all people. Thus, the faith community seeks to gather those who wish to serve others and to bring healing to those in the academic world who are restricted by artificial barriers and wounded by alienating practices. The Church gains credibility when the dream of community produces genuine commitment and intelligent effort. In the ideal community of faith, the Mystery that rules over our lives is named and worshiped. Dedication to Christ is fostered, and openness to all truth, goodness, and beauty is maintained. The life of the Spirit is nourished and discussed. Positive images of God, Christ, Mary, and the afterlife warm the heart and structure the imagination. The common good is emphasized and personal development encouraged. Individuals experience true freedom and at the same time accept responsibility for the well-being of the group. Traditional wisdom is available and the best contemporary insights are valued. Prayerful liturgies enable us to praise God with full hearts and create a sense of belonging, as well as nourish people for a life of service. Members are known by name and newcomers are welcomed. Unity of faith is celebrated while legitimate pluralism is recognized. Individuals find both support and challenge and can share their joys and sorrows. The members hunger for justice and have the courage to fight the dehumanizing tendencies in the culture. The community knows the sorrows of life but remains a people of hope. In this ideal community of faith, the members are of one heart and mind (Acts 4:32) and receive the spirit of wisdom which brings them to full knowledge of Jesus Christ who is the head of the Church (Eph 1:17-23).

38. By working toward the dream of genuine community, campus ministry unleash-es human potential and contributes to the common struggle against the forces of alienation. A Church serious about building community reminds others of the beauty and nobility of a life lived in harmony and peace. The baptized who experience acceptance, healing, and empowerment in the faith community are better prepared to bring an understanding ear, a reconciling touch, and an encouraging voice to alienated persons on campus.

3. The Challenge of Forming the Faith Community

39. When the dream of a genuine faith community is alive, then the search for effective strategies is intensified. Attitudes are crucial. Campus ministers whose personal outreach is warm and welcoming are likely to gain the active participation of others in the community. The ministry of presence in which leaders of the faith community make themselves available by being on campus regularly and getting involved in activities and events is a valuable way of making initial contact with potential members of the faith community and of enhancing existing relationships. Administrators, faculty members, and students who sense that they are valued as persons and that their talents and initiatives are appreciated, will find involvement more attractive.

40. On many campuses, Mass and communion services have proven to be powerful means of building community. Ministers who put a great deal of effort into preparing liturgies that are in accord with the Church's liturgical directives and are prayerful, coherent, and aesthetically pleasing, generally find an enthusiastic response. If they keep in mind the sensibilities of the academic community and strive for wide participation, the broad use of legitimate liturgical options, and a flexible style, the inherent community-building power of the eucharist is enhanced. There is a greater recognition today that stimulating homilies that apply the Gospel realistically and convey positive religious images are especially important in fostering genuine religious conversion and a sense of closeness to the worshiping community and the Church as a whole.[29] It is a sign of hope for the future that so many collegians are

gaining a deeper appreciation of the power of the eucharist to rise the mind and heart to God and to serve as "a sacrament of love, a sign of unity, a bond of charity."[30]

41. In many sacramentally oriented campus ministries, the adult catechumenate process has become an especially valuable means of incorporating new members into the Catholic Church and strengthening the faith of those who are already members. As a result, the Catholic faith community becomes stronger, more attractive, and inviting. The presence of adults who have freely chosen to join the Church moves some members to think more deeply about their own relationships to the Church. Those who serve as sponsors often gain a new appreciation of their faith and a renewed sense of the Church as a community of committed believers. A community will attract newcomers as more and more of its members demonstrate enthusiasm for the faith and an attractive style of Christian living.

42. On other campuses, different forms of community building predominate. For example, campus ministers at some commuter colleges form community through bible study programs. Through personal contact, they gather together faculty members and students for shared reading and discussion of the Scriptures. This leads into group prayer and joint projects to serve others. Such programs reveal the power of the Scriptures to call individuals out of their isolation and to give them a sense of solidarity as they struggle to live out the Christian life in the academic world.

43. The experience of Christian community on campus is important to the life of the whole Church. Students who have such a positive experience and are taught their responsibilities to the larger Church will continue to be a very valuable resource for family, parish, and diocesan life when they leave school. Campus ministers can prepare for this by maintaining good ties with local parishes and giving students the opportunity to be of service there.

44. Building up the community of faith on campus is the responsibility of all baptized persons. The desire to serve and the hunger for community must be tapped. Individuals who are personally invited to join in this task and given freedom and encouragement to use their gifts and talents for the benefit of the community are more likely to respond. It is the duty of leaders to provide vision and encourage others to accept their responsibilities. The task of forming Christian communities on campus encounters great difficulties but also brings deep satisfaction. This crucial aspect of campus ministry is worthy of vigorous and creative efforts so that the Catholic community can be an authentic sign and instrument of the kingdom on campus.

B. APPROPRIATING THE FAITH
1. The Challenges to Faith on Campus

45. Campus ministry has the task of enabling Catholics to achieve a more adult appropriation of their faith so that they can live in greater communion with God and the Church, give more effective witness to the Gospel, and face the challenges to belief that exist in the academic world. In the classroom, students learn to question traditional assumptions and to tolerate diverse opinions on important questions that cause some to doubt their religious beliefs. Most students eventually encounter the modem critics of religion who charge that belief is either infantile or dehumanizing. In some classes, the scientific method that has advanced human learning so effectively is presented as a total world view, which supplants religion and renders obsolete other approaches to truth. Some professors give the impression that maturation involves rejection of religious beliefs. In these and other ways, the academic world challenges the traditional belief systems of many students.

46. Campus life tends to reinforce these intellectual challenges. Catholic students, at times, find their faith shaken by encountering peers who profess widely divergent world views and life styles. Today, a significant number of Catholics are attracted away from their religious heritage by fundamentalist groups that employ aggressive proselytizing tactics and promise clear answers and instant security in the midst of a frightening and complex world. When students learn more about the harsh realities of life and monstrous evils that have been part of human history, they are, at times, forced to question their belief in a God who seems callous in allowing such human suffering. Finally, the whirl of campus life, with its exhilarating freedom and the pressure of making good grades, can so dominate the attention of students that they drift away from their faith without much real thought.

47. Many Catholics on campus, including faculty members, are unprepared to deal with intellectual challenges to the faith. They are unable to explain their belief to interested friends or to defend it against attacks by hostile critics. Their understanding of the faith has not kept pace with their knowledge in other areas. The legitimate pluralism of theology and spirituality in the Church confuses them. They have not achieved an adult appropriation of their religion that would enable them to speak about it not only with conviction but also with intelligence. At times, this produces frustration and anger over the inadequacy of their religious training.

48. These problems are intensified by the general religious illiteracy in our culture. Public education is not committed to passing on the religious heritage. Many good people do not recognize the importance of religious knowledge for a well-rounded education. Most colleges and universities still do not have departments or programs of religious studies, nor do they provide adequate opportunities to explore the religious dimension of various disciplines in the curriculum. In the academic world, there are still those who think that teaching about religion necessarily involves proselytizing and that it cannot be done in an academically sound way. This attitude compounds the problems of campus ministers who seek to promote a more mature appropriation of the faith among Catholics.

49. On the positive side, the challenges on campus prompt some Catholics to explore and deepen their belief. Doubts, which are frequently a part of faith development, at times lead to further study and renewed convictions. The academic world provides intellectual stimulation and helpful resources for those who want to explore their religious tradition. There is a growing interest in religious studies and an increase in programs and courses around the country. Some public

institutions have excellent departments or programs in religious studies that demonstrate that this can be done legally and according to proper academic standards. Today, within the academic community a few voices are heard insisting that a well-educated person should have a knowledge of religion. At some institutions, campus ministry has produced excellent programs in theological studies that supplement the offerings in the curriculum through a wide variety of credit and noncredit courses, seminars, and lectures. The faculty members and students who have achieved a more mature appropriation of their faith provide important witness on campus and are a sign of hope in the struggle against religious illiteracy.

2. Principles for Appropriating the Faith

50. By its very nature, Christianity calls us to an ever-deeper understanding and appreciation of our faith. Baptism initiates us into a lifelong process in which we are gradually formed anew in the image of our Creator and thus grow in knowledge (Col 3:10). The Scriptures remind us that this process means moving beyond childish ways to more mature approaches: "Let us, then, be children no longer, tossed here and there, carried about by every wind of doctrine that originates in human trickery and skill in proposing error. Rather, let us profess the truth in love and grow to the full maturity of Christ the head" (Eph 4:14-16). The Scriptures also call us to move beyond illusion to a deeper way of thinking and relating to God: "You must lay aside your former way of life and the old self which deteriorates through illusion and desire, and acquire a fresh, spiritual way of thinking" (Eph 4:22-23). Members of the faith community who achieve a more mature grasp of their Christian faith are in a better position to understand themselves and their world. Those who continue their theological education are better able to reflect on their experiences in the light of the Gospel. By assimilating the meanings and values in the Christian tradition, believers are better equipped to affirm the positive meanings and values in the culture and to resist those who are opposed to the Gospel. Individuals who are well grounded in their own Catholic heritage are better prepared to enter into ecumenical and interfaith dialogue and cooperation. The Second Vatican Council reminded us that Christians have the task of achieving "a public, persistent, and universal presence in the whole enterprise of advancing higher culture."[31] The council called upon Christians to "shoulder society's heavier burdens and to witness the faith to the world."[32] Those best qualified for this great work are the believers who have understood the implications of their faith and are able to articulate their deepest beliefs. The Scriptures offer us this advice: "Should anyone ask you the reason for this hope of yours, be ever ready to reply, but speak gently and respectfully" (1 Pt 3:15-16). To respond credibly, intelligently, and sensitively to honest inquiry requires careful and systematic preparation. All the members of the community of faith have a right to the kind of theological education that prepares them to meet this responsibility.[33] When we consider the demands of the academic world, it is clear that the Church on campus has a special responsibility to enable all of its members to appropriate the faith more deeply in order to give effective witness to the academic community.

51. The importance of achieving an intelligent appropriation of the faith can also be established by examining the nature and purpose of education. As we have noted elsewhere, "a truly liberating and elevating education is incomplete without the study of theology or religion."[34] We must continue to encourage the study of religion in our society as a whole because, as Cardinal Newman insisted, religious truth has an inherent value and is "not only a portion but a condition of general knowledge."[35] Educated persons should know something of the history, teachings, and practices of the various world religions and be especially versed in the Judeo-Christian tradition, which shaped Western civilization in general and our own culture in particular. Furthermore, they should be aware of the religious aspects of other disciplines, such as literature, history, and art, as well as the religious dimension of our contemporary culture.[36]

52. Traditionally, theology has been known to the Church as the "Queen of the Sciences." Today, we must emphasize its continuing power to keep alive the great questions of meaning, purpose, and identity and to provide a coherent vision of life, which serves as a framework and unifying principle for all learning. Theological study helps to produce the kind of intellect described by Cardinal Newman "which cannot be partial, cannot be exclusive, cannot be impetuous, cannot be at a loss, cannot but be patient, collected, and majestically calm, because it discerns the end in every delay; because it ever knows where it stands, and how its path lies from one point to another."[37] The study of theology not only helps us gain this kind of perspective, but also helps us to understand in greater depth Jesus Christ who reveals to us the secrets of the Father. In a well-rounded Christian education, the teachings of the Church are presented with fidelity to the magisterium and with the contemporary situation in mind. This kind of solid theological training enables the members of the faith community to achieve a genuine synthesis of their rich religious heritage and the best in the contemporary culture.

53. A Christian faith that fails to seek a more mature understanding is not faithful to its own inner dynamism. A culture that is unaware of its religious roots and substance is impoverished and weakened. Educated Christians who have not grown beyond an adolescent level of faith development are limited in their ability to achieve personal integration and to make a contribution to society. These dangers remind campus ministry to maintain its dedication to forming the best possible learning community. The goal is that all of the members of the community achieve a deep understanding of their faith so that they are better prepared to witness to the kingdom of truth in the world.

3. Strategies for Appropriating the Faith

54. In order to move toward these goals, it is vital that campus ministry creates a climate in which theological learning is respected. Campus ministers help to produce this climate by reminding all the members that they need an adult appropriation of the faith that matches their learning in other areas, in order to function as effective Christians in the world. This message is strengthened if the campus ministers are perceived as being serious about continuing their own theological education. The presence of faculty members and students who are already finding enlightenment and satisfaction in theological studies is a powerful motivation for others. A tradition of pursuing theological learning must be established in which all the members sense their responsibility to achieve a more mature understanding of their faith.

55. If the faith community shares this broad appreciation of the importance of religious studies, then individual programs are more likely to be successful. Program planners should be aware of the courses on campus that deal with religious matters, as well as the current needs and interests of faculty and students. For example, the existence on campus of an increasing number of fundamentalist groups has intensified the need for Scripture courses that combine the historical-critical method with opportunities for personal application and shared prayer. Such courses tap the current interest in relating the Scriptures to everyday life and prepare members of the faith community to deal with the aggressive recruiting methods employed by some fundamentalist groups. In general, campus ministry should supplement the religious offerings in the curriculum and provide a wide variety of opportunities for Catholics to study and appropriate their religious heritage and to reflect critically on their experiences in the light of the Gospel.

56. Effective strategies must deal realistically with the situations of the targeted audiences. Theological studies can be made more attractive for students by arranging credit for courses offered by the campus ministry program. For example, through a theologian-in-residence program, students on a state university campus could gain academic credit from a nearby Catholic college for theology courses taught at the campus ministry center on the state campus. Programs for faculty members and administrators must respect their vast experience while, at the same time, taking into account their general lack of systematic theological training.

57. Campus ministry has the responsibili-

ty not only to provide theological education for Catholics, but also to work with others to improve the response of higher education to the problem of religious illiteracy in our culture. The key to making progress in this idea is to overcome the unfortunate assumption that the study of religion cannot be a genuine academic discipline. The academic community must be shown that religion is worthy of careful and systematic study because it is central to human existence and is an important wellspring of our culture. Professors who deal with religious questions in their courses can help to overcome this bias by teaching this material according to rigorous academic standards of objectivity and with obvious respect for opposing opinions. If the bias against religion as an academic subject can be overcome, then a variety of positive steps might be possible, such as establishing a religious studies program, organizing a lectureship devoted to religious questions, and founding an endowed chair for Catholic thought. If the climate on campus were more open, then campus ministers with advanced degrees might find opportunities to teach part time in appropriate departments or programs. Even if some of these larger initiatives are not possible, campus ministers still can provide a valuable service for students by identifying the courses on campus in which the religious aspect is treated well and fairly.

58. In the faith community, it is understood that religious literacy is for the well-being of society and that theological learning is for the sake of a deepened faith. The goal is an adult appropriation of the faith that fosters personal commitment to Christ and encourages intelligent witness in the world on behalf of the Gospel.

C. FORMING THE CHRISTIAN CONSCIENCE
1. Moral Relativism on Campus
59. The Church on campus must facilitate the formation of a Christian conscience in its members so that they can make decisions based on gospel values and, thereby, resist moral relativism. Many questions of personal values and ethics inevitably arise for individuals in the academic community. Students are concerned with the moral

dimension of such matters as relating to family members, abortion, sexual conduct, drinking and drugs, forming friendships, honesty in their studies, and pursuing a career. At times, faculty members experience a conflict of values as they try to balance their research and teaching and attempt to remain objective in the classroom while expressing their personal opinions. Their integrity can be tested as they fight against grade inflation and struggle to maintain academic freedom while accepting external funding for research. Individual courses often produce particular ethical and value questions. This occurs in obvious ways in philosophy, literature, and the life sciences and in more subtle ways in the physical sciences and technology courses. For example, a computer course may be based on assumptions about human nature that need to be discussed. Ethical questions also arise in relation to institutional policies and practices, such as whether a particular college or university is demonstrating a proper respect and care for the athletes it recruits and utilizes.

60. As members of the academic community deal with these questions, they unavoidably come under the influence of the moral climate that dominates their particular college or university. The eyes of faith discern, in the academic world as a whole, the predictable mixture of grace and sin that characterizes all institutions. On the one hand, the climate is shaped by high idealism, dedicated service, a long tradition of civil discourse, great tolerance for opposing views, sensitive care for individuals, hard work, and a deep love for freedom. Examples of personal virtue are evident in students who resist intense peer pressure and maintain their high moral standards; in faculty members who make financial sacrifices to stay in the academic world and who carry on their teaching and research with responsibility and integrity; in administrators who consistently speak the truth and treat all members of the academic community humanely. Organizations and groups often help raise the moral tone of the campus by being involved in charitable activities and espousing high ideals. In some fields, such as business, medicine, law, and the life sciences,

more courses are being offered that deal with ethical questions. Periodically, a wave of idealism sweeps our campuses which reminds us of the great potential for goodness in the academic community.

61. On the other hand, Christians recognize in the academic world a strong strain of moral relativism that tends to reduce genuine freedom to license and an open-minded tolerance to mindlessness. Rational discourse about ethical questions degenerates into nothing more than sharing personal feelings. Sin is reduced to neurosis or blamed on societal pressures. The project of forming a healthy conscience is neglected in favor of a selfish individualism. In this climate, some persons assume that it is impossible or useless to make judgments about whether particular actions are right or wrong, whether some values are better than others, and whether certain patterns of behavior are constructive or destructive.

62. If this philosophy predominates on campus, Catholics are hard-pressed to maintain their values and principles. They find it harder to mount an effective critique of institutional practices that violate the high ideals of higher education and fail to respect the dignity of human beings. Young adults who are moving through various stages of moral development are often confused by mixed messages and conflicting philosophies. Students must contend with peer pressures to enter into the drug scene, to cheat on exams, to engage in promiscuous sexual activity, to have abortions, and, in general, to adopt a hedonistic lifestyle. Some other students find that their commitments to spouses and families are called into question. Faculty members and administrators, at times, experience subtle pressures to go along with morally questionable institutional policies and practices.

2. Conscience in a Catholic Perspective

63. In this situation, campus ministry has the crucial task of assisting in the formation of Catholic consciences so that individuals who will continue to face very complex ethical issues throughout their lives are prepared to make good moral judgments according to gospel values. The Scriptures remind us: "Do not conform yourself to this age but be transformed by the renewal of your mind so that you may judge what is God's will, what is good, pleasing and perfect" (Rom 12:2). Conscience formation involves just such a transforming renewal of mind in accord with the will of God.[38] For, conscience is that "most secret core and sanctuary of a person where one is close with God."[39] There we hear the voice of God echoing in the depths of our being and calling us to heed the law written on our hearts. As Cardinal Newman wrote in the last century: "Conscience does not repose on itself, but vaguely reaches forward to something beyond itself and dimly discerns a sanction higher than self for its decisions, as is evidenced in that keen sense of obligation and responsibility which informs them."[40] "Conscience, then, though it is inviolable, is not a law unto itself."[41] It is rather through our conscience that we detect a call from God, summoning us to love the good and avoid evil. It is in response to this call, heard in the secret recesses of our hearts, that we make the judgments of conscience required by the concrete circumstances of our daily lives. This requires an informed conscience, one nourished in prayer, enlightened by study, structured by the Gospel, and guided by the teachings of the Church. Self-deception is all too easy; blindness and illusion can easily mislead us. "Beloved, do not trust every spirit, but put the spirits to a test to see if they belong to God" (1 Jn 4:1). Thus, we need the community of faith to challenge our illusions and to call us to greater self-honesty.

64. In emphasizing the objective call from God, mediated through the Church, we do not want to lose sight of the fact that the divine summons must be answered freely and intelligently. "Morality, then, is not simply something imposed on us from without, but is ingrained in our being; it is the way we accept our humanity as restored to us in Christ."[42] Thus, all human beings are bound to follow their conscience faithfully in order that they may set the course of their lives directly toward God.[43] We are freely responsible for ourselves and cannot shift that burden to anyone else. We come to the full measure of freedom by putting on the mind of Christ. When Christ freed us, he meant us to remain free (Gal 5:1). By preaching Christ

and his message of freedom, the community of faith seeks to inform the consciences of all of its members. The Christian who possesses a conscience structured by the Gospel of Christ and who is guided by the continuing presence of Christ's spirit in the Church is better prepared to deal with the rapidly changing complexities of the world today. When genuine virtue is acquired, then good actions flow more spontaneously and new strength is found to live according to one's ideals. Individuals whose conscience has been tutored by the Gospel understand that their task is not only to resist evil but to help transform the world.

65. This portrayal of the informed Christian conscience stands in stark contrast to moral relativism. If morality is based on the call of God, then it cannot be totally arbitrary. Moral relativism betrays the essential structure of human persons who are ultimately dependent on a God who calls all of us to account. A conscience that remembers its source and is nourished and supported by the community of faith is the best resource for dealing with the complex questions of personal values and ethics.

3. Methods of Conscience Formation

66. Campus ministry is called to bring the Gospel of Christ to bear on the moral problems faced by members of the academic community. This can be done by personal encounters such as spiritual direction and counseling, as well as through homilies, classes, and seminars. When campus ministers address these questions, it is vital that they are perceived as being in touch with the texture and complexities of the moral problems generated by campus life. They also must have a working knowledge of the wisdom found in the Catholic tradition on particular moral questions. A good way for campus ministers to multiply their effectiveness is by facilitating peer ministry programs in which individuals who have successfully dealt with particular moral problems can help others in similar situations. For example, a senior athlete who managed to keep a healthy perspective on sports and maintain good grades could be prepared to speak with other athletes struggling to keep their values intact in highly pressurized situations. Students who have freed themselves from the drug scene could help others interested in breaking their drug habits. For older students struggling to keep their marriages together, conversations with faculty members who kept their commitments in similar circumstances could be mutually beneficial in enriching their married lives. In all such peer ministry approaches, it is important that those serving others are well prepared through a proper grounding in gospel ideals and church teachings on these moral questions. Engaging members of the faith community in such peer ministry programs is a valuable way of extending the effort to form Christian consciences.

67. Courses or seminars provide a more structured approach to the formation of conscience. For example, undergraduate students can be gathered for a seminar on the question of premarital sex, contraception, and abortion. An open atmosphere is needed so that the students can speak freely about the prevailing attitudes and peer pressures on campus, as well as about their own outlooks and modes of decision-making. A skillful leader can use the discussion as a basis for bringing out the Christian teaching that insists that sexuality is best understood in terms of personal relationships and that intercourse is a sign of the total commitment associated with marriage. In dealing with this and all areas of personal morality, the Catholic tradition must be presented as containing a wisdom that illuminates the mystery of human existence and encourages behavior that is in the best interest of the individual and society.

68. A good deal of conscience formation must be done on an individual basis. Counseling, spiritual direction, and the celebration of the sacrament of reconciliation provide excellent opportunities to apply Christian teachings to an individual's precise situation and current stage of moral development. Through these means, persons can gradually discover the illusions and destructive patterns that impede the development of a conscience fully attuned to the Gospel. Such settings also provide the occasion to proclaim the great mercy of our God, who deals patiently with our weaknesses and guides us gradually to full growth in Christ.

69. If campus ministry hopes to deal effectively with questions of personal values and ethics, it must be concerned with the general moral climate on campus. When individuals maintain high moral standards despite pressures, they make an important personal contribution to the moral tone of the academic community. Since colleges and universities have the task of fostering critical thinking and transmitting our cultural heritage, they should include questions of values and ethics in this general mission. Members of the faith community who understand the importance of the moral dimension of life are called to join with others in promoting a more extensive and informed discussion of ethical issues on campus. This can be done in a great variety of ways, such as facilitating an appreciation of the need for courses on ethics in each department and program, encouraging professors to treat the questions of ethics and values that arise in their courses, and sponsoring lectures and seminars on particular moral questions. It is especially helpful to get the whole academic community involved in concentrated discussions. For example, campus ministers could join with other interested groups in sponsoring a "Values and Ethics Week" on campus, designed to deal directly with moral issues. During this week, all professors are encouraged to spend class time discussing the ethical implications of their courses. Informal discussions and structured seminars are arranged throughout the week. In order to give the whole program momentum and status, major speakers are brought in to address current ethical concerns. The important element in these strategies is to move the academic community to carry on its proper task of promoting critical thinking in the area of values and ethics.

D. EDUCATING FOR JUSTICE
1. The Search for Justice on Campus
70. Campus ministry is called to make the struggle for social justice an integral part of its mission. The academic world generates questions not only of personal morality but also of social justice, which includes issues of peace and war, as well as reverence for life in all phases of its development.

Some questions arise as colleges and universities determine their internal policies and practices. How, for instance, should they balance their concern for quality education with a policy of open access that gives disadvantaged students the opportunity for higher education?[44] Issues also emerge as higher education interacts with other institutions. A prime example is whether universities can maintain their integrity, freedom, and a balanced research program while accepting massive funding from the Department of Defense for research on weapons systems. Periodically, a social justice issue captures the imagination of a significant number of students on campus, producing demonstrations and an appeal for direct action. A more sustained commitment to particular justice issues is demonstrated by some individuals, such as those who remain active in the peace movement over a long period of time and those who maintain the effort to gain legal protection for unborn human life. Such persons of conscience often encounter apathy, misunderstanding, and rejection and therefore deserve the special support and encouragement of the Church.

71. The academic community could generate intense debate over all these issues. In general terms, some want the university to remain detached from social issues, while others look for more active involvement to achieve a more just society. Most agree that higher education makes a valuable contribution by providing a forum for discussing the great questions of the day in a civil and reasoned fashion so that constructive solutions can be worked out.

72. Finally, it must be admitted that there is a great deal of apathy in evidence on campus today. Many are caught up in their own concerns and have little if any interest in social matters. Others who have been actively involved are now weary of the battles and have retreated into less demanding activities. Most students do not even think in terms of altering unjust structures through political action or social involvement. In general, alongside striking examples of personal commitment to justice, we sense a strong current of individualism that undercuts concern for the common good and eclipses the urgency of social concerns.

2. Principles of Catholic Social Teaching

73. Campus ministry is called to be a consistent and vigorous advocate for justice, peace, and the reverence for all life. All the baptized should understand that "action on behalf of justice is a significant criterion of the Church's fidelity to its missions. It is not optional, nor is it the work of only a few in the Church. It is something to which all Christians are called according to their vocations, talents, and situations in life."[45] With this in mind, campus ministers have the responsibility of keeping alive the vision of the Church on campus as a genuine servant community that is dedicated to the works of justice, peace, and reverence for life, in all stages of its development.

74. As we noted in our pastoral letter on peace, "at the center of all Catholic social teaching are the transcendence of God and the dignity of the human person. The human person is the clearest reflection of God's presence in the world; all of the Church's work in pursuit of both justice and peace is designed to protect and promote the dignity of every person. For each person not only reflects God but is the expression of God's creative work and the meaning of Christ's redemptive ministry."[46] In our day, the sanctity of the life of the unborn calls everyone to protect vigorously the life of the most defenseless among us. When we reflect further upon Christ's redemptive ministry, we see that he demonstrated a special care for the poor and the outcasts of his society. He came "to bring glad tidings to the poor, to proclaim liberty to the captives" (Lk 4:18). In identifying himself with suffering persons, he provided us with the strongest motivation to work for justice for all (Mt 25:31-46). In word and deed, Jesus taught us the essential unity between love of God and love of neighbor. His followers understood that if you claim to love God and hate your neighbor, you are a liar (1 Jn 4:20). The Gospel he proclaimed and the Spirit he sent were to transform and renew all of human existence, the social and institutional dimensions, as well as the personal.[47] This analysis suggests a rationale for the commitment to justice, a rationale that should be known and understood by all members of the Church.

75. In the struggle for justice, we need Christians who understand that "knowledge of economics and politics will not in itself bring about justice, unless it is activated by human and religious ideals. However, religious ideals without the necessary secular expertise will not provide the kind of leadership needed to influence our complex society."[48] The faith community on campus, which includes individuals with significant academic achievements, is especially well equipped to achieve the integration of an informed faith with knowledge and skill in the social arena. To accomplish this, there must be great emphasis on "teaching and learning the tradition of Catholic social thought, the creation of an environment for learning that reflects a commitment to justice, and an openness on the part of all Catholics to change personal attitudes and behavior."[49] We call special attention to the coherent body of Catholic social thought developed during the past century in papal encyclicals and reflected in our pastoral letters.[50] It is especially important for Catholics on campus to assimilate these teachings and to use them in their work for justice.

76. As the faith community carries on this educational task, it must remember that the goal is not learning alone, but constructive action to eradicate injustice and to transform society. Christians must learn how to empower individuals and groups to take charge of their own lives and to shape their own destinies. The sin that infects the social order must be not merely analyzed, but attacked. Unjust structures and institutions must be changed, as must policies and laws that fail to respect human life. To be a credible partner in this task, the Church on campus should remember that "any group which ventures to speak to others about justice should itself be just, and should be seen as such. It must therefore submit its own politics, programs, and manner of life to continuing review."[51]

3. Working for Justice

77. Considering the apathy on campus, the faith community has the vital task of raising consciousness on social issues and providing motivation for study and action.

Leaders in the faith community who are already actively committed to the struggle for justice are a valuable resource in this effort. Drawing on their own experience, they can try to recruit others to work on specific justice issues. The very presence in the faith community of a core group dedicated to justice serves as an example and invitation to others to contribute their own talents and gifts to create a more humane society. Since apathy and excessive individualism are such pervasive problems, it is important for all those who are concerned about social justice to sustain their efforts even in the midst of limited successes.

78. Education for justice can be carried out in a variety of ways, ranging from scripture studies and liturgies with a justice orientation to seminars and guided readings on a particular justice issue. Education for justice is enhanced by including an action component. For example, a seminar on hunger that raises consciousness on the issue should include suggested actions, such as joining an appropriate organization, writing congresspersons, or helping out in a local food distribution center. Given the gravity of the nuclear threat, it is especially important to study the issue of peace and war. Such studies should include a discussion of ways to implement the summons to peacemaking contained in our pastoral letter *The Challenge of Peace: God's Promise and Our Response.*

79. Since the struggle for social justice demands involvement and not simply objective analysis, the Church on campus should provide ample opportunities for all of its members to work directly in programs and projects designed to create a more just social order in which peace and reverence for life are possible. Students who are involved in service projects, such as visiting nursing homes, tutoring disadvantaged children, or helping out during vacations in impoverished areas of the country, often grow in appreciation of the people they serve, as well as discover more about the complexity of institutional problems. Systematic reflection on such experiences in the light of the Gospel and the social teachings of the Church enhances their learning and prepares them to be life-long seekers after justice.

80. Campus ministry has the responsibility to work with others to enable higher education to live up to its commitments and ideals in the area of social justice. Individuals have many opportunities to speak on behalf of those who are powerless. For instance, administrators and faculty members who are helping to set admissions policies or who are involved in hiring decisions can raise up the concerns of the disadvantaged and underrepresented. Students in various organizations can be vigilant so that the rights and sensibilities of international and minority students are respected. Individuals and groups who are attuned to the social dimension of the Gospel can raise ethical questions about institutional policies.

81. Periodically, issues arise that call for a more public response by the Church on campus. Campus ministers, for instance, may be asked to be advocates for a group of students who are seeking redress of legitimate grievances or to provide leadership on a particular issue, such as combating the problems of racism and sexism. These are important opportunities, and campus ministers should respond by drawing on the social teaching of the Church and giving public witness to the Church's concern for justice and peace.

82. Finally, the faith community can touch the conscience of the academic world by sponsoring programs on campus designed to raise consciousness and to promote justice and peace. For example, the Church could organize a day of fasting on campus, with the meal money saved going to help feed hungry people. This is a means of alerting individuals to the magnitude of the problem, of offering concrete help to the hungry, and of witnessing to the social dimension of the Gospel.

E. FACILITATING PERSONAL DEVELOPMENT

1. Self-fulfillment in the Academic World

83. Campus ministry has the task of promoting the full personal development of the members of the academic community in a setting that is filled with rich, if often neglected, resources for self-fulfillment. Colleges and universities provide marvelous opportunities for healthy personal growth. Classes, lectures, and seminars provide intellectual stimulation. Cultural and social events broaden horizons and facilitate emotional growth. The greatest catalyst for development comes from interaction with the concerned people who make up the academic community. There are campus ministers who can provide guidance for the spiritual quest; administrators who possess broad visions and sensitive hearts; faculty members who are generous in sharing the results of their scholarship; international students who bring the richness of different cultures; and peers who are willing to share friendship and the common struggle for greater maturity. With all of these resources, many individuals find the academic world to be an ideal setting for establishing their identities, forming relationships, developing their talents, preparing for leadership, discerning their vocations, and charting the direction of their lives

84. On the other hand, this vast potential for growth is often ignored or impeded. Some students think of college only in terms of opening the door to a good job and a secure future. They attend classes, gain credits, and manage to graduate. Learning to think critically and achieving a well-rounded personality through involvement on campus are not part of their program. For these students, the call to self-fulfillment either falls on deaf ears or is interpreted exclusively in terms of a lucrative career and material success. The great potential of higher education to promote personal development can also lie dormant because of the policies and practices of colleges and universities themselves. The traditional task of producing well-rounded individuals who are prepared to serve the common good can recede into the background, as policy decisions are made on the basis of declining enrollments and financial pressures. Recently, voices from within the academic community have been raised, claiming that higher education has not remained faithful to its traditional goals and is not living up to its potential. Some say this is because students are not involved enough in the whole learning process.[52] One report claims that administrators and faculty have lost their nerve in the face of cultural trends and student pressures. It charges that leaders, by failing to insist on the systematic study of the humanities, have effectively deprived students of the cultural heritage that is needed for a well-rounded education.[53] Others decry the lack of a coherent curriculum and call for diverse learning experiences that foster critical thinking and help produce integrated persons who can live responsibly and joyfully as individuals and democratic citizens.[54] Among the critics, there is general agreement that reform is needed so that colleges and universities can achieve their proper goal of facilitating the full personal development of students.

2. Christian Perspectives on Self-fulfillment

85. The Church has the task of distinguishing and evaluating the many voices of our age.[55] Campus ministry must be attuned to the voices of reform in the academic community and be prepared to function as the friend of genuine personal development and as an ally in the quest for healthy self-fulfillment. Our Scriptures remind us that the Spirit calls us to put aside childish ways and to live with greater maturity (1 Cor 14:20). For us Christians, Jesus Christ is the perfectly fulfilled human being.[56] In him, we see the depth of our potential and sublime character of our call. "He blazed a trail, and if we follow it, life and death are made holy and take on a new meaning."[57] By following this path of truth and love, we can grow to full maturity in Christ (Eph 4:15). The Spirit of Jesus, poured out through his death and resurrection, energizes us for the task of developing our potential. The same Spirit enables us to recognize and overcome the selfishness in our hearts and the contradictions in the culture that distort the quest for healthy self-fulfillment. When individuals pursue personal development within the community of faith, they are constantly challenged to use their talents in the service of others and to stay open to the Spirit, who accomplishes surprising things in us (Jn 3:8).

86. The Second Vatican Council has given contemporary expression to these biblical insights.[58] Human dignity demands

that persons act according to intelligent decisions that are motivated from within. We should pursue our goals in a free choice of what is good and find apt means to achieve these laudable goals. The Christian vision of human existence safeguards the ideal of full human development by rooting it in the sacredness of the person. All persons are worthy of respect and dignity and are called to perfection because they are "a living image of God"[59] and possess a "godlike seed" that has been sown in them.[60] This intrinsic relationship with God, far from limiting the drive for personal development, frees human beings to pursue their fulfillment and happiness with confidence.[61] Furthermore, life in community teaches us that personal freedom acquires new strength when it consents to the requirements of social life, takes on the demands of human partnership, and commits itself to the service of the human family.[62]

87. These principles remind us that Christians must proclaim an ideal of self-fulfillment that is solidly rooted in the sacredness of persons, is placed in the service of the common good, and stays open to the God who is the source of all growth.

88. When campus ministry brings the light of the Gospel to the educational process, the search for personal development leads to a Christian humanism that fuses the positive values and meanings in the culture with the light of faith.[63] Genuine Christian humanists know that the heart is restless until it rests in God and that all persons are unsolved puzzles to themselves, always awaiting the full revelation of God.[64] Thus, for them, personal development is perceived as a lifelong adventure, completed only in the final fulfilling union with the Lord. Christian humanists know that history and all cultures are a mysterious mix of grace and sin[65] and that where sin exists, there grace more abounds (Rom 5:20). Thus, while rejecting the sinful elements in the culture, they are able to assimilate the grace-inspired meanings and values in the world into a comprehensive and organic framework, built on faith in Jesus Christ. As individuals pursue their personal development, the ideal of Christian humanism lights the path and sets the direction.

3. Achieving Personal Development in a Christian Context

89. Campus ministry can facilitate personal development through vibrant sacramental life, courses, seminars, and retreats that enable Catholics on campus to integrate their collegiate experience with their Christian faith. Through pastoral counseling and spiritual direction, campus ministers can encourage individuals to make use of the resources on campus and guide them on the path toward a Christian humanism. This important work is enhanced when the ministers are perceived as persons of prayer who are serious about their own personal growth.

90. It is helpful to multiply these efforts by bringing together, in a personal encounter, those who share the journey toward Christian maturity. A program that enables an individual faculty member to meet on a regular basis outside the classroom with a particular student for friendly conversation and serious discussion provides great opportunities for the kind of exchange that is mutually enriching. Faculty members who are inspired by gospel ideals and undergo training for this kind of program are in an excellent position to be role models for students and, perhaps, spiritual mentors. Students, in turn, bring to the relationship their distinctive experience and challenging questions, which can be a catalyst for mutual growth. A great variety of such programs is possible. The key is to increase the opportunities for more personal contact between members of the faith community so that they can assist one another in the quest for a genuine Christian humanism.

91. Since there is a temptation to reduce self-fulfillment to a selfish individualism, campus ministry provides a valuable service by keeping alive the ideal of Christian humanism, which recognizes that personal growth must be open to the transcendent and in service to the common good. Through prayer groups and liturgical celebrations that link life and worship, in lectures and seminars that relate current questions and the Christian tradition, by service projects and actions for justice that put personal gifts at the service of others, the community of faith publicly manifests the Christian ideal of self-fulfillment. The sacrament of reconciliation is a powerful means for personal development since it enables individuals to confront the sins and destructive patterns that inhibit their progress and to hear again the compassionate summons to grow into greater maturity in Christ. Communal penance services that encourage an examination of the distinctive challenges and opportunities for personal development presented by campus life are especially effective in making the ideal of Christian humanism more concrete.

92. Inspired by this ideal, individual members of the faith community have the responsibility to assist their colleges or universities in the task of educating whole persons for lifelong growth and responsible citizenship. This is done in obvious ways by students who study hard and take advantage of cultural opportunities on campus and by faculty members who teach well and take a personal interest in students. In addition, there is the challenge of establishing institutional policies and practices that better facilitate these goals. Today, there is a general consensus that undergraduate education must be improved by various means, such as setting higher standards for classroom work, establishing a more coherent curriculum, and improving teacher performance through better preparation and proper incentives.[66] As the precise shape of the reforms is debated on particular campuses, it is vital that the voices of Christian humanists be joined with others of good will, on behalf of reform, which makes possible the education of the whole person. Trustees, administrators, and deans, as well as faculty members and students who serve on appropriate committees can promote policies that clearly place the well-being of students in the center of the academic enterprise. The opportunities are many and varied for members of the faith community to work with others in an effort to improve the quality of higher education so that a healthy personal development is facilitated. What is needed is the conviction that this is an essential aspect of bringing Christian witness to the campus.

F. DEVELOPING LEADERS FOR THE FUTURE

1. Potential Leaders on Campus

93. Campus ministry has the great opportunity to tap the immense pool of talent in our colleges and universities and to help form future leaders for society and the Church. Large numbers of intelligent and ambitious young people are on campuses, gaining the knowledge and skills needed to launch them into eventual positions of leadership in the world. Many of the older students at our colleges and universities are acquiring new knowledge and skills that will enhance their opportunities to influence their world for the good. The intense course of studies pursued by graduate students equips them with specialized knowledge that can be used for the common good. When international students, trained on our campuses, return to their own countries, they carry with them knowledge and skills that can be extremely valuable in promoting progress in their own societies. While not all of the students on campuses today will assume prominent leadership positions, everyone will have opportunities to provide some leadership in their various communities.

94. The large numbers of Catholics attending colleges and universities are potential leaders not only of society, but of the Church as well. Parishes require women and men who, in actively proclaiming the Gospel, combine commitment and good will with knowledge and skills. The Catholic community is in great need of more priests who will dedicate themselves to serving the needs of others. The religious orders are looking for new members who will live a life of dedicated service. In searching for this kind of church leadership for the future, we naturally turn to our colleges and universities, where so many of our talented young people are being educated.

95. The search for church leaders on campus should also extend to Catholic administrators and faculty. The local Church should make every effort to train individuals to carry out campus ministry on campuses where there are no professional campus ministry personnel. These men and women who are blessed with extensive education perform an important Christian service in the academic world and constitute an immense resource for church leadership. Not all of these individuals have the time or calling to assume leadership positions within the faith community. However, as a whole, they constitute a valuable pool of leadership talent that could be better utilized for the benefit of the Church.

2. Leadership in the Christian Perspective

96. From the perspective of faith, the Scriptures present a distinctive understanding of leadership. Jesus told his followers, "You are the light of the world . . . your light must shine before all so that they may see goodness in your acts and give praise to your heavenly Father" (Mt 5:14-19). This suggests that all the disciples of Jesus carry the responsibility of offering personal witness in order to make a difference in the world and using their influence to bring others to a greater appreciation of the goodness of God. His kind of leadership is to be carried out according to one's own unique talents. As the Apostle Paul indicated: "Just as each of us has one body with many members, and not all the members have the same function, so too we, though many, are one body in Christ and individually members one of another. We have gifts that differ according to the favor bestowed on each of us" (Rom 12:4-6). Paul also reminds us of the deep purpose involved in such gifts when he says, "To each person the manifestation of the Spirit is given for the common good" (1 Cor 12:7). In the Christian community, genuine leadership is based not on coercive power or high status, but on loving service that leads to the empowerment of others (Mk 10:42-45). Thus, the clear teaching of Scripture is that gifts and talents are not given simply for personal advantage; they are to be used generously for the benefit of others and for the good of society and the Church.

97. The Second Vatican Council recognized the great opportunities for this kind of Christian leadership and called on all adult Christians to prepare themselves for this task. "Indeed, everyone should painstakingly ready himself [or herself] personally for the apostolate, especially as an adult. For the advance of age brings with it better self-knowledge, thus enabling each person to evaluate more accurately the talents with which God has enriched [each] soul and to exercise more effectively those charismatic gifts which the Holy Spirit has bestowed on [all] for the good of [others]."[67] Thus, from the perspective of faith, it is clear that effective leadership in the contemporary world is connected both with a sense of loving service and with a more mature development in self-knowledge.

98. The nature of Christian leadership can also be understood from the viewpoint of the vocation we all receive from God. Through baptism, "all the faithful of Christ of whatever rank or status are called to the fullness of the Christian life and to the perfection of charity. By this holiness a more human way of life is promoted even in this earthly society."[68] This baptismal vocation gives to every Christian the special task "to illumine and organize" temporal affairs of every sort "in such a way that they may start out, develop, and persist according to Christ's mind."[69] Individuals may choose to live out this general vocation as single persons, as members of the clergy or religious orders, or as married couples. In all of these states of life, there are opportunities large and small for exercising a leadership that is based on service and helps to humanize our world.

3. Strategies for Forming Christian Leaders

99. Campus ministers can facilitate the development of Christian leaders by encouraging members of the faith community to identify their gifts and to use them for the common good. Individuals must be helped to overcome their fears and to gain confidence in their abilities. They need proper training and opportunities to improve their leadership skills. For example, retreats for liturgical ministers can help them sense the importance of their roles at Mass and enable them to perform these roles prayerfully and competently. A leadership training session for officers in Catholic student organizations, at the beginning of the academic year, can give them added confidence and practical skills. Campus ministers who work with student organizers of a social justice project can provide them with Christian principles and practical advice that will enhance their effectiveness as current and future leaders.

100. In addition to developing leaders within the faith community, campus ministers should also encourage students to exercise their influence in other groups and activities. It helps to remind them that involvement in the life of their college or university is a significant factor in getting more out of the collegiate experience and that all Catholics on campus have the responsibility to work for the betterment of the academic community.

101. The development of leaders involves helping students to discern their vocations in life and to prepare for them. Most young people on campus today need guidance in preparing for marriage and family life. The preparation should include programs that encompass the following elements: the sacrament of marriage as an interpersonal relationship; the identity and mission of the family; the role of human sexuality and intimacy; conjugal love as union and as sharing in the creative power of God; responsible parenthood; and the couple's responsibilities to the larger community.[70] A significant number of collegians seriously consider vocations to the priesthood or religious life.[71] Campus ministers are in an excellent position to promote these vocations. A program in which campus ministers gather interested students together regularly for discussions and prayer is a valuable way of helping them discern the promptings of the Spirit. Students moving in the direction of the single life often need personal assistance in order to deal with societal pressures and cultural stereotypes.

102. In order to get more faculty members and administrators to exercise leadership in the faith community, campus ministers need to establish personal contact with them, offer them opportunities that fit their particular expertise, and provide them with training, if necessary. For example, counselors on campus could run marriage preparation and enrichment programs for the faith community, after studying the Church's teachings on marriage. It would also be helpful to gather the Catholic faculty and administrators together, on occasion, to give them a sense of group identity and to encourage their active participation in the Church on campus. This could be

done through a retreat in which they explore ways of integrating their faith with their professional concerns. The more this integration takes place, the better role models they will be for students, who are the emerging leaders of society and the Church.

Epilogue

103. In this pastoral letter, we have placed campus ministry in its historical and cultural context and have examined it from the viewpoint of the persons who carry it out, as well as the tasks they perform. We are convinced that this ministry is vitally important for the future of Church and society. As bishops, we recognize our responsibility to "see to it that at colleges and universities which are not Catholic there are Catholic residences and centers where priests, religious, and [lay persons] who have been judiciously chosen and trained can serve as on-campus sources of spiritual and intellectual assistance to young college people."[72]

104. The revised Code of Canon Law has reinforced this responsibility by reminding us that the diocesan bishop is to be zealous in his pastoral care of students, even by the creation of a special parish or, at least, by appointing priests with a stable assignment to this care.[73] We know it is important to find dedicated persons for this ministry who have a solid faith, a love for the academic world, and the ability to relate well to both inquiring students and an educated faculty. They need proper training, which includes personal development, practical experience, and theological study. Advanced degrees are helpful in order to gain credibility in the academic world. We are committed to providing the best professional campus ministers possible and intend to hold them accountable for dedicated and creative service to the academic community. Our responsibilities extend to ensuring that within each diocese adequate funding is available for campus ministry and that there is an overall plan for allocating resources.

105. Our hope is that this pastoral letter will mark the beginning of a new phase in the history of Catholic campus ministry in the United States. In our vision of the new era, campus ministry will succeed more than ever before in forming the faithful into vibrant communities of faith and in empowering them to bring the light of the Gospel to the academic world. Campus ministry will be better understood and supported by the Church as a whole and will therefore be strengthened to make its voice heard in the center of campus life. The spiritual life of the Church on campus will be renewed so that it can be a more potent force, enabling the academic community to live up to its own ideals. The faith community will be more in touch with its Catholic roots so that it can confidently enter into deeper dialogue and more productive relationships with other religious groups on campus. A contemporary Christian humanism will flourish, which will demonstrate to all the value of an adult faith that has integrated the best insights of the culture. The Church on campus will be seen more clearly as a genuine servant community, dedicated to social justice, and therefore will be a more effective sign and instrument of the kingdom of peace and justice in the world. In the new era, the Church and higher education will find more productive ways of working together for the well-being of the whole human family. In our vision, campus ministry, empowered by the Spirit, faces a future bright with promise.

Notes

1. "Catholic Higher Education and the Pastoral Mission of the Church," in *Pastoral Letters of the United States Catholic Bishops*, 4 vols., Hugh J. Nolan, ed. (Washington, D.C.: United States Catholic Conference, 1983-1984), vol. IV, 1975-1983, no. 64, footnote 32. (Hereafter all pastoral letters will be cited from the Nolan text.)
2. Ibid.
3. There are more than 3,300 institutions of higher learning in the United States. The 1985 fall enrollment was 12,247,000 of which approximately 9.6 million attend public colleges and universities and 2.7 million attend private institutions. In the total student population, 43 percent are 25 or older and 45 percent attend part-time. In recent times, Catholics have constituted around 39 percent of the

freshman class. For these statistics, see *Chronicle of Higher Education,* September 4, 1985.

4. "Catholic Higher Education," nos. 45-46.

5. See John Whitney Evans, *The Newman Movement* (Notre Dame: University of Notre Dame Press, 1980).

6. Among the many consultations with administrators, faculty, students, selected experts, and others, we found especially helpful the close to 300 responses received from presidents and elected faculty leaders representing institutions of higher education from all 50 states who informed us of their hopes and concerns.

7. In both 1983 and 1984, 39.3 percent of college freshmen were Roman Catholic. See Alexander W. Astin, *The American Freshman National Norms for Fall 1983* (and 1984), published by the American Council on Education and the University of California at Los Angeles. Catholics constitute about 25 percent of the general population in the United States.

8. Cf. "Involvement in Learning: Realizing the Potential of American Education" (National Institute of Education, 1984); William J. Bennett, "To Reclaim a Legacy" (National Endowment for the Humanities, 1984); "Integrity in the College Curriculum: A Report to the Academic Community" (Association of American Colleges, 1985); and "Higher Education and the American Resurgence" (Carnegie Foundation for the Advancement of Teaching, 1985).

9. "To Teach as Jesus Did: A Pastoral Message on Catholic Education," in *Pastoral Letters*, vol. III, 1962-1974, no. 63.

10. "Pastoral Constitution on the Church in the Modern World," in *The Documents of Vatican II*, Walter M. Abbott, SJ, ed. (New York: America Press, 1966), no. 57. (Hereafter all documents from Vatican II will be cited from the Abbott text.)

11. Ibid.

12. Ibid., no. 92.

13. "The Church of the University," *The Pope Speaks*, vol. 27, no. 3 (Fall 1982): 252.

14. "Declaration on Christian Education," in *Documents of Vatican II*, no. 1.

15. John Paul II, *On the Family* (Washington, D.C.: United States Catholic Conference, 1982), no. 37.

16. "The Church of the University," p. 250.

17. Ibid., p. 252.

18. "To Teach as Jesus Did," no. 67.

19. Ibid., no. 49.

20. "Dogmatic Constitution on the Church," in *Documents of Vatican II*, no. 10.

21. "Decree on the Apostolate of the Laity," in *Documents of Vatican II*, no. 3.

22. More than two-fifths of the current student population are 25 years of age or older. See footnote 3.

23. "Called and Gifted: The American Catholic Laity," in *Pastoral Letters*, vol. IV, 1975-1983, no. 19

24. Ibid., no. 27.

25. "The Church in Modern World," no. 44.

26. "Dogmatic Constitution on the Church," no. 9

27. Ibid., no. 4.

28. Ibid, no. 48.

29. Fee et al., *Young Catholics* (New York: William H. Sadler, Inc., 1980), pp. 154-155.

30. "Constitution on the Sacred Liturgy," in *Documents of Vatican II*, no. 47.

31. "Declaration on Christian Education," no. 10.

32. Ibid.

33. Ibid., no. 2.

34. "Catholic Higher Education," no. 22. In this regard, it is important to distinguish theology, which involves a faith perspective and commitment, from religious studies, which can proceed in a more neutral fashion.

35. John Henry Cardinal Newman, *The Idea of a University* (Garden City, N.Y.: Image Books, 1959), p. 103.

36. "Catholic Higher Education," no. 22.

37. Newman, *The Idea of a University*, p. 159.

38. "The Church in the Modern World," no. 16.

39. Ibid.

40. Cited in "The Church in Our Day," in *Pastoral Letters*, vol. III, 1962-1974, no. 205.

41. Ibid., no. 206.

42. "To Live in Christ Jesus," in *Pastoral Letters*, vol. IV, 1975-1983, no. 22.

43. "Declaration on Religious Freedom," in *Documents of Vatican II*, no. 3.

44. See the report by the Southern Regional Education Board's Commission for Educational Quality, "Access to Quality Undergraduate Education," *Chronicle of Higher Education*, July 3, 1985, p. 9 ff.

45. United States Catholic Conference, *Sharing the Light of Faith: National Catechetical Directory for Catholics of the United States* (Washington, D.C.: United States Catholic Conference, 1979), no. 160.

46. "The Challenge of Peace: God's Promise and Our Response," in *Pastoral Letters*, vol. IV, 1975-1983, no. 15.

47. "The Church in the Modern World," no. 26.

48. "Catholic Higher Education," no. 39.

49. "To Do the Work of Justice," in *Pastoral Letters*, vol. IV, 1975-1983, no. 8

50. For important papal documents, see David J. O'Brien and Thomas A. Shannon, eds., *Renewing the Earth: Catholic Documents of Peace, Justice, and Liberation* (Garden City, N.Y.: Doubleday, 1977). Among our more recent pastoral letters and statements on social justice and peace, we call attention to: "The Challenge of Peace: God's Promise and Our Response"; "Brothers and Sisters to Us"; "To Do the Work of Justice"; and our forthcoming pastoral letter on the economy. Finally, we note the valuable insights in the pastoral letter *What We Have Seen and Heard: A Pastoral Letter on Evangelization from the Black Bishops of the United States* (Cincinnati: St. Anthony Messenger Press, 1984).

51. *Sharing the Light of Faith*, no. 160.

52. See "Involvement in Learning."

53. See Bennett, "To Reclaim a Legacy."

54. See "Integrity in the College Curriculum."

55. "The Church in the Modern World," no. 44.

56. Ibid., no. 22.

57. Ibid.

58. Ibid., no. 17.

59. "Pastoral Letter on Marxist Communism," in *Pastoral Letters*, vol. IV, 1975-1983, no. 14.

60. "The Church in the Modern World," no. 3.

61. Ibid., no. 21.

62. Ibid., no. 31.

63. This term, *Christian humanism*, has been used in the Church to suggest the ideal of integrating positive cultural values and meanings in a faith perspective. For a recent usage of this term, see "Catholic Higher Education," no. 19.

64. "The Church in the Modern World," no. 21.

65. Ibid.

66. We recall the four reports cited in note 8.

67. "Decree on the Laity," no. 30.

68. "Dogmatic Constitution on the Church," no. 40.

69. Ibid., no. 9.

70. John Paul II, *On the Family*, no. 66.

71. Fee et al., *Young Catholics*, pp. 154-155.

72. "Declaration on Christian Education," no. 10.

73. *Code of Canon Law* (Washington, D.C.: Canon Law Society of America, 1983), cc. 813, 814.

A Letter to College Students from the Catholic Bishops of the United States

Dear College Students,

We write to you as your coworkers in Christ, and we congratulate you on all you have done to arrive at this point in your life. Already you are leaders, because in a very real sense you have begun to lead, especially if you are an older student with family and work responsibilities.

Your college years are a very significant time for you. In these few years you will greatly expand your knowledge and your skills. At the same time, you will be making many important choices—about vocations, relationships, and careers.

These years will also provide a wonderful opportunity for you to grow in your faith, a faith that is rooted in your own personal relationship with Jesus and nourished by prayer, reading the Scriptures, and participating in the sacraments. As you grow in faith, you will recognize the important responsibility of sharing your faith with others.

We realize that foremost among the many priorities in your life is the time devoted to study. Your study is not unrelated to your life of faith. Through your exploration of history, language, science, and art, you can also deepen your faith and your understanding of our religious tradition. In the future, what you study now can help transform business, academia, culture, and the mass media into places where the Spirit of God truly lives and works. And there is always the possibility of a career of ministry and leadership in the Church.

But you do not have to wait. Think of the impact you as a Catholic college student can have even now on others who may not know the rich tradition of Catholicism. Working with students of other faiths and religious traditions on campus, you can make important contributions toward peace and justice, reminding the whole academic community of the presence of those whom society neglects or marginalizes. By your involvement as a Catholic, you can help others see the face of Christ in the faces of the poor.

It is a fact of campus life and life everywhere that many people today experience a deep sense of uncertainty and confusion. It seems that for some the world is filled with questions and even discouragement. While we have to admit that the future, as always, is uncertain, we also have to recognize that it is full of possibilities. And as Catholics, we have the added certainty and hope that comes from our faith in the victory of Jesus' death and resurrection. You can be witnesses of that hope for everyone you meet, sharing with them the hope that is based on the Gospel and the abiding presence of the Spirit. By your care and concern, you can also reassure other people that they are really loved and that Christ's love is always present for them.

There are many specific ways that you can minister on campus to create a climate of hope and a community of welcome. Begin by inviting your friends and neighbors to join you at Sunday Mass, the most important celebration of the Catholic community. It is easier for them to respond to the prompting of the Spirit when someone else is willing to go with them. Also, offer to be a reader, server, eucharistic minister, cantor, or musician, according to your gifts.

Strengthen your own spirituality by searching for answers and by becoming more knowledgeable about your faith. Start with the Scriptures, God speaking to us. Then the *Catechism of the Catholic Church* is a wonderful reference that can help to answer both your questions and those others might have. And campus ministers, with their special training, want to help you with your questions, spiritual growth, and religious identity.

There are so many other ways to serve. Volunteer to help out in the local community or improve the quality of life on campus by becoming involved in peer ministry or by tutoring your fellow students. Working together with campus ministers, you can organize or participate in small prayer or faith groups in your residence hall or local community. By your efforts on behalf of life, you can remind others that a lived Christian faith begins with a profound respect for human life from conception to natural death. By simplifying your lifestyle, you can be a reminder that our resources are not without limit and ought to be used wisely.

Jesus commissioned us to be his witnesses by the testimony of our lives when he said, "You will receive power when the Holy Spirit comes upon you, and you will be my witnesses in Jerusalem, throughout Judea and Samaria, and to the ends of the earth" (Acts 1:8). We bishops of the United States enumerated in our pastoral letter on campus ministry of 1985, *Empowered by the Spirit*, six ways in which the Church on campus can be a faithful witness to the message of the Gospel: forming the faith community, appropriating the faith, forming the Christian conscience, educating for justice, facilitating personal development, and developing leaders for the future.

Since 1985, many campus ministries have reported increased student involvement in liturgy, community service, retreat opportunities, and justice concerns. Now as the Church approaches the two-thousand-year mark in its history, we challenge you to reflect, using these categories from *Empowered by the Spirit*, on the ways in which you have revealed the Church on campus to be a faithful witness to the truth of the Gospel, a "servant community, dedicated to social justice, and a more effective sign and instrument of the kingdom of peace and justice in the world." This will be especially challenging for you who do not have the help of an organized campus ministry program.

You have so many gifts to offer the Church: your faith, your desire to serve, your spiritual hunger, your vitality, your optimism and idealism, your talents and skills. We can all learn from you, so we ask you to expand your leadership role in witnessing to the Gospel on campus. We promise you our prayerful support and encourage your future involvement in the mission of the Church through a parish faith community. We look forward to working more closely with you to make the Church ever more effective in announcing the reign of God. We ask for your prayers for us in our work of shepherding the Church.